Elementary Social Studies

Elementary Social Studies

Teaching for Today and Tomorrow

Jack M. Evans
Central Michigan University

Martha M. Brueckner
Earle Brown Elementary School
Brooklyn Center, Minnesota

Allyn and Bacon
Boston   London   Sydney   Toronto

Copyright © 1990 by Allyn and Bacon
A Division of Simon & Schuster, Inc.
160 Gould Street
Needham Heights, Massachusetts 02194-2310

Series Editor: Sean W. Wakely
Series Editorial Assistant: Carolyn O'Sullivan
Production Administrator: Annette Joseph
Production Coordinator: Susan Freese
Editorial-Production Service: TKM Productions
Text Design: Denise Hoffman, Glenview Studios
Cover Administrator: Linda K. Dickinson
Manufacturing Buyer: Tamara Johnson
Photo Credits: page 51, Laima Druskis; pages 72, 371, and 385, Ken Karp; page 118, Irene Springer; all other photos by Jack M. Evans and Richard C. Brueckner

Library of Congress Cataloging-in-Publication Data

Evans, Jack M.
    Elementary social studies : teaching for today and tomorrow / Jack
M. Evans, Martha M. Brueckner.
        p.   cm.
    Includes bibliographical references.
    ISBN 0–205–12241–8
    1. Social sciences—Study and teaching (Elementary)—United
States.   I. Brueckner, Martha M.   II. Title.
LB1584.E93   1989
372.83′044′0973—dc20   89-27031
                                                                                              CIP

Brief Contents

V   The New Teacher   379

Contents

II   How Children Learn   41

Chapter 2 How Children Learn Social Studies   43

Chapter 3 Introduction to Methodologies   69

III   What Children Learn   95

IV Planning for Instruction   129

V The New Teacher   379

Preface

Two old friends who had not seen each other for many years met at a conference of the National Council for the Social Studies in Chicago. One was an elementary classroom teacher and the other a university social studies methods professor. They had dinner, and the discussion that ensued was the beginning of this book.

As is usual when teachers meet, the conversation turned to shop talk. The topic centered on preparing future teachers for the classroom, most especially for teaching elementary social studies. The consensus was that social studies instruction tends to be more "read about and recite" and is often perceived to be more boring than most other subjects. The next question was Why? To us, the two old friends mentioned above, social studies topics are interesting, and the people and places studied are certainly not boring. So maybe the problem is not social studies itself but the way it is taught. *Elementary Social Studies: Teaching for Today and Tomorrow* is an effort to prepare the future teacher to do a more interesting and effective job of planning and teaching social studies.

We, the authors, represent two distinct teaching environments: the elementary classroom and the university classroom. Too often, there is little communication between the two. Those at the university level are more often concerned with research and theory, while those at the elementary level focus upon what works with children. We think both views have much to offer to the preparation of future teachers. We've spent much time deliberating the needs of the beginning teacher from both theoretical and practical aspects. The result of these deliberations was to produce the topics that are the core of this book.

As you read this book, keep in mind the following assumptions:

- This is a true elementary social studies methods textbook. It is about *how* to teach social studies, not a short course in the content of social studies. We have purposely omitted the history of social studies, various organizational structures, and other historical but not very useful information. We assume that students have had courses in the social sciences as an integral part of their university experience.

- Social studies can be learned by personal involvement as well as by reading. According to Piaget, children of elementary school age are in the concrete operational stage. They need hands-on experiences. Educators have applied this concept to science and mathematics with good results. Why not apply it to the teaching of social studies? To go one step further, why not apply it to the preparation of social studies teachers? The format of this book is designed to involve you, the student, in the learning process. Therefore, each chapter concludes with activities that will help you teach and reinforce the instruction of social studies concepts.

- Good planning is the core of good teaching. Organizing a lesson or a unit; planning the teaching, questioning, and evaluating strategies; and carrying them out is what teaching is all about. We have included questioning and evaluating as an integral part of the planning process, not as an add-on.

- Social studies is important, alive, and definitely not boring. All that is needed to make it so is a well-prepared teacher who is willing to go beyond the textbook and explore the real world with her or his students.

We have enjoyed writing this book because we believe social studies is important. If only one person becomes a better social studies teacher as a result of our efforts, then all the time and energy spent producing this text will have been worthwhile.

ACKNOWLEDGMENTS

Upon completion of the writing task, there is finally time to reflect on the project and the many people who have been either directly or indirectly connected with it. We thank all of you who have helped in any way, and we apologize to those we may have inconvenienced.

We express gratitude for the support of Ruth Evans and Richard Brueckner. Only those who have written can truly appreciate the value of a supportive spouse.

We also thank the people at Allyn and Bacon for their help and support, especially our editor, Sean Wakely, who believed in us and our book. Thank you to our copy editor, Lynda Griffiths, for making sense of our manuscript and keeping us on schedule. Thanks also to our reviewers for their helpful criticisms, comments, and suggestions: Buckley R. Barnes, Georgia State University; Keith D. Berkeley, University of South Carolina; JoAnne Buggey, University of Minnesota; and Don Varner, Northeast Oklahoma State University. We have had differences of opinion and, in some instances, of basic philosophy, but you have strengthened the book with your sometimes blunt, sometimes humorous, and always sincere comments.

Last, but most important of all, we want to thank the children of Earle Brown Elementary School in Brooklyn Center, Minnesota, and Hanna Vowles Elementary School in Mt. Pleasant, Michigan, who served as models for photographs and, in doing so, represent all children in all schools. Children are the reason for the existence of the teaching profession. Without them, teachers would have no one to teach, and there would have been no need for this book. A special thanks to all children just for being children and to all teachers who teach.

Finally, we want to dedicate this book to all the elementary teachers who are indeed ''teaching for today and tomorrow.''

UNIT I

Introduction

1

Introduction to Social Studies

PROJECTIONS

What will social studies education be for the 1990s and beyond? Making predictions regarding what is important, relevant, or usable for any future time is not an easy task. It is safe to say that social studies is a significant content area and will remain so. Teachers, administrators, and various professional organizations are continually examining, evaluating, and reordering educational goals. We are involved in an ongoing process of short- and long-range planning: Where are we now and where do we want to be five or ten years from now? Will our social studies goals be directed toward more intense instruction in the cognitive and affective skills or become more content oriented?

The impact of technology is evident in the elementary schools across the nation. Students are interacting comfortably with computers, interactive television, and other hardware. The potential of these media is impressive. Large amounts of information can be stored and retrieved quickly by using a computer or a laser disk. Radio, television, and telephone technology permit instant access throughout the world. A computer, modem, and telephone line allow access to many data sources. You may not use them yet, but your students do.

With all of this wealth of data at our fingertips, is it practical to direct a large portion of social studies instruction to information gathering and retention? Should we expect youngsters to maintain a myriad of facts at the level of instant recall? On the other hand, we are appalled at the lack of basic knowledge when our graduates cannot name the countries that border ours or locate the United States on a globe. A basic foundation of factual information will continue to be important.

It is conceivable that in the 1990s our social studies goals will be directed more toward the process and human relations skills. The primary goal will continue to be to develop good citizens. Elementary teachers must assume a proactive role in teaching students the vital skills that will enable them to function as contributing members of our society. The skills of interpretation, planning, cooperative participation, higher-level thinking and processing, decision making, problem solving, selective choosing, and others are crucial to a successful, contributing life-style.

The social dynamics of contemporary elementary classrooms provide a natural setting conducive to practicing and learning these life skills.

Social studies topics are difficult to project with certainty. Events and attitudes of today indicate that certain issues such as environmental education and consumer education will be continuing concerns. Undoubtedly, global awareness will expand considerably. Geographical areas such as Central America, the Persian Gulf countries, and the African continent are undergoing significant changes politically, socially, and economically. The needs and requirements of the growing Spanish-speaking community in the U.S. Southwest and other areas is a concern, as are those of other growing ethnic groups such as the Amerasians. Racial equality will continue to be a goal. Our consuming, producing, and servicing economic society is undergoing significant changes. Fewer laborers are needed to produce the goods we need to survive. Indications are there will be a greater need for persons in the servicing industries and professions. Are we adequately preparing students to meet this reality? Cogent curriculum planning and development must address these social studies issues.

A particularly exciting issue for the 1990s and beyond is the education and training of teachers. Important changes and modifications are being made in teacher preparation, licensing, certification, and performance. Social studies teachers need a strong academic preparation in the foundation courses. Social studies methods courses are accentuating the teaching aspects more (What will you do in the classroom?), not merely the knowledge aspects (What do you know about social studies?).

A continuing concern for teachers, administrators, parents, and politicians is the funding of quality education for all children. This important concern is a substantial issue for the future. Educators and parents want and support a strong social studies program and are willing to work toward getting it. It is a fact of life that these programs cost money, and public funds are not always readily available.

Social studies teachers must be flexible, adaptable, and committed to maintaining the role of social studies in the elementary curriculum. You, the social studies teacher for the 1990s and beyond, can expect to encounter some innovative changes in your content areas. It is critical that you investigate, contemplate, evaluate, and, most importantly, participate in these changes so that you can become the strong social studies teacher you want to be.

Welcome to the wonderful world of the social studies. You are going to be responsible for teaching children how to live and survive in the future. Since we do not know precisely what each person will encounter in his or her travels from infancy to adulthood to old age, it is impossible to teach each person exactly what he or she will need to know. However, we do know that people who can think, solve problems, communicate, understand, make decisions, and act upon those decisions can survive and make contributions to their society. Your task as a teacher is to prepare children to become effective students in school and contributing members of our society. This is also the goal of the social studies.

The purpose of this book is to help you become the best social studies teacher you can possibly be. It is a methods textbook designed to emphasize those methods and strategies that are characteristic of good teaching. You will obtain social studies information from content courses in political science, physical geography, history, and other similar courses. Teaching social studies is different than teaching reading, math, or music. Techniques, plans, materials, methods, organization, and other factors address these differences. This book will increase your awareness of these factors and help you meet the challenge.

What are the social studies? Why are they important? What are the goals of social studies education? How are the social studies influenced and modified by new knowledge and new technology?

These are interesting questions that should be answered, but even as answers are formulated, new information is changing those answers. Such is the fluid nature of the societies and the world in which we live. If you accept this as fact, you will know that social studies is alive and constantly changing. Social studies will never be a dead, dull, boring topic to be read from a book and memorized. Active involvement by the students can develop the knowledge and flexibility necessary to live and function in today's changing world.

The Social Studies Teacher

The Role of the Teacher

The most important role of any teacher is to teach students what they do not know. More specifically, it is to teach the required subject content and skills to students. In most elementary schools every teacher must teach social studies a certain number of minutes per day/week as required by state and local mandates. The teacher's role is to perform this duty with a high degree of professionalism. Teaching only the topics or skills you enjoy or just "covering the basics" is not acceptable. The teacher's role is to plan for teaching social studies content using a wide variety of materials, methodologies, strategies, and techniques that will make social studies interesting and challenging for the students.

The social studies teacher must have more than a minimal knowledge of the various social sciences that comprise elementary social studies. This basic knowledge set is acquired by college course work, participation in related seminars and workshops, reading current research, and other individual professional activities. An excellent resource for increasing your knowledge base is the teacher's manual that accompanies your social studies textbook. It will contain a multitude of information that will help focus your role as a teacher of the social studies. Keeping a clear focus means the teacher must give a 100% effort to teaching social studies during the class period.

The role of the social studies teacher includes two major components: responsibilities to the students and responsibilities to the curriculum. Responsibilities to the students are a high priority, including such things as effective planning, imaginative lesson presentations, fair and realistic evaluations, meeting individual needs, and exhibiting a positive, professional attitude and role model. Teaching the accepted curriculum is a big responsibility. Responsibilities to the curriculum area or department are also important. In a small school the social studies curriculum committee may consist of one teacher and the principal who meet periodically to monitor how the curriculum objectives are being accomplished. In larger schools there may be one teacher per grade level who meets monthly with the curriculum coordinator and the principal to perform countless planning and managing duties. In either case, all of the teachers must act responsibly to: (1) teach the content; (2) achieve grade-level objectives; (3) use the recommended tools and materials; (4) provide feedback to the curriculum committee; (5) share and promote the use of materials, techniques, and strategies that are particularly effective; and (6) be willing to serve on the curriculum committee when asked. Any curriculum is only as strong as the teachers who teach it. Your role is to make your contribution to energize the social studies.

Attitude and Its Effect on Students

The attitude of the teacher is an important factor in the success or failure of any program in the classroom setting. It is necessary to have an effective, thorough program, complemented by various supplemental instructional materials. This program is then enhanced and strengthened by a teacher with a positive attitude who plans and presents lessons with enthusiasm. Teaching social studies is part of the elementary teacher's job, but not every teacher feels strongly about teaching social studies. Having individual preferences for certain subject areas is normal. Feeling unsure or apprehensive about one's own ability to teach all the social studies areas effectively is understandable. Spending time studying the program will diminish these insecurities.

It is important that teachers model a positive attitude toward learning all the subjects that are integral parts of elementary education. A teacher who openly shows enthusiasm, while maintaining a healthy respect for the seriousness of learning itself, will project several clear messages to students:

- Learning and experiencing the social studies is necessary.
- Learning is exciting and personally rewarding.
- I care enough to plan my lessons carefully, so I can relax and enjoy teaching my students.

- If I am positive, the students will receive positive reinforcement and develop a positive attitude.

- A positive attitude toward social studies teaching is both necessary and professional.

A positive attitude reflects the degree of commitment a teacher invests in the preparation of lessons and activities. A well-planned lesson enhances good classroom management. Weak lessons that are mainly reading about social studies with little or no depth of focus give the message that "This isn't really very important, let's get on to other things that really matter." These kinds of lessons do not keep students on task and do contribute to weak and shallow learning of social studies objectives. Teachers who are unsure of their abilities to teach social studies effectively must work toward developing a positive attitude that will add to, not detract from, the positive learning experiences of students.

The Preparation of a Teacher

Academic. Preparing to teach at the elementary level requires that you receive classroom instruction in many academic areas. A strong background in child growth and development, educational psychology, and the psychology of learning and instruction are essential elements in the process of learning how to teach. Courses in the social sciences provide you with content background for what to teach. Teacher education programs usually require courses in methodologies for each of the academic areas. Some of those methodologies are specifically designed and prepared for one subject, just as this book is for social studies. Others have instructional elements that can be cross-referenced among several subject areas.

The elementary classroom teacher is a specialist in academics and in the management of children. Proficiency in the academics is a requisite for successful teaching. The various methods and core curriculum classes provide a basic foundation for readiness to teach. This basic foundation is strengthened by continual reading, studying, and researching throughout your teaching career. Elementary classroom teaching is more than teaching subjects. It is teaching children. The group dynamics of teaching for extended periods of time within a relatively confined, structured physical area necessitates acquiring strong management skills. Individualizing to meet specific learner needs has always been the responsibility of teachers. How do you present a lesson to a group of 25 students and provide for those with special needs? The management organizational skills that are needed to do this are taught in new, creatively designed classes at the university level, as well as through various continuing education programs, workshops, and other professional groups that specialize in staff development.

Professional.   Preparing to enter a profession is an exciting, challenging process. Choosing the field of education in itself indicates you are a caring, serious person. Your academic preparation will be very complex and will continue long after graduation from a four-year institution. Academic preparation provides the knowledge and skills base you will need to teach children. Personal preparation is vital. Educators have traditionally been viewed as the extension of the family unit upon which our democratic society is based. They are respected and trusted to guide and instruct children for a large portion of their day. Establishing a strong commitment to be consistent in doing the best job you possibly can is the mark of a true professional. Build a mindset to do what is good for children, not what merely is required.

When you enter the teaching profession you will be enriched by active participation in professional organizations that work to establish and maintain standards for the profession or a specific academic field. Becoming an active member of professional organizations can benefit you in several ways:

- Membership provides opportunities to interact with others in the profession—new teachers as well as senior teachers.
- Membership enables you to contribute valuable input to the organization and to receive needed support and assistance from other members.
- Membership allows you to learn leadership skills from the local to the national level.
- Membership enables you to stay current in the research studies that pertain to a particular academic field.
- Membership provides a way for new teachers to make a contribution to their professional organizations.

Some professional organizations that you may consider are:

- The National Council for the Social Studies
- The National Geographic Society
- The National Science Teachers Association
- The Council for Basic Education
- The state-level organizations of these

Practical.   From a realistic standpoint, your practical preparation for teaching social studies has begun. Once you decide to become a classroom teacher, the sooner you begin to prepare, the better it is for you. As a prospective teacher it is very helpful to acquire the habit of reading in the social studies areas. Keeping current on the many issues that are of special concern to educators is a strong asset for those new to the profession.

Thinking about assuming the role of teacher is a good way to plan for instruction. Having some general plans established well in advance of the actual opening of school makes specific planning that much easier. Initial previewing of textbooks and supplementary materials gives you a general overview of what is being taught in social studies at the present time. This kind of general knowledge facilitates your transition into actually using a particular set of materials. Start a social studies notebook or journal for yourself and record your ideas and thoughts. Such things as bulletin board ideas, unit topics, special interests, events, evaluation thoughts, motivational techniques, creative lesson extensions, and any other spur-of-the-moment ideas can be quickly entered in your journal. Ask other teachers for some of their special ideas that have been successful. When you begin to teach, you will appreciate these notations.

The Social Studies: What Are They?

Elementary social studies for the next decade will encompass a wide range of content areas, human relations experiences, and process skills. Students will progress from a basic knowledge of local neighborhoods and primary map and globe identification skills to a variety of global issues and concerns of and for our expanding environment. Preparing our children to function effectively in the twenty-first century is of the utmost importance.

What are the social studies? It is hard to give a specific definition to the term because it is comprised of so many disciplines, each having its own definition. The dictionary defines social studies as: "a part of a school or college curriculum concerned with the study of social relationships and the functioning of society and usually made up of courses in history, government, economics, civics, sociology, geography, and anthropology."[1]

The National Council for the Social Studies (NCSS) articles of incorporation state: "The term 'social studies' is used to include the social science disciplines and those areas of inquiry which relate to the role of the individual in a democratic society designed to protect his or her integrity and dignity and which are concerned with social issues and human relationships."[2] This definition goes beyond the study of various disciplines by including the role of the individual in social issues and human relationships. Current trends in social studies emphasize more humanistic aspects of learning. The cluster of social science disciplines includes history, geography, economics, anthropology, social psychology, sociology, philosophy, and political science. At the elementary level, however, the more traditional disciplines of history, geography, government, sociology, and economics remain eminent. Social psychology, philosophy, and anthropology are common threads that examine various human intellectual characteristics. Social studies is the total involvement of individuals and human groups in their past, present, and future.

Social Studies Skills

The building of a base level of knowledge and skills is primary for children if they are to act and react responsibly. Reading social studies information, internalizing data, formulating attitudes, having opportunities to practice various human relations skills, and participating and sharing in group activities are all ways in which elementary students experience the social studies. Current social studies programs attempt to correlate many learning skills into their scope and sequence. For a brief preview of content areas presently in use, the topics can be divided into three main categories: product skills, process skills, and human relations skills.

Product Skills.   Teaching content information is a necessary part of the elementary curriculum. Product skills can be viewed as the topic or subject matter content being taught. A review of current textbooks reveals the following topics as main focal points. Note the variety of topics and the potential for lesson extensions in each.

Geography: The natural, physical aspects of an area or region are explored in this content area. Students examine mountains, plains, forests, river systems, regions, and weather, as well as other features of the earth's surface area.

History: The chronological history of a country, continent, or specific region is investigated. Students will come to realize the effect of historical events upon such things as population growth, ethnicity, development, government, and pride in one's heritage. The role of inventions in a society should be investigated with emphasis on the consequences they produce. Time movement is an important part of instruction in the teaching of history.

Famous Americans: In an effort to initiate national pride and to encourage citizenship and patriotism, studying famous U.S. citizens gives children a theme to focus on in establishing their own identities as Americans. George Washington and Abraham Lincoln are standards for what it means to be an American; present-day programs may feature contemporaries such as Shirley Chisholm (political leader), Sally Ride (astronaut and scientist), or Chuck Yeager (pilot).

Government: The role of government (local, state, national, and world vision) is emphasized in most social studies texts. Students are presented with the various forms of government and the processes that allow them to function effectively. The process of governing fairly and efficiently can be actualized for students by presenting activities at the classroom, school, and community levels.

Economics: It is important for elementary-aged children to realize the supportive role economics plays in the functioning of a group. Currency, labor, products, and trade each play a role in the economics of an area. Consumer education is included in this domain.

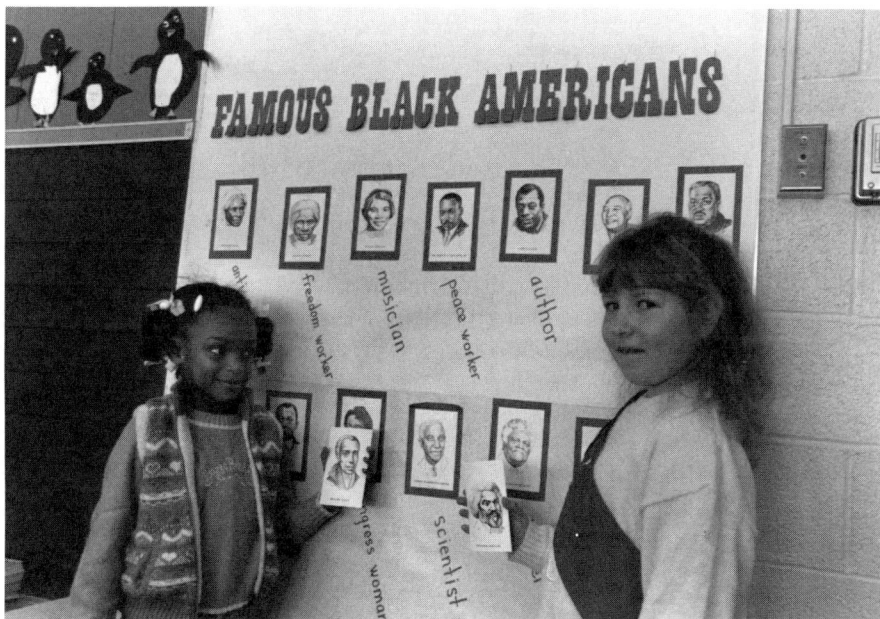

Investigating the contributions of U.S. citizens helps children to learn their cultural identity.

Cities: The characteristics of large and small cities, how and why they develop in certain locations, and the effect of cities on the environment, population, and jobs are part of a complete understanding of the social studies. Large cities in our own part of the world as well as those in other areas are explored.

Labor: Children are taught about the advent of the U.S. worker, unions, jobs, the work ethic, the Industrial Revolution, the change from a producing to a servicing labor force, career education, and children's work. Career knowledge may help children select the position they will occupy in the labor force.

The World: An understanding of the interdependence of all peoples is important for children to develop and maintain. Emerging new nations, environments, populations, governments, trade leadership, decisions made in the past and in the present, global concerns, and neighbors all affect our present world scene.

States and Regions: Specific regions (e.g., the North Central states) are examined in terms of special and sometimes unique characteristics and how they affect other areas in contributing to the overall growth of a country. Making products, industry, farming, land use, communities (specifically your own community), river systems, foods, and ethnic heritage are all part of learning about states and regions.

Maps and Globes: Historically, the study of maps and globes has comprised a very large portion of the social studies curricula. Facility in map and globe content would include exposure to various types of maps and their uses (location maps, distance and product maps, directional maps), different types of globes, map-making experiences, and map-reading skills.

These are some of the major topic areas in current social studies curricula. Although each of them is timely and important in and of itself, each becomes more significant when encompassed within the overall K–12 social studies program.

Process Skills.   Process skills are those skills necessary to be able to do social studies. To *do* social studies means to collect, organize, and use the content material from the social studies disciplines. Process skills are best taught when presented with product skills. Children retain information over longer periods of time and apply that information more effectively when several modalities operate at the same time.

To experience the social studies fully, a wide variety of skills are needed. Many can be introduced as early as kindergarten and expanded upon each succeeding year. A listing of these process skills is presented here and will be elaborated on in Chapters 3 and 4.

Read graphs, diagrams, time lines, charts

Recognize and use specific social studies terms

Interpret graphics

Plan and participate in research projects

Write and present reports

Participate actively in a group or committee

Think, plan, and do

Recognize main ideas, sequencing of events

Outline

Make decisions

Read social studies textbooks to determine important information and supporting details

Utilize the inquiry process when appropriate

Use the library and media centers appropriately

Transfer social studies knowledge into other subject areas (art, math, language arts, technology, music)

Recognize points of view, bias, generalizations

Compare and contrast

Estimate

As you can see from this list, many skills must be taught to a child as he or she becomes fluent in the social studies. Learning and doing social studies is a complex undertaking and should not be taken lightly.

Human Relations Skills. Whereas the social studies product and process skills are more readily observable, the human relations skills tend to be more empathic. The most important skills needed to develop acceptable human relationships are accepting, becoming, and feeling. For children to acquire and use human relations skills, it is necessary to provide opportunities to practice and to observe role models exhibiting them.

Accepting: Accepting yourself as a functioning member of society is an important characteristic. Each child must come to know himself or herself as an important person with particular strengths and weaknesses and to feel secure having the knowledge of both. At the primary level of instruction, the presentation of individual likenesses and differences reinforces for children that it is okay to be different in some ways and alike in other ways. Citing specific common bonds of various family groups, sects, culture, life-styles, and societies affords students additional opportunities for accepting themselves and others. In their jobs at school and home children learn acceptance of personal responsibilities and contributions to the overall good of the groups in which they function. Understanding the need for rules in social situations is a long-term goal that may take several years for true acceptance to occur.

Becoming: The process of becoming a good citizen begins at home prior to entering school and is continually reinforced in school, beginning in kindergarten. Functioning successfully within the classroom is a foundation upon which to build higher-level socialization skills. Growth and change at differing rates is to be expected. Young children exhibit the process of becoming responsible by being attentive, participating in group play activities, taking turns, caring for and about others, showing respect for school property, and making contributions to the class. The roles of children in play groups, learning groups, and the at-large school population need to be examined as vital concerns in the process of becoming.

Feeling: As a human relations skill, feeling includes such characteristics as caring, understanding, loving, making friends, and empathizing. Children experience and readily exhibit the depths of their feelings. Recognizing and accepting this aspect of growth and development is important for teachers and other adults who interact with youngsters in the academic setting. Encouraging feeling as a necessary human characteristic can be presented in the classroom quite simply by informally talking about feelings, identifying various feelings, accepting feelings, and understanding appropriate behaviors related to them. Many different feelings are entirely normal—even those feelings children cannot verbalize.

Elementary social studies gets its content from the various disciplines of sociology, economics, anthropology, history, geography, political science, philosophy, and social psychology. These disciplines provide a foundational base of theory and research, and the content for what children will learn in school. This content is comprised of facts, concepts, generalizations, and other data. Learning information must be accompanied with the appropriate and necessary process, product, and human relations skills (see Figure 1–1).

Social studies for elementary students include skills in the cognitive and affective domains. Teaching to the affective domain requires special planning and preparation. It is easy to fall into the pattern of teaching the cognitive content and only incidentally or occasionally teaching the affective skills. Affective skills have a special role in the social studies and should be given full attention in the curriculum.

Figure 1-1   Social Studies and Technology

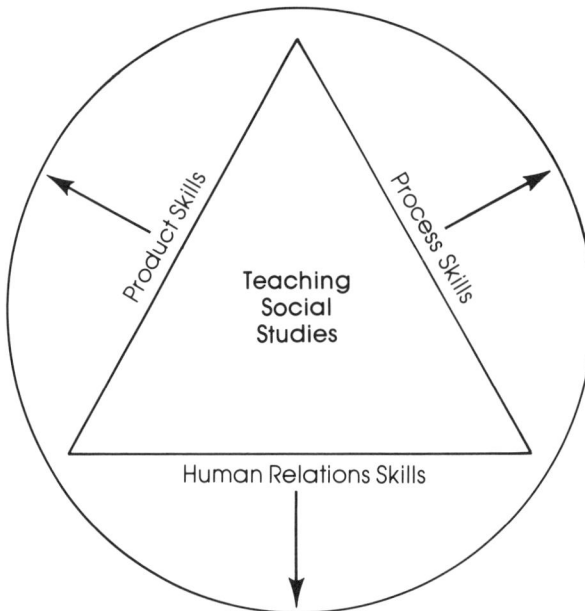

The Need for Social Studies

Why teach social studies at the elementary level? Do youngsters really need to learn about cultures that are foreign to their own? Can they truly relate to time periods from the past? Will they cope effectively with an unknown future time?

As educators we need to look at these issues in a responsible manner. Our communities and governmental bodies are actively promoting, even demanding, that the education systems provide up-to-date information and timely issues in all subjects. Human concerns within the social studies curriculum perhaps facilitate more timely issues than some other subject areas. Such topics as fire prevention, safety, environmental education, consumerism, career exploration, and others have found their niche in the social studies. These units may not be in every textbook, but they are in the curriculum. Parent groups and other forces in our communities are making a significant impact on what is taught in our schools. Educators do not make curricular decisions unilaterally. Advisory groups and committees are actively voicing their needs and wants to local school boards and administrators. Educators should work with these groups to establish the curriculum content, goals, and objectives for the local school community.

One example of corporate input into the social studies is the "Officer Friendly"® program, which has been in operation since 1966. Officer Friendly is a nationwide kindergarten through third-grade program sponsored by schools and local law enforcement agencies, in cooperation with the Sears-Roebuck Foundation. The national goals are:

1. *To establish rapport among students, teachers, parents, and the uniformed police officer by providing students opportunities to learn about law enforcement through visits by Officer Friendly, special instruction by the teacher, and parental involvement.*
2. *To provide students with opportunities to learn about their rights and responsibilities as citizens and to encourage them to form positive attitudes toward their own welfare and the welfare of others.*
3. *To foster more supportive attitudes toward law enforcement by informing students about the many services that police officers provide in the community.*
4. *To show students how to cope with physical hazards and other dangers in their environment.*[3]

This program is an organized series of lessons that provide students with important information related to positive growth in the areas of good citizenship and personal safety. The classroom teachers are provided with lessons to teach such as "Stranger Danger." Officer Friendly (a member of the local police department) visits the classroom to reinforce and further emphasize lesson content. Follow-up activities are then presented to culminate each series of lessons. The goals are specific, the information and children's activity sheets are appropriate for the age levels, and the personal appearance of a local police officer at regular intervals contributes to an effective program.

For more information write to:

The Officer Friendly Program
The Sears-Roebuck Foundation
Dept. 903, BSC 51-03
20 Sears Tower
Chicago, IL 60684

Why do we teach social studies? The multidisciplinary aspects of modern social studies affords countless opportunities for educators to civilize our youth. In cooperation with the home and family, we teach social studies to inform, to establish awareness, to challenge, and to teach coping skills for the present and the future.

Elementary students need to learn the human relations skills of getting along with others, caring, recognizing likenesses and differences, functioning successfully in their particular family structure, and feeling secure within themselves. Children learn about themselves and their place in the family of humankind by learning about their culture, race, religion, and roots. Learning the specific vocabulary inherent to the social studies is necessary for comprehension of material. Facility with particular learning/study skills traditionally allocated to one subject area (reading graphs, estimating, interpreting graphics in mathematics) is now used for cross-curricular experiences. Such skills as recognizing main ideas, sequencing events, determining point of view, and making generalizations, which are highly stressed in reading instruction, are now used for processing social studies information.

Many ethnic groups feel strongly about the younger generation knowing who they are and where they come from. Such groups want to keep the culture alive and give the children a sense of belonging. Tradition, history, and religion form a link between the young and the old. Children can enjoy learning crafts that are peculiar to a specific nationality, family recipes, and stories about "how it was before electricity," among other things. Some regions in the United States have very active, vocal cultural groups that work diligently to keep their heritage alive. The Swedish Council of America,[4] the Italian-American Cultural Society,[5] and the National Council of U.S.-Arab Relations[6] are three such organizations.

Goals: An Overview

If indeed we are mandated by the community to teach social studies, what specific learning goals should we establish? What can we expect students to do, which behaviors should they exhibit, and exactly what should they learn in class?

The goals for elementary social studies can be stated as general and individual. Some general goals presently included in major social studies programs are:

1. To acquire basic map- and globe-reading skills (location; identification of physical areas; understanding and using keys, symbols, and legends; classification) and the application of these skills to real-life situations
2. To apply library and research skills for gathering information and to participate in social studies simulation tasks and group projects
3. To acquire a basic knowledge and appreciation of history, your own cultural heritage and those of others, and the various functions of our society and the child's role in it
4. To appreciate the impact and interdependence of global concerns and situations

In addition, specific teacher goals are:

5. To participate in the socialization of each new generation into the American way of life and the institutions that allow it to function successfully (home, church, school, and our democratic values systems)
6. To use out-of-school experiences when appropriate

Some individual goals of the student may include:

1. To use a variety of social studies informational materials (factual data, adequate supplementary materials to reinforce that data)
2. To recognize and accept their roles and responsibilities within various social groups (play groups, family, at school), neighborhoods, and the community at large
3. To employ decision-making and "think, plan, and do" activities
4. To acquire a sense of productivity (I can do things well!)
5. To work toward creative producing, risk taking, and the stretching of ideas
6. To work toward good citizenship

There are many general, individual, and specific goals in social studies for each grade level. Individual programs develop goals intrinsic to their structure and/or scope and sequence. When viewing social studies as a multidimensional curricula, it is necessary to keep in mind those goals which are both inclusive and individual. The goals of a particular program must fit the needs of the students.

The NCSS Goals

The National Council for the Social Studies (NCSS) is a professional organization that focuses exclusively on the social studies. Educators from all levels participate in the council to promote and advance the goals and directives of social studies education. The council adopts essential elements for teachers to address in their state and local programs and curriculum guidelines. The following elements are proposed by the NCSS for instructional programs:

1. *The Social Studies program should be directly related to the age, maturity, and concerns of students.*
2. *The Social Studies program should draw from currently valid knowledge representative of human experience, culture, and beliefs.*
3. *The Social Studies program should deal with the real social world.*
4. *Objectives should be thoughtfully selected and clearly stated in such form as to furnish direction to the program.*
5. *Learning activities should engage the student directly and actively in the learning process.*
6. *Strategies of instruction and learning activities should rely on a broad range of learning resources.*
7. *The Social Studies program must facilitate the organization of experience.*
8. *Evaluation should be useful, systematic, comprehensive, and valid for the objectives of the programs.*
9. *Social Studies education should receive vigorous support as a vital and responsible part of the school program.*[7]

Each of these broad recommendations has several specific elements for implementation at the classroom level. These specifics can be examined in the publications listed in the Reading Resources at the end of this chapter or a copy can be requested from the NCSS. These curriculum guidelines recommend that the social studies programs be appropriate, realistic, current, multidimensional, and purposeful. Goals and objectives should be achievable and incorporate a variety of active learning experiences.

Good Citizens

One of the goals of public education is to teach and guide each new generation of young people. This process occurs over a period of years. Its purpose is to pass along the accepted dogmas and principles for living that represent our democratic way of life. The expected outcome of this process is a recurring group of responsible citizens.

What are good citizens? Although the adjective *good* is admittedly overused, an appropriate modifier must accompany the word *citizen* to further clarify our goal. Merely to educate a new generation of citizens is unclear. Citizens, persons born in a particular region or country, can be either a credit or a detriment to that country depending upon their behavior. Our goal is to raise and educate persons who will be responsible to themselves and others. They will make significant positive contributions to the local neighborhoods, thereby strengthening the very foundation of the country itself. We aim to create a sense of pride, dignity, and self-worth in each person. A good citizen is active, not passive. He or she is reactive at different times and under different circumstances.

Teaching citizenship is an important goal of social studies. If it is not taught at school, it may not be taught anywhere else. This is not to diminish the role of parental training in the areas of acceptable behavior and personal responsibility. Quite to the contrary, school goals build upon those very important foundations that are established before the child enters kindergarten. When these home foundations are solidly in place, the teaching of more formal citizenship goals is enhanced.

What are citizenship goals and how are they taught in elementary schools? Citizenship goals, the behaviors we expect to observe and teach, are part of the scope and sequence in textbooks and other teaching materials. Specific goals and behavioral objectives are given for each grade level. Teaching citizenship to young children can be a difficult task. The conceptual aspects are foreign to them, but the concept of civilized behavior is not. Civilized behavior makes the citizen. Identifying the behaviors of a good citizen is a necessary task if teachers expect to teach and, more importantly, to model the behaviors to students. Teaching citizenship must begin by identifying the qualities and characteristics of good citizens in terms the students can understand and internalize. As a beginning exercise, a list of classroom behaviors might be developed.

Citizenship Goals

1. Share with others.
2. Don't run in the hall or classroom.
3. Don't yell at the teacher.
4. Don't swear in school.
5. Vote in all elections.
6. Do your own work.
7. Always be honest.

The process of identification is followed by teacher modeling, role playing, and many opportunities to practice the behaviors that good citizens possess. Positively reinforcing the desired behaviors is very important if they are to be retained for more than a short time.

It is essential to be realistic in establishing goals that are both observable and obtainable for elementary students. Students are members of a school population. Look at this fact from a citizenship point of view: they are citizens of their school group. What do we expect the citizens of our schools to do and under what circumstances? Are these things consistent with home and community standards and expectations? Consider some qualities and characteristics of good school citizens:

1. They participate in group, class, and school activities.
2. They are responsible for personal and school property.
3. They are kind and respectful to others.
4. They do their job to the best of their ability.
5. They are cooperative and helpful.
6. They make contributions for school improvement.
7. They make good decisions for their age.
8. They obey class and school rules.

It is reasonable to expect students of all ages to exhibit these behaviors in the school setting. It is easy to observe when they do, and equally observable when they do not. The personality, the working relationship between all the adults and the students, and the school culture itself are affected when civilized behavior is actively pursued.

The Social Sciences

Elementary social studies derives its substance from the social sciences. The facts, knowledge, concepts, generalizations, and hypotheses of the various social sciences contribute significantly to form that core content. In addition to the content of the social sciences, the processes are also incorporated into the scope and sequence. Students are expected to learn a great deal of factual information in social studies. Learning these facts is very important for their ability to solve problems. Learning the processes used by the various social scientists in their daily work adds a new dimension to the learning of facts. Students often ask "How do historians know what happened so many years ago?" or "How do scientists know so much about dinosaurs?" Learning and having opportunities to practice the processes used by contemporary social scientists is the necessary counterpart of rote learning.

There are eight major divisions of the social sciences that contribute to elementary instruction. Each makes contributions to the vast body of knowledge we label social studies. Briefly examine each of the social science disciplines and their roles in social studies curriculum.

Anthropology

Anthropology is the sudy of humans and how they have evolved from simple hunter-gatherers to the complex social beings of today. Why do elementary students need to know about the condition of humans thousands of years ago? They need to know it so they can develop clear concepts and ideas about then and now. Concepts of change and adaptation are important. Early Man is a favorite topic of recreational reading for children. The appearance, life-style, and tools of this period hold a great fascination for them. Learning some basic concepts about early man gives students another building block for their informational set.

Cultural heritage is also an important part of the social studies. In almost every curriculum, multicultural studies is emphasized. The diversity of cultures in our schools and communities make it imperative that children learn about cultures other than their own.

Economics

Economics is the study of goods and services, their production and consumption, and the allocation of the earth's limited resources. The study of economics helps children understand the relationships between goods and services, money, barter, supply and demand, and other principles of economics. Needs and wants, work and wages, and decisions regarding the use of resources are some other topics in this category.

Economics is highly relevant to the everyday lives of individuals and members of a family unit. Economic education contributes facts and guidelines for establishing responsible attitudes toward the acquisition and the disposition of resources. This presents a broad spectrum of possibilities for children. They are concerned with how to get money (a job, allowance, gift), what to spend it on (records, clothes, junk food, toys), how to get the best value (where to shop, how much to pay), and thrift (saving for a future purchase). One of the more recent contributions in economics is the emphasis on consumer education. On the national scale, economics helps children understand that the United States is driven by a free enterprise, capitalistic system.

Geography

Geography is the study of the earth's form and its physical properties. The contributions of geography to the social studies are extensive. Geographic conditions have a significant impact on the settlement, growth, and development of regions. The livelihood of social groups depends largely on the physical features of the area where they locate. The relationship of people to the physical environment is affected by the geography of the area in positive and negative ways.

Geography provides students with information on the physical characteristics of the place where they live, as well as areas that are very remote from their everyday lives. Some of the physical characteristics that are of concern are climate, elevation, landforms, place location, and shape. Maps are one of the best-known tools of the geographer. Geography provides an informational background on the earth and its physical characteristics.

History

History is the study of past events. It tells us of wars and peace, disasters, inventions, buildings, people (great and small), life-styles, experiences, and human struggles. It tells of greatness and of the mundane, of the rich and poor, and it is never dull.

Children must have an understanding of past events if they are expected to understand present events. History contributes significantly to citizenship education. It provides opportunities for students to examine our U.S. history and that of other countries. Teaching history is an important way of teaching our heritage.

Parents teach their children family history and cultural heritage in various ways.

Philosophy

Philosophy is the study of knowledge. It is what we know and what we believe. Two of the more important aspects of philosophy are how to think and values. Thinking skills are an important part of the social studies. They are in use when a child makes a decision, puts data into logical sequence, or analyzes a problem. Values are what we believe. Religion, morals, ethics, and right and wrong are based on values. One major task of the teacher is to teach a child to know right from wrong. Each individual has a philosophy that guides his or her moral and ethical behavior.

Political Science

Political science is the study of how we govern ourselves. At the elementary level, we usually refer to political science as government. The study of government teaches students how our democracy works from the local to the national level. The various forms of government at the international level are difficult to understand, even for adults. However, it is necessary for students to begin learning them if they are expected to participate in the political process as adults. The operations of government at all levels is an everyday topic in the news. Current events contribute significantly to the study of governments.

Another important part of political science is the making and enforcing of laws. Children learn what laws are, why we need them, how to make them, and why we obey them.

Psychology

Psychology is the study of human behavior. Some psychologists study animal behavior to understand how learning takes place; others study people. Teachers are interested in learning how to modify behavior in their classrooms. Children learn about the uniqueness of the individual and about self-concept. Although psychology may not be considered as important as history or geography is to the social studies, it is important.

Sociology

Sociology is the study of problems confronting the human population and the interaction of group structure. Sociology provides a way for students to learn some effective ways to confront and solve human problems. A major task will be to solve problems such as overpopulation, hunger, and shortages of resources. Sociological concepts are woven throughout the social studies. The human aspects of social studies are the primary focus of this area. Children learn to use group skills when doing projects. They also learn individual responsibility to themselves and to the group.

The social sciences are closely interrelated. It is difficult to imagine the development of principles and practices in each of these sciences occurring in isolation from each other. Logic tells us there had to be some effects that altered the development of others in some way(s). In a very practical sense, the social sciences have existed from the beginning of human history. Decisions and actions affect other decisions and actions, and people learned from their successes and failures long before written history began. Consider this scenario and the social science implications.

It is the prehistoric time of Early Man. A group of about 25 adults and children have lived and worked together for a period of time, hunting and gathering to maintain an existence. Two families decide to leave the clan and join a distant clan. One of the adults was the Leader and his mate was the clan Healer. They left with the best of everything.

Some possible social science implications and effects include:

Anthropology
1. The growth of the clan may be altered.
2. Moving to a new area may be delayed.
3. What are the interpersonal effects?

Economics
1. The same amount of food may be available, but there are fewer adults to collect it.
2. The best tools for hunting were taken by those who left.
3. Some necessary survival skills may not be available now.

Geography
1. Over time, there will be more of some vegetation and less of others.
2. The physical appearance of nearby terrain may or may not remain the same.

History
1. In the clan's oral history, this departure have never before occurred.
2. The security of a precedent is not available.
3. The oral history predicts doom and destruction for those who leave.

Political Science
1. One of the adults who left was the Leader of the clan.
2. There are four fewer adults to contribute to decision making.
3. A procedure must be developed to select a new Leader.

Sociology

1. One of the women who left was the Healer.
2. Offspring are a valued resource; the clan has lost three.
3. The clan has lost two strong males who are important for the safety and protection of the clan.

In all probability the clan would not caucus and say, "We are now going to make a political science decision and elect a new Leader." But somehow the process would occur and a new Leader would emerge. It is easy to see how one event, the departure of some key clan members, would directly and indirectly force some dramatic decisions and actions to occur. The health needs, safety, food gathering, human relations matters, mobility, decision making, dealing with change, and many other group matters had to be addressed. It is not inconceivable that situations similar to this may have happened. They were dealt with in ways that were consistent with the social culture of the group. The decisions and actions were the beginnings of social science processes.

In modern times the developing curriculum of our social sciences is very pronounced. The global characteristic of world events dramatically emphasizes the interrelatedness of economic situations in one area to the political effects of another area. Current world events are constantly providing content material for the social studies. A major drought that continues over a period of years has serious consequences for the geography of the region, as well as economic, social, and political ramifications. As governments deal with a situation such as this, it requires planning, negotiating, and adapting processes on both the regional and the international levels. Within the elementary school curriculum, social studies is the place to study people and the environment.

Social Sciences in Current Texts

Teachers use textbooks as an important tool and resource for instruction. As a resource, those textbooks have the necessary information teachers need to present content to students. As an instructional tool, the textbooks must be organized and designed in ways that contribute to effective teaching practices. Authors and publishers attempt to do both of these things in their printed materials.

Social studies textbooks contain information and processes inherent to the social sciences. Some texts attempt to give an equal emphasis to each of the major topics. Others teach designated topics only to the primary grades. Still others introduce all major topics in the first grade and then emphasize them more heavily each successive year. It is helpful to know the content and processes that are contained in some of the current textbook series.

Current Trends in Social Studies

The standard traditional teaching of social studies has its foundation in the social science fields that are closely connected with the study and the progress of humankind. These fields have contributed significantly to the formation of social studies curricula for children in elementary schools. The work currently being done in these areas will affect what children learn in the social studies in future years.

Teaching the traditional social studies is both valid and justifiable. Such things as learning about Early Man, the family, decision making, problem solving, and other social studies topics are exciting for students, and involve all of the social sciences. These and other standard topics will continue to be taught and included in elementary programs. A program that relies primarily on these standard topics will soon become stagnant and dated. Although the defined learner outcomes advance at each successive grade level, without some new topics the teaching of social studies can easily evolve into mundane routine.

Current trends in social studies education are timely issues and ideas of some importance that contribute to education by providing a needed impetus for change. Current topics might include world population, aging, energy sources, computers, and cultural diversity. If indeed we are educating children to function, to be aware of and concerned about the world around them, and to be cognizant of what is and will continue to be relevant for some period of time, then this evolvement process—this adaptation to change—is necessary. Educators, professional groups, parents, publishers, politicians, and students provide input into the social studies curricula. Our educational system is accountable to the people we serve, and these people do have a voice in what exactly is being taught in their schools.

Current trends should be viewed as issues, ideas, and content areas that will endure over some time; they should not be confused with current events which may or may not be short-term matters. Social studies must remain current and up to date in its content and process. At one point, the study of Africa made its impact in social studies from the geographical standpoint (the deserts, the animal populations). It continues to be a very important area of study with a major movement toward the political and sociological sciences (emerging nations, global relations, human rights, business). Another major trend is the study of modern China. The entrance of China into world affairs and trade, the modernization of the country, and changes in culture continue to provide very important learning for children.

Aside from the expansion and updating of content areas for students, current research is making its impact on education. Research-oriented educators are telling us that social studies issues such as valuing, thinking skills, affective and cognitive skills, and other higher-level processing should be emphasized and evaluated more closely than is presently the case. Classroom teachers are voicing concerns about the informational and processing levels of learning. Is each being evaluated fairly? Parents and special interest groups are concerned about the teaching of citizenship and national pride. Some feel these should be the major focus of social studies education in elementary schools.

Futurism as a social studies concern is more than an exercise in "let's pretend" at the primary level. The advent of the technological age—the Third Wave era—gave a monumental burst of growth to almost all aspects of our society, including education. Social studies encompasses the various social sciences focusing on the human condition, the forces that shape and affect humankind. This shaping, changing, and adapting to the high-tech age has been significant. The concept of futurism as a continuing force is being addressed by the education community at all levels of instruction. As with other concepts and ideas that emerge with little or no base upon which to build, futurism as a content and process presents a particular set of problems and concerns for educators. Some of these concerns are:

1. What exactly is futurism? Can we define it? Whose definition do we use?

2. Should futurism be taught as a content skill? If so, from which sources do we draw our information?

3. Should futurism be taught as a process skill? If so, are there special processing skills unique to it?

4. What is the status of futurism in the social studies curriculum? How much emphasis does it merit?

5. Are we teaching futurism from the psychological standpoint of coping with constant change or from the mechanical standpoint of technology?

6. How can we prepare ourselves as educators to teach futurism?

Current trends in social studies education can be viewed as emerging priorities that have their origin in areas such as global conflicts, economic pressures, ecological disasters, and technological advances. The role of education in this scheme can be active (providing the leadership skills and the knowledge base to adequately address issues) or the role can be reactive (responding or taking a course of action, frequently after the fact). Clearly, an active role is the better choice. Why are emerging priorities important? They are important because they are a reflection of changes and modifications that affect our everyday lives. They are important to the social studies in particular because this area of curriculum is the one that assimilates these issues and concerns. They are important in education because they present opportunities for growth, expansion, and accommodation in areas beyond the scope of the textbook. New life and vitality are necessary if our education offerings are to be current.

Topics

There are many topics available for study. Local topics such as garbage disposal, traffic, or the homeless may provide more interest and more chance for direct application of solutions. Global topics such as human rights, world hunger, or population control have more far-reaching effects on world population. Here are several topics that are of importance today. As with all current trends, they may or may not be the more important directions of tomorrow. As a teacher, you must remain aware of change in the course of events.

Citizenship. The teaching of citizenship has always been a part of the social studies. Becoming and being a good citizen is very beneficial for school children. At the primary level, for example, teaching citizenship includes such things as:

1. Learning about the flag
2. Saying the Pledge of Allegiance regularly
3. Learning the social skills of getting along with each other
4. Practicing how to be a friend in school, at home, and in play groups
5. Learning some basic sociopolitical concepts such as respect for lawmakers, rules and laws, freedoms and responsibilities, group dynamics, and choices
6. Cooperation for the good of the group
7. The value of work
8. Learning respect, loyalty, and values

Patriotism is not an old-fashioned, outdated idea. National pride and a renewed surge of consciousness is being seen all over the country. The most current educational materials are focusing heavily on citizenship, history, and a strong sense of Americanism. Although our national ideologies are certainly discussed and encouraged in the home, in church groups, and in social groups of various types, the school setting remains a major influencing force for the teaching of our democratic way of life and values systems.

Characteristics of national pride, loyalty, working hard to make your country stronger, cooperation, self-sacrificing for the betterment of the group, and many other characteristics of citizenship are part of the teaching and promoting of citizenship. Long after the informational data or the school learning is forgotten, the skills that are learned remain.

New teachers of social studies may ask, "What are some things I can do to teach citizenship in my classroom?" The textbook and the teacher's guide usually have recommended unit plans. The scope and sequence of the text will make recommendations for the order and the extent of instruction. Here are some ideas that can be used in the classroom to supplement textbook suggestions:

1. Identify the term *citizenship* in a way that the students can understand. This will be different for primary and upper elementary grades. Use the term frequently and in appropriate circumstances.
2. For primary students, identify some characteristics of a good citizen. Model these characteristics yourself as frequently as is appropriate. Young children emulate their adult role models.

3. Recognize these good citizen behaviors and concepts whenever you see the students exhibiting or practicing them. Positive reinforcement increases the probability that they will occur again.

4. Recognize and celebrate local, state, and national events in special ways. This would include not only holidays, but such things as anniversaries of scientific and other kinds of inventions, discoveries, and personal contributions that have enriched our lives. Honoring people that have given of themselves in special ways helps children relate to real, positive models, and to think "Maybe I could do something like that when I grow up."

5. Point out current events items that exhibit citizenship at a very tangible level.

6. Compare and contrast some topical issues that the students can understand; for example: "Is this good or bad for our country, for our immediate neighbors, for the world?"

7. Brainstorm ideas on such things as: What makes me proud to be an American? Are values systems that differ from ours necessarily undesirable?

Multicultural Education.   Studying and examining cultural groups other than our own is a part of the elementary social studies program. At one time the study of the Mexican culture received great impetus; it still does in cities and states with a large Hispanic population. At another time the various African cultures were emphasized. What culture will be the next focal point? Multicultural education focuses on the language, religion, customs, manners, values, attitudes, dress, foods, holidays, and the everyday way of life of peoples and cultures from all over the world. The arrival of large numbers of immigrants from non-Western countries has made this current thrust a matter of immediate concern for many areas in this country. Accommodating and assimilating non-English speaking children into the foreign atmosphere of our school system presents real challenges for educators. Although various English as a Second Language (ESL) programs contribute to the teaching of language, a large portion of language learning occurs in the regular classroom. The communication skills (verbal and nonverbal) of the teacher are a very important part of multicultural education.

Multicultural education strives to teach children to accept and respect cultures that are different, while maintaining a pride in their own culture. It strives to establish a personal, cultural identity for each child. Building an American society that is rich in its cultural diversity remains a vital social studies goal. In this case, education must be an active, forceful agent that is responsive to the needs of a particular area or region. Each social institution should ask, "How can we help groups that move into our community?" Multicultural education should provide students with some information and practical skills they can use at their own level of experience and understanding.

People and Places in the News.   The news media (radio, television, magazines, newspapers) are a constant source of social studies material. The media relate information to the public about events and concerns that are happening on a daily, moment-to-moment basis. The emphasis here is on what people do, such as participate in elections, make discoveries or achievements of some importance, participate in conferences or peace treaties, mediate or trade—all of these actions are content for teachers to highlight. Such things as natural disasters (floods, drought, famine, earthquakes), less-than-democratic elections, wars, conflicts, terrorism, the enactment of laws, and other events are open items for scrutiny in the social studies classroom.

Particular places in the news may be areas, regions, or newly developing nations that are both obscure and totally foreign to the experience of most U.S. children. Although some of these places seem to appear on the world scene almost overnight, their role in world affairs may become significant in a few short years. Surely, teachers cannot be expected to emphasize every place that appears in the news. However, it is a good way to get children to look for geographic locations on a world or local map. Have the students find the locations of the Olympic Games or trace hurricane routes, for example. Some initial background information is certainly a basic responsibility of the social studies teacher. Here are four basic goals or purposes for people and places in the news:

1. To incorporate people and places in the news as a function of, and a content area within, current events

2. To focus on people and places as short- or long-term topics for investigation as appropriate

3. To establish people and places as more than a show-and-tell item

4. To seek out appropriate teaching and learning materials for classroom use

Consumer Education.   A continuing current trend is consumerism. Consumers are people who purchase, use, and participate in products and services. Children of all ages represent a significant market for goods and services of all types. Books, comics, food, clothes, movies, toys, games, and cosmetics are some of the things they purchase. The business community certainly recognizes and strategically gears their marketing and advertising campaigns directly at young consumers. The purchasing power of children cannot be ignored.

How children learn to become intelligent consumers is the job of consumer education in the schools. The role of family and media influence in consumer socialization is significant. Consumer education includes such things as the use of money, product safety, quality, advertisements, managing money (how to get it, how to spend it), making choices, and values. It attempts to teach purchasing skills and the skill of recognizing advertising.

Children should learn about the economic effects of their purchases on the U.S. economy. Should we "buy American" to support U.S. workers and businesses, keeping our money here? What affect does the importation of foreign goods have on our economy? Could continuing purchases of imported goods eventually affect our standard of living and/or our job prospects?

The power of consumers is also a focus: What can you do if a product or service is not acceptable? What can you do if a product or service is very good? Young consumers are becoming more aware of the producer/manufacturer's responsibilities. Writing letters to complain or compliment is one way youngsters can demonstrate their rights as consumers, as well as use language arts and communications skills. *Penny Power* is a bimonthly publication of Consumer Union[8] that addresses consumer concerns for young children. Some goals for consumer education at the elementary level are:

1. To develop educated, aware consumers in the marketplace
2. To increase awareness of choices, alternatives, consumer responsibilities, and recourse
3. To identify the relationship between the producer and the consumer
4. To clarify the environmental aspects of consumerism

Environmental Education.   Teaching children responsible attitudes and skills they can use to interact safely with their immediate and distant environment is the purpose of environmental education. Environmental education is a very broad category of curriculum. It encompasses the scientific issues of pollution—air, water, soil—as well as the use of resources (conservation). Many social issues of everyday living are "bumped" into environmental education. Some of these issues include packaging, waste disposal, nuclear energy, expansion of cities, consumption of products, planning for the future of natural resources, and others.

Correlation of the scientific and the social studies aspects of environmental education is necessary and inevitable. Examining the scientific properties without the social responsibilities and ramifications is incomplete. Is it reasonable to expect elementary-aged children to comprehend such complex ideas as these? Yes, it is. Even youngsters at the kindergarten level are alert and aware of environmental concerns that are easily recognized. Although the matter of pollution seems overworked and dated, it continues to be a major concern. Activities and lessons can be designed and planned to emphasize its effects on our everyday lives. Within the classroom and the school itself, the matter of littering, paper disposal, use of detergents or cleaners, and other daily practices can be examined firsthand. Such concerns as "What does the custodian do with the trash when he empties our wastebaskets?" or "Where does the food go after we clean our lunch trays?" and other relatively simple matters can lead to environmental investigations or become part of the culminating experiences in a unit.

What are some reasonable, attainable goals for environmental education for the elementary school? Here are some very general goals to consider:

1. To develop in children an awareness of and appreciation for environmental issues

2. To provide opportunities to practice some decision-making and problem-solving strategies for environmental issues that are relevant

3. To establish safe, sound life-style practices that will be socially responsible

4. To educate an ongoing, concerned, and active citizenry for the cause of the environment

Other goals and objectives can be obtained from organized environmental groups.

Global Education.   Chase and John state:

> *People all over the world are rising up to be counted as people. It is people who make events. It is people who are poor and hungry. It is people who decide to make war. It is people who are friendly, indifferent, or hostile. It is some people in a country who run its government, not always representing the majority of their countrymen but dealing with people running other governments. Teaching our children about the world means building images of real people living in a real country who are like themselves in many ways and different in others. Teaching children about other cultures also helps clarify some of the elements within one's own.*[9]

While much is being written and discussed about global education, the above is a good summation of what global education is truly all about. It strives to give students a realistic picture of ourselves as a nation of individuals, as well as give a view of how other nations and individuals see us. It helps youngsters try to make some sense out of the world as it is and, yes, to provide them with both cognitive and affective skills to affect change. Global education is both cross-cultural and intercontinental. It encompasses the physical environment on a global scale, the politics of many diverse nations, economic systems, values systems, educational processes, and many other issues.

A major purpose of global education is to develop global citizens who can view their world and its events with an international perspective. Preparing youngsters for global citizenship takes time. One unit on global issues will not result in a classroom of totally informed global citizens. The concepts of interdependence, responsibility, cooperation, empathy, values clarification, and others require time and repeated exposure to develop. The teaching of global awareness need not be grandiose to be effective. Understanding cultures that are very distant in terms of time and space is difficult, especially for very young children, but it is not impossible to provide them with valuable learning experiences. Primary teachers start building the foundation for content and concepts that are explored at each successive grade level. They begin with experiences and activities that focus on family life, foods, games, roleplaying, and reading and listening to stories, poems, and folk tales. These active learning experiences provide the format for presenting the global content.

Robert G. Harvey proposes five dimensions of teaching for global perspective: perspectives consciousness, state of planet awareness, cross-cultural awareness, knowledge of global awareness, and awareness of human choices.[10] Each of these incorporates physical, human, and values orientations and each has structure for the teaching of content and concepts. To summarize, the goals and purposes of global education are:

1. To introduce students to cultures and people different than our own
2. To establish a basis of content and concepts upon which further knowledge and studies are built
3. To introduce and develop the interrelatedness and interdependence of all peoples and countries
4. To develop the skills, attitudes, and understanding necessary for responsible decision making

Integrating Current Trends into the Social Studies Program

It is the responsibility of the classroom teacher to teach the established curriculum as determined by the designated textbook series, state and local requirements, and any special topics of local tradition. Integrating current trends into the social studies curriculum is similar to any other integration process. Coordinate and correlate the key factors to highlight the most important properties of each area. Current trends may or may not be integral to the text that is being used. The media, trade books, and special interest organizations are the sources for obtaining teaching materials. Many schools now have developed a curriculum guide for the social studies that provides the structure and content to be taught.

Teaching topics of current trends can be done by presenting them as specialized or supplementary units to the established curriculum. Some will be examined more carefully than others and at different times during the year. The information must be current and up-to-date and not stereotypical. Searching and gathering pertinent information is a time-consuming teaching responsibility, but knowing where to look can ease the task considerably. Prepared teaching packets are sometimes available and should be used if they meet your teaching criteria. See Chapter 13 for some suggestions.

ACTIVITIES

The following class activities are designed to afford you the opportunity to interact with your fellow teachers-in-training under the guidance of your instructor.

In some cases you will work alone; other times you may pair with two or three others. There will be times when you will see another point of view, expand your personal horizons, explore the effects of controversial issues, roleplay, and practice some teaching skills you will need when you enter the classroom. Look on these activities as a chance to take some risks, share ideas, and seek advice from your instructor. She or he is there to assist you in becoming a skilled teacher.

1.1   Controversial Issues

Choose a controversial issue that is currently on the educational scene (note that some are ongoing). Here are a few topics to consider:

Evolution
Human rights
Role of censorship
Religion[11]
Values

Consider your choice. Do you think it should or should not be taught in the elementary school?

Prepare your case and present it to the class or your group. This activity could be designed in a debate format, perhaps three or four persons on each side of the issue with your instructor acting as the moderator. The audience will roleplay the taxpayers who are involved in deciding whether or not your issue will remain in or be eliminated from the curriculum.

1.2   Futures

Project five or ten years into the future. What role do you see for the social studies within the larger curriculum? Keep in mind the balance of our producing and servicing society. Should the scope be scaled down or expanded? Will the valuing and citizenship aspects be diminished? What about first amendment rights?

Divide into small discussion groups and share ideas with each other. As a group, write down on large pieces of paper all the ideas that are given. At the end of the discussion, these ideas will serve as the basis for a class discussion activity.

1.3 *Current Trends*

A Scenario (Upper Grades)

Examine the following scenario in terms of its current trend content. Although this situation is contrived for an example, similar situations occur in world events and are concurrent with social studies programs.

> Countries A, B, and C are in the midst of a serious economic disaster. Their economic base is largely agricultural. Periods of extended drought have resulted in crop failures. Foreign aid is inconsistent at best. The trade base has declined due to the lack of agricultural products to export. A sense of despair and hopelessness pervades.

Now think of the various ramifications of this situation in terms of the topics listed below. Think of regional and worldwide considerations. Working alone or with another person, list three concerns, outcomes, consequences, or topics that would be appropriate for classroom investigation.

Citizenship
1.
2.
3.

Multicultural Education
1.
2.
3.

People and Places in the News
1.
2.
3.

Consumer Education
1.
2.
3.

Environmental Education
1.
2.
3.

Global Education
1.
2.
3.

Integrating current trend items into the social studies curriculum is further enriched when the skills of other subject areas are used in the lessons. Using the above scenario and the items you have listed, write some ideas for lesson extensions in the following curriculum areas:

Language Arts
1.
2.
3.

Math
1.
2.
3.

Art and Music
1.
2.
3.

Now examine your ideas with a partner or your group. For which grade did you plan your activities? Were the math ideas easier to plan than the others because the situation had an economic base? Share with your instructor.

A Scenario (Primary Grades)

Now examine this scenario for primary-aged students.

A group of Arabic families has moved into the school neighborhood. Up to this point, the school population has been mostly Caucasian, with life-styles that are familiar. Some ''educating'' of the school population is clearly needed.

Helping the newcomers adjust to life in an American school is clearly a big job. Helping our children accept the newcomers in school and in the neighborhood is the other side of the task. This situation provides an excellent opportunity to teach multicultural education firsthand. It gives us a chance to learn about the Arabs' culture and it gives them a chance to learn about ours. For each of the areas below, record some activities you could do in the classroom with a primary grade of your choice.

Language   *Roleplay*

Dress   *Customs*

Literature   *Foods*

Family Life   *Play Groups*

In your activities did you plan what the teacher will do and what the students will do? Activities that are new to young learners require guided practice sessions, especially for the students who come from a totally different background. Providing for a smooth transition into your school setting should be the guiding force for all that you are planning. Share your ideas with your group or your instructor.

These activities give you some insights into the material presented in Chapter 1. As a new teacher, you will encounter situations wherein issues are questioned, challenged, or debated. Knowing how you feel about social studies issues enables you to help your students clarify and understand the issues that concern them.

Summary

Elementary social studies gets its content from the various disciplines such as sociology, economics, anthropology, history, geography, and political science. These disciplines provide a foundational basis of theory and research. From these basic structures, the content of what children learn in school is derived. This content is comprised of facts, concepts, generalizations, and other data. The learning and experiencing of social studies is not complete with informational learning alone. This learning of content must be assimilated and accompanied by using the appropriate process skills in the teaching procedures. Skills facilitate and actualize the learning of data. Most of these process skills are also used in other curriculum areas.

Social studies for elementary students includes both cognitive and affective material. Teaching to the affective domain requires special planning and preparation. It is easy to fall into the pattern of teaching the informational content and only incidentally or occasionally teaching the affective skills. These skills have a special role in social studies and should be given full attention in the curriculum.

READING RESOURCES

Clark, T. "Teaching About Apartheid in South Africa." *Social Education, 51* (1987): 94–100.

Fleming, D. B. "Social Studies Goals: U.S. Department of Education Style!" *Social Education, 77* (July/August 1986): 141–144.

Hahn, Carole. "Advocating Early Childhood Social Studies." *Elementary School Social Studies: Research as a Guide to Practice,* Bulletin No. 79. National Council for the Social Studies, 1986, pp. 165–174.

Kniep, W. M. "Social Studies Within a Global Education." *Social Education, 50* (1986): 536–542.

Kniep, W. M. "Global Education: The Road Ahead." *Social Education, 50* (1986): 415–416.

Newmann, F. M. "Social Studies Education: A Look Ahead." *Education Digest, 52* (1986): 36–40.

Parker, Walter C., and Kaltsounis, Theodore. "Citizenship and Law-Related Education." *Elementary School Social Studies: Research as a Guide to Practice,* Bulletin No. 79. National Council for the Social Studies, 1986, pp. 14–30.

Rachlin, Jill. "Putting God on the Reading List." *US News and World Report, 105* (1) (July 4, 1988): 57.

"Social Studies for Young Children." National Council for the Social Studies Position Paper, 1983. *Elementary School Social Studies: Research as a Guide to Practice,* Bulletin No. 79. National Council for the Social Studies, 1986.

Stone, Lynda. "International and Multicultural Education." *Elementary School Social Studies: Research as a Guide to Practice,* Bulletin No. 79. National Council for the Social Studies, 1986, pp. 34–50.

ENDNOTES

1. Webster's New Collegiate Dictionary (Springfield, MA: G. and C. Merriam Company), 1977, p. 1103.

2. National Council for the Social Studies, *NCSS Articles of Incorporation.* Washington, DC, no date.

3. *Officer Friendly Program Guide,* p. 4. The Sears-Roebuck Foundation, Dept. 903, BSC 51-03, 20 Sears Tower, Chicago, IL 60684.

4. Swedish Council of America, 2600 Park Ave., Minneapolis, MN 55407.

5. Italian-American Cultural Society, 28111 Imperial, Warren, MI 48093.

6. National Council of U.S.-Arab Relations, 1625 Eye St., Washington, DC 20006.

7. "Revision of the NCSS Social Studies Curriculum Guidelines," *Social Education* (1979): 261–273.

8. *Penny Power,* Consumers Union of U.S., Inc. Mt. Vernon, NY.

9. Chase, W. Linwood, and John, Martha Tyler, *A Guide for the Elementary Social Studies Teacher,* 2nd ed. (Boston: Allyn and Bacon, 1973), p. 139.

10. Harvey, Robert G., "An Attainable Global Perspective." Global Perspective in Education (pamphlet), 218 E. 28th St., New York, NY 10003.

11. A suggested source is "Religion in the Curriculum: A Report from the ASCD Panel on Religion in the Curriculum," August 1987.

UNIT II

How Children Learn

2

How Children Learn Social Studies

PROJECTIONS

You are one of the persons who will be teaching social studies in the decade of the 1990s and beyond. How you prepare yourself now will, to a large extent, determine the type of social studies teacher you will ultimately become. Securing a strong foundation in the established learning theories and learning styles of children is very important. This foundation forms the structure from which your social studies instructional practices will emerge. Instructional practice is grounded in your particular beliefs regarding the myriad ways children learn curriculum content, more specifically, social studies content and thinking skills.

Cognitive instruction in the social studies will adapt to a variety of strategic teaching models. Much research is being conducted in the area of cognition and school learning. Debates continue regarding such things as automaticity, behaviorism, metacognition, learning and prior knowledge, holistic teaching, and other aspects of learning theory. The controversy over content skills and thinking skills continues: Should content be taught first and then followed with thinking skills, or should we teach the thinking skills to facilitate the content learning? This issue needs to be addressed.

Teachers are concerned that curriculum and instruction focus on the various ways that children learn. It is not easy for adults to revert back to early childhood and consciously elicit the ways they actually learned new things as a child, especially school-related learning items. One of the most immediate recollections is "I simply had to memorize everything"—a successful strategy for those individuals with keen visual and auditory memory, a frustrating, less productive strategy for many others.

Teachers observe many things in their classrooms. One very important observation is the various things children do while they perform given classroom tasks. Those tasks may or may not follow the planned prescription for learning as designed by the teacher, but the given tasks will ultimately be performed and the skills will be learned. It is important that teachers take their cues from students in the classroom and thus plan learning activities that are child-centered and not adult-centered.

The stages of learning as identified by Piaget are a continual influence in education. There is a need in the social studies for a concentrated effort to provide more learning experiences in the area of concrete formations. It is unfortunate that in some cases the male students are allowed and encouraged to *do* the social studies lessons, and the female students are allowed and encouraged to *read about* the lessons. Another unfortunate practice is the relegation of concrete experiences to the primary grades, more specifically to the kindergarten. The rush to move primary students into formal operations is unnecessary and usually unproductive. More hands-on experiences and activities are needed for longer periods of time. Concerned teachers are planning and providing more of these experiences for older students as a way to teach both product and process skills.

One very exciting innovation in education is in the field of learning styles. It is making inroads in textbook materials, professional courses and seminars, as well as graduate degree programs. This chapter examines McCarthy's 4MAT System Model as one example of a usable format for classroom teachers. There are others with slightly different approaches. It is imperative that schools, teachers, and parents incorporate the learning styles of children into their plans.

One of the most important developments that will drastically affect the teaching of social studies is the ongoing research on how the brain works. As new information is gained, new procedures for teaching will be developed. It is not inconceivable that our entire educational structure may be altered. We know too much about learning to continue teaching in our present mode. Your challenge will be to encourage the change and adapt to it.

We know so much about learning and use so little of it. It is unfortunate that, to a large extent, educational research has affected so few classrooms in any signifiant way. Why? Elementary classrooms are very much the same as they were fifteen or twenty years ago—not only in physical appearance but most importantly in the interactions that are occurring. This practice cannot continue; children must be taught to cope with the future, not the past. There are always some teachers who are moving forward, applying newer educational innovations. These pacesetters are to be commended for their self-confidence, courage, dedication, and open-minded philosophy of teaching and learning. Many other dedicated individuals are conducting research to assist all teachers in the ever-present challenge to do a credible job of educating our youth.

Researchers are constantly gathering new data about how the brain functions and learns, optimal learning sequences, development of learning patterns, intake of data through the senses, and numerous other areas that help us better understand the learning process. Teachers should make every effort not only to read the research but to apply it in the classroom. The things we know about how children learn are effective when we apply them to our teaching. If you are to be a successful teacher you must learn everything you can about how children learn, and then make every effort possible to plan your lessons in ways that apply this knowledge.

In this chapter you will be introduced to how children learn. It is an overview, not a comprehensive account. Learning theories and learning styles are complete courses unto themselves and we recommend that you read extensively in these areas. *Learning theories* and *learning styles* will be introduced here. In the succeeding chapters, reference is made to the material in this chapter as we show you ways to incorporate this information into your social studies lessons.

Learning Theories

There are three areas of learning that are presented in this section. Behaviorism and cognitive theory are concerned with how children learn. Cognitive development is more concerned with mental development.

Learning is usually defined as a change in an individual caused by some experience. It can be induced in a variety of ways. The experience may be planned (after a carefully taught lesson in history, the student now has knowledge of the event that she did not possess before) and it may be incidental or accidental (on the way to school a child was bitten by a dog and he now has a fear of dogs). Learning is occurring all the time. Teachers are faced with the task of providing structured learning situations.

Behaviorism

Behaviorists are primarily concerned with observable changes in behavior. They want to see visible evidence that learning has taken place. They look for new skills that can be performed or knowledge that can be measured.

Behaviorism had its beginning with the classic study by Ivan Pavlov. He observed that a dog would salivate when meat powder was place on its tongue. A bell was rung as meat was placed in front of the dog, causing the dog to associate the bell with the meat. Soon, the dog would salivate at the sound of the bell. A stimulus (the sound of the bell) would cause an observable response (salivation). This was referred to as *classical conditioning*.

E. L. Thorndike followed with the *stimulus-response theory*. A stimulus produced a response. He also found that a behavior that produced a desired effect was repeated, whereas those behaviors that did not produce desired effects were not repeated. This developed into his *Law of Effect*, which stated that if an act was followed by a satisfying effect, it would probably be repeated, but if it was followed by an unsatisfying effect, it would probably not be repeated. Can you see any implications for classroom behavior here?

B. F. Skinner proposed a theory of *operant conditioning*. His work was based on the relationship between behavior and the consequence of the behavior. Pleasant consequences would cause the individual to repeat the behavior, whereas unpleasant consequences would not.

Present-day behaviorists focus on the *consequences* of behavior. As a result of an act, what will happen? The person will receive either a reward or a punishment. A reward is defined by behaviorists as a *reinforcer* because it reinforces the behavior. In effect, it is a pleasant consequence that makes the individual repeat the act. If a child answers a question correctly (a desirable behavioral act) and as a consequence receives praise (a reinforcer) then the behavior (answering correctly) is strengthened. On the other hand, undesirable consequences tend to receive an undesirable reinforcement called *punishment.* Since punishment is not a pleasant reward, the behavior is not likely to be repeated. If a child refuses to do his classwork (an undesirable behavioral act) and as a consequence must remain after school (a punishment) then the behavior will be diminished. It should be noted that the desirability or undesirability of the act is determined by the giver of the reinforcement or punishment. Reinforcement makes the behavior desirable and punishment makes it undesirable.

The teacher who inadvertently rewards undesirable behavior can expect that behavior to continue. For example, a child seeks attention by disrupting the class (undesirable behavior). The teacher stops the class and spends several minutes reprimanding the child. This is supposed to be a punishment, but is it? Actually, the child received the attention he wanted and it proved to be a reinforcer. The next time the child wants attention, he will disrupt the class again.

One more point about behaviorism should be made: The administration of a reinforcement or punishment should immediately follow the act. Delayed consequences are not always perceived as being a result of the behavior. The longer you wait, the less impact you will have on the behavior.

Behaviorists are concerned with observable behavior. This is why we usually associate behaviorism with classroom behavior. It is much more difficult to observe the learning that occurs from mental activities such as concept formation or reading a textbook.

Cognitive Theories

Cognition is how we process information. The cognitive theorists are concerned with how we intake information, remember it, and then use it as the need arises. The emphasis seems to be more on *how* we learn than *what* we learn.

One of the earlier forms of cognitive theory was the Gestalt theory, *Gestalt* being a German word loosely translated as form, shape, or configuration. Kurt Koffka, Wolfgang Kohler, and Max Wertheimer studied the way perception was influenced by the context or configuration of the elements perceived. They theorized that the relation among components rather than fixed characteristics of the objects determine what is perceived. Present-day interpretations maintain that the separation of the body and the mind is artificial and the human organism responds holistically to life events. The general principle of Gestalt is that of *perception* or how we see things. Two concepts are linked to perception. The first is the concept of *closure*. We tend to see wholes, not parts. Our mental set automatically fills in blanks or omissions, even at times when we do not want it to. The whole ends up being greater than its parts.

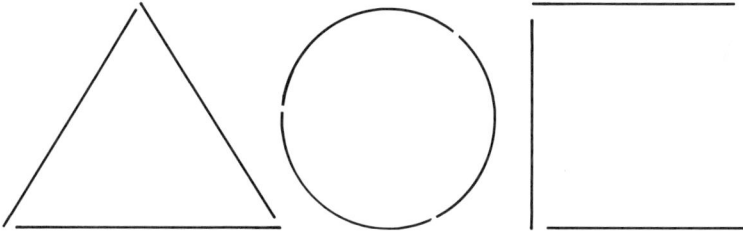

Do you see a triangle, circle, and square, or disjointed figures?

The second concept is *figure-ground*. We tend to focus on the main figure, obscuring the background. For example, if you meet a friend in the library, you will focus on the friend's face or form and ignore the shelves of books in the background. In general, Gestalt theory says that we cannot break the learning environment into neat categories; it must be viewed as a whole. The total experience determines what is learned.

Current cognitive theory stresses the total learning situation of the student. There are three main areas of concern: *attention, memory,* and *problem solving.*

Attention.   In order to learn, the student must be able to screen out all outside distractions or stimuli. When we ask a child to ''pay attention'' we are asking him or her to disregard all external distractions and attend only to those we provide. Attention is hard to control. It is directly related to interest; interesting stimuli attract attention. The sound and sight of a fire engine passing the classroom often attracts more attention than a boring lecture that has dragged on for an unreasonably long time. To get and hold a child's attention so that he or she can receive information requires teacher stimulation that overrides all other external stimuli. In actual practice, this means that you must do a good job of motivating, followed by an interesting lesson, or you will lose the student's attention.

Memory.   Memory is concerned with how we store and retrieve information for later use. *Short-term* memory is where we store our conscious thoughts. It is very volatile and limited. Small amounts of information are retained for only a short time, perhaps for as long as 20 or 30 seconds, but usually less. A conscious effort must be made if we want to keep information in short-term memory for any length of time. Short-term memory is the receptacle where incoming information is processed. As information is received, it goes into a small storage area where it is sorted, processed, then dumped. As it is sorted, important or usable information is separated to be either processed or stored in long-term memory. Extraneous data are promptly dumped or forgotten. Short-term memory also serves as an outlet for long-term memory. As we process information, we can search our long-term memory for pertinent data, retrieve it to short-term memory, and then use it in our current processing efforts.

Long-term memory is where we store all we know. It has room for a lot of information that can be stored for a long period of time. We seem never to fill it or to empty (forget) any of the information stored there. You may have trouble locating some seldom used information, but other data can be recalled decades later. How many times have you heard an elderly person recalling events of his or her childhood or, more appropriately to education, their ABCs that they learned in the first grade? The real challenge is to get information from short-term memory into long-term memory. The processing of information and the subsequent movement of that information into long-term memory is learning. There are several strategies for memorizing (committing data to memory), but the most common is practice. The more something is practiced, the more apt it is to be committed to memory. With enough practice, recall becomes automatic.

Problem Solving. The main concern of cognitive psychology is the mental process of learning. Obtaining and storing information is not enough. We must process it to make it useful and meaningful. And then we must be able to apply what is learned to the solution of other problems. This is called *transfer* of *learning.* Our goal, as teachers, is for students to be able to learn on their own, to identify problems, and then to solve them. Problem solving involves the use of knowledge and skills (memory) to produce an acceptable answer. The ability to use skills and knowledge to solve new problems is an example of *transfer.*

As a teacher, you may not be as concerned with the theoretical aspect of learning as you are with the application. Jerome Bruner, David Ausubel, and Robert Gagné have each developed teaching models based on cognitive theory.

Jerome Bruner. Bruner developed a model called *discovery learning.* The students learn by being actively involved in using concepts, skills, and principles to solve problems and answer questions. The teacher structures the learning environment so this can occur, then acts as a guide to help the students discover new information and applications. Discovery learning has been used extensively in teaching science, but the imaginative teacher can find many ways to apply it to social studies as well as to any other subject matter. Advantages are that it is very motivating. It arouses curiosity, makes learning a challenge, and forces students to develop and use independent learning skills. Students have to *use* information rather than only store it. Critics find that discovery learning takes a lot of time, careful planning, and is difficult to use. As a result, it is used more as a supplement to traditional methods rather than as a replacement.

David Ausubel.   Ausubel proposed an alternative to discovery learning that he called *reception learning*. It calls for the teacher to structure the learning activity, select and provide the appropriate materials, and then present a well-organized lesson that starts with general ideas and proceeds to specific details. The central focus of receptive learning is *expository teaching*, which consists of three phases:

1. *Presentation of advance organizer:*   A preview of the lesson relates what is to be learned to the prior knowledge of the child.
2. *Presentation of the material or learning task:*   The teacher presents the information to the students in a structured lesson, using a variey of methods.
3. *Strengthening cognitive organization:*   The lesson is related to the advance organizer. Students are questioned about the relationships and are encouraged to ask and answer extending questions.

Expository teaching is very similar to many of the traditional teaching strategies and it emphasizes the role of the teacher in directing the learning experience.

Robert Gagné.   Gagné proposes that there are a series of eight learning events required to transmit information to a class: (1) motivation, (2) apprehending, (3) acquisition, (4) retention, (5) recall, (6) generalizing, (7) performing, and (8) feedback. These events are paralleled by instructional events that are designed to accomplish the event. Teachers plan so they can lead students through the events in sequence so that learning can occur.

Cognitive learning is based on the premise that learning is internal and most effectively takes place when the student is directly involved. The teacher may follow any of several approaches, but all are concerned with the involvement of the student in the learning process. In general, the following list summarizes the beliefs of cognitists as related to teaching.

1. Students are active processors of information. They must be involved in learning if learning is to occur.
2. Learning is most likely to occur when the information is meaningful to the learner.
3. *How* students learn may be more important than *what* they learn.
4. Skills and processes become automatic with practice.
5. Internal motivation is the best motivation.

Cognitive Development

Swiss psychologist Jean Piaget is a name familiar to almost everyone in education. He studied the behavior of children and developed his theory of *cognitive development.* Two important ideas come from this theory: the concepts of *schemes, accommodation, assimilation,* and *equilibration* and his *stage development theory.*

Schemes, Accommodation, Assimilation, and Equilibrium. In cognitive development, knowledge comes from the child's interaction with the environment. Schemes are patterns of behavior that a child develops as he or she learns. They may be simple, such as crying for attention, or complex, such as using a map to locate a place. When a new event or object enters into a scheme, the learner must *assimilate* the new data into his or her scheme. Sue Ann has learned to use a Michigan road map to locate places and is given an Oklahoma road map to use. She has to process these data into her scheme. She makes minor adjustments in her map-reading scheme and uses the Oklahoma map. When data do not conveniently fit into a scheme, the learner must *accommodate* by changing the existing scheme into a new scheme. Sue Ann locates places on a map by looking for the name randomly. The concept of latitude and longitude is introduced and the cities are now to be located using this concept. Her old scheme of random searching no longer works, so she must change her scheme, thereby changing her behavior pattern for locating cities. Learners are constantly striving for *equilibrium,* a state of mental comfort where everything is in place and fits there. When an event occurs that upsets this balance, the learner goes into a state of *disequilibrium.* Sue Ann knows that she can locate a city using latitude and longitude and feels comfortable in this knowledge. But she is given a state highway map that does not have latitude and longitude on it, and she knows that random searching is inefficient and time consuming. She is not comfortable. The teacher can now introduce the grid concept and Sue Ann will want to learn to use it to regain her equilibrium. This knowledge is of great value to teachers. If we can upset the equilibrium by introducing new ideas, concepts, or events in a controlled learning environment, we can direct the child's learning as he or she strives to regain equilibrium.

Stages of Development. The second and best-known idea to come from Piaget is his stage development theory, which says that children proceed in an orderly, sequential manner through four learning stages. No stage can be skipped, and many learners never completely attain the formal operations stage.

It is necessary to understand and recognize the particular stage of development where students are functioning before we can properly establish usable and obtainable objectives for them to meet. The four stages of development are briefly discussed:

Sensorimotor (Birth to about 2 years):   At this time the infant can visually track an object in space, such as a rattle, objects on a mobile, or someone's finger. The infant progresses from merely looking at the object to actually trying to grab it with his or her own hands.

Preoperational Thought (Ages 2 to 7 years):   The thought process of the preoperational child is static and he or she lacks reversibility. The child's thoughts are irreversible and he or she is attentive to limited amounts of information. The child is in the static state of reality.

Period of Concrete Operations (Ages 7 to 11 years):   At this stage of development the child touches, uses, and organizes objects in different ways. He or she can take a set of five objects and order them from smallest to largest.

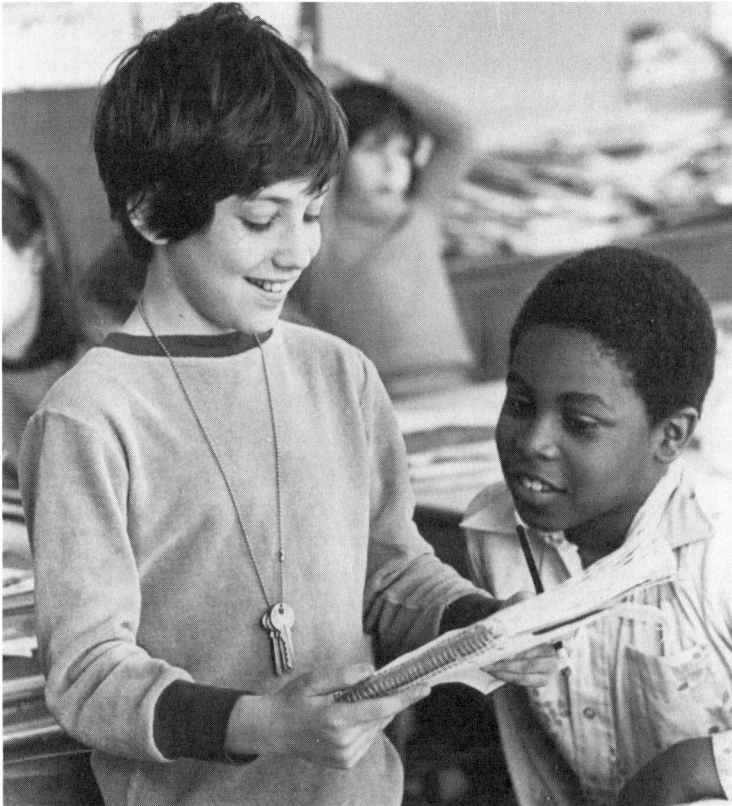

These students are sharing an enjoyable activity. Teachers provide opportunities for students to share and learn from each other.

Manipulating, building, and using the whole body during learning activities are ways the child learns at this particular period. He or she can see and understand the logic of certain reactions or functions in situations that are familiar. This stage generally coincides with the elementary grades in school.

Period of Formal Operations (Ages 12 to adolescence):   During the stage of formal operations the youngster is developing the ability to think abstractly. He or she can see and understand the logical progression in new situations that have not been encountered previously. The child can make inferences. This period of development extends into adulthood.

A primary class will have a number of children who are at or approaching the concrete operations stage of intellectual development. Some of the slower-developing children may still be functioning at the preoperational level. A few of the advanced children may be moving toward formal operations. Related criteria for early identification of high-potential children are the ability to use logical reasoning, to think in terms of future events, and to project into the arena of possibilities and alternatives, critical thinking, and "maybe this might work."

A child's elementary school experiences will encompass the concrete formation period of development. The opportunity to touch, feel, act out, and use one's whole body in the real world is an importat part of early school learning. When observing lower-grade children in their school environment, they are noticeably up and about much of the time. The large-motor skills are still developing and the fine-motor skills are not as advanced. Children enjoy doing things as opposed to having the teacher tell them about it. How many times have you heard a child say "Let me do it, teacher!" Recognize this period of high motivation and interest in learning, and then take advantage of it.

The use of concrete experiences is very important during these years. A social studies teacher should incorporate a variety of objects and artifacts into her or his lessons, creating projects and otherwise involving the students in hands-on learning situations. Remember that "reading about" or "listening to" are abstract activities and many of your students are not quite ready for this form of instruction. Keep in mind that young children learn more efficiently when they are actively involved in the process. The objectives set for them to master should in some way address their particular stage of development.

This overview of learning theories is a brief condensation of a very important subject for you to learn if you want to be an effective teacher. You may favor one theory over another, but you will probably use a combination of all as you are concerned with results and not with labels. Using learning theory to plan your lessons and to manage your classroom can make a lesson much more effective.

Learning Styles

In 1968 John DeCecco defined learning styles this way: "Learning styles are personal ways in which individuals process information in the course of learning new concepts and principles."[1]

There are other definitions of the term in various educational publications. This particular one focuses on several key elements that are important in teaching elementary social studies. These elements are:

- *Personal ways:*   The ways students learn are very personal and individualized. Not all students in the class learn in the same ways. Each student's preferred ways are important factors in his or her educational progress.

- *Process information:*   Students receive and process verbal and printed information in different ways and at varying rates. Some children process and retain information in small, sequential steps; others are capable of receiving and retaining larger informational sets in one instructional sequence.

- *Learning new concepts and principles:*   Various social studies notions, truths, moral laws, and ideas are difficult for students to understand and eventually to learn. The personal ways that students approach these concepts and principles are the learning styles that enable them to learn new things.

The term *learning styles* summons a variety of ideas for teachers. Such things as students who want to work alone, group activities, paper and pencil lessons, lecture style, working on the computer, listening to tapes and cassettes, experiential activities, and many other educational terms are grouped under the learning styles umbrella. Some are indeed learning styles-oriented, some are actually teaching styles, and others are simply conversational jargon.

It is important for teachers to know how children learn and to use that knowledge in their instructional planning. Knowing that seven students in the class learn most efficiently when they can work together is a valuable piece of information. However, it is not particularly useful (to you or those seven students) unless they have opportunities to learn by working together. The point is, we know a great deal about the psychology of learning and classroom applications. It is necessary for all teachers to implement these applications in order to meet the various learning styles of all students.

David Kolb's *Learning Style Inventory* is one instrument that identifies these four styles of learning: the *diverger, converger, assimilator,* and *accommodator.* Briefly, the strengths of these four learning types are:

> *the accommodator gets things done, is a risk-taker, has strong leadership skills*
>
> *the diverger has imaginative ability, understands people, recognizes problems, is a brainstormer*
>
> *the converger can define problems, uses deductive reasoning, makes decisions, solves problems*
>
> *the assimilator develops theories, defines problems, creates models, plans well* [2]

From a theoretical standpoint, a working knowledge of these four learning styles is certainly beneficial. Learning styles includes the modalities of learning: visual, auditory, and tactile-kinesthetic from the psychomotor point of view. Some professionals interpret a learning style as the particular response a student exhibits after the teacher presents a lesson, such as working alone to internalize the information, talking it through in a small group, or participating in large group activities. Student pairing is another learning style that is commonly practiced in elementary classrooms. The left, right, and whole brain learning styles are part of classroom application.

From a functional, everyday classroom standpoint, preferred learning styles can be viewed as the specific, observable ways that students learn. The teacher's observation skills are a key factor in determining just exactly how individual students seem to learn or perform certain skills most efficiently and with the least amount of stress. With practice, a new teacher will recognize that Chris functions best when he works alone at a study carrel and Jenny needs the interaction of two or three other students to learn new concepts or data. The objective in this process of identifying the various learning styles is to provide students with opportunities to learn within a particular mode. Further reading and study in the field of learning styles is recommended for a more thorough understanding of the various applications for planning and instruction.

Modalities of Learning

The modalities of learning are the ways, methods, and manners in which children learn. They are the methods whereby the external bits of information that bombard children during periods of learning become internalized. There are basically three learning modes: visual, auditory, and tactile.

Visual Mode. The visual mode enables children to learn by what they see. Children today tend to be very visual, due in part to the impact of early exposure to television and other audiovisual technology. School learning can be highly visual in nature. The bulletin board, the chalkboard, filmstrips, movies, computer programs, visual aids such as charts and fingerplays, textbooks, and selective paper-pencil lessons all depend heavily on the child's ability to process information through the visual mode.

The newspaper provides information in the visual mode.

Auditory Mode.   The auditory mode enables children to learn through the sense of hearing. It is very important for young children to listen in order to learn effectively. Primary teachers must verbalize a large amount of information during the average school day. The adjustment-to-school stage alone entails a great deal of telling children what to do. Procedures, organizational skills, acceptable school behavior, and many beginning behaviors are verbalized by teachers. Teachers must attempt to create a classroom atmosphere wherein external stimuli are kept at a minimum during optimal learning periods so that listening and attending can occur.

Tactile Mode.   The tactile mode is in operation when children touch, feel, manipulate, order, and use their fine-motor skills. An example of students operating within the tactile mode might be when the class is learning about cities in a mapping lesson. The teacher makes available a large variety of manipulative materials such as building blocks, Lincoln logs, twigs, various kinds of paper, cardboard, yarn, empty containers, boxes, and paints. The children use these materials to construct the buildings, trees, streets, hills, mailboxes, playgrounds, and other physical features of their city on a map layout. Think of all the touching, scrutinizing of textures, spacial experiences, and manipulating this activity affords the tactile sense.

The visual, auditory, and tactile modalities are critical for learning. Primary teachers are masters at providing opportunities to use all three modalities in their lessons. It is not an overstatement to say that dynamic learning occurs when these three modalities are employed simultaneously. It is unfortunate that as children move up through the elementary grades, they get fewer tactile experiences and more visual and auditory experiences. The effectiveness of the tactile-kinesthetic modality is not limited to primary-aged students, nor should it be. Social studies curriculum is particularly well suited to utilize all three of these modalities: the visual (reading printed materials, viewing movies and filmstrips, examining photos and maps), the auditory (listening to each other, lectures, cassettes, records), and the tactile (building, sorting, ordering, experiencing texture).

Left-Right Brain

The human brain has two very important components: the right hemisphere and the left hemisphere. Conversationally they are referred to as the left side and the right side. Research into the specialized functions of these two sides of the human brain has been occurring for a number of years. Research that initially focused on dyslexia and brain-damaged persons has expanded to investigate other areas. The findings of these studies have significant implications for education at all levels.

The left and right hemispheres of the brain have specialized functions that receive information in certain ways. Tables 2–1 and 2–2 identify some specific left and right brain functions. Some learning activities that draw upon the left side of the brain are convergency, logic, reality, textbook activities, sequencing events, and ordering. Some activities that are characteristic of right brain processing are visualizing, seeking divergent solutions to a problem, spontaneous planning, mysticism, tactile learning, and emotional interpretations.

Teaching to the left and/or right brain is desirable. Calling upon the particular processing functions of each ultimately enhances and enriches the learning experience. Current research studies are focusing on whole brain teaching strategies that employ the processing characteristics of both brain hemispheres simultaneously. Courses and seminars are available to teach the special instructional strategies that are needed to do this in the classroom.

Determining a student's general left or right brain preference can be accomplished in two very basic ways: by using a formal testing instrument or by informal teacher observations. For elementary students, the most practical method is probably the teacher observation method. Formal testing-evaluative procedures are costly, time consuming, and frequently not an established component in the school district's testing and evaluation program. Professional course work, seminars, and workshops prepare teachers to implement teaching strategies that fo-

Table 2-1   Specialized Functions of Left and Right Sides of the Brain

Left Brain

 1. Controls the right side of the body
 2. Verbal/numerical
 3. Logical/vertical
 4. Rational
 5. Linear time
 6. Focus
 7. Sequential/orderly
 8. Analytic, the arrangement of parts
 9. Explicit
10. Active
11. Literal
12. Convergent
13. Fact/reality

Right Brain

 1. Controls the left side of the body
 2. Visual/spatial
 3. Perceptual/sensual/lateral thinking
 4. Intuitive
 5. Space, infinity
 6. Diffusion
 7. Spontaneous/creative
 8. Gestalt, viewing the whole
 9. Tacit
10. Receptive
11. Metaphorical/symbolic
12. Divergent
13. Dream/fantasy/mystical

Source: Margaret Hatcher, "Whole Brain Learning," *The School Administrator* (June 1983): 9.
Reprinted with permission.

cus on the strengths of both right and left brain learners. The purpose of these is to prevent isolating and permanently labeling individual students as either a left or right brain learner exclusively. Becoming familiar with the peculiarities of left and right hemispheric processing is valuable to the degree that this knowledge guides the teacher toward an instructional expertise that helps students to learn.

How does a teacher informally determine the hemispheric preferences of the students? Teachers spend a lot of time with their students. They observe many behaviors, both social and academic, everyday. Using the basic knowledge and skills they acquire from the professional literature and course work, teachers

Table 2-2 Right/Left Mode Characteristics

Left Mode	Right Mode
Rational	Intuitive
Responds to verbal instructions	Responds to demonstrated instructions
Controlled, systematic experiments	Open-ended, random experiments
Problem solves by logically and sequentially looking at the parts of things	Problem solves with hunches, looking for patterns and configurations
Makes objective judgments	Makes subjective judgments
Looks at differences	Looks at similarities
Is planned and structured	Is fluid and spontaneous
Prefers established, certain information	Prefers elusive, uncertain information
Analytic reader	Synthesizing
Primary reliance on language in thinking and remembering	Primary reliance on images in thinking and remembering
Prefers talking and writing	Prefers drawing and manipulating objects
Prefers multiple choice tests	Prefers open-ended questions
Controls feelings	Free with feelings
Responsive to structure of environment	Essentially self-acting
Prefers hierarchal (ranked) authority structures	Prefers collegial (participative) authority structures
Sequential	Simultaneous
Is a splitter: distinction important	Is a lumper: connectedness important
Talks, and talks, and talks	Is mute—uses pictures, not words
Is logical, sees cause and effect	Is analogic, sees correspondences, resemblances
Draws on previously accumulated, organized information	Draws on unbounded qualitative patterns that are not organized into sequences, but that cluster around images of crystallized feelings

observe and make notations regarding students behaviors in the classroom. The two organizational charts listed in Tables 2–1 and 2–2 are helpful sources to use.

In the elementary classroom, left brain preference students are the teacher pleasers. When the teacher has all the lesson components laid out in a particular manner, these children will carefully follow them in the way the teacher wants. Their reactions and/or responses are predictable in many situations. They will reach the lesson goal in an organized fashion. The right brain preference students are adventurous, forging ahead into an activity without a step-by-step pattern. They may make mistakes along the way, but if one approach doesn't work they will simply try another. To some adults, this appears to be a random, inefficient use of time, but these students will also ultimately reach the goal. It may just take them longer. Both the left and right brain preference children are successful when the observant teacher makes provisions for them to succeed.

Cycles of Learning

Dr. Bernice McCarthy has used the research of learning styles and brain functioning to formulate a model for classroom teachers. This model is called the 4MAT System. It combines the four learning style types of David Kolb with the left and right brain functions to form a specialized "cycle" the teacher moves through in planning and teaching lessons. The model consists of four quadrants that correlate with the four learning types: concrete experiences, reflective observation, abstract conceptualization, and active experimentation. In each of these McCarthy imposes a left and right brain component, so learners have opportunities to draw upon both hemispheres. Figure 2–1 shows the Complete 4MAT System Model.

In quadrant 1 the teacher sets the stage for the learning sequence. She or he estalishes the objective and the "why" factor. In quadrant 2 the teacher gives significant input and does the modeling of "what" the students are to learn. The teacher is the most active in these two quadrants. In quadrant 3 the students become more active. They perform guided practice activities with the teacher acting as a coach and facilitator. Quadrant 4 provides learners with opportunities for independent applications, to experiment with "what if" situations. This capsulizes the roles of teachers and students in each of the 4MAT areas. To fully appreciate and apply the components of this or any other model, it is necessary to participate in training seminars or workshops. However, it is possible to begin using the components for social studies activities. Learning styles-brain hemispheres teaching models are helpful teaching tools; they assist the insightful teacher in coordinating research and curriculum to affect dynamic instruction.

The McCarthy model incorporates left and right brain components into each of the four quadrants of the cycle, as shown in Figure 2–2.

The following activities show some suggested applications for an elementary mapping lesson.

Quadrant One

Left brain
The teacher introduces maps.

The teacher identifies the cardinal directions NSEW in the room.

The teacher establishes reasons why maps are needed.

Various maps are shown and discussed.

The students locate various places on the map.

Figure 2-1   The Complete 4MAT System Model

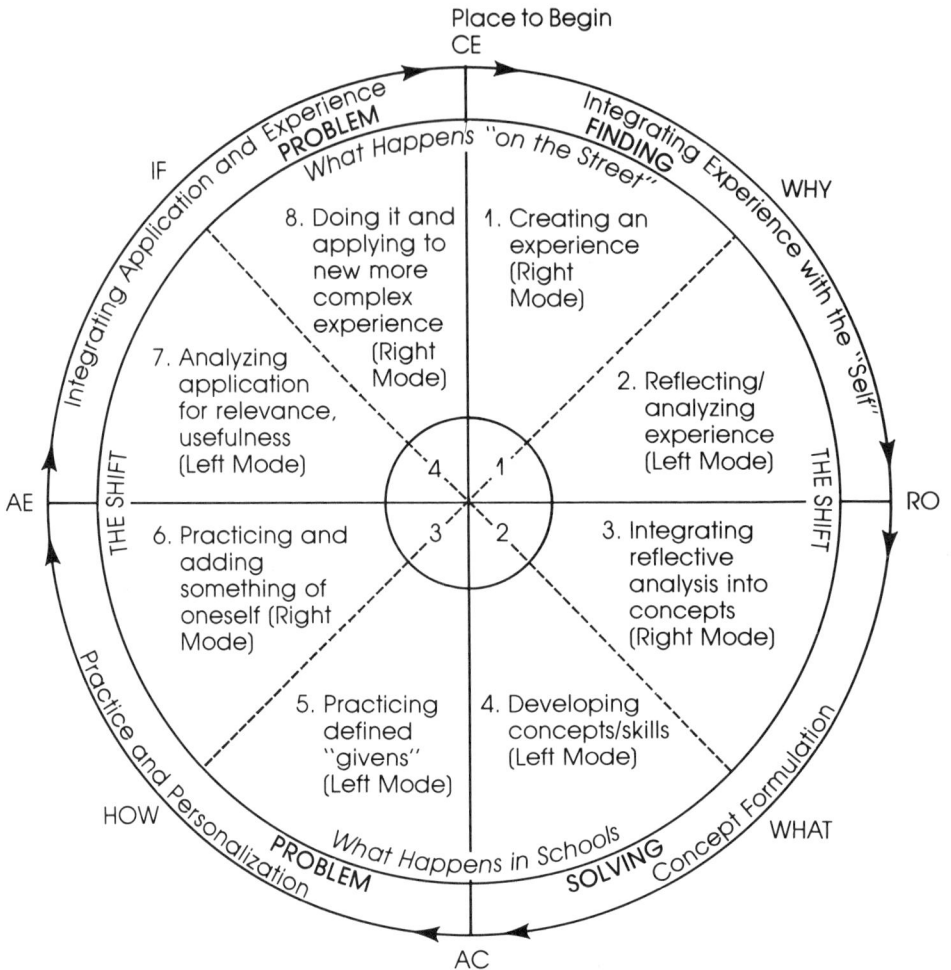

Place to Begin
CE

IF

Integrating Application and Experience
PROBLEM
What Happens "on the Street"

Integrating Experience with the "Self"
FINDING

WHY

8. Doing it and applying to new more complex experience (Right Mode)

1. Creating an experience (Right Mode)

7. Analyzing application for relevance, usefulness (Left Mode)

2. Reflecting/ analyzing experience (Left Mode)

THE SHIFT

AE

4 1
3 2

THE SHIFT

RO

6. Practicing and adding something of oneself (Right Mode)

3. Integrating reflective analysis into concepts (Right Mode)

5. Practicing defined "givens" (Left Mode)

4. Developing concepts/skills (Left Mode)

HOW

Practice and Personalization
PROBLEM
What Happens in Schools
SOLVING
Concept Formulation

WHAT

AC

Figure 2-2   Skills of the Four Learning Styles—The 4MAT System

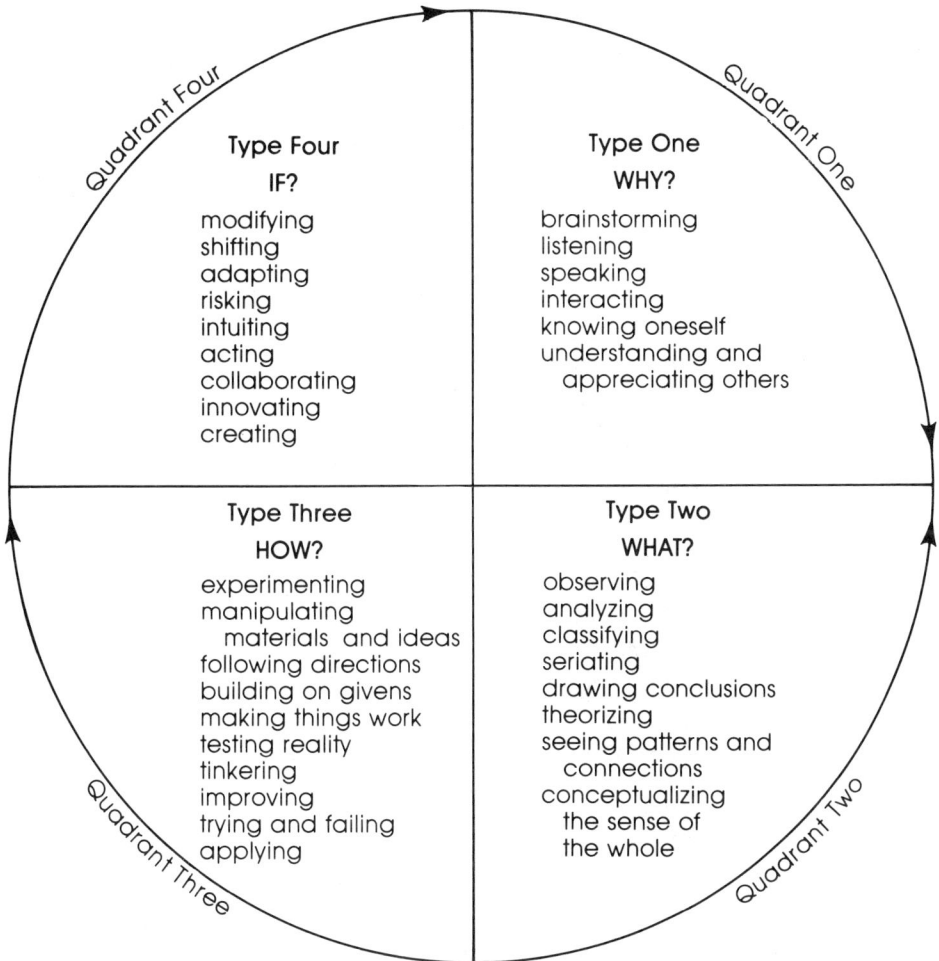

Type Four
IF?
modifying
shifting
adapting
risking
intuiting
acting
collaborating
innovating
creating

Type One
WHY?
brainstorming
listening
speaking
interacting
knowing oneself
understanding and
    appreciating others

Type Three
HOW?
experimenting
manipulating
    materials and ideas
following directions
building on givens
making things work
testing reality
tinkering
improving
trying and failing
applying

Type Two
WHAT?
observing
analyzing
classifying
seriating
drawing conclusions
theorizing
seeing patterns and
    connections
conceptualizing
the sense of
the whole

Quadrant Four · Quadrant One · Quadrant Three · Quadrant Two

Source: Bernice McCarthy, "Skills of the Four Learning Styles—The 4MAT System," *Educational Leadership, 42* (April 1985): 63. Reprinted with permission of the Association for Supervision and Curriculum Development. Copyright © by ASCD. All rights reserved.

Right brain

The teacher gives verbal commands to the group to locate particular places.

The student places objects in the room; others locate the objects.

The students manipulate objects on the desk.

The students perform given tasks on a bulletin board display or at a three-dimensional learning station.

Quadrant Two

Left brain

The teacher and students read textbook material together.

The teacher directs the class to follow certain paths on mapping pictures or illustrations.

The teacher takes the class outside to locate NSEW.

The class views filmstrips or movies.

Right brain

The students make a map of their room (or house).

Furniture, entrances, and windows are located according to their directional locations.

Each student makes an oral presentation of his or her project.

The students talk-through their projects in small groups.

Quadrant Three

Left brain

The students read printed materials under the direction of the teacher.

The students know what to look for and how to recognize pertinent information.

Application activities are practical.

Right brain

The students discuss how maps are used and why they are needed.

Brainstorm consequences of having no maps available.

The students try following paths with no given directions.

The students practice giving written or verbal directions through a given maze.

Quadrant Four

Left brain

The students cooperatively design maps from the classroom to various locations in the school.

The students list the practical reasons for following each of the given paths to particular rooms.

The students classify paths into two categories—practical or impractical—and state their rationale for each choice.

The students list possible conflicts for each path.

Right brain
The teacher and students evaluate the activities and projects.

The students experiment with "what if" applications.

The students try out each other's directions and maps.

The students transfer their information to a new and different situation.

This series of social studies mapping experiences demonstrates how the teacher can plan to meet the various learning styles of the students in his or her class. Some specific activities are planned for both the left and right brain preference individuals, as well as opportunities for experiences in the learning style that is not dominant. This cycle of learning has application possibilities in all curriculum areas. The model can be seen as an eight-step process wherein the teacher guides and directs the activities and experiences in the first four steps of the cycle, and then makes the transition to a facilitator-resource person in the last four steps. The students are receivers and users of information in various parts of the cycle to a greater or lesser extent. The 4MAT System also provides opportunities for left and right brain learning style teachers to adapt their teaching styles.

ACTIVITIES

Internal motivation is the best motivation. It is encouraging and exciting to observe motivated, enthusiastic students engaged in learning activities. Many elementary students are interested and enthused about participating in almost every lesson the teacher plans for social studies. They are motivated to learn.

Teachers are aware that some students are not interested in every aspect of the social studies curriculum. Recognizing this apparent lack of motivation and planning to manipulate it is the teacher's responsibility. Motivation is the first of eight learning events as proposed by Robert Gagné. It is suggested that you read *The Conditions of Learning* by Robert Gagné and *Motivation Theory for Teachers* by Madeline Hunter as a preparation for the first activity. If we subscribe to these sequential learning events, then we can agree that being motivated to learn is a critical step in the process. How do teachers motivate students, particularly those who most need it? Working with a partner or a small group, you are going to have the opportunity to list and identify some possible activities to establish or increase the motivation level(s) of students. You may consult other learning theory sources for this activity.

2.1 Strategies for Developing Extrinsic and Intrinsic Motivation

Teaching the social studies reading skills is one strand of the scope and sequence in various textbook series. Some of the reading skills taught in the Silver Burdett series *The World and Its People*[3] are:

Distinguishing between relevant and irrelevant data
Distinguishing between fact and opinion
Recognizing and identifying the author's or speaker's purpose
Recognizing propaganda
Reading and interpreting facts from tables
Skimming

Your objective is to teach these social studies reading skills to a fifth-grade class. What motivational strategies could you use? Your group will list five possible approaches for each type of motivators.

Extrinsic Motivators	*Intrinsic Motivators*
1.	1.
2.	2.
3.	3.
4.	4.
5.	5.

Your goal is to motivate your students to use the social studies reading skills. You have listed some possible motivational strategies to use. Now extend these further. What is the relationship of the motivators to the objective? State this relationship for each item on your lists. Discuss these with your instructor for verification.

2.2 Using the 4MAT Model

When you are teaching social studies there will be a variety of students in your classes. These students come to you for instruction with diverse learning needs and learning styles. One teaching style or strategy will not be compatible with every student. Flexibility and creativity are necessary to meet diverse student requirements.

There are many social studies concepts that students need to learn. Concepts are abstractions and are somewhat difficult to understand. Some concepts are more difficult to teach than others, but as professionals we are required to teach them regardless of difficulty. Two examples of concepts are *Regions* and *Government*. These are your unit topics for this activity.

Kolb identifies four learning-style types: accommodators, assimilators, convergers, and divergers. No one type is more desirable than another, and each has singular admirable qualities. Select the primary or the intermediate grades for a target group as you proceed with this activity.

Learing-Style Type

List four student activities that could be used for each learning style type in your Regions and Government units.

Accommodator
Example: Terri will organize a research group for the semi-arid regions.

Regions	*Government*
1.	1.
2.	2.
3.	3.
4.	4.

Assimilator
Example: Ben will write the work plan for the research group.

Regions	*Government*
1.	1.
2.	2.
3.	3.
4.	4.

Diverger
Example: Casey will brainstorm this proposal: What if semi-arid regions suddenly had large increases in rainfall?

Geographic outcomes	*Political-social outcomes*
1.	1.
2.	2.
3.	3.
4.	4.

Converger
Example: Melissa will propose solutions to five of the situations Casey identifies.

Regions	*Government*
1.	1.
2.	2.
3.	3.
4.	4.

Left Brain and Right Brain Functions

Refer to the specific left and right brain function charts shown in Tables 2–1 and 2–2. Now construct some left and right brain activities for these style preference children in your class.

Left Brain
Example: Amy constructs a multiple-choice self-quiz on Regions to be placed in the social studies learning center.

1.	1.
2.	2.
3.	3.
4.	4.
5.	5.

Right Brain
Example: Jeremy will construct a three-dimensional model of a tropical region of his choice.

1.	1.
2.	2.
3.	3.
4.	4.
5.	5.

4MAT System

Reexamine the 4MAT System on pages 60–61. Use this information to help you construct student activities that are germane to the four quadrants of the system.

Quadrant One (Why?)
Example: The class listens to the teacher lecture on the topic of political and physical regions.

1.	1.
2.	2.
3.	3.
4.	4.
5.	5.

Quadrant Two (What?)
Example: A small group classifies a given list of characteristics as belonging to either a political or a physical region.

1.   1.
2.   2.
3.   3.
4.   4.
5.   5.

Quadrant Three (How?)
Example: One team devises a plan to measure and record the rainfall at their homes for 30 days. Are the results realistic for the region?

1.   1.
2.   2.
3.   3.
4.   4.
5.   5.

Quadrant Four (If)
Example: A pair of students will create a model agricultural region in a semi-arid region. List reasons why this is a good model.

1.   1.
2.   2.
3.   3.
4.   4.
5.   5.

Summary

As you gain experience in teaching children of different ages and performance levels, you will become increasingly aware of their diverse learning styles and preferences. These activities provide an initial opportunity to begin thinking about these learning styles and to plan some workable classroom activities for children to perform. Some student activities are easier to plan and design than others—if your personal brain dominance is the right side, then right brain activities will probably be easier for you to plan and teach. However, as professionals we must provide instructional activities for all the children in our classes. Discuss the above activities with your classmates. Which section was the most difficult to complete? For what reasons? As adults it is beneficial to experience some frustration with a particular assignment. It helps us to be more understanding of students who are unable to complete assignments, for whatever reason, in our classrooms.

READING RESOURCES

Ausubel, David. *Educational Psychology: A Cognitive View.* New York: Holt, Rinehart and Winston, 1968.

Bruner, Jerome. *Toward a Theory of Instruction.* New York: Norton Publishers, 1966.

Cain, Sandra, and Evans, Jack. *Sciencing an Involvement Approach to Elementary Science Methods,* 2nd ed. Columbus, OH: Charles E. Merrill, 1984, pp. 10–17, 176–179.

Cuccia, A. "Developing a Learning Styles Classroom—From A to Z." *Early Years, 17* (1986): 81–83.

Gagné, Robert. *The Conditions of Learning,* 3rd ed. New York: Holt, Rinehart and Winston, 1977.

Glover, John, and Bruning, Roger. *Educational Psychology,* 2nd ed. Boston: Little, Brown and Co., 1987.

Hunter, Madeline. *Motivation Theory for Teachers.* El Segundo, CA: TIP Publications, 1984.

McCarthy, Bernice. "What 4MAT Training Teaches Us About Staff Development." *Educational Leadership, 42* (1985): 61.

Renzulli, Joseph S., and Smith, Linda H. *Learning Styles Inventory: A Measure of Student Preference for Instructional Techniques.* Mansfield Center, CT: Creative Learning Press, 1978.

Slavin, Robert. *Educational Psychology.* Englewood Cliffs, NJ: Prentice-Hall, 1986.

Springer, Sally P., and Deutsch, George. *Left Brain, Right Brain,* rev. ed. San Francisco: W. H. Freeman, 1985.

ENDNOTES

1. DeCecco, John P., *The Psychology of Learning and Instuction* (Englewood Cliffs, NJ: Prentice-Hall, 1968), p. 75.

2. Kolb, David A., *Learning Style Inventory* (Boston, MA: McBer and Company, 1976).

3. "Neighborhoods and Communities," in *The World and Its People,* Annotated Teacher's Edition, T25 (Morristown, NJ: The Silver Burdett Company, 1986).

3

Introduction to Methodologies

PROJECTIONS

Social studies methods and strategies for the future—what will they be? There are no crystal balls or guarantees for education, only possibilities. In the recent past, some content areas such as reading and math have undergone major changes in instructional strategies. Individually guided instruction, ability grouping, performance grouping, large and small group instruction, and cross-grade and mixed-age groupings are some of the management strategies various schools have employed to attain maximum student performance. Each has achieved varying degrees of success. An individualized social studies program is not as yet accessible, practical, or teachable.

There is no question that students have more to learn in several content areas. Social studies is one of them. To teach all the required material successfully, teachers must be prepared to use those methods and strategies that will enable them to achieve goals in an efficient manner. Methods and strategies that are somewhat "tried and true" are not necessarily outdated or negative. Large group instruction for some units or topics will continue to be a positive, usable way to teach social studies. Smaller project groups and individualized-adaptive instructional sequences are establishing a niche in elementary classrooms. Social studies is a natural instructional setting to develop cooperative learning experiences.

It is essential for social studies teachers to provide both product and process experiences for students. Learners must have a substantial background in both facts and concepts if they are to be educated in the social studies. There is simply more to learn, and teachers in the 1990s must be prepared to teach it. How students approach learning this material is critical, and the process of learning will be a major concern. Teachers need to plan their instructional strategies to allow these various processes to flourish.

Teaching students how to think is presently a major educational objective and indications are that it will be a continuing trend in the 1990s. Teaching thinking skills is accomplished by establishing a firm foundation of facts and concepts and then using them to move students toward upper-level thinking. Social studies is conducive to providing students with opportunities to experience application, analysis, and synthesis. The trend is to encourage even primary-aged children to experiment with forecasting, projecting, and evaluating. A strategy based solely on fact gathering and assimilating will not survive.

Social studies teachers are constantly using traditional instructional strategies, changing, modifying, adjusting, and perfecting them to more adequately instruct students. Futurists envision the elementary classroom as being significantly different from those we know and recognize today. The student in front of a computer screen for a large part of the instructional day is one scenario that is commonly predicted. Although this idea is decried by many people, it is a fact that even now students are interfacing with technology (computers, interactive television, and other innovations) more than the public may realize. Technology is impacting virtually every content area. Elementary libraries have the card catalogue on the computer system and students are using it comfortably.

As teachers address the issue of methods and strategies, it is necessary to examine those we are currently using. Professional responsibility demands that we also examine those methods and strategies we should be using to teach social studies. It is our responsibility to be proactive in assessing the future needs of learners. More importantly, we need to be assertive in designing and devising innovative, creative instructional strategies to meet those future needs effectively. That is part of the challenge you will face as a social studies teacher.

What Are Methodologies?

What exactly are teaching methodologies? In academic environments there is a plethora of educational terms, jargon, phrases, and/or labels that relate to what teachers do. Such terms as *methodology, strategy, techique, instructional procedures, modeling behaviors,* and others are commonly heard. It is easy to understand how confusing it can be to differentiate between them. Consider this dictionary definition of methodology: "The principles, practices, of orderly thought or procedure applied to a particular branch of learning, and arrived at by systematic analysis and application of the techniques of logic."[1] This concise definition doesn't quite get to the heart of methodology. We prefer the definition given by J. A. Battle: "When we speak of method we are talking about everything (and we do mean everything—all the knowledge) that the teacher utilizes to get the pupil better educated."[2]

The methodologies that teachers use are those materials, questions, activities, applications, presentations, and explanations that help children learn. The procedures and processes the teacher plans to use to present a lesson is her or his methodology for that lesson. The specific methodology the teacher may decide to use could be one or a combination of any of the following: contracts, demonstration, inquiry, lecture, problem solving, or programmed instruction.

One teacher may decide to use the lecture method to teach global issues, and another colleague may elect to use a combination of lecture and inquiry. Both teachers will have successful presentations using the methodologies that fit their particular situations. Whereas the demonstration method may be appropriate for a particular primary-grade lesson, it may be ineffectual for a sixth-grade group. No one method is the best for every teaching situation or for every teacher. Any methodology is only as effective as the teacher who uses it.

Why Are They Important?

Teaching methodologies are important because they are the active phases of teaching that make lesson content come alive for students. The preplanning of lessons is important—the objectives, materials, activities, and evaluation procedures—but without an effective methodology to activate those elements, learning will be difficult to achieve.

Methodologies are important because they are the observable, specific actions and behaviors that teachers perform while attempting to teach a lesson. The importance of these various teaching methodologies lies in the fact that the individual teacher plans ahead of time exactly what he or she will do to present information to students in a step-by-step manner that is orderly, sequential, and logical. A systematic approach to determine the appropriate methodology contributes to a smooth lesson presentation, as well as a positive learning atmosphere and good classroom management. Specific teaching methodologies motivate and activate lesson content.

Organizational Strategies

What is an organizational strategy and how does it affect teaching? An organizational strategy is the systematic order within which the teaching of lessons can occur. It is the planned structure that molds all parts of the lesson plan into a solid foundation for presentation to students. An organizational strategy is organized in the sense that it is preplanned and integral to the lesson components. It is strategies in the sense that each lesson part is intended to occur at the most opportune moment. Your methodology is the mode you select to present the lesson. Your organizational strategy is the framework. Sound lesson plans are necessary for good teaching. Those plans become more effective when accompanied by an effective organizational strategy. Good plans and an effective organizational strategy result in effective teaching.

Every teacher has a preferred way to organize and prepare a lesson. We are going to investigate three of the more widely used organizational structures: those developed by Madeline Hunter, Carol Cummings, and Benjamin Bloom. It is important that you become familiar with these structures for two reasons: (1) they provide an organized format for a lesson that incorporates accepted principles of learning and (2) many schools use these formats and expect their new teachers to be knowledgeable about them.

Madeline Hunter

Madeline Hunter has worked with school districts, administrators, teachers, and students of all ages for many years. Her work and research include how children learn, clinical supervision, increasing the effectiveness of teachers, working with principals to affect better schools, designing and implementing teaching models, and consulting with other countries to improve their educational systems. Teachers can agree on what to teach, as goals and objectives are stated in curriculum guides. The methods used to teach all subject areas, including materials to use, provisions for special needs students, time allotments, schedules, and other decisions, are made every school day by the individual teacher. The countless decisions teachers must make are directed at facilitating and aiding the learning of students.

In recent years the Madeline Hunter "Effective Teaching" workshops and

This student is busily engaged in an activity. Encourage appropriate on-task behaviors.

classes have been held in cities across the country. These are in-depth training and guided practice sessions that give educators opportunities to recognize and learn the elements of effective teaching. Research shows that certain things teachers do are effective and others are ineffective. It is easy to continue doing things that you think help students to learn, without really knowing if they do.

Hunter's effective teaching strategies focus on the positive behaviors of teachers that are oftentimes done automatically. All good teachers do these things a countless number of times everyday. Hunter's strategies and methods also focus on helping teachers recognize ineffective behaviors and how to eliminate them or at least decrease their frequency. The strategies are used for evaluating teaching, not the teacher. The teacher is not rated.

The effective teaching program consists of a preobservation conference between the supervisor (coach) and the teacher. The purpose of this conference is either to plan jointly a particular lesson wherein certain teaching behaviors will be exhibited, or to merely talk about those behaviors in a random lesson of the teacher's choice. The observational visit then takes place. The coach uses a script-tape or audiovisual tape to record what is happening during the lesson. Some coaches write the observed behaviors (verbal and nonverbal) to be discussed at the postvisit conference. It is important that the notes are written. It is easy to forget the many right things teachers do. During the instructional conference the coach and the teacher review the notes together. Appendix A contains an example of a script-tape.

The role of the observer is to direct the teacher toward more effective teaching. When a certain trust level is established, the observations and the instructional conferences are nonthreatening.

Critical Behaviors.   The critical behaviors of teachers are those that contribute to effective teaching. Part One of Hunter's effective teaching plan focuses on the components of a lesson presentation that keep the teacher on task while she or he is teaching. Here is a brief explanation of these critical behaviors for effective teaching.

Teach to an Objective: Good lesson plans begin with a clear objective: What are you going to teach? Once you clearly decide what to teach, you can proceed with planning how to teach it. The teacher must keep the objective clearly in mind throughout the lesson. It will be obvious to the students if he or she does. It is not uncommon to hear teachers remark, "I don't know if this (concept or fact) will ever get through to the kids" or "The students act like they don't know what I'm talking about." Both of these conditions may very well exist. Assuming these teachers are conscientious and have planned their lesson reasonably well, it is possible that, due to oversight, uncertainty, or lack of sufficient planning time, a clear objective was never really determined.

Having a definite objective in mind at all times clarifies lesson components. The questions, statements, examples, modeling behaviors, and diagrams will all converge toward the objective. Even young children can recognize your objective, though they may not be able to verbalize it. Teaching to an objective is clearly evident to the coach. It is surprising how accurately the coach can identify the teacher's objectives by systematically observing the teaching process.

Teach to the Appropriate Level of Difficulty: Teaching to the appropriate level of difficulty means providing instruction and lesson content that students can reasonably be expected to achieve. The level of difficulty can be interpreted as a performance level that is comfortable for the individual student, group, or class. Establishing or identifying this performance level requires some means of determining what that level is. New teachers can use these resources to determine a good place to start.

1. Records of performance from previous years are helpful. Look for specific skills that are mastered. Keep in mind that letter grades are not always helpful.
2. Pretesting indicates what previous knowledge is already established. Do not teach what students already know.
3. Consult with other teachers, grade chairpersons, or curriculum coordinators.
4. Take the necessary time to establish your entry behaviors. Know what the students must be able to do before you introduce new material.

It isn't easy to know exactly the correct instructional level of students. Try these four steps and see what information they provide. When the lesson is underway, adjustments in the goals, objectives, and expectations to higher or lower levels are easily made. The important thing is to set the instructional level so that students can be successful. Nothing is more motivational than the feeling of success. During the classroom observation, the coach will readily recognize if lesson presentations are too difficult (frustrating for the students, resulting in nonproductive behaviors) or too easy (true learning is not occurring).

Monitor and Adjust: The monitoring and adjusting behaviors of teachers are those actions in which the lesson content, flow, and objectives are balanced to meet student needs more adequately. As lessons progress, the teacher must be cognizant of how the students are receiving and responding to his or her presentation. The observant teacher knows how this happens by listening carefully to the types of questions that are being asked, by watching for students staying on task, by evaluating the responses and comments of students, and by using other verbal and nonverbal indicators of various kinds.

If the lesson is not going well for one reason or another, make the necessary adjustments as soon as possible. Try a new approach, a different technique, or a more familiar mode to clarify the lesson for the students. Monitoring and adjusting the strategies and/or content of a lesson is a mark of teaching flexibility. If something is not working, do not hesitate to change it.

Use, Don't Abuse, the Principles of Learning: Effective teachers use established principles to enhance learning. Abusing or overemphasizing one or more of those principles is both unnecessary and unproductive. The principles of learning as used in the Staff Development Cycle of Hunter's "Effective Teaching" are motivation, rate and degree (how much is learned and how fast), retention, and transfer.

Motivation is defined as that within a person that incites action. It is impossible to make a student motivated, but effective teachers do strive to create a positive classroom environment to increase motivation. The feeling tone of the student, the interest, and the knowledge of results (How am I doing?) are factors in motivation.

The *rate and degree* factor is composed of the following elements of learning: motivation and reinforcement (teacher responses that are positive strengthen the behavior). The rate of learning (how fast or slowly a child learns) and the degree of learning (how much is learned) are highly individualized. Active participation is the student involvement in learning accompanied by the teacher modeling (demonstrating) the desired behavior. Meaningful practice sessions of appropriate length and duration are important. The concept of transfer means the student needs many opportunities to apply one learned behavior

A teacher can be effective when teaching a large group if he or she is well prepared.

(skill, fact, relationship) to other situations. Use acquired skills to assist in the learning of new skills.

Retention is remembering what has been learned. The practice periods, the relevancy of the learning, and the opportunities for transfer will increase the level of retention.

Transfer operates effectively when the various similarities of new and old learnings are emphasized. The transfer factors should be clear and obvious (don't use remote similarities) to work to the advantage of the students. When many opportunities to generate transfer are given, the probability of new learning is increased.

Although the Madeline Hunter strategies have been in existence for some time, teachers today are finding her methods very useful in organizing their lesson for teaching and learning. The main strength of this approach is that children learn. It forces the teacher to plan and organize for teaching. The less left to chance in teaching the better your possibility for a successful teaching experience.

Carol Cummings

In her book *Teaching Makes a Difference,*[3] Carol Cummings builds a teaching model upon the classification of instructional skills adapted from the works of Madeline Hunter. These instructional skills are: selecting the objective, teaching to an objective, monitoring and adjusting, and principles of learning. The skills emphasize that teaching is decision making. The planned, careful decisions that teachers make develop and refine those instructional skills.

The organized plan (the strategy) a teacher uses determines what she or he will do to insure that this process called learning will occur in the classroom. The developmental level of the teacher's personal instructional skill will contribute positively or negatively to the quality of learning. To develop an instructional skill level of high quality is the goal of every professional. This process admittedly requires commitment and a conscious decision to work at it over a period of time. New teachers begin to develop instructional skills the first day of professional service.

Instructional skill—teaching expertise—is the mark of the master teacher. Combine a strong knowledge base (subject matter) with a firm commitment to concentrate on those instructional skills, and you are on the track toward good teaching. Even master teachers are constantly evaluating their skills and working to improve!

A good place to start in the process of developing instructional skill is to decide what you want the students to learn in a given lesson. This decision is the selecting of your objective. To show cooperative behavior in a group, to name and locate the four cardinal directions on a given map, to find the longitude and latitude of five major cities in the Northeast, to list ten products of the southern states are examples of appropriate objectives. They state clearly which behaviors the teacher wants to observe. While selecting objectives, the teacher will have considered and determined the level of complexity and difficulty for a particular child or group.

Once the objective is selected, the task is to determine which teaching behaviors will guide the students most directly toward it. Some relevant teacher behaviors for the longitude and latitude objective would be: demonstrating how to write degrees of longitude and latitude correctly, showing how to locate various cities on regional and U.S. maps, and designing lessons that focus on other locational skills (transfer). Through lecture and discussion, the teacher will build a rationale for learning this particular skill and will provide opportunities for the students to practice the skill under her or his supervision.

Carol Cummings recommends using a task analysis to assist in selecting and teaching to objectives skills. What is a task analysis and how can it help? A task analysis is "an identification of the sublearnings necessary to accomplish a given objective."[4] Cummings proposes this task-analysis process as relevant to the first three instructional skills listed previously. By definition, a task analysis forces the teacher to identify carefully the individual learning steps that are needed in order for the student to learn the objective. Those necessary sublearnings may not be as extensive as you think. Sometimes two or three may be all that are really needed; other times it may be more. If you have identified too many sublearnings, perhaps the objective needs to be revised to a more manageable form. Viewing a task analysis in a process chart format (Table 3–1) will help you understand how it can help your teaching strategy. Here is one from Cummings.[5]

Long-Range Objective
Able to use parts of a book
1. locates title, author, publisher, copyright date
2. understands meaning of copyright date
3. uses table of contents
4. uses glossary
5. uses an index
6. uses a bibliography
7. can discriminate which part of book to use to locate information

Daily Instructional
Uses an index
1. knows location of index
2. knows/understands attributes of index
    –arranged in alphabetical order
    –gives page numbers
    –identifies topics and subtopics
    –abbreviations used
    –may give many page listings
    –may refer you to another topic
    –may identify illustrations
3. given a topic, can locate pages that information is found on, using index
4. given a question, learner can identify topic, then use index

Table 3-1   Example of a Task Analysis
Objective: The student will be able to use an index to locate information.

Task Analysis	Teacher Behaviors	Student Behaviors
1. Knows location of index	1. Explains where index is found; shows several examples in different books	1. Locates an index in his or her reading book
2. Knows/understands attributes of an index	2. Shows and explains each attribute of an index	2. Lists . . .

Note how this example starts with the long-range objective and then breaks it down into smaller steps, the daily instructional format. Also note the specific key words—*locate, arrange, identify*—that are used to further specify the details of the objective. Formatting in this fashion clarifies the teacher behaviors that are needed for the lesson, as well as what the student is expected to do after instruction.

The third part of this strategy is monitoring and adjusting. Your instructional objective is clearly defined and you have selected relevant teacher behaviors that focus the students directly toward it. Now they begin to practice and/or perform the skill under your direct supervision. This monitoring is very important. It is not uncommon for a student to practice a particular skill for a period of time, feel confident that he or she knows it, only to discover at a later time that he or she had practiced or drilled incorrectly. The end result is a lot of wasted learning time. Not only must the correct skill be learned, but what was practiced must be unlearned! The teacher who monitors and guides the practice periods will catch misunderstandings and problems quickly. Correct monitoring eases the task of making adjustments when and if they are needed. The teacher must move about the classroom and check the students' work while they are doing it, not hours later.

The principles of learning—motivation, retention, active participation, and reinforcement—are very closely correlated with psychology, child development, and brain functioning. *Motivation* is that inner desire, drive, and interest that directs the student to learn, perform, practice, and participate in instructional activities. Recognizing and encouraging this motivation is an important skill for teachers. Not every student is sufficiently motivated to invest a 100% effort into every lesson. Strategies and techniques for motivation are necessary factors in your organizational plan. Something that is highly motivating for one student may be meaningless for another. Knowledge of these personal motivators for specific students will help to eliminate endless searching for something that works.

Retention simply means remembering what has been learned. Once a new skill has been introduced, practiced correctly, and used for some purpose, we want the skill to be remembered for more than a day. Retention is strengthened when the student's attention is centered specifically on the task at hand and auxiliary factors are kept at a minimum. Retention is also enhanced when the skill makes sense to the student. Even nonsense nursery rhymes make sense to young children! Of course, watching the teacher demonstrate the skill correctly and then practicing the skill with the teacher is helpful.

Active participation gets the student involved. Can you imagine learning to ride a bicycle by watching someone else do it? How could you possibly establish the sense of balance, control, and body in space without actually getting on the bike and experiencing it? Active participation will probably involve more than one modality of learning, thereby making the experience even more meaningful.

In addition, active participation in a purposeful lesson makes it easier for *reinforcement* to occur. While the students are engaged in the activity, the teacher can reinforce successful efforts while they are occurring. The old saying "Nothing succeeds like success" is true for school learning too. It is important that verbal and written reinforcement focuses on skill performance, not superfluous factors. For example, say "You did that exactly right."

To bring all of these principles of learning together in a compact format, Cummings proposes the following strategy.

> *READY:*   How can I focus the learner with something novel or different?
>
> *SET:*   How can I transfer (associate) what the learner already knows to the new learning? Instead of the student wondering "What's this all about?", how can I help the student experience: "Ah ha! I see what this is all about!" Is there a logical relationship between any old learnings and this new learning?
>
> *GO:*   How can I actively involve all the learners (either covertly or overtly) so I can speed up the new learning?[6]

Getting yourself ready and determining how you will get the students ready is the first step (motivation). Itemizing previous learnings and establishing connectors with the new skill helps to make sense out of the lesson (retention). Providing the active participation with the appropriate reinforcers increases the probability that the new learning will occur more readily. This *Ready, Set, Go* strategy is an easy, workable structure that will help you concentrate on the principles of learning as you work through your organizational strategies for teaching. Print *Ready, Set, Go* in bright red letters and learn the definitions. Attach the sign to your desk as a constant reminder.

Teaching is decision making. The decisions you make correlate directly to the kind of teaching you will do and the lesson delivery. These educated choices distinguish the professional teacher from any other person who enters a classroom and attempts to teach children. Choosing effective instructional strategies can only result in more effective learning situations for students and more professional growth and satisfaction for you.

Benjamin Bloom

Organizational strategies are important teaching structures to formulate and define. A clear strategy helps to state and organize the events that will occur during your instructional periods. Some things to weigh carefully while organizing your strategy are the observable teaching behaviors (what you will do), your expected learner outcomes (what you want the students to do), the instructional level of the lesson, specific questioning strategies, the student-teacher interaction processes you want to initiate, and other components of strategic planning.

Bloom's taxonomy of educational objectives is not an organizational strategy in itself. It is a hierarchy of levels of thinking and processing. It can, however, be used as a basic structure to formulate your strategy. In 1956 Benjamin Bloom published *The Taxonomy of Educational Objectives.* This was a major work that had a significant impact on education; it is still a benchmark of educational practice today. The taxonomy gave a systematic procedure for identifying educational objectives. These educational objectives, the observable learning behaviors of students, are systems of thought processes from simple to complex. There are six categories in this taxonomy. Each one is more complex and requires a higher level of thinking than the previous one(s), and each utilizes some or all of the skills/processes of preceding levels. The taxonomy can be viewed as structural sequences for developing thinking skills. Here are the six levels of thinking as identified by Bloom.

> *The Levels of Thinking*
> - Level One—*Knowledge:*   The lowest or beginning level of thinking or cognition. This level requires the student to recall facts, information, or processes. Much book learning is at this level.
>
> - Level Two—*Comprehension:*   Requires the student to use materials or explain ideas based on given information. To demonstrate understanding is the indication that comprehension is occurring.
>
> - Level Three—*Application:*   Requires the learner to use abstract ideas or thoughts and apply them to particular concrete situations. Using abstract ideas in a new setting demonstrates application.
>
> - Level Four—*Analysis:*   Students are asked to identify explicit relationships of individual parts, to recognize patterns, and to explain the significance of those parts.
>
> - Level Five—*Synthesis:*   Asks the student to do creative processing and to assemble parts into a whole by arranging and combining in significant workable ways.

- Level Six—*Evaluation:* The highest level of cognition in the taxonomy. In evaluation, the student must be able to make quantitative or qualitative judgments. To perform an evaluation activity, the skills of the preceding five levels are used. Could you really make valid judgments without basic information (knowledge level)?

These levels of thinking are arranged sequentially and purposefully from the basic gathering and remembering of facts and information, to using and applying them at increasingly higher levels of thought processing. The teaching of social studies at the kindergarten and first-grade years begins at the knowledge level. Without a basic foundation of facts and other information, a student is unable to use or understand (comprehension level) very much of what is taught. This does not mean, however, that primary teachers limit their instruction to the teaching of facts. Given an appropriate background of experiences and information, primary students are capable of seeing essential relationships, identifying parts, creating new arrangements, and even learning how to make some initial judgments. The "right answer" approach to learning is not the goal here, but rather the opportunity to experience higher thought processing.

An Instructional Strategy. Examine the taxonomy as the framework for building an instructional strategy. Remember: The strategy a teacher selects is the organized plan wherein lesson elements are included. The strategy will consider both content and process—what is to be taught/learned and at which levels of functioning. Designing a strategy using the taxonomy as a basis incorporates lesson activities (questions, projects, tasks) that guide students toward upper-level thinking skills. It determines what the teacher does (plan specifically for more complex processing) and what the students do (experience many opportunities to develop these processes and skills). Such strategies include the science of teaching (sound pedagogy and significant content) and the art of teaching (creative, carefully designed methods for presenting it to students).

An instructional strategy that strives to incorporate levels of thinking beyond knowledge (memory, oftentimes simply stated as recall) functions best in a classroom environment that is accepting. The teacher is flexible and understanding, secure enough to encourage free responses and open-minded enough to realize that there may be no right answers for some situations. A significant amount of risking and stretching of ideas will occur, especially at the upper levels, and students must experience a safe learning environment for this to happen. Such a strategy facilitates the coordination of content and performance levels more accurately. Teachers cannot assume that upper-elementary students already have acquired all the knowledge they need, concentrating instruction only on the upper levels of the taxonomy. In some content areas, the first level is the place to start for particular students or classes. The taxonomy provides a framework for building experiences, one upon the other, to build sequence into the curriculum.

Here are some student activities that are suitable for each level of thinking on the hierarchy.

Knowledge

Late

1. Define these terms: *longitude, latitude, meridian.*
2. List the export products of Maine.
3. Label all the parts of a given map.
4. Give three school safety rules.

Comprehension

Couldn't

1. In your own words, explain the library procedures.
2. Explain why the lumberjacks lived in camps.
3. Using given terms, paraphrase their meanings.
4. Describe a typical day in the early days of Boonesborough.

Application

Approach

1. Locate various cities using given latitudes and longitudes.
2. Design a frontier village and roleplay various community helpers.
3. Demonstrate how pollution is like lung cancer.

Analysis

Annie

1. Contrast the villages of woodlands and plains Indians.
2. Examine the components of the transportation system on the Mississippi River.
3. Compare the St. Lawrence Seaway with the Panama Canal.
4. Make a diagram of the Rocky Mountain region and examine the sections.

Synthesis

soon

1. Design a more usable water fountain.
2. Describe the effects of a pollution-free environment.
3. Set up a different traffic pattern for the lunchroom.
4. Project some ways to get to school in the year 2010.

Evaluation

Group

1. Rate these terms qualitatively and state your criteria: *pollution free, crime free, disease free.*
2. Explain why we should or should not have school rules.
3. Assess the values of freedom.
4. State the best way to study for a test and defend your opinion.

The varieties of student activities and experiences that are suitable for a particular level of thinking are both expansive and challenging. Although the evaluation level requires some concentrated thought on the part of students and teachers (planning for this level is thought provoking, too), it is by no means beyond the ability of elementary students. The particular examples given above could generate some very insightful discussions or debates.

New teachers are challenged to assimilate more than one level of mental processing into their lessons. If memory-recall knowledge is the only ultimate objective of elementary social studies, book reading will probably accomplish a large part of that objective. That alone is not an acceptable goal, however. Teachers must prepare specialized lessons and activities to encourage, guide, and even push students toward learning how to think. Using your thinking skills is a life-long process. Start with two or three activities that are above the knowledge level. Give students a chance to experience working at a higher level. Then add more higher-level activities. Many introductory lessons will be at the levels of knowledge and comprehension. These two lower levels of the hierarchy are good places to start.

Knowledge lessons and activities include reading for information; recalling facts in written, oral, or performance formats; and identifying materials. The teacher acts as a coach, guiding students toward information gathering, recording data, and responding in various ways. Significant verbal interaction such as explaining, questioning, verifying, and discussing occurs at this level. The comprehension level is organized around activities that clarify the student's understanding of the information that is gathered. You will organize lesson elements that give students many opportunities to demonstrate what they know. There is more student involvement with each successive level in the hierarchy.

An organizational strategy helps you determine where to begin and provides a plan to help you reach the lesson culmination. Not every strategy you devise will be perfect, but you will learn and adjust.

Process and Product Teaching

When you are considering your methodologies and strategies you must decide whether to teach process or product or both simultaneously. The social studies has been organized toward product teaching. It is important that we teach process. Other areas such as science, math, and reading stress the process approach and find it very effective.

Product Teaching

The simplest way to define product teaching is to say that it is teaching toward or for a specific answer, with the end product or answer to a question or a problem being the important goal. The teaching of factual material readily lends itself to product teaching. Students learn facts and concepts then use them to answer the questions we ask to test their knowledge. Answers are right or wrong and are evaluated accordingly.

As an example, you might ask the following true-false question on a quiz: America was first discovered by Columbus in 1492. True or False? If Max answers true, you mark it correct. If he marks it false, you mark it wrong. The student either knows the answer or he does not.

Process Teaching

Process teaching centers on the process used to obtain answers. The answer is not as important as how the student arrived at the answer. This is why we teach problem-solving skills. We want our children to ask questions and then be able to find ways to answer them to the best of their ability. As they become more proficient in the use of the processes, the quality of the students' answers improves. This is another reason why it is important that you teach skills in social studies. They are the tools of process teaching.

Let's return to our true-false question about America first being discovered by Columbus in 1492. Suppose that Teri, Tammy, and Shirley all answered false. In product teaching, they would all be wrong. In process teaching they are still wrong, but you ask one more question: How did you get that answer?

> *Teri:* "I didn't know, so I guessed."
> *Teacher:* "Maybe you should go back and reread the assignment or go to the library and do a little research."

The process of guessing is not always a good way to solve a problem. Try another way. Teri did not do the research that she should have, so she must go back and redo the process of getting an answer.

> *Tammy:* "I thought it was 1493. Remember the rhyme we learned? 'In 1493 Columbus sailed the deep blue sea'?"
> *Teacher:* "Back up and think again about the rhyme—it wasn't 'deep blue sea,' it was 'the ocean blue.'"

Tammy based her answer on incorrect information that she had gathered. It is necessary for the teacher to help the student correct misinformation. Was Tammy completely wrong or was she right based on her information?

> *Shirley:* "It is true that Columbus made his first trip to America in 1492, but new evidence indicates that he actually landed in the Caribbean and not in America. I read that the Vikings were here much earlier. And the Indians discovered America in prehistoric times and have been living here ever since."
> *Teacher:* ???

What could you say here? Is Shirley's answer right or wrong? It is right if she is thinking and has gone beyond recall of the fact you taught, but wrong if you want only a true-false answer. Would you give Shirley zero credit for her response of false to your true-false question?

Shirley based her answer on more than recall of information. She used your lesson on Columbus as a challenge and expanded the problem to determine who really discovered America. And she solved it.

The important point is that you ask the children how they got their answers. We want to know the process(es) they used and why they came up with a particular answer. How would you teach about elections? Would you have students read a book, then you lecture and ask questions? No! Use process teaching. Have an election and let the students describe what happened. Yes, process teaching takes a lot of time, but can you imagine that the children might actually enjoy school!

Fortunately, you do not have to pick one methodology or the other. You can teach product as well as process in social studies. There is a time and place for both, but remember that it is very easy to concentrate on product and forget to include process.

Expository and Discovery Teaching

A good teacher will use a combination of expository and discovery teaching. There are times when you want to give your students some information and there are times when you want them to find out for themselves. The key is knowing which is most appropriate at a given time.

Expository Teaching

In expository teaching the teacher presents the material to be learned. The teacher's role is that of information giver and the student's role is that of a receiver. In this type of teaching the teacher has the active role and the student is more passive. On the surface this appears to be a negative situation, but that is not necessarily so. There are several good reasons for using expository teaching.

- Expository teaching is efficient. It allows the teacher to present necessary information to an individual, group, or entire class in a quick, concise manner. The students may need certain information before they can proceed. Present a quick expository lesson and the students are ready to continue their work.

- Expository teaching allows the teacher to present information not found in the textbook or references available to the students. You can update information, present different points of view, or add new data as necessary.

- You can overview a topic to prepare your students for what is to come. They need a starting point and direction before they can proceed. A quick introduction and overview will provide that direction.

- You can share personal experiences. You or a resource person can tell about experiences that you have had, places you have visited, things you have done, and lessons you have learned. The only way this knowledge is available is through an expository presentation.

Expository teaching is the central focus of David Ausubel's work on receptive learning. (See the discussion of Ausubel on page 49.) Lecture and demonstrations are the two best known examples of expository teaching.

Lecture.   When you think of a lecture, you usually visualize a teacher in front of a room, reading or speaking from a set of notes. Can you lecture to young children? Yes; teachers do it all the time. A lecture is nothing more than a teacher presenting information orally to a group of students. To be effective, there are several points to remember.

1. Make your lectures short and to the point. Young children have short attention spans and, more importantly, limited intake capacities. It is better to give small amounts of information, then allow students to absorb and/or use the information before giving them more. Do not confuse them with extraneous materials; get to the point.

2. Plan your lesson. Knowing what you want to present will help you keep on task and get through quickly. Make provisions for questions and interruptions by your students.

3. Use good public speaking techniques. A well-modulated voice and frequent eye contact with your audience will increase the reception of your information.

4. Use audiovisual materials to enhance your presentation. You must reach your tactile and visual learners as well as your auditory learners.

You will lecture to your class just as you will use other techniques. Be sure to make it effective so that you are teaching, not just "talking at" them.

Demonstrations.   Demonstrations are usually used for two reasons: to show how something works and to present a special skill. You might have a resource person, a student or team of students, or even yourself give a demonstration. You may ask someone, perhaps a grandparent, to bring a spinning wheel to class and show how it works. The children will watch him or her spin, ask questions, and then try it themselves with the help of the resource person. They have a concrete experience with the spinning wheel and can now relate to that experience whenever they read about, hear, or see a spinning wheel.

On occasion, when the children are working on a project or activity, they need a special skill to continue. The teacher can quickly demonstrate how to operate a piece of equipment or to perform a specific skill. For example, the students are doing a lesson that requires them to construct a map. They need a larger version of the map than what appears in the textbook. The teacher can stop the lesson for a short time and show them how to use the opaque projector to make a copy. The students can then return to work and use the opaque projector to make their map.

Discovery Teaching

In discovery teaching the teacher sets the stage, helps define a problem or formulate a question, then steps back and allows the students to gather the information needed to solve the problem or answer the question. The teacher acts as a guide and a resource person. Students are active participants in the learning process.

The strength of this approach is that it involves the students in the learning process. They define their own problem, use the appropriate skills to gather data, and then analyze the data to get an answer. They learn how to solve a problem with minimal help from the teacher. The information learned has mean-

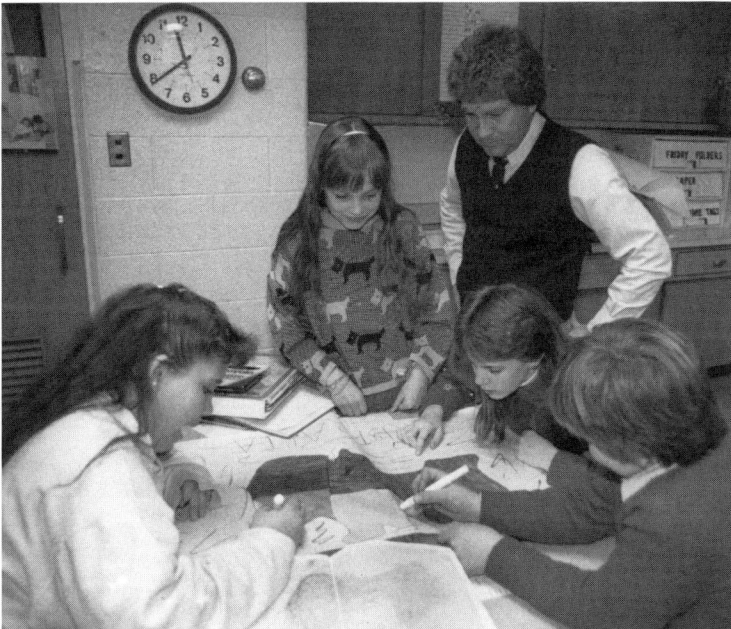

As the students work on the problem, the teacher monitors the progress and is available if needed.

ing to them because they gathered it for a purpose, and then applied it to their problem.

The main drawback to this approach is that it is not as efficient as expository teaching. It takes a lot of time. The students have to do all of the research and data gathering that the teacher does for them in expository lessons. Not all children learn or discover at the same rate. Discovery teaching is an experience that cannot be hurried. A good discovery lesson will produce new problems to be investigated, many times raising more questions than answers. This allows the students an option for more concentrated study or for a broader look at the topic being studied. However, the teacher must control the focus of the class in order to obtain her or his objectives. The teacher must decide what learning is applicable and what is not, and if a sidetrack is profitable or not.

At first glance it may appear that discovery teaching is not structured and that the teacher has very little to do. This is not true. The teacher must plan very carefully before starting a discovery lesson, as well as plan for contingencies that arise during the course of the lesson.

Generally, a good teacher will use a mixture of expository and discovery teaching, varying the lessons and using expository and discovery teaching as the need arises.

ACTIVITIES

As you do these activities, you will need a topic. Choose one of the following; they represent material commonly taught at the grade level indicated. Your instructor may want you to choose a topic from a particular textbook series or he or she may choose one for you.

Grade 1: Holidays honor some event or person.

Grade 2: There are many family structures.

Grade 3: There are many kinds of communities.

Grade 4: There is a need for conservation of natural resources.

Grade 5: The first Americans (Indians) needed many skills to survive.

Grade 6: The countries of the western hemisphere depend on one another for many different things.

3.1   Using the Hunter Model

In this activity you will work with the components of effective lesson presentation as used by Hunter. Choose a topic from the list above and answer the following questions:

1. Which topic did you select?

2. What specifically are you going to teach? (Teach to an objective)

3. How will you pretest to find where to start? (Teach to the appropriate level of difficulty)

   What are some other ways to find the appropriate level for your lesson?

4. How are you going to know during the lesson if your students are learning? (Monitor and adjust)

   What will you do if your lesson is:
   a. Too difficult?

   b. Too easy?

5. Use these three areas from Hunter's Cycle of Learning to decide what you will do. (Use, don't abuse, the principles of learning)
   Describe specifically what you would do in your lesson to:
   a. Motivate

   b. Reinforce

   c. Transfer

Discuss your answers with your group, class, or instructor. Be prepared to defend your choices.

Did you find better alternatives when you discussed your answers with others? What were they? Did you present only answers for each of the above questions or did you give several possibilities? There are many possibilities for every one of the topics, and the best one may depend entirely upon the children that you are teaching. Did you remember to consider the grade level of your topic?

3.2 A Task Analysis (Cummings)

In this activity you will work with the components of effective lesson presentation as used by Cummings. The purpose is to help you take a close look at your topic and how you can teach it. A task analysis is an exercise in subdividing a topic into components, further subdividing each component, repeating again and again as many times as necessary to get teachable steps. To make this activity manageable, assume that you will have one week (five days) to teach the objective. Use the objective that you developed in Activity 3.1, question 2.

1. What is your objective?

2. Subdivide your objective into long-range goals. Write an objective for each day.
   Monday:

   Tuesday:

   Wednesday:

   Thursday:

   Friday:

3. Pick one of the daily goals above. Subdivide it into components. What specific objectives will you teach on that day?

    a.

    b.

    c.

    d.

    e.

4. Select one objective from question 3 above and perform a task analysis. (The teacher behavior is what the teacher will do to teach the objective. Student behavior is what the students will do.)

Task:

Teacher Behavior:

Student Behavior:

You should know what you want to teach the learner, what you will do, and what the learner will do. Share your analysis with your group or your instructor for their reaction. Your instructor might ask you to share with the class.

You could probably subdivide your tasks further; every task is made up of smaller tasks. You do reach a point where it is no longer practical to subdivide further, however. A task analysis forces you to break a task down into teachable components. It also forces you to take a close look at what you are actually teaching and how you will teach it.

3.3   *Using Bloom's Taxonomy*

This activity will help you to better understand the levels of Bloom's taxonomy. Choose a grade level and one of the topics suggested at the beginning of the activities. You may want to continue using the same one you have been using or work with a different one.

State three student activities that you might use for each of the levels of Bloom's taxonomy. Be ready to explain why the activities are appropriate to teaching on that particular level.

Knowledge

1.

2.

3.

Comprehension

1.

2.

3.

Application

1.

2.

3.

Analysis

1.

2.

3.

Synthesis

1.

2.

3.

Evaluation

1.

2.

3.

Which level did you find the most difficult to plan? The easiest? Did you need to go back and reread some information about the levels? Could you go back through your activities and put together a lesson incorporating at least one activity from each level? It may prove to be difficult because some lessons lend themselves more readily to one or two levels. Share your examples with your group or instructor.

Summary

Teaching social studies is a challenge. It requires a strong foundation in the content areas. This foundation, accompanied with a repertoire of various methodologies and strategies, is the core of successful social studies instruction.

Beginning teachers must formulate a personal working philosophy of social studies education. This philosophy includes such things as attitude, commitment, involvement, and the characteristics that comprise good teaching. Your personal philosophy will guide you in making decisions, such as: What is the place of social studies in my total educational responsibility? How much time and effort will I invest? Will I use those methods that are "tried and true" or will I use some nontraditional innovative techniques? Will I teach to the test? Which behaviors will I expect as a result of my teaching? These decisions and many others are made by you, the social studies teacher.

This chapter has examined some strategies, methodologies, and teacher behaviors that will enable you to teach social studies effectively. Obviously, a strategy you may select to teach consumer affairs might not be equally effective when used to teach a unit on anthropology. Strategies must be planned to fit each lesson. The task of planning and implementing these strategies is somewhat easier to manage when you know the components of strategic planning for instruction.

Using a variety of methods, strategies, materials, techniques, and approaches adds vitality and interest to your lessons. Some lessons may indicate that you should begin with several classes of process teaching, and then use those process skills to guide the students toward product experiences. Another series of lessons may indicate that an expository approach is needed. Your strategy might include a variety of hands-on manipulative activities that lead students to discover certain things during discovery lessons.

At first, it is difficult to determine which approaches are the best. Beginning teachers are wise to follow the suggestions and guidelines as presented in the teacher's manual and then expand upon them as experience is acquired in the classroom. Social studies teaching is open to many teaching styles. There is a wide area for you to interject your innovative and creative ideas. The way you plan a lesson is based on the decisions you make. Your students will benefit from your flexibility and you will grow professionally.

READING RESOURCES

"The Methods of Teaching." *Journal of Teacher Education, 37* (July/August 1986): 2–35.

Banks, James A., with Clegg, Jr., Ambrose A. *Teaching Strategies for the Social Studies.* Reading, MA: Addison-Wesley, 1973.

Banks, James A., with Clegg, Jr., Ambrose A. *Teaching Strategies for the Social Studies: Inquiring, Valuing, and Decision Making,* 3rd ed. New York: Longman, 1985.

Frankel, Jack R. *Helping Students Think and Value: Strategies for Teaching the Social Studies.* Englewood Cliffs, NJ: Prentice-Hall, 1980.

Maxim, George W. *Methods of Teaching Social Studies to Elementary School Children,* 3rd ed. Colombus, OH: Merrill Publishing Company, 1987.

Rooze, G. E. ''A Strategy for Helping Students Draw Conclusions.'' *Social Studies,* 77 (March/April 1986): 74–76.

Ryan, Frank L. *Exemplars for the New Social Studies.* Englewood Cliffs, NJ: Prentice-Hall, 1971.

VanSciver, J. H. ''Sweet Success in Social Studies: A Process Approach.'' *Social Studies,* 77 (September/October 1986): 208–209.

ENDNOTES

1. *Standard College Dictionary,* Text Edition (New York: Harcourt, Brace, & World, Inc., 1963), p. 853.

2. Battle, J. A., ''The Content of Method and the Method of Content,'' in *The New Idea in Education* (New York: Harper and Row, Publishers, 1968), p. 153.

3. Cummings, Carol, *Teaching Makes a Difference* (Edmonds, WA: Snohomish Publishing Company, 1986).

4. Ibid., p. 186.

5. Ibid., pp. 67–68.

6. Ibid., p. 147.

7. Bloom, Benjamin, *The Taxonomy of Educational Objectives: The Classification of Educational Goals: Handbook 1: Cognitive Domain* (New York: Longman, 1956).

UNIT III

What Children Learn

4
Content, Concepts, and Skills

PROJECTIONS

Identifying and planning for the curriculum projections for any specific area is an exciting undertaking for teachers, coordinators, and administrators. It is an especially challenging task for the social studies because of the various disciplines it encompasses. The traditional social sciences of anthropology, geography, history, government, economics, and sociology will undoubtedly remain the cornerstone of elementary social studies. The particular emphases within each of the individual disciplines may undergo major transformations, however. Traditional topics, although they are certainly important and valid, may not occupy a large portion of the curriculum. Does the topic Community Helpers really need to be taught for three years—in first, second, and again in third grade?

While some traditional topics may be deemphasized, the areas of current events, global realities, multiethnic issues, nationalism, governments, and other topics may occupy a larger part of the curriculum. Studying the "here and now" is a trend that needs to be examined carefully. There is so much social studies occurring everyday that students can readily witness the drama of events and processes simply by tuning in to the evening news or reading the daily newspaper. Present-day social studies events and topics need to be emphasized for students to be truly informed about the environment in which they live.

Teachers are expected to teach more to students and at an earlier age. Structured preschool programs and the instruction programs of daycare centers are becoming more important in the socialization of many young children and in teaching readiness skills to them. The school is becoming more important in teaching the social skills as parents and children spend less time together. The old argument that the parents have the child for eighteen hours a day while we only have them for six hours is no longer true. If you do not count sleep time, we have many children for a much longer period of time than the parents do.

The new social studies programs offer exciting materials that introduce not only factual matter but also activities that challenge young minds to examine, classify, interpret, decide, participate, judge, accept, and perform other social studies process skills. The classroom is the setting where youngsters learn many social skills that are usable in the play group, the family group, and other out-of-school groups.

There is a critical need for a more concentrated effort in the teaching of affective skills. So often students approach teachers and say, "But how can I do this?" It continues to frustrate and baffle teachers. The students honestly have little or no idea how to approach a project, assignment, or lesson. Teachers must make a concentrated effort to teach specific affective skills. We cannot assume that students have the necessary affective skills to approach given tasks successfully.

There is a fluid aspect of social studies education. The standard, traditional content areas are somewhat constant; other topics flow into and out of the curriculum at various times. The world scene, economic changes, social situations, family values systems, and other forces give impetus to particular educational trends. These trends are mirrored in curriculum goals and content. A topic that is heavily emphasized today, such as racial relations, may or may not be the major emphasis tomorrow. Newer issues and topics, such as the technology of space, immigration, conflicts in Central America, or apartheid in South Africa, move to the front of public consciousness.

What will the content and concepts be in the near future? No one can state them emphatically. We can, however, thoroughly teach the skills and content material we are presently required to teach. Using this as a foundation, whenever curriculum adaptations and adjustments become necessary, our students will have at least minimal skills and understandings to cope with them adequately.

One of the most important decisions a teacher makes is *what to teach*. It is important to know how to teach, but before you can decide how, you must decide what to teach. In this chapter you will be introduced to three areas from which lessons are drawn. The first is the area of content. The majority of teaching is centered on content and the ability of the child to use that content in everyday situations. Closely related to content is the second area: the teaching of facts, concepts, and generalizations. We teach the child how to organize facts into useful categories (called concepts) and to develop generalizations based upon them. Last, but very important, we teach children the skills that are necessary for learning. Without basic skills, all other learning is seriously hampered, if not impossible.

Selecting Subject-Matter Content

Teachers are concerned with what is required in the curriculum. It is impossible to determine specifically what to teach before you know your grade level, the school district, or the textbook series that is adopted. Regardless of the grade level or textbook, there is no substitute for having a strong content background. You cannot expect to teach well what you do not know. Would you try to teach

French if you cannot read or speak French? If you are weak in an area, then you must do some homework before you try to teach it. There are four main sources for the subject-matter content that is taught in social studies programs: textbooks and curriculum guides, traditional, current events, and special-interest groups. Each of these sources has an effect on the content and on how and why it is taught.

Textbook and Curriculum Guides

The bulk of the content material taught comes from textbook and curriculum guides. Some schools have curriculum guides that set the social studies program for the school and specifically state what to teach in each grade level. Other curriculum guides are less specific and refer primarily to the textbook. Textbooks generally are the curriculum guides for most school systems. When you are given a grade-level assignment in a school, you are told what textbook(s) to use. It then becomes your responsibility to become familiar with that textbook and, more specifically, with the subject matter content therein. You may choose methods and materials other than those suggested by the textbook, but you cannot ignore teaching the content. Remember that other teachers build on what you teach.

Look first at the Table of Contents of your textbook. It overviews the content areas to be taught. Next, go to the Unit and/or Chapter. Look at the material presented, the objectives, and the special sections such as vocabulary or review. This information tells you what material is to be taught. It is a good idea to look at the textbooks used in the grades below and above yours to see what the larger curriculum may be. It is advisable to review those texts before you start teaching new material, then you will know the foundation skills of your class.

Traditional

In every school there are traditional topics that are taught. For example, it may not be in the textbook, but in some grade levels, we traditionally teach about Thanksgiving, Labor Day, and Christopher Columbus. Some material is taught simply because "We have always taught that." Tradition is probably the weakest reason for including certain content in the curriculum. Do not be afraid to challenge this material and discard it if there is no reason other than "We have always taught this." All content taught should have a purpose, or else it is a waste of our time and the students' time.

Current Events

It is very important that we teach material from current topics. Textbooks cover structured material that gives students an overall view of their world and their place in it. But we are also concerned with the events of today. It is critical that children be exposed to global issues; we do not live in isolation from the rest of the world. As transportation and communication improve, the world becomes our backyard. Live telecasts from everywhere on the earth (and from space too) bring the world into our living rooms.

Air travel can put anyone anyplace on earth in a day. Migration for such reasons as marriage, jobs, religion, political persecution, wars, and famines have intermixed racial, ethnic, social, and political groups throughout the world. It is not difficult to find someone from almost any country in an average-sized town. This is a point to remember when you need help to teach about a certain culture or country. State and national heritage are stressed in textbooks; now we must deal with global heritage. It is important that you read current materials on global education. Professional periodicals such as *Social Education* and *The Social Studies* are good sources. Professional conferences and workshops will also keep you informed of current thought in the field.

Current events are an important source of content materials. The issues and events of the day are of concern to all informed citizens. It is important that we teach children how to become informed and how to participate in the issues that concern them. Local issues are always important. Should we or should we not construct a new landfill? Who should we vote for? Which taxes do we need to support the schools? Elementary students cannot vote on these issues, but as students in a democracy, they must begin to establish an awareness of matters that will face them as adults. Social studies teachers must teach those social re-

Everyone in the class is working and learning when they know what they are expected to learn.

sponsibility skills that build a solid foundation for a responsible citizenry. The most important thing we can teach our children in social studies is how to make intelligent decisions. By using current events as classroom content, we can make social studies pertinent for students. Schedule a specific time each week for discussing local concerns.

Special-Interest Groups

It is impossible to gauge the impact of interest groups on the selection of the subject-matter content that you will teach. There are many subtle pressures as well as specific overt demands that dictate your choice of content. You only have to look at some of the recent court decisions as to what can and cannot be taught. The most famous was the Scopes trial concerning the teaching of evolution. The so-called Scopes II trial of *Bob Mozert et al.* v. *Hawkins County Public Schools et al.* (October 1986) allowed parents to withdraw their children from a reading program because of their religious objection to a reading series. There are religious fundamentalist groups that censure textbooks, business groups that promote inclusions of their product or service in the curriculum, service organizations that want to promote their special messages or solicit support, racial or ethnic groups demanding equal or special consideration, and state, local, and even your own personal demands to be considered. As a teacher, it is often tempting to say to yourself, "I'll stick to the text and be safe." You do not always have that option, however, even if it were a valid choice. You will find that you are required to include content other than that found in the textbook.

State and local requirements are matters of concern. Many states have specific content that is mandated by state statute. School districts must include this content material if they are to be accredited and funded by the state. Local districts may also have special content that is required. If you do not comply, you may not be teaching there next year! It is up to you to determine from your principal or curriculum coordinator if any of these special requirements exist.

One last source of subject-matter content is you and your personal, professional judgment as to what needs to be included in your program. You may see omissions in the text material, or you may have special expertise that allows you to go beyond what is included in the textbook. You may have students with special needs that must be met. Special situations may arise that call for attention. You may want to include special topics that are not included in your regular program. You do have the freedom, within reasonable limits, to expand the knowledge base of your students. Remember that with this freedom comes the responsibility to do the job you were hired to do, and not to use the classroom for your private forum.

In the final analysis, you are the professional in charge and you alone must make the decisions as to what subject-matter content will be taught in your classroom. You must choose wisely to insure that your children have the factual knowledge necessary to learn the concepts and generalizations they will use throughout their lives.

Teaching Facts, Concepts, and Generalizations

Facts

To most people, teaching is the imparting of knowledge to students in the form of factual information. Students are asked to learn, memorize, gather, discover, and/or regurgitate facts. Teachers ask questions concerning factual information obtained from books, films, lectures, and other resources. Even some of the more popular games such as Trivial Pursuit and Jeopardy are based on a knowledge of facts.

Facts are verifiable, true statements—or at least they are considered true at the moment. Time and additional knowledge has disproved many of our previously known facts. For example, consider this fact: Columbus discovered America in 1492. This is true in a sense, but additional information has shown that (1) he discovered the West Indies, not the mainland of the American continent, (2) the Vikings were on the continent several hundred years prior to the arrival of Columbus, and (3) the Native Americans found the continent and permanently settled here in prehistoric times. All of these statements are true in the proper context.

Teaching Facts.   Knowledge is based on facts. It is very important that facts are taught in school; they are the building blocks of concepts and generalizations. Without factual information, it is impossible to make intelligent decisions or evaluations. Every child should learn as much factual information as they are mentally capable of doing, starting at a very early preschool age. The more facts they have at their disposal, the greater the potential for the useful acquisition and employment of knowledge.

Facts are an integral part of teaching. The social studies are often criticized for the emphasis placed on factual information. We can avoid this criticism by making sure that the facts we emphasize are meaningful and not trivial. It is important in the United States to know that the Declaration of Independence was signed on July 4, 1776. But is it important to know the name of the horse ridden by General Washington's third in command? When testing student knowledge, ask for significant facts. Trick questions based on inconsequential facts really do not help you or the students in evaluating a lesson; however, they do discourage learning. Other content areas such as English, math, and science expect memorization of facts, so you should not feel guilty about expecting students to learn facts in social studies.

Concepts

A concept is a concrete or abstract category of meaning. Concepts provide the means for organizing facts into useful categories. Consider concepts as a filing cabinet with drawers and folders, as seen in Figure 4–1. Each folder has a name.

Figure 4-1   Concept File

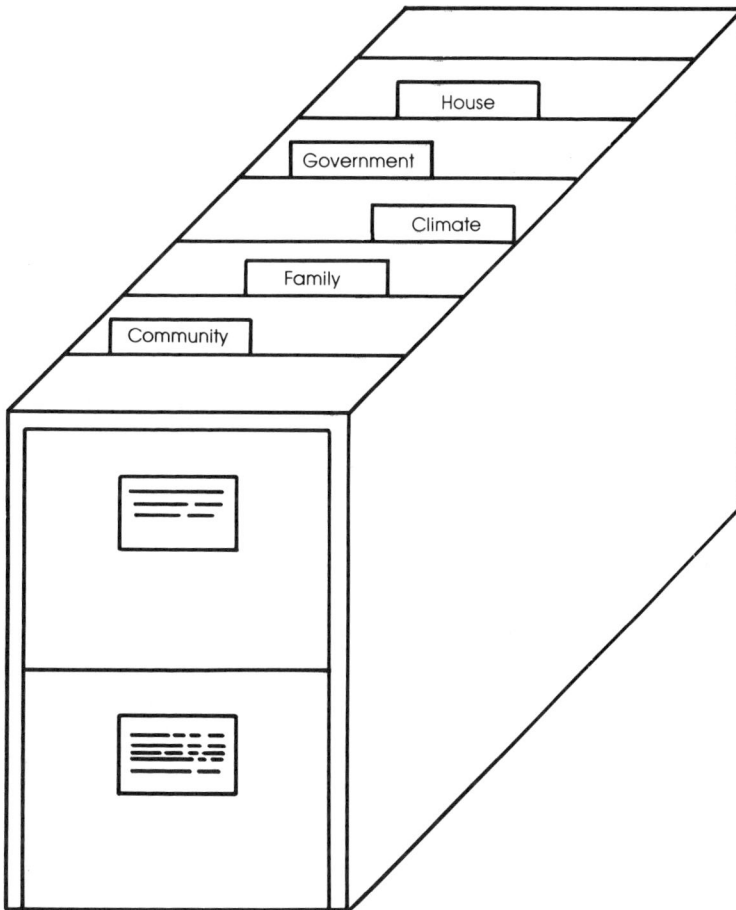

This name is usually a single word like *family* or a double word like *community helpers.* In reality, double-word titles are more complex than single-word titles because they are the result of combining several concepts into a new concept. The concept *community helpers* combines the concept *community* and the concept *helpers* to form a new meaning.

Concepts are names of categories. Note the list of examples below that relates to climate. All are familiar and have special meanings. Put a meaning to each of them.

snow	weather	hot
hail	land	cold
rain	sky	wet
sun	cloud	dry
ice	tornado	humid
wind	storm	clear

They are all common words, but each carries a meaning for the person using the word. Could you explain climate without using several of these terms?

When a folder is given a name, it forms a category under which we can classify facts relating to the concept. Using the concept *family* as an example, we might file the following facts:

1. I am a member of a family.
2. My brothers and sisters are part of my family.
3. My father and mother are part of my family.
4. My friends have families of their own.
5. A family is a group of related people.

Now whenever you hear the key word *families,* you have a mental picture of certain facts relating to that key word. The most important function of concepts is to facilitate communication. The ability to communicate is one of our most important skills; it allows us to share information. Concepts are a form of shorthand that makes communicating easier. If you are told to read a book, you already know something about the book from your concept of the category labeled *book.* List some facts that the word *book* brings to your mind.

1.

2.

3.

4.

How do these facts describe a book? How many other concepts are used in your list of facts? Facts and concepts are closely interrelated. Concepts are a way of categorizing facts, but facts are loaded with concepts. Consider the two facts listed below and the concepts contained in them. Can you add other concepts to the list?

Fact: Daniel Boone was a hunter, explorer, and soldier.
Concepts: hunter
explorer
soldier

Fact: Many settlers traveled west on the Oregon Trail.
Concepts: settlers
travel
trail
west

Very young children start developing their own set of concepts as soon as they start learning. The concepts are very simple to be sure, but they are the basic concepts upon which all future facts and concepts will be based. Youngsters may not be able to verbalize their concepts but they can use them. Parents use a concept and the baby begins to put meaning to it. The mother asks, ''Are you hungry?'' and the baby reacts to the concept *hungry.* As soon as the baby can talk, he or she will use the word to denote need for nourishment. As the child grows mentally, he or she will add many other facts to the category *hungry* and will use it many ways, depending upon the specific need. Concepts are learned and continually refined. This refining process never really ends because learning never really ends. There is always new information to be processed and categorized, either into existing categories or newly formed ones.

Types of Categories: Simple and Complex.   Concepts can be either simple or complex (also called concrete or abstract). Simple concepts are real and specific; they are defined in a very precise manner with a concrete definition. An example of this is the concept *house.* It is specifically categorized as a building in which people live. It is very concrete, without any emotion or undertones. Simple concepts are easy to develop and comprehend.

Complex concepts are abstract; they are defined in terms of emotion (feelings) or behavior. Can you give a simple, factual definition of *happiness?* Clearly this concept is based on emotion. It is a feeling, perhaps of satisfaction or pleasure, and it may elicit a behavior such as smiling or laughing. A dictionary might define *happiness* as pleasurable satisfaction. Synonyms are *contentedness, satisfaction, cheerfulness, gaiety,* and *delight.* Any facts filed under this category will be stated in abstract and/or emotional terms.

Public and Private Meanings.   Most concepts carry a dual meaning. A meaning that is shared by many people is public, common to everyone who uses it. This is the critical factor in using concepts as a means of communication. We can hear or read a concept such as *home* and apply a common meaning—a place where we live. On the other hand, private meanings are also given to the same concept. These meanings are personal, having special meaning to one or a few individuals. Using the concept *home* again, privately it may invoke feelings of a particular house, a group of people, or even a state or nation. Further explanation might be needed to convey the private meaning you attach to a concept when you use it.

Time and Space Concepts.   There are two important concepts in social studies that deserve special consideration: time and space.

Time: Simple time concepts are difficult for young children until they have had enough experience to develop a relative base. Have you ever promised a child an ice cream cone "later in the afternoon" and then spent the rest of the morning answering the question "Is it time yet?"

Children begin to develop a time sense when they start school, relating time to specific activities being carried out in a normal daily routine. The real problem comes when we introduce such social studies time concepts as *long ago, eon, century, decade, era,* and *prehistoric times.* How can you give meaning to these words when the child has nothing more than a dictionary or textbook definition with which to relate? As a part of teaching this concept, it is necessary to present concrete examples that can be used to understand the concept of time. Shorter time periods such as *morning, afternoon,* and *night* are a starting point for younger students. They can relate to how long before lunch, the end of the school day, or until a favorite TV program comes on. They know how old they are but they really have no concept of the length of a year. When you are five or six years old, a ten-year old is an "old person." Grandparents and teachers may be considered "real old, maybe 19 or 20." Upper-grade children have a better time sense and can relate more easily to the concept of *year,* as they can look back at the number of years in school or the number of birthdays they have had.

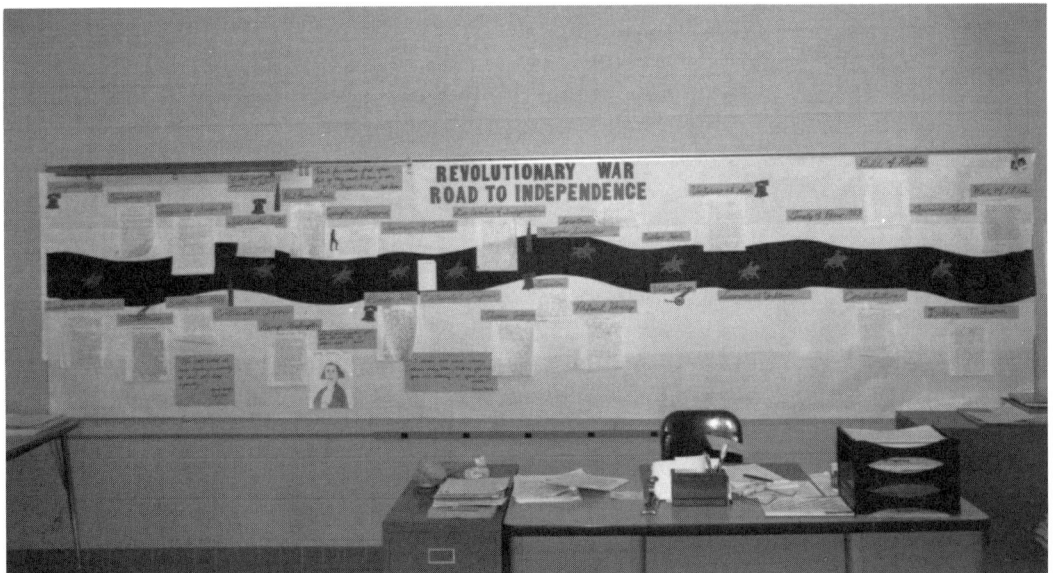

A time line can put historical events in a time sequence that children comprehend.

Another aspect of the concept of time is the concept of chronological order (or time sequence). Many children need special help in putting events in sequence. Concrete references such as time lines are very helpful in giving visual and tactile meaning to the concept. Exercises that force the child to think and act sequentially are beneficial. For example, learning to remember and follow a series of directions or to analyze a task and put it into sequence helps the child understand the need for sequential order.

Space: The concept of space is as abstract as time. For example, how are distances taught? Can a child relate to the concept of a mile or a thousand miles if he does not really know how far a mile is? What does the child use as a benchmark? In actual practice you may want to measure a mile or half mile distance that is easily seen by the student, then use this as a reference point.

Space as it relates to area is also a difficult concept to develop. How big is an acre? We measure land this way and study settlers who bought or claimed land by the acre or by the section (640 acres). Try explaining this to a child. How wide is the continent? It might be just as easy to explain "How high is up?" The spatial concept must be developed carefully, beginning with a small, known base. Concrete experiences such as measuring the classroom and playground or outlining the acual size of something such as a cabin or tepee on the playground can develop size relationships. Walking a set distance, such as one mile, will give a feeling for the distances traveled in early days when walking was the major means of transportation.

Time, space, and distance are excellent examples of concepts that must start at a very low level of cognition. They develop as the child matures and gains new insights and adds new meaning to the concept. Facts, as they accumulate, are filed under the proper categories, adding meaning to the concept. These abstract concepts are always being modified as new experiences provide new facts. Growth in understanding is the result.

Teaching Concepts.   Concepts, like subject-matter or factual content, must be taught, especially if those concepts are needed to communicate the subject-matter content being taught. Children and adults are constantly learning and/or refining new concepts. This brings up an important point: Most concept learning is done informally and not by conscious effort by either the learner or the teacher. This does not mean that teachers should not and do not actively teach concepts. It does mean that sometimes the teacher needs only to offer clarification or a quick definition to make the concept usable. At other times though, it is important that the teacher actively teaches new concepts, especially when new material is being introduced. New material may necessitate the teaching of completely new concepts or the addition of new data to old concepts. Either way, usable concepts must be learned by students before they can really grasp new material and use their new knowledge.

Concepts are learned in two ways: by observation and by definition. Learning concepts by observation is mostly self-instructional. The learner observes the way other people use a concept and then develops his or her own definition. He or she may listen to the way words are used or watch the actions of others. The learner may apply the other senses—tasting, smelling, touching—to add more data to his or her interpretations of the concept. To illustrate this way of learning, consider a small child learning the concept *hot.* Parents tell her, "No! No! Don't touch—*Hot.*" She knows that *hot* has something to do with something she is not to touch. She may not be sure why just yet, but when the parents say, "It will hurt you," she knows to relate *hot* to personal discomfort or danger. She may even try it—if the parents allow it—on a warm but not dangerously hot item. The uncomfortable feeling causes her to draw her hand back quickly; thus, the concept *hot* has more meaning for her. Sometimes concepts are best learned through observation since a definition may not convey many of the subtle or hidden meanings of a particular concept.

Learning concepts by definition is more formal. Sometimes observations do not make sense to the learner and it is necessary for him or her to get help to understand the concept. Other times, the concept cannot be learned by observation because it is unobservable and must be learned by definition.

It is important to remember that before a concept can be taught, either by observation or by definition, the child must have experiential background upon which to base the concept. Sometimes the teacher finds that the most difficult task is to find what the child knows so she or he can build upon it. Many children come to school with a very poor experiential background. You may have to spend a lot of time providing experiences to use as a base upon which to build the concepts that your students will need to know. How would you teach a child the concept of *ocean* if he or she has never seen one or even pictures of one? In the classic book *Moby Dick,* Herman Melville uses many pages to describe the ocean to his readers who have never seen one. Through the media of television and motion pictures, most people have seen pictures and even heard the sounds of oceans, thereby allowing them to develop a usable concept.

Dr. Troy Sullivan,[1] a teacher in a remote Indian school in Alaska, once told of the problem of using a basal reader with his students. The simple statement, "Father got into the automobile to drive to the office to work," created problems. First, what is an automobile? There were no roads or automobiles around. The closest vehicle was a lone Jeep 20 miles away, which they might see once a year if the river froze solid enough for someone to drive it down to their village. Second, what does "go to work" mean? No one in the village except the teachers held jobs and went to work in the way we understand the concept. All of the villagers worked hard hunting, fishing, trapping, making clothes, and preparing and storing food to survive, but they did not "go to work." Third, what is an office? The nearest one of those was on a military air base 40 or 50 miles away. None of the villagers had ever been in one. Try to explain these concepts to a child who has no experiences upon which to build.

While teaching at the University of Alaska at Anchorage, Dr. Sullivan was involved in a project to use Indian and Eskimo students from remote villages as teachers in their village schools. His task was to provide as many experiences and to develop as many concepts as possible in a summer, so they could explain to others the concepts found in the textbooks. Experiences included such things as riding in an automobile, visiting offices, riding elevators, going to a restaurant, eating hamburgers, shopping in stores, and visiting small industries. Can you imagine the task? Your task is just as difficult because many students do not have the experiential background they need for school learning. We often take for granted that they do.

To teach a concept, follow a four-step procedure: Rule–Example–Rule–Application.

1. *Rule:*   Define the concept, being sure to link it to the learner's experience. The definition may be obtained from a dictionary or textbook, or it may be formulated by the teacher. You may want to write it on the chalkboard or overhead so the students can use visual as well as aural cues. Give the attributes of the concept to clarify what is involved in the concept. It is a way of breaking the concept down into usable detail and to clarify the rule.

   Example: Concept—Family
   - *Rule*—The most fundamental social or mating group: parents and their children
   - *Attributes*—Usually consists of:
     a. Mother and father
     b. Siblings—brothers and sisters
     c. May include grandparents
     d. May also includ persons related by blood or marriage: relatives, kinfolks

2. *Example:*   Use examples and nonexamples of the concept to illustrate the rule. Start with examples that clearly illustrate the rule then follow with a nonexample. As the rule becomes clear, examples and nonexamples that are not as clear cut can be introduced to help the learner make the necessary distinctions. After the teacher has given an example or nonexample, students should be given the opportunity to talk about their interpretations and to ask questions. The primary purpose of using examples and nonexamples is to further define and clarify the concept and rule.

   Example: Concept—Family
   - *Example*—Your mother and father are your family.
   - *Nonexample*—Your teacher is not a part of your family.
   - *Example* (less distinctive)—If your grandparents are living with you or you are living with them, they are family.
   - *Nonexample*—A parent who left the family unit may or may not be considered family.

3. *Redefine Rule:*   Given the rule or definition again. Ask the students to repeat the rule orally while you write it on the chalkboard. If they have the
necessary skills, they can also write it. Ask different students to put the
rule in their own words and give an example and nonexample to illustrate
their rule. The purpose of this step is to give all of the children a chance
to verbalize the concept.

Example: Concept—Family

- *Repeat the Rule*—The most fundamental social or mating group: parents
  and their children

- Children repeat the rule.

- *Student Version*—A family is all the people living at my house. My brother
  and my Mom and Dad are my family. My friend Beverly is not part of my
  family.

4. *Application:*   Find a way for the students to use the concept in a meaningful way. Applying knowledge is the best way to commit it to permanent
memory and to make that knowledge usable. You might have several students roleplay a family and give the position of each person within the
family. Develop the lesson that you started when you introduced the concept. You had a reason for teaching the concept and now you are ready for
it to be used. Be sure to point out how the concept fits into the lesson and
why it had to be learned.

Example: Concept—Family

- *Roleplay*—Sarah Jane, pick a team and have each play the role of a member
  of your family. How many boys and how many girls will you need? What
  name will each person have? Who is that person? Is he or she older or
  younger than you?

- *Apply to Lesson*—We are studying about a pioneer family. Why do we want
  to know about the family? Why are families important? How big was a
  family?

It is important to learn concepts so that easier communication can be accomplished. They allow all of us to share common ways of grouping knowledge
into usable categories. Concepts often have many meanings that develop out of
a simple core as the experiences and knowledge of the user expands, but the
core allows us to understand the new meanings. Teachers must help the child
to develop the core concept. Concepts are not always taught by the teacher;
many are self-taught by observation. The teacher may only have to clarify and
apply a concept that is already known, or to help the learner put new meaning
to a known concept, or to develop a new concept. However the teacher does
it, the new insight into the concept allows the learner to proceed with learning
new materials.

Generalizations

Often called the "Big Idea," generalizations are the core or basic idea of a lesson. Usually they are stated in the form of a summarizing statement, expressing relationships among concepts. Generalizations have a broad degree of applicability, allowing them to be transferred to many situations. This broad applicability is what makes them so important.

Generalizations are based on facts and concepts. Consider the following definitions:

- *Fact:*   One unique event or happening.

  Example: The Declaration of Independence was signed on July 4, 1776.

- *Concept:*   Categories in which we place facts; a filing system for facts.

  Example: Freedom (Facts under this category: self-rule would be possible; would not be dependent on England; oppressive taxes would be revoked).

- *Generalization:*   Relationships among concepts; usually refers to more than one example.

  Example: When a government forces excessive rules and regulations on its subjects, they will rebel against that government and establish a new one in its place. There are many examples of this occurring: The United States and England's King George, Russia and the Czar, France and the Monarchy, Iran and the Shah.

Facts and generalizations have a common bond—they represent propositions believed to be true. Both can be verified or refuted by observation. Consider the fact: The state of Texas was once an independent nation. This is a single unique event. It can be easily verified by consulting various historical sources. A generalization such as "Large cities are usually located on major waterways" can be verified by locating major cities on a map and determining if a major waterway is there. Even though we believe facts and generalizations to be true, time and new discoveries have disproved many of them. Concepts, on the other hand, are definitions. They define the elements of facts and generalizations and tend to remain stable even as new information is gathered and filed. (See Figure 4–2.)

Generalizations have two main purposes: to summarize and organize and to predict. A child gathers facts from many sources and must find a way to make all of them useful. The first step is to file them under headings called concepts. Then a higher level of thinking occurs as the child begins to look at the similarities, differences, and interrelationships among those concepts. Generalizations are then formed to summarize and organize the interrelationships into a workable proposition. Once the generalization is established and accepted as true, it can be transferred to many other situations, predicting outcomes or relation-

Figure 4-2 Facts, Concepts, and Generalizations

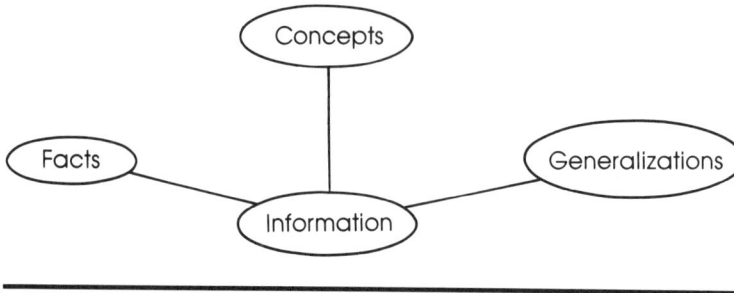

ships. The generalization now has value to the learner; he or she can draw conclusions about cases and situations not yet encountered.

There are four types of generalizations that may be developed. Each is useful in its own way.

- *Descriptive:* A relationship is described. This is a very straightforward description of the way things are for good or ill. That's the way it is.

  Example: A large city cannot exist without a good water supply.

  This is a statement of reality; there's not much to argue about. People must have water to live and a large city with lots of people must be able to supply water to all of its inhabitants.

- *Cause and Effect:* One concept causes another. Many times this may be expressed as an "if . . . then" relationship.

  Example: If one country violates the borders of another country, armed conflict is likely to occur.

  Here the action of one country, a border violation, causes a reaction by the other country. Without one action the other does not occur.

- *Correlations:* One concept is likely to occur in the presence of another. They do not cause each other, but usually one may not exist without the other.

  Example: Technological advancement occurs more rapidly in affluent societies.

  Technological advancement can occur in a poor or underdeveloped country and there are examples of this. Usually the necessary time, work force, and expertise can be found only in more affluent societies.

- *Value Judgment:* Claims are based on values. Truth and the relationship is based on the perception of the claimant.

Example: The further development of nuclear power-generating plants is unwise.

Who can really say if the development of nuclear power is or is not wise? It seems so to many, but it is based on emotion and judgment, not on fact.

Teaching Generalizations.   Generalizations, like concepts and facts, need to be taught. Quite often the reason for teaching facts and concepts is to provide background for a generalization that is the "Big Idea" of a lesson. Your text may supply the generalizations that are the basis of the lesson, or a curriculum guide may provide them. You may make up your own as needed, or the students may generate them. They are all around you and easy to find.

Care must be taken in selecting the generalizations to be taught—they can be very simple or very complex. It is imperative that the teacher develops appropriate generalizations. They must relate to the experiences of the student and develop from those experiences, if the generalization is to be usable and valuable. It may sometimes be difficult to find an experiential base so you may have to provide some experiences. Without that base, the generalization will have little or no meaning to the student.

The complexity of the concepts contained in the generalization must also be taken into consideration. They must be appropriate to the grade level. Many textbooks do not state specific generalizations but do provide the main idea of the lesson. These are written in simple language appropriate to the student's level of comprehension.

Generalizations are learned in one of two ways: inductively or deductively. *Inductive learning* proceeds from facts to generalizations. The teacher presents a problem to the students and they then gather facts from various sources. Analysis of the facts shows commonalities that allow the students to form generalizations.

An understanding of the generalization is based on the premise that if the learner develops it, then she or he understands what it means. As an example, a teacher might give the class a list of cities, such as Chicago, Detroit, Philadelphia, New York, St. Louis, San Francisco, and Seattle. The class is then asked to find what all of these cities have in common. Using maps and other reference materials, the students find that all are located on major rivers or bodies of water. From this, they generalize that major cities are located on major waterways.

Deductive learning of a generalization is opposite of inductive learning; it proceeds from generalization to facts. A generalization is presented to the students and they must gather factual information to support the generalization. Understanding takes place as the students try to prove or disprove the generalization. Using the same generalization as before, the teacher tells the students that without a major waterway present a city cannot develop. The students then start compiling lists of cities and testing the generalization, trying either to verify or refute it. As they gather their information, they begin to understand the meaning of the generalization.

Both of these methods are effective. In either approach the teacher must help establish the problem and then guide and direct the students toward an understanding of the generalization.

The teaching of facts, concepts, and generalizations is a major task of the social studies teacher. As children learn content and how to use concepts to communicate their knowledge, they become more aware of the world and their place in it. This allows students to begin to develop the generalizations they will use as a basis for future beliefs.

Teaching Learning Skills

Too often the teaching of skills is glossed over or neglected entirely. This is unfortunate because the learning of skills is a vital part of the education of a child. With a good skills foundation, children can learn and function on their own. Affective skills provide the ability to think and to solve problems. Academic skills provide the means for obtaining, sharing, and processing information. Social skills permit us to function in our society. Without the skills necessary to use them, factual material, concepts, and values are useless. What good

Map skills are an important tool for children as they investigate the world around them.

is it to know something—a cure for cancer, for example—if you cannot communicate this knowledge to anyone else?

The main focus of the science programs of the 1960s (Elementary Science Study, Science Curriculum Improvement Study, Science—A Process Approach) was on the teaching of the process skills (i.e., the tools of science). This practice of teaching children how to use the tools of science is still stressed today in all current science materials.

The social studies should put equal emphasis on the tools of social studies. We tend to emphasize map and globe skills and maybe group skills, but we must expand to include all phases of skill development. With the necessary tools, a person can make intelligent decisions, actively participate in a job, and be a productive member of society. The acquisition of skills by a student cannot be overemphasized. Facts may change or become obsolete, but skills are useful forever.

There are many ways to group skills but we prefer to separate them into three categories: affective skills, academic or process skills, and social skills. These will be examined further.

Affective Skills

Affective skills encompass two areas, thinking skills and problem-solving skills, that are basic to the child's ability to function as a productive adult. These skills must be taught; they cannot be learned as a by-product of subject-matter teaching. Teachers must provide opportunities for children to develop and use thinking skills. As the class gathers data they can evaluate, compare, classify, criticize, and summarize the information gathered from various sources. They can analyze problems and make hypotheses. There is so much a teacher can do to get the children to do more than read and/or listen then memorize the information provided. It is important to structure lessons so that memory is not the critical factor. Have children put their thoughts in their own words and then learn to critique these thoughts. The key to developing thinking skills is continuous opportunity to practice them.

Children and adults are faced with a continual onslaught of problems to be solved: How can I do this homework? How can I get the money for an ice-cream cone? How will I pay the bills if I lose my job? Who shall I vote for? Children are not isolated from problems such as a parent's loss of a job. When a parent loses his or her job, the entire family is affected in many ways. Youngsters are acutely aware of how adults approach problem-solving situations, even though they may not verbalize their observations and thoughts. The parents respond in a certain way and the children see it. Problems range from the trivial to personal enormity, from personal to global. All problems have one commonality—they must be solved.

We usually learn to solve problems by one of two ways. First is by trial and error. Try something, see if it works; if it doesn't, try something else. Maybe you will get lucky and find an answer, maybe not. The second method is to think logically and come up with one or more possible solutions and try them.

In teaching problem solving, several steps are followed.

1. *Define the problem.*   What are you trying to find out? This seems like a very elementary step, but it is not always easy to get to the real problem involved, to sort it from others, and to be specific as to what you really want to know. Two other factors must be considered: (a) Degree of difficulty: Is it too hard for the problem solver or too easy? and (b) Can the problem be solved with the materials at hand and with the expertise available to the problem solver?

2. *Try a quick solution.*   A quick answer may be all you need. You might ask someone, such as a teacher or a friend, for an answer, or you might refer to a source, such as your textbook or an encyclopedia. If this works, you have solved the problem. If not, proceed to step 3.

3. *Gather data.*   Start getting information together from many sources. You might choose to do an experiment. (Yes, you can do experiments in social studies!) Go to the library, contact resource people (parents, teachers, authorities), or use any number of other data-gathering activities. The task at hand is to get as much information as possible.

4. *Process the data.*   Try to make sense out of the data. Think about the data and put them into usable form. Classify the information into pros and cons or as rational/irrational data. Order them chronologically, sequentially, or by importance. Make charts, graphs, and tables.

5. *Analyze the data.*   Think. What do the data tell you? Carefully weigh the information that you have to come to a conclusion. Does it make sense?

6. *Formalize an answer.*   Reexamine your problem and relate your answer to it. Is your answer reasonable and in accordance to your data? Have you let emotional or preconceived beliefs get in the way of a valid and logical answer? Are you ready to defend your answer even if it contradicts what others, including your teacher, believe? Are you satisfied with your answer? Has your investigation raised any new problems that you want to answer?

The affective skills of thinking and problem solving are high-order skills. They must be carefully taught in the schools so that children can become independent thinkers and doers when they are adults. We have, in the past, taught children to think and we must continue to do so. Just be forewarned: As each generation matures and learns to think, they do not always think what we (the older members of our society) think they ought to think! That is the price of producing independent thinkers.

Academic or Process Skills

These are the skills that allow a person to do social studies. A statement concerning science skills from the *Essential Performance Objectives for Science Education (Grades K–9)* provides a rationale equally valid for social studies skills: "These processes are actually labels for collections of productive intellectual behaviors or skills. And these intellectual skills describe what individuals *can do* (italics added) rather than what individuals can verbalize."[2]

Arthur Ellis provides a list of skills (or processes) for elementary social studies. They are worth examining. Think of the skills on Ellis's list as the tools of social studies. See how they describe what a child can do.

> *Observing: Observing phenomena, events, and interactions, both alone and with a partner; eyewitnessing; listening.*
>
> *Recording: Recalling information or observances, photographing, mapping, drawing, illustrating, writing, tape recording, listing.*
>
> *Describing: Creating written, oral, photographic, and graph descriptions; identifying attributes.*
>
> *Defining: Defining terms and procedures, developing precise meanings, communicating, stating problems.*
>
> *Measuring: Using standard measures, developing one's own measures, counting, quantifying data, using mathematical computations, developing rating scales, using and developing map scales.*
>
> *Classifying: Grouping, labeling, categorizing, differentiating.*
>
> *Comparing/Contrasting: Noting differences and similarities, identifying attributes, describing.*
>
> *Data Gathering: Identifying and selecting data sources; determining appropriate methods; conducting surveys, historical studies, experiments, and interviews.*
>
> *Data Processing: Quantifying data, performing graphic analysis, mapping, making charts, writing summaries.*
>
> *Communicating: Communicating orally and in writing, through pictures and through graphics; engaging in group activities; expressing oneself.*
>
> *Constructing: Building models, dioramas, relief maps, murals, displays, and exhibits.*
>
> *Analyzing: Discriminating, categorizing, finding patterns, identifying attributes, detecting structures.*
>
> *Synthesizing: Planning, producing, documenting, theorizing, developing systems.*
>
> *Hypothesizing: Guessing in an educated way, developing hunches, testing assumptions.*
>
> *Inferring: Making statements from data, reaching conclusions, making decisions.*
>
> *Predicting: Determining relationships, forecasting outcomes, correlating variables.*
>
> *Generalizing: Conceptualizing, identifying supporting data, testing relationships, finding patterns, summarizing.*

Evaluating: Making judgments, making decisions, determining validity, detecting errors and fallacies.

Question Posing: Developing questions, identifying researchable problems, defining terms.

Verifying: Checking sources, validating ideas and sources, referring to authority[3]

The best way to teach these skills is by continual use. Plan your lessons to include them. You may not be able to teach each skill separately, but you can make sure that your students use them. If your textbook does not make provision for the inclusion of these skills, find a way to get them in. When children use a skill, point it out to them. Tell them they are classifying or generalizing. Make the students aware of the processes and terminology, and how they help learning and problem solving.

Social Skills

The development of social skills permits an individual to function in our society. One of the primary functions of the kindergarten is to socialize the child so that he or she can function in a school setting. The kindergarten child learns to work with others, take directions, share, and develop self-control. Without these skills present, the first-grade teacher cannot start the academic instruction of the child.

Roleplaying and participating in various ceremonies and programs are exciting educational experiences for youngsters of all ages.

As children grow older, additional social skills become necessary and must be developed with the aid of the teacher. Children learn to work in groups and with partners. They learn social skills and social obligations. They learn manners. They also learn to lead and follow and to become aware of responsibilities and rights. Children must also learn the necessary skills for relationships with the same and opposite sex. As cultural, ethnic, and racial awareness develop, so must the skills necessary to cope with this new awareness. You must help your students develop and become socially acceptable citizens.

Social skills can be categorized as relationships.

1. Relation to Others
   Respect for others
   Respect for individual rights and responsibilities
   Manners
   How to share
2. Relation to Self
   Self-control
   Self-direction
   Self-concept
   Self-awareness
3. Relation to Cultural, Ethnic, and Racial Groups
   Tolerance
   Respect for differences
   Acceptance of others

As you look at these skills, you can see that most of them are complex skills and many of them are interrelated. They are taught by example, by inference, and by direct inclusion in your class lessons. They must be repeated and expanded over many years. When a child has mastered these skills she or he is called socially competent.

Skills are the tools that allow a person to learn and function in our society. We use affective skills to think and solve problems. The academic skills are the tools we use to do social studies. The social skills allow us to interact with others. All three types of skills are very necessary to every one of us, child and adult, if we are to be useful and productive members of our society.

ACTIVITIES

The primary focus of this chapter has been on *what* you are to teach. These activities will give you the opportunity to select some content, concepts, and skills to teach and then to determine how you would teach them. You will select content topics using established criteria, show how you will teach a concept, then select a problem and show how you will solve it by using various learning skills. Refer to the appropriate material in the first part of the chapter if you need help. Remember to look for real material that would actually be taught when you select a topic or concept.

4.1   Social Studies Topics

In this activity you will learn about selecting social studies materials other than textbooks.

Teaching Traditional Topics

Thanksgiving is a U.S. holiday that is traditionally taught in elementary schools. Your group is to develop an argument for or against teaching this topic. Be prepared to present your case to the class. Your instructor may choose to have a representative of each group be a part of a panel discussion.

Arguments for Teaching Thanksgiving
1.
2.
3.

Arguments against Teaching Thanksgiving
1.
2.
3.

What are some other traditional topics that might also be argued?

1.
2.
3.

Self-Check.   It may not be popular to argue against topics such as Thanksgiving, but were you able to come up with some valid reasons for or against teaching it? What were some of the arguments that your classmates produced? Could you give at least one argument for and one against each of the other traditional topics that you listed?

Selecting Current Topics

Use a newspaper or your knowledge of a current event to select a topic that you would teach in your classroom. Build a rationale for including it in your social studies lesson. Be prepared to convince others (such as a parent or your principal) that it is worth teaching.

Current Event Chosen: _____

1. Why is it important?

2. Why should it be taught?

3. What do you expect to accomplish by teaching it?

Roleplay with a partner or your group a situation in which you have taught the current event. One or more parents want to know why you taught that topic to their children.

Self-Check. Was your reasoning for teaching the topic sincere or was it rationalized? Did you pick an event because it was important or because it was interesting? They are not always the same. For example, a newspaper report of a shark attacking a swimmer off the coast of Australia might be of high interest to your fifth-grade class, but is it important to them?

Special-Interest Groups

Your local bank has managed to get the school board to include economics in the curriculum. The teachers of the even-numbered grades are required to teach a unit on Thrift and Saving. Speculate on the appropriateness of this requirement and your reaction to it.

1. What is your reaction to the requirement?

2. How would you meet the requirement?

Be prepared to explain your position to your group or your instructor.

Self-Check. Is your reaction to the requirement based on reason or emotion? Were the reactions of others in your group based on reason or emotion? Did you look at the requirement as reasonable, adding to the education of your children, or as an imposition on your teaching time? Why would a requirement such as this be included in a curriculum?

Identifying State and Local Requirements

If your state has developed social studies objectives and they are available, pick one grade level and examine the objectives closely. Your instructor may want to lead a class discussion on this topic.

> ***Grade Level Chosen:*** _____
> Major topics covered
> 1.
> 2.
> 3.
> 4.

4.2 Teaching Facts and Concepts

The facts, concepts, and generalizations that you will teach are the core of your social studies program. In this activity, you have the opportunity to learn what is taught in a social studies textbook program. You will also devise your own procedure for teaching a concept.

Locating Content to Be Taught

Select a textbook from a social studies series. Look at the Table of Contents and supply the following information:

> Title and Series: _____
> Grade Level: _____
> What are the major topics to be taught?
> 1.
> 2.
> 3.
> 4.
> 5.

Select one of the above topics. Look carefully at one chapter and list the factual information that is to be taught.

Topic:_____
Facts

1.	6.	11.
2.	7.	12.
3.	8.	13.
4.	9.	14.
5.	10.	15.

Group these facts under appropriate concepts. There may be more than four, so add space as needed.

Concept: _____   **Concept:** _____

Facts   *Facts*
1.   1.
2.   2.
3.   3.
4.   4.

Concept: _____   **Concept:** _____
1.   1.
2.   2.
3.   3.
4.   4.

Go back over the chapter. Locate the main generalization that is the focus of the chapter and list it here.

Generalization:

Self-Check.   Were the concepts listed as concepts in the textbook you used, or did you have to hunt for them? Did the textbook give you any information about developing them? Was the generalization or main idea stated clearly? Did the concepts relate to the generalization?

Teaching a Concept

Pick a concept from the list above. Explain how you would teach it using the Rule–Example–Rule–Application approach.

Concept to Be Taught: _____
Rule:
Definition

Attributes

Example:
Example

Nonexample

Example (less distinctive)

Nonexample (less distinctive)

Redefine the Rule:
Student version

Application:
Relate to student experience

Apply the concept to the lesson

Explain your example to your group, to the class, or to your instructor.

Self-Check. Did you have any trouble developing examples and non-examples? Did you think to consider the grade level of the lesson and the appropriateness of your example for children in that grade? Would it make a difference in your choice of examples and applications if your children were from an inner-city school? A rural school? A particular ethnic or cultural group? You do have to take all of these criteria and more into consideration when you are developing examples and applications for a lesson.

4.3 *Skills*

This activity will help you to understand better how skills are taught and learned. As you do the activity, keep thinking about the process you are going through. This activity will work best as a small group activity, using one member of the group as an observer while the other members go through the thinking and problem-solving activity. The observer can then help the rest of the group analyze the process.

Pick one of the following problems. Use whatever resources that are available to get a solution that satisfies all members of your group and your instructor.

1. You have a 3 × 5 index card and at least five social studies books. Using only one 3 × 5 index card, find a way to support all of the books at least one half inch above the desk. Only the card can touch the top of the desk. It must be free standing (no hands touching) when you are through. Try adding more of the various items that you brought to class to see how much weight you can support.

2. You are going to take the family out for the evening. There is one male adult, one female adult, and two children (ages six and nine). You have $20.00 to spend for food and entertainment. Develop an agenda and a budget for the evening.

3. Your sixth-grade team of five persons is required to teach the rest of the class about weaving. How are you going to do it?

4. You and your family are going on a two-week vacation to the Grand Canyon. How much will the trip cost you?

With the help of the observer, analyze your actions in solving the problem. Try to identify specific steps and actions.

Analysis of the Process Used to Solve the Problem

Using the selected problem you chose above, answer the following questions.

1. State the problem in your own words:

2. What were your first thoughts or comments?
    a.
    b.
    c.
3. What attempts were made at a quick answer or using trial and error?
    a.
    b.
    c.
4. What were your data sources?
    a.
    b.
    c.
    d.
5. How did you process your data?
    a.
    b.
    c.
    d.
6. Explain your answer:

Using the Process Skills

Look at the list of process skills on pages 117–118. List those that you used and explain how you used each.

    1.

    2.

    3.

    4.

    5.

Using Social Skills

Analyze your use of the social skills during this activity.

1. How did you relate to others?
   a.
   b.
   c.
2. How did you relate to self?
   a.
   b.
   c.
3. How did you relate to cultural, ethnic, or racial groups?
   a.
   b.
   c.

Self-Check.   In this activity, the answer that you obtained was not important, but the process involved in obtaining it was. Knowledge of the way skills are learned and used will make it that much easier for you to teach them to others.

Summary

The main topic of this chapter was *what* to teach. Three areas of concern were presented. First, the teacher has to make a decision regarding the content to teach in the course of the year. Basic subject matter can usually be found in the textbook. Other factors also influence the choice of content. The teacher must be aware of content that is traditionally taught in the school, special-interest requirements, and current events that affect the students.

Second, it is important that the teacher develops a strategy for teaching the concepts and generalizations relating to the factual content. Understanding the "Big Picture" is the main reason behind the teaching of a topic.

Third, for your students to learn, they must possess the skills that allow them to solve problems and to function as a part of their group or society. These skills are not acquired automatically but are learned. The teacher has to teach the skills and provide opportunities for the skills to be applied and practiced.

READING RESOURCES

Birchell, G. R., and Taylor, B. L. "Is Elementary Social Studies Curriculum Headed 'Back to Basics'?" *Social Studies,* 77 (March/April 1986): 80–82.

Brady, M. "In Search of a Social Studies Discipline." *Social Education, 51* (April/May 1987): 266–268.

Haas, J. D. "The Social Studies Curriculum: Can It Be Changed?" *Education Digest, 52* (October 1986): 28–31.

Middleton, H. et al. "Popular Peers as Change Agents for the Socially Neglected Child in the Classroom." *Journal of School Psychology, 24* (Winter 1986): 343–350.

Reyes, D. J. "Critical Thinking in Elementary Social Studies Text Series." *Social Studies, 77* (July/August 1986): 151–154.

Thayer, Louis, with Beeler, Kent D. *Affective Education: Strategies for Experiential Learning.* San Diego, CA: University Associates, Inc., 1976.

ENDNOTES

1. Sullivan, Troy, Professor Emeritus, University of Alaska at Anchorage, Anchorage, Alaska, approximately 1964.

2. *Essential Performance Objectives for Science Education (Grades K–9),* Michigan State Board of Education, October 1985.

3. Ellis, Arthur K., *Teaching and Learning Elementary Social Studies,* 3rd ed. (Boston: Allyn and Bacon, 1986), pp. 101–102.

UNIT IV

Planning
for Instruction

5
Planning, Objectives, and Teaching Strategies

PROJECTIONS

Planning remains a major teaching responsibility. What are some possible ramifications of planning for social studies? It is uncertain if the elementary classroom as we know it, one teacher and 25 to 30 students, will exist in the next century. If dramatic organizational and managerial changes occur in the elementary schools, then equally pertinent changes must take place throughout the system.

Elementary specialization is a concept that continues to surface. Proponents of this concept maintain that if a person is very skilled at teaching social studies, then she or he should spend the large portion of the school day teaching social studies. Students benefit from instruction by a person who has special skills and talents in this area. The teacher benefits by achieving greater job satisfaction from teaching what he or she knows and does very well. Specialization affects planning in these ways:

- A teacher who works in a chosen special area is highly motivated to focus on teaching explicit content and skills.
- Specialization keeps planning directed in one content area, not seven or eight each day.
- A teacher would feel less "pulled in too many directions" with too much to teach and too many content areas in which to keep current.
- Planning may be more efficient and ultimately directed more toward student needs.

Staff differentiation, creative staffing, cooperative staffing—each term is used to describe many of the newer instructional management schemes. One plan is for master teachers to supervise and train newer teachers, teacher assistants, paraprofessionals, aides, and others who work directly and indirectly with students. The planning for social studies instruction would be rather intense. The teachers would be responsible for planning not only what they would teach (new material, skills, processes) but also all the activities the students would perform under the supervision of teaching assistants or other paraprofessionals. Planning in this situation would have to be very specific and organized, concise, and easily understood by everyone on the instructional team.

As we approach the twenty-first century, many of our goals will change as the needs of society change. Basic goals such as becoming a good citizen will always be with us; however, new goals will be developed as our social and physical environment changes. As we look ahead to shortages in nonrenewable resources, our attitude toward the allocation and use of those resources must change. Nationalism may have to give way to globalism. Some freedoms may have to be exchanged for the common good. For example, do we have to give up our right to keep arms to obtain the right to live without fear of being shot? Certainly, this is a controversial issue, but times change and so do goals. Pressure groups and educators will continue to influence our goals, each professing to know what is best for our children to learn. Objectives will continue as they are now, ever changing as we seek the best way to achieve our goals.

Teaching strategies will change as new technology and new insights into learning are developed. The computer is an example of technology that is changing our methods of teaching. As more teachers become skilled in using them and as improved software becomes available, children will become more involved in learning by computer. It is conceivable that homebound or isolated students using a computer and modem will soon be able to do their lessons electronically. Some isolated parts of the world are already using interactive television so students can "attend class" with a real teacher present. What will our next new technology be? How will we change our teaching strategies to use it? It will be exciting to find out.

In a previous projection new advances in learning theory were discussed. How will insight into the brain and how it works affect our teaching strategy? We are looking forward to an exciting decade of changes that will affect our organization, goals, objectives, and teaching strategies. The only constant is that planning will still be of utmost importance if we are to take advantage of the changes.

Planning

Why do teachers spend so much time planning? Isn't everything laid out specifically in the teacher's manual? Why can't teachers just teach? Teaching manuals do provide background information, suggestions for individualizing instruction, lists of materials needed for each lesson, key concepts to develop, and many other useful tools for the teacher to use, but planning is necessary to optimize your teaching skill and the students' learning experiences.

Planning for instruction can be tedious, whether it is for social studies, reading, or math. Writing lesson plans is not usually a teacher's favorite use of preparation time; neither is paper checking. However, both of these are professional responsibilities. The reward appears sometime later when you can see the students successfully performing a skill that you taught them.

Long-Range Planning

A long-range plan may encompass the teaching and learning of a chapter or unit of instruction. It also can be a semester or even a year-long undertaking. All planning should be carried out with the goals and objectives of the entire year well in mind. Individual units or chapters have specific performance objectives that must be taught. They build on the skills from previous units and prepare for new skills to come. The building of skills, both informational and performance, must be approached from a developmental standpoint. Each particular skill is planned at a slightly more advanced level than previous ones.

Long-range planning at the primary level may be as short as a one-week unit. Although planning for one week may not seem complicated, it can be very difficult to condense all the required skills into five or six lessons of perhaps 20 minutes each. These lessons will affect other lessons that will be presented next week and even next month.

In the intermediate grades long-range planning will be for a longer period of time, usually from several weeks to perhaps an entire marking period. This

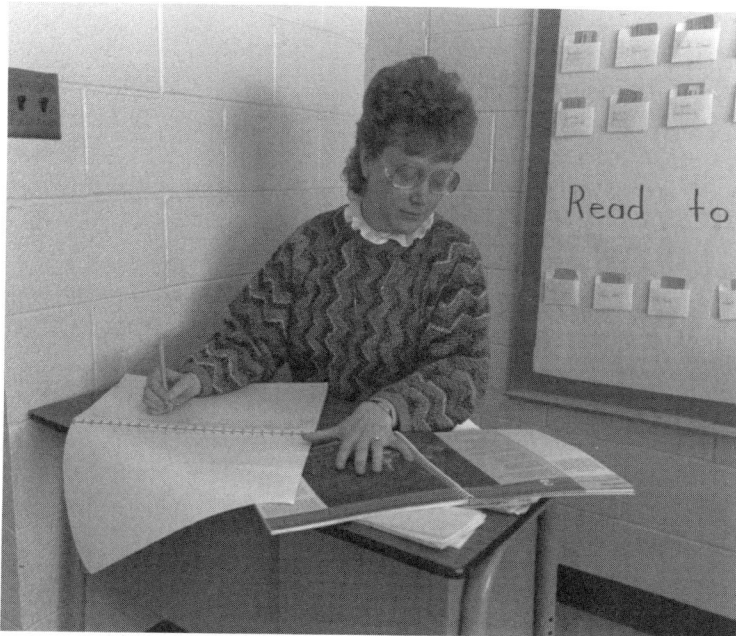

Teachers frequently plan lessons one week in advance.

process must take into consideration the numerous skills that are taught in a particular unit and the approximate time it will take to teach each one. A specific unit of study, such as "The Revolutionary War Period" in a fifth-grade class, includes a large amount of material. Planning for such a unit forces the teacher to isolate each objective and to designate an amount of time to accomplish it. Specific developmental activities can tentatively be planned and then applied to a particular lesson when appropriate. It is always a good idea to think in terms of what the students might be able to do at some point, and then work toward making those possibilities a reality.

Unit Plan. Most long-term planning in social studies is based on a unit plan. The unit plan is the long-range blueprint of what the teacher needs to do and it includes such things as the topic, objectives, background information, skill requirements, a time allotment, suggested materials, activities, teaching strategies, and evaluation. An average social studies unit takes two or three weeks to complete. Primary units may take less time, whereas some intermediate units will need a month or more. When teachers plan a unit for the first time, it is difficult to determine exactly how much time will be needed. Adjustments and adaptations are easily made as the unit progresses.

The following two examples give you an idea of what to include in a unit plan.

A Primary Unit Plan

Title: Communities

Goals: To develop the concept of community
To identify the ways various communities meet people's needs

Suggested Time: Three weeks

Background Information: Self, family, friends, work and jobs, school environment, needs and wants, cooperation and sharing, decision making, producing and servicing

Skill Requirements: Reading, following paths, tracking, thinking, brainstorming, accepting, risking

Suggested Materials: Textbook, workbook, primary maps and globes, library books, filmstrips, computer programs, art supplies

Activities: Research project, make a collection, interviews, consult the learning-center teacher, roleplay, fieldtrip.

Teaching Strategies: Read and discuss, make predictions and generalizations, explain, model, supervise cooperative learning activities, demonstrate

Evaluation: Written and oral questions, chapter test, informal observation, home questionnaire

Unit/Lesson Extensions: Oral reports, at-home project, art activity, higher-order thinking activity, concrete experiences.

An Intermediate Unit Plan

Title: Our World Neighbors

Goal: To become aware of the interrelatedness of all people on earth

Suggested Time: Nine weeks

Background Information: Local, state, and national cultures; the social sciences; producing and servicing; planning; cooperation; conflict resolution; responsibility

Skill Requirements: Product and process skills, inductive and deductive reasoning, thinking skills, research skills, written and oral communications, group skills, creative producing, risking

Suggested Materials: Films, books, textbook, workbooks, maps and globes, media resources, teacher's resource book, reproducibles, learning center folders, art supplies, blank cassettes

Activities: Research project, oral reports, cooperative learning activities, reading, panel, debate, artistic representations, creative dramatics

Teaching Strategies: Discussion leader, resource person, lecture, research guide, use of learning center

Evaluation: Chapter and unit test, spot quiz, informal and formal observations, oral questions

Unit/Lesson Extensions: Community resource persons, upper-level thinking skills, formal operations, research projects, interactive television experiences

There are many components of a complete unit plan. Each major part includes a variety of individual items the teacher will use during an instruction period. As you plan for a specific unit of work, you will work to include specific materials, such as the names of films, pages or chapters to be read, titles of supplementary materials, and resource people. The unit plan for social studies is a helpful scheme for general long-range planning.

Calendar Plan. Designing a calendar plan is the next step in good planning. The unit plan establishes the general overall teaching responsibilities and activities that are needed to teach the unit successfully. A calendar plan is a valuable exercise in stating in more specific terms which instructional activities you will perform each day. It is a method of organizing ahead so that you can know the sequence and timing of your lessons. You can look at your calendar and know when to prepare materials, give advance assignments, and check to see if you are somewhat on schedule. Figures 5–1 and 5–2 show plans in a calendar format.

Figure 5-1   A Calendar Plan for Primary Grades

	Monday	Tuesday	Wednesday	Thursday	Friday
Week 1	Introduce the unit Read text	Lead discussion Read text Do one workbook page	Small group activity	Library research for book reports	Administer short quiz Go to computer lab
Week 2	Whole class activity Send ''home activity'' with students	Short lecture View a filmstrip and discuss	Fieldtrip	Collect homework activity Do unit review activities	Unit test Closure activity

intermediate
↑

Figure 5-2   A Calendar Plan for Immediate Grades

	Monday	Tuesday	Wednesday	Thursday	Friday
Week 1	Introduce the unit	Read textbook material	Start discussion	Lecture lesson	Plan for library research
			Assign out-of-class reading materials		
Week 2	Administer first quiz Start oral reports	Do workbook pages	Start projects in class	Guest speaker and discussion	Chapter test
Week 3	Cooperative learning group activity	Panel discussion	Learning center resources day	Fieldtrip Write quiz for Friday	Administer quiz Computer lab
Week 4	Introduce lesson extension (extra credit)	Watch a video, discuss and evaluate	Study period, work on projects	Unit test	Projects Fair

Short-Term Planning

Short-term planning at the primary level usually means one or two lessons at a time. When teaching beginning process and product skills, it is difficult to determine exactly how many lesson presentations it will take for a certain skill to be learned. It is sometimes necessary to plan one lesson, teach and evaluate it, then plan the next lesson. Tentative plans can be written for a week in advance (this is required in many school systems), knowing they will probably be altered somewhat on each succeeding day.

Short-term planning for the intermediate grades is not necessarily as short as that for the primary grades, but it usually involves one week or less. Short-term planning allocates specific time frames for each individual lesson or activity. The skill and lesson outcomes can then build on each other. Planning what you expect to accomplish in five days is very practical and manageable.

Preface your short-term planning by careful thought regarding the lesson topic and each individual segment of a structured lesson plan. For instance, how much time will be needed for the introduction alone: One 20-minute period? What if another period is needed after that? Planning makes provisions for supplemental or backup plans for each phase of the lesson in the event the initial plan needs modifying.

Daily Plan.   The daily plan specifies what the teacher will do during the social studies period and what activities are expected from the students. The daily plan concentrates on teacher and student responsibilities yet always allows for flexibility. It helps to know exactly what you need for today's lesson, as well as what will be needed for tomorrow. Such things as textbooks, library materials, filmstrip projector, a blackline master, or art supplies must be located and ready for the lesson.

Examine the teacher's role for the first three days of the primary class on the calendar plan. This is not a complete daily lesson plan, but it will give you an idea of what you will do and what materials you will have to get ready.

Monday

Teacher's role:

1. Have textbooks ready.

2. Introduce the unit in these ways:
   Tell the class we are starting a new unit on Communities.
   Question: What is a community? Solicit many ideas and list all on chalkboard.
   Identify your own community and name some surrounding communities.

3. Locate the first page of the unit, lead discussion of the pictures, and solicit many details.

4. Tell the class what the objective is: To name the ways communities meet people's needs.

5. Respond to each student's questions and contributions.

Tuesday

Teacher's role:

1. Repeat the objective.
2. Have some convergent and divergent questions prepared ahead of time.
3. Read the textbook pages aloud, or pair the students to read with each other.
4. Have the textbooks and workbooks available.
5. Give each student an opportunity to participate in the discussion or answer a question.
6. Give clear verbal directions for completing the workbook page.
7. Be available to assist those students who need help.
8. Collect the books and workbooks.

Wednesday

Teacher's role:

1. Restate the objective.
2. Have four large pieces of white paper and crayons ready.
3. Review the class rules for working in groups.
4. Divide the class into four work groups. Designate a leader for each group and assign each group the theme they are to illustrate (farming community, our community, a suburb, an industrial community).
5. Monitor all groups as they work.
6. Lead a brief evaluation of the group experience.
7. Display the projects.

Although the specific details of the daily plan are not shown in these examples, it is necessary to be aware of these roles and tasks before starting to teach a lesson. The teacher must select and gather all equipment and materials required for a lesson; otherwise, the smooth flow of her or his presentation will be interrupted if something is forgotten or mislaid. The daily plan helps to foresee many of the details and responsibilities of both the teacher and the students.

Incidental Teaching

Occasionally, a teacher must make a decision to teach without previous planning. For instance, imagine that you are teaching a third-grade class. One of your students comes to class with a family crest that his grandparents brought back from a trip to Europe. He wants to share it with the class. Do you make time for his sharing or do you respond apologetically, "I'm sorry, Josh, but you will have to put that away. We are studying about Mexico right now." Is there a place for Josh's contribution? *Absolutely!* You can feel the excitement and the immediacy of this sharing experience for this particular child. Perhaps it is the most positive, highest-interest level he has exhibited all year, and furthermore the rest of the class shares his excitement! The teachable moment is here and it is now. Robert Havighurst describes the teachable moment as:

> *When the body is ripe, and society requires, and the self is ready to achieve a certain task, the teachable moment has come. Efforts at teaching, which would have been largely wasted if they had come earlier, give gratifying results when they come at the teachable moment, when the task should be learned.*[1]

Of course you will take advantage of the opportunity and build upon it. Think of the bonding you establish with this particular child. You care enough about him to accept the personal offering he wants to share and to experience with others.

This kind of human relations—teacher-student recognition—cannot be overshadowed by some predetermined schedule or lesson plan. This is not to say that you should routinely cancel all planned lessons to build experiences around every Show-and-Tell item that is brought to school, but your judgment identifies a true teachable moment. It can be an event in the news, a personal experience (as in this case), or an item brought from home. Think of each event in terms of:

1. How valuable is this from an educational standpoint?
2. Is it appropriate and worthwhile for this age group?
3. How much time can I reasonably devote to this?
4. How important is the need for recognition for the child involved?

Incidental teaching activities are always at the discretion of the teacher and are controlled and directed by her or him.

Let's return to Josh for a moment. Here he is with the family crest he wants to share with the class. Show and Tell is not a part of the regular third-grade day, but you give him a few minutes to report "My grandparents took a trip to Europe and brought back our family crest." Just that little activity gives the child recognition and makes him feel important. But have you permitted some good learning opportunities to escape by not recognizing this teachable moment and elaborating upon it? A viable and valuable lesson can be gleaned from this moment. Think about these possibilities:

1. Invite the grandparents into the class to show other objects, slides, or pictures of their trip. As a side benefit, you promote positive school-community relationships.

2. It is possible that the grandparents have explored their family tree. Ask them to bring that to class and make a presentation. This will show your students that adults study too. It might also provide the impetus for your students to explore their family trees.

3. The class can prepare a time line to show the information represented in their family trees. You can teach process skills, time concepts, and mathematical transfer.

4. Explore the whole area of family crests. Learn how they began as well as which countries have them in the greatest or fewest number. Are new ones being designed today? This is a great opportunity to teach and reinforce library skills.

5. Each student can work on a mini family tree that will include the extended family, such as parents, grandparents, aunts and uncles, cousins, and brothers and sisters. This is a good time to prepare a display for open house or parent-teacher conferences, and it will give the children a real outlet for their work.

6. Each student can design a family crest appropriate for their family. Art activities provide lesson transfer to the social studies. Combine subjects whenever you can.

7. Compare and contrast such specifics as: family sizes, nationalities represented, recent immigration, and foreign languages spoken in the home or at family gatherings. Use your process skills. You might also bring in cultural attributes and language problems.

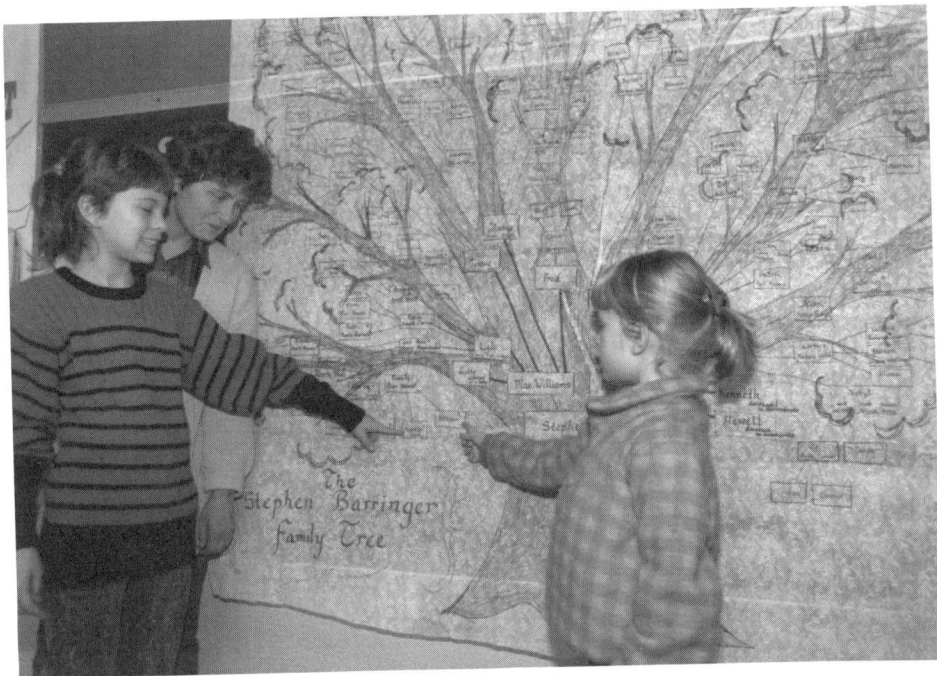

A family reunion was the impetus for researching this family tree.

8. What other suggestions or ideas can the students or you suggest? There are a lot of possibilities to explore.

The activities suggested are but a sample of those that can be designed by the creative teacher to develop a worthwhile series of lessons from a relatively simple sharing by a particular student. All of this, and more, can evolve naturally during incidental teaching opportunities. An incidental opportunity may last for only a short period of time, in which case you will have to improvise. It may present an opportunity for a prolonged lesson, in which case you will have to do some fast outside planning to get the most out of it. Recognize incidental teaching opportunities when they occur and turn them into great lessons. Incidental teaching may result in some of the best teaching of the school year.

Why Plan?

Effective teaching requires a strong commitment to spend the time that good planning demands. Planning what to teach and how to teach it is a major responsibility of teachers. It is necessary that objectives be appropriate, that methods and strategies be carefully selected and applied, and that the evaluation criteria fit the objectives. The teacher's manual will include valuable information necessary for teaching the daily lessons. Individuals new to the profession should study and use this information. Creative teaching requires that you meet the specific learning needs and learning styles of the students. Quality planning is necessary to effectively meet a wide range of educational needs.

When planning, you cannot overlook the learning needs of special education students who may be in your class. The Education of All Handicapped Children Act (Public Law 94-142) mandates school districts to provide special education facilities and/or materials to all handicapped children. The least-restrictive environment clause ensures that many of the students will be mainstreamed into the regular classroom. It is reasonable to assume that a GLD (Generally Learning Disabled) student and perhaps a physically disabled (visually impaired, hearing impaired, or language delayed) child will be in your room. What provision will you make for that child with limited English proficiency?

Achieving balance while ensuring quality learning must be the goal of all teachers. Like students, teachers must take the necessary time to think, to plan, and to do. To summarize, the following are some reasons for thoughtful, precise planning:

1. Sound planning enables the teacher to set reasonable goals for the day, the week, and the marking period, and to monitor these goals at periodic intervals to determine if the students are achieving.

2. When goals are set as a result of sound planning, the teacher can make necessary adjustments in materials, strategies, and expectations without redoing the entire planning structure.

3. Effective planning based on a thorough understanding of the adopted curriculum enables the teacher to set expectations for the different ability and performance levels of the students.

4. When the basic lesson planning is done well, creative lesson extensions can proceed.

5. Planning enables the teacher to feel more confident and the students to recognize that the teacher is prepared for class. Discipline problems and lack of motivation or direction are often directly related to weak planning or preparation on the part of the teacher.

6. Planning carefully can result in actually getting more done in less time. You have a given amount of teaching time available and you must use it advantageously.

7. Good planning helps to keep teaching and learning on a specific course and minimizes sidetracking.

8. Planning enhances positive relationships with other staff members in the grade level or department. All of us are working together to meet school and/or district goals.

Planning Considerations

Learning how to plan effectively and efficiently is a prime objective for new teachers. Knowing the content and the skills to be taught is essential. Remember: If you do not know the content, you cannot teach it. Knowing how students learn enables you to plan effectively to teach content and skills. You know your students best. You know their specific learning and emotional needs, rates of learning, strengths and limitations, and growth areas. Valuable assistance can be obtained from fellow professionals, principals, curriculum coordinators, and other immediate supervisors, but you are the person most qualified to plan your students' learning experiences.

The learning styles of children vary, as do the teaching styles of educators. No one style or method is necessarily better or more desirable than another. Ideal teaching provides children with many opportunities to employ a comfortable learning style while also providing opportunities to experiment with other learning styles. Lessons that are continually designed for only one learning style (usually the teacher's personal learning style) become repetitive, dull, or frustrating for those students with a different preferred style.

When planning social studies lessons and units, think about the visual, auditory, and tactile modalities and how they activate learning in those lessons. For example, consider the frustration of a visually impaired student who is taught by using mostly reading and visual materials. What are the chances of success for this student? Consider presenting the same lesson with a minimal amount of reading material (provide for individual differences!) and maximize the tactile and auditory modalities. This may be accomplished by:

Tactile Opportunities

1. Provide models, kits, and realia for the student to manipulate.

2. Design individualized learning materials that allow the student to use his hands for touching, assembling, or building.

3. Incorporate the board game concept whenever possible; younger students enjoy handling puzzle pieces for matching and identification skills.

4. For older students, use more complex learning station activities with a variety of materials such as building supplies, fabrics, cardboard, wallpaper, books, tissue rolls, boxes, and paints.

Auditory Opportunities

1. Provide cassettes, records, or tapes for listening experiences.

2. Ask another student to read textbook material to this student.

3. Seek out appropriate student learning materials from the agencies that service the visually impaired.

4. Make arrangements for the student to be with a small group that is discussing the printed material from textbooks and other sources.

This is one example of ways to meet individual needs in the classroom. Always be cognizant of the fact that not all students learn the same way. Provide opportunities for students to use all of their senses during the learning process to develop and strengthen psychomotor and mental processes.

Local Requirements

Most school districts have a curriculum handbook that outlines the scope and sequence of each subject area and specifies the goals and objectives. The curriculum handbook may not include all that you need to know. It is not uncommon for districts, or even locales within larger districts, to have unwritten requirements that must be taught. For example, if your school is named after an individual who made significant contributions to the community a hundred years ago, you may be expected to teach that heritage to the younger generation. Ask about local requirements. They are important to the people in your school neighborhood.

State Requirements

Many states have developed state goals and objectives for the social studies. Some states require that the objectives be met in order to receive state aid or accreditation. In other states, the objectives are advisory. These goals and objectives may be written by a state agency or officer; a task force of concerned citizens such as parents, teachers, administrators, professional people, and pressure groups; or a group of social studies teachers.

Required state objectives may be categorized as skills or knowledge to be introduced at each grade level or to be emphasized for mastery. For example, the state of Texas has a document called *State Board of Education Rules for Curriculum: Principles, Standards, and Procedures for Accreditation of School Districts* that was produced in compliance with a state law. The document is commonly called "The Essential Elements" and specifically states the required objectives for all content areas in all grade levels. All Texas schools must conform or lose accreditation and state funds.

The objectives for the elementary grades in Texas are grouped by grade level, with seven common categories:

1. Personal, social, and civic responsibilities

2. The American economic system

3. Historical data about Texas, the United States, and the world

4. Institutions and processes of local, state, national, and other political systems

5. Local, state, national, and world geography

6. Psychological, sociological, and cultural factors affecting human behavior

7. Social studies skills

From two to eight job objectives are specified for each category. Look at this excerpt as an example. It is not complete, but it will give you an idea of what is required as Texas's state objectives.

> *(c) Social Studies, grade two, shall include the following essential elements:*
> . . .
> > *(2) The American economic system. The student shall be provided opportunities to:*
> > *(A) distinguish between goods and services;*
> > *(B) describe how people depend on each other to supply economic goods and services;*
> > *(C) identify persons who provide goods and services to the community;*
> > *(D) distinguish between making (producing) and using (consuming) things; and*
> > *(E) identify the kinds of income people receive (wages, salaries, rent, profits).*
> > . . .
> *(f) Social studies, grade five. Social studies, grade five, shall include the following essential elements:*
> . . .
> > *(5) Local, state, national, and world geography. The student shall be provided opportunities to:*
> > *(A) describe how the various geographic regions of the United States are similar and different;*
> > *(B) understand how people have adapted to and modified the physical environment of the United States;*

(C) *understand the geographic interrelatedness of the United States and adjacent countries;*

(D) *describe the landforms and climates of various regions of the United States;*

(E) *locate major geographic features of the United States on maps and globes;*

(F) *use latitude and longitude to determine directions and locations on a United States map; and*

(G) *use scale to determine distance within the United States.*[2]

Examine your state objectives. They may not be as specific as those in the Texas Essential Elements, but the skills that are indicated for mastery at your particular grade level are the ones that should be stressed in your teaching.

Textbook Requirements

Usually there is an instructional planning chart in textbooks that identifies the goals and specific learning objectives for each grade. You can see what you are expected to teach, what has already been taught, and what content and skills from the previous year may need an intense review. Frequently there are a number of optional cognitive or affective objectives. These optional objectives can be the source of some excellent planning that goes beyond the regular lesson plan.

Goals and Objectives

One important premise of this book is that teachers must know very specifically what they are to teach before they can teach it and what they expect students to learn as a result of their teaching. The first step in preparing a lesson is to decide what you are going to teach. The previous information in this chapter gives you some sources to use in making your decision. To use that information, you must be aware of two terms that are used to describe what we want children to learn: *goals* and *objectives*. They are not the same.

Teaching to a specified objective is a basic premise of teaching itself. Without a definite objective in mind, the act of teaching becomes an exercise in random teacher talk and aimless student activities that lead to no clear conclusion. An understandable objective actually makes the planning process more manageable. Once the goal or objective is set, it should not be viewed as irrevocable. Teachers expect to change some objectives during a lesson. Monitoring the objective enables the teacher to regulate the material presented. It is always better to make adjustments than to continue working toward an objective that is too easy (boring) or too difficult (frustrating) for students.

Goals

Goals are long-term expectations and are written in very general terms. We find them in our textbooks and curriculum guides. Goals usually do not require observable behavior, as an instructional objective would, so nonmeasurable affective verbs may be used. Consider these examples:

1. The students will be able to read a map.
2. The students will understand our economic system.
3. The students will know how we select our president.
4. The students will appreciate their cultural heritage.

All of these goals describe desirable expectations, but ask yourself:

1. Can I teach them in one or two lessons? Map skills are taught repeatedly throughout all grades.
2. Can I verify learning? What criteria would you use to determine if a student appreciates his or her culture?
3. Can I see a change in behavior? What observable behavior would a student exhibit as a result of knowing how to select a president?

We do not specifically teach a goal—we teach toward it. Goals are used to guide instruction and learning, forming a base from which we derive instructional objectives.

Objectives

The social studies teacher uses objectives to focus directly on what must be taught in the curriculum. "I am going to teach current events" is an admirable goal. Specific objectives put the various aspects of the goal into a usable format. The social studies teacher's guide gives terminal (or instructional) objectives for each unit and, in many cases, for each lesson in the textbook. These are designed to correlate with the major points that are emphasized in the text. These terminal objectives tend to be general in nature for large group classroom instruction and are structured to enable the average student in the class to experience success. Enabling (or learning) objectives are the specific objectives each teacher writes and uses to achieve the terminal objective.

Writing Objectives.   The enabling objective states concretely what you want the students to be able to do as a result of your teaching and the students' experiences during the lesson. Before you start writing objectives, consider the following definitions developed by Robert Mager.

> *Objective: An objective is an intent communicated by a statement describing a proposed change in a learner; a statement of what the learner is to be like when he has successfully completed a learning experience.*
> *Behavior: Behavior refers to any visible activity displayed by a learner.*
> *Terminal Behavior: Terminal behavior refers to a behavior you would like your learner to be able to demonstrate at the time your influence over him/her ends.*[3]

Keep in mind the general focus of these three definitions. For purposes of manageability and practicality, a good working definition of an enabling objective is: An *enabling objective* is a statement of the behavior a learner will demonstrate at the end of a lesson. To write usable objectives, keep these factors in mind:

1. What do I want to teach? (curriculum decision)
2. How can I state it clearly? (semantic decision)
3. Is it achievable? (developmental decision)
4. Is it observable? (planning decision)
5. What are the time limitations? (management decision)
6. What are the criteria for success? (evaluation decision)

You can write a beautifully stated objective and still have nothing. A well-written objective does not guarantee that learning will take place. It must be appropriate and achievable.

A good objective states what the student must demonstrate, the criteria for success, and the given conditions and materials. Both primary and upper elementary-grade students can meet objectives with these three elements. Look at this objective: The student will correctly identify and locate the capitals of five northeastern states on a given map in a given time. Do you know what the learners are expected to do? The key terms in this particular objective are *identify, locate, given map*, and *given time.*

The process verbs in the objective give a special direction to teaching and the learning that evolves from it. It is helpful to have some words that can assist in the writing of social studies objectives. The following list is not complete, as there are many word choices that can apply specifically to social studies. These are some that can be used for content, process, or affective objectives.

Some Process Verbs for Social Studies Objectives

Content	Process	Affective
tell	operate	appreciate
discuss	apply	enjoy
name	solve	believe
list	develop	think

define	design	know
locate	estimate	feel
find	diagram	value
identify	sequence	share
illustrate	utilize	help
state	incorporate	perceive
	compare	trust
	contrast	experience
	reproduce	accept
	plan	conceptualize

Content verbs indicate that specific information will be required, such as: *List* five Indian foods, *Name* three Indian leaders, or *Define* the term *medicine man*. Process verbs require the performance of a task, such as: *Design* an Indian costume, *Compare* the food-gathering methods of two tribes, or *Plan* a hunt. The affective verbs are used more for goals than for specific objectives because they are difficult, if not impossible, to measure. We also want to achieve affective objectives, such as: *Value* the Indian culture or *Appreciate* Indian music and art. To make them measurable, we may have to combine them with a process verb, such as *Show appreciation* of Indian art or *Demonstrate knowledge* of Indian culture.

The observable behavior is the true basis of evaluating enabling objectives. Can the student meet your objectives? This should be foremost in your mind when planning the lesson. Care must be taken to set the objectives at a challenging level. They should not be so easy that true learning is not really occurring, and not so difficult as to be unrealistic. Finally, did the students know from the outset what they were expected to learn? Objectives should be made known to all of the students from the very beginning of the lesson. This cannot be overemphasized.

To write objectives, consider using the following formula. An example will be given, then you try one or two. The topic is Maps.

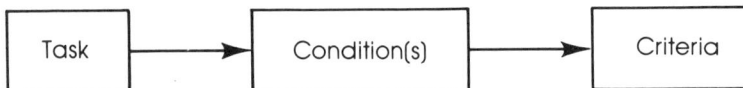

The child will:

Task:

1. Locate his home state on a United States map

2. (content verb)

3. (process verb)

Condition:

1. when asked to do so by the teacher

2.

3.

Criteria:

1. within one minute

2.

3.

When writing a good objective, you must consider the subject matter and skills in the lesson to determine what you want to teach, and then write the objective in a usable form. Writing objectives for the primary and upper grades is not very different, but upper grades do require consideration for ability. You must state what the learner will do to show that he or she has learned and you must state the conditions.

The next two sections present a lesson description followed by some objectives that could be used with the lesson. Look at the lesson and decide what should be taught. Then analyze the objective to find the task, conditions, and criteria.

Social Studies Objectives for a Primary-Grade Lesson.   Look at the following sample lesson for a primary class and the objectives that follow. What are students expected to do?

The Lesson

A second-grade class is required to study the family roles of persons in the United States and Africa. The textbook presents two families in various situations, such as how decisions are made, the schooling of children, recreation, and the effects of climate on such things as clothing, housing, foods, customs, and rules. The manual suggests reading all of the pages in the text for this particular lesson. Several children's books that pertain to family life in these two countries are recommended to be read to the class. Some group discussion questions and a "what if . . ." situation can also be presented. There may be a workbook page or two that has a short lesson reinforcement for the children to do independently.

The Objective

Taking into consideration the material given in the manual, what might be an acceptable, workable, and attainable objective? A class that is heterogeneously grouped may require that the teacher set the objective at a very basic level to insure success for even the lowest-performing students. Such an introductory-level objective might be one of the following.

1. Given a list of 12 short phrases, the student will identify (circle) those that are shared by the American and the African families they have studied.

2. The student will correctly identify, verbally or in writing, at least five ways that school life is the same (or different) in the U.S. and the African schools.

Discussion

What is the content or skill being taught?

        Objective 1.   Task:
                       Condition:
                       Criteria:

        Objective 2.   Task:
                       Condition:
                       Criteria:

        Add your own objective:

Comparing and contrasting the elements of family life is a common strand in primary social studies curricula. The cultural setting might be in Mexico, China, Southeast Asia, or Canada, but the objectives are similar. The appropriate level of difficulty is largely determined in the objective itself by the choice of verbs and other structural selections. Knowing the performance level of the students in other subject areas makes the level of difficulty for social studies lessons somewhat easier to determine. Knowing the expected outcomes of the previous grade level is also helpful.

The first sample objective requires some reading facility, so the developmental stage of the lesson must provide opportunities for the students to practice reading the vocabulary that will be used to test the objective. Note that even though some reading is required, the objective is still at the recall level (recall of information already presented during the lesson). The second objective is also at the recall level, but the nonreaders can successfully meet the requirement by making oral responses to the teacher. These children will be using the auditory modality in significant ways during this lesson.

After a student has met the basic objective(s), expand the objectives for higher-level learning. Here are some examples of additional objectives based on the lesson:

Extending the Objective

1. Given 10 statements about U.S. and African family life situations, the student will respond with true and false answers with 95% accuracy.

2. Given appropriate materials, the student will construct a model of an African village to represent at least 10 specific characteristics stated in the lesson.

3. The student will list 10 specific problems an African family would face if they came to our community to live for a year, and give a solution for each problem.

Social Studies Objectives for an Upper-Elementary Grade Lesson. Formulating a usable objective for an upper-elementary grade employs the same basic criteria as those for the primary grades. Is it appropriate for the age group, the ability of the students, and the lesson material? What is the observable behavior? (What must the students be able to do at the end of the lesson?) Can the students reasonably be expected to meet the goal? How will success be measured? Can the students recognize what I want them to learn?

The Lesson

A fifth-grade class is required to study the chronological history of the United States. The time period extends from the colonial period to the present time. At the elementary level the depth of content cannot be expected to be on a par with a secondary American History course. The background information includes such areas as politics, farming, the role of invention, population, conflicts, international relations, and other major factors vital to the formation of our country. The basic text makes several recommendations regarding additional readings for both students and the teacher, group activities, audiovisual reinforcers, report writing, and study questions to answer.

The Objective

The focus of this lesson is the movement of time in history. Considering a time span of over 200 years, it is necessary to organize the time into smaller sets. In general terms, the teacher wants the students to comprehend the progression of time, understand the sequential nature of historical events, and acquire facility using time as a learning tool. How then can an objective be formulated? A possible objective that would meet the criteria could be one of the following:

A sixth-grade group prepares a time line to depict the important events of a historical sequence.

1. The students will construct a time line to include all significant information covering a (how many years?) time period (as directed by the teacher).

2. Given a specific time span, the student will interpret the information, stating the relevancy of the events in the sequence. At least two pertinent facts for each section must be given.

Discussion

What is the content or skill being taught?

Objective 1. Task:
            Condition:
            Criteria:

Objective 2. Task:
            Condition:
            Criteria:

Add your own objective:

The topic of this lesson, the chronological history of the United States, is generally included in intermediate social studies programs. Objective 1 states clearly what you want the students to do. They will make their own time line and show the events that were important for a particular time period. The word *construct* is an open term that enables the learner to make some judgments. (Do I choose to construct my time line in one dimension with paper and pencil, markers, or paint? Do I decide to construct my time line using a three-dimensional method with a papier mache model or other appropriate materials?) The word *all* indicates a high achievement/performance level of expectation from the teacher. It also indicates that during the instructional segments, care will be taken to distinguish between significant information and supporting information.

Objective 2 may be viewed as more of an entry-level objective. The time line is designed by the teacher and the learner expectation is recall and interpretative. The standard for success is stated clearly in the second statement in the objective: At least two pertinent facts for each section must be given.

To meet either of these objectives, it is necessary for the teacher to provide several opportunities for the students to experience and to experiment with time lines as a learning tool, progressing from a simple diagram to more complex representations.

Extending the primary objective provides enrichment for high-potential students in your class. You also have an additional objective or two available if your class has no trouble meeting the basic objectives. Remember that everyone must accomplish the basic objective before they go on to the extension objectives. It is better to overplan than to be unprepared. Examine these objectives that might be used to extend the lesson:

Extending the Objective

1. The student will convert the information on a given time line into a paragraph format. A minimum of two well-organized paragraphs is required. (Note that this type of optional objective is a valuable learning tool for students who express themselves more easily in a written lesson as opposed to a verbal presentation.)

2. As a part of a live time line presentation for the class, the student will read or recite the important factual information for his or her assigned period of time. Costumes, signs, background scenery, and other visuals are optional. (Note that this creative dramatics format may appeal to those learners who are very self-motivating and work well with others.)

A good objective states what the student must demonstrate, the criteria for success, the given conditions, and materials. Both primary and upper-elementary grade students can meet objectives with these three elements. Primary objectives may appear to be easy because they are at the level of "building a background," but they are challenging to the students who are working to achieve them. Upper-grade objectives do not have to be lengthy or contain a lot of complicated semantics to qualify as an effective objective. A usable objective must not impair the teaching process. It is usable if it provides direction to the process. Write your objectives so they will serve as a teaching tool, not as a hindrance.

Teaching Strategies

A teaching strategy (also called a teaching method) is defined as a plan for achieving an educational goal or objective. Goals and objectives define what you want the students to learn or achieve. A teaching strategy is how (process) you will teach it to the learner. As a part of planning, you must select appropriate strategies that will efficiently teach the lesson.

Why Are Strategies Necessary?

The elements of effective teaching include several areas, such as a thorough understanding of child development, well-developed lesson plans, selective supplementary materials, a positive learning environment, caring, and effective group dynamics. To write your lesson plan, carefully examine your social studies goals and state precisely, as objectives, what the students are to learn. You then select an appropriate strategy to achieve those objectives.

Teaching strategies are a necessary element of planning to insure a good lesson presentation from the motivational level to the lesson culmination and evaluation. All of the pertinent lesson information can be firmly set in your mind, but if it is presented ineffectively or inefficiently, the best-planned lesson may ultimately fail. For example, if a strictly lecture-type strategy is chosen to teach a citizenship lesson to primary-age children, their shorter attention span alone will contribute to loss of interest, tuning out, discipline problems, and, at best, short-term retention of information. On the other hand, if a short informational presentation is made followed by an active learning exercise, chances are that control will be more acceptable, motivation factors will be more evident, and retention will be longer lasting.

Teachers of the elementary grades are involved heavily in establishing a knowledge base upon which future learning is built. This necessitates a certain amount of information giving, but that can be accomplished in ways other than by lecturing or giving reading assignments. A constant strategy of expository teaching is not always effective either. Children anticipate variety in lesson presentation and experiential learning.

Varying your teaching strategies to fit a particular lesson is necessary because children can process and retain only so much information at a given time. Sitting at a desk and listening to the teacher present a large amount of factual data for a long period of time will probably result in a large portion of the class being off task and bored. That same information can be received in audiovisual presentations, class activities, a cooperative learning setting, or a computer lesson. Boredom, lack of interest, time off task, other distracting behaviors, and, yes, even low achievement may be due to teaching failure rather than learning failures.

Teaching strategies are necessary so that you know exactly what you are going to do to teach the lesson. It is vital that a step-by-step approach be firmly in mind so the flow of the lesson will be constant. Floundering, changing course in midstream, and losing momentum upset the balance of the lesson and contribute to time off task. This is not to say that teachers cannot display flexibility and change directions during a lesson. The difference is that the new tactic is planned (always remember to have a planned, anticipated technique ready as a backup) and can be initiated with relative ease. This is better than choosing something randomly and hoping that it will indeed work.

To summarize, planning your teaching strategy (your plan for achieving an educational goal) is necessary for these reasons:

1. One mode of lesson presentation is not appropriate for every lesson. Varying the teaching style adds to lesson appeal and helps to maintain interest.

2. Strategies are a necessary part of a lesson's organizational structure. Good objectives and stimulating materials have limited value without a dynamic method of presentation to learners.

3. A specific teaching strategy will increase the probability of a smooth progression of teaching and learning.

4. A planned strategy decreases the use of trial-and-error methods that are time consuming and distracting.

5. Appropriate teaching strategies ultimately accentuate the strengths of the lesson.

6. Competence with various teaching strategies broadens your level of expertise and signifies professional growth.

7. Most of all, a teaching strategy establishes your method for presenting new learning to your students.

By considering the above rationale for planning strategies, the importance of a carefully thought-out teaching strategy becomes clear.

Planning a Teaching Strategy

When planning your strategy for a lesson, it is helpful to take several things into consideration. Here are a few important elements.

1. What is the learning objective?
2. How much time will this lesson require?

3. Does the topic indicate that a particular strategy would work better than all others?

4. What strategy will this particular class respond to best?

5. Do I have extensive knowledge of this topic? If I do, perhaps more risk taking would be a challenge. If I do not, then maybe I should use a strategy with which I am more comfortable.

6. Is this topic new to the class or is it a review item from the previous year?

7. How extensive are the supplementary materials that are available for class use? Am I limited to the textbook and workbook only?

8. How many modalities, learning styles, and performance levels should I consider as I plan this lesson?

There are many factors to be examined when deciding on a particular method of presentation for any lesson. It is helpful to keep in mind that we are teaching subject content to children. The human factor in teaching must always be top priority. Use what works for you as the teacher, and for your children who want to be learners.

In planning teaching strategies, the teacher makes choices regarding what he or she will do to teach a lesson. A simplified formula for an instructional strategy is:

1. What will the teacher do/say? (planned behavior)

2. How will the students respond? (anticipated behavior)

3. If acceptable, what will the teacher do/say? (planned behavior)

4. If not acceptable, what will the teacher do/say? (planned behavior)

The strategy selected should be appropriate for the age level of the learner, the objective, and the specific topic. For example, would an expository (teacher acts as a giver of information) strategy be an acceptable choice for a lesson on population graphing, or would you select a strategy that employs a short teacher presentation followed by a longer hands-on practice session of actually making some population graphs? Planning a specific strategy increases the probability that the objective(s) will be more efficiently met, trial-and-error tactics will be at a minimum, management skills will improve, and the anticipation factor of children will be more positive. Examine some applicable teaching strategies for the social studies.

Expository Teaching Strategy.   Expository teaching is basically the lecture style of teaching. The instructor tells the students or has them read almost every-thing they are expected to learn. The students repeat the information back, using a written or recitation format. Rote learning and sole dependence on the text-book are examples of this strategy. Expository teaching is largely teacher controlled and students are generally passive receptors of information with minimal involvement. Before the advent of modern educational research and child psychology, much of elementary education was conducted in this fashion. The teacher told and the students received. This method did offer an advantage to the auditory learner, but ignored the visual and kinesthetic learner. Expository teaching is efficient. A great amount of information can be dispensed quickly and students are not distracted by extraneous material or information.

Teacher-Student Interaction Strategy.   The teacher-student interaction strategy involves both teacher and student and lends itself to creative and informative exchanges. Some quiet think time when no one is talking is an integral part of the strategy. This strategy can be extended into an exercise of interaction analysis wherein teacher-talk, student-talk, and silent times are tabulated by an observer to determine the quantity and quality of interactions. This method provides opportunities for students to learn from each other by sharing thoughts and ideas in a spirit of cooperation with the teacher.

Left Brain, Right Brain, Whole Brain Strategy. Research on brain function has significant impact on many areas of education, ranging from special education to physical therapy for handicapped children. Much is being written in the pro-

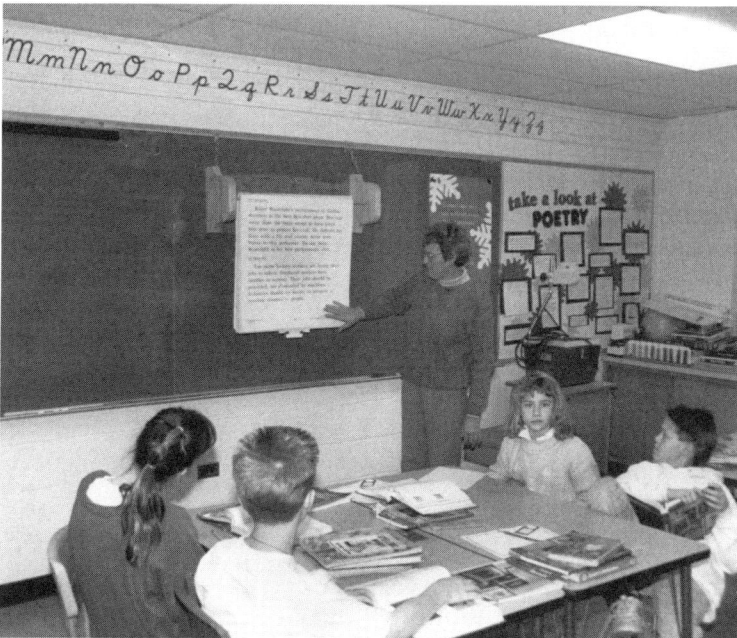

The teacher uses many methods to present information to students, including lecture.

fessional journals about the left and right brain teaching and learning methods. Teachers are learning to adapt their strategies to incorporate this knowledge.

The right brain learners accommodate very easily to creative learning situations. When given an opportunity to find new ways to do things, the right brain learners will probably excel. They tend to be very imaginative, adventurous, and welcome risk-taking situations. The left brain learners function well within a more organized, predictable framework. They are comfortable with book-oriented lessons and when they are assigned a specific task they will perform it as directed. The whole brain learners are capable of learning equally well using left brain and right brain activities. They can draw upon the strategies of both sides of the brain. Most children operate somewhat as whole brain learners as lessons are not always presented to their specific strengths.

Teachers must not only be aware of the left or right brain preference of their students, but should also be aware of their own preference. Teachers tend to teach to their own preference, and children of another preference will have problems. You must be aware of your preference so that you can conscientiously plan activities for both left and right brain learners. If they cannot learn your way, then you must teach their way.

Adapting a teaching strategy that emphasizes right or left brain processing necessitates particular classroom management decisions, such as providing a place for the book learners to work quietly and a place for the creative problem solvers to have space to try out their ideas. This strategy works well with all age groups. Even primary-age youngsters operate successfully when drawing on the learning style that suits them.

Computer Teaching Strategy.   The impact of the computer as a learning tool at the elementary level is significant. Many youngsters are as comfortable with the computer monitor as they are with the television in their homes. Access to computers in the classroom creates a very stimulating, effective learning situation if the teacher uses them properly. You may have access to a computer lab or to only one or two machines in your classroom. Either way, you can use the computer to have effective lessons. Use it to stimulate interest, present information, provide drill and practice, or for evaluation and closure.

A computer-based strategy is a good choice when considerations have been carefully weighed. Consider these:

1. What is the student's level of proficiency in operating the computer?
2. How skilled is the teacher in operating the computer?
3. How skilled is the teacher in using the computer as a teaching device?
4. What types of programs are available? Are they appropriate for your objective and are they educationally sound?
5. Are students required to think, or are the responses on the memory-recall level only?

6. Does the program require or teach decision-making skills?
7. Does the lesson content come across clearly or will the color graphics and sound effects overpower or distract the learner?
8. Is the program too "gimmicky"—all show and no real learning?

Most of the software packages available today meet effective teaching standards, but it may be necessary to modify an existing program or to write and program your own lesson. Writing your own program enables you to implement your objective fully, incorporate sufficient practice opportunities, and guide the lesson toward the closure you have planned. Programming your own lesson may be beyond your computer expertise, but it is not difficult to find someone who can help you.

Cooperative Learning Strategy.   Organizing children into groups for particular learning experiences has been evident in classrooms for many years. A heterogeneous group of students working together on projects is a valuable technique. Everyone in the group can experience varying degrees of success. The interaction and sharing of ideas may result in even better group dynamics than those planned by the teacher. Team learning is based on the assumption that the whole is greater than the sum of the parts.

This strategy requires that the members of the groups be selected carefully to insure that not only will the group experience success, but each individual will make significant contributions and experience personal satisfaction. The composition of the group may be the greatest single factor in the success or failure of the activity. To implement a group learning experience, the teacher must have the objective prepared in advance. Each group must understand its goal and have some plan in mind to achieve it. In some cases each group may have a different objective to pursue, covering a different dimension of the general goal. This will require that all groups come together and share information at the conclusion of the lesson. This particular adaptation of group learning is excellent for older children.

A cooperative learning strategy requires establishing working groups and organizing and implementing usable procedures for students to follow, while at the same time allowing for student input. This demands a great deal of projecting, anticipating student needs, and making accommodations. Once the groups begin to function, the role of the teacher is largely that of facilitator, guide, and resource person.

Total Student Response Strategy.   The total student response technique is used by many teachers. It is especially effective for primary-age children because it is a very direct, close proximity approach. This particular method is an example of a nearly perfect ratio of interaction between teacher and student. Here is how to use this technique:

The teacher asks a question, makes a statement, or points out something particular in the room.

All the students respond either orally (choral or by holding up a particular card to answer the question or respond to the statement.

The obvious value of this strategy is that all of the students are responding as opposed to the children raising their hands and the teacher calling on only one to respond. In essence, it fosters thinking for everyone. It gives all the children an opportunity to respond to every statement or gesture given by the teacher.

A variation of this technique is used in the schools of other countries, especially those where teaching materials are in short supply. The teacher questions, and all students respond orally—noisy, but effective. The more opportunities children have to respond to the teacher, the more reinforcement they get. This is very gratifying for young children because each time they hold up their card, they are visually, and often verbally, recognized by the teacher who visually monitors responses and participation by looking at all the cards the children are holding up.

There are several strengths of the total student response strategy:

1. All students are given the opportunity to respond, increasing the probability of internalizing the skill.

2. Slower-learning children feel they are part of the group because they can hold up a card and not risk embarrassment by verbally calling out a wrong answer.

3. The teacher can monitor responses and adjust the level of difficulty of her or his questions or statements.

4. It uses all of the modalities of learning: visual (the learner must visually sort through his or her cards and choose the correct one); auditory (the learner must attend carefully to process what the teacher says before responding); and tactile (touching, feeling, sorting, and holding the card provide tactile reinforcement).

5. Making the set of cards can be a class project. Updating and adding to the set continues participation in the strategy.

6. This strategy can be used in different phases of the lesson: pretesting (in a few moments the teacher can readily determine the class's previous knowledge of a particular topic); reinforcement (after a few lessons have been presented the teacher can use this approach to find out if the students are understanding the information presented); and evaluation and closure (at the end of the lesson a nonwritten test can be administered easily and all of the learners can participate and experience a degree of success).

ACTIVITIES

You have read about planning, objectives, and teaching strategies. Now you will put that knowledge to use. In Activity 5.1, you will have the opportunity to write some objectives and then customize them to fit individual needs. Preparing a teaching strategy follows in Activity 5.2. As you do these activities, keep in mind what you want to teach then plan your lessons to achieve that goal.

5.1 *Objectives*

The identification and implementation of enabling objectives at the classroom level is a primary responsibility of individual elementary teachers. Becoming aware of specific local, state, and national terminal objectives that must be taught at some time during the year is also the responsibility of the elementary social studies teacher. This activity is designed to help you focus on enabling objectives that are usable with elementary students and are adaptable to a specific social studies curriculum.

Lesson Objectives

Think of a general learning objective for a first-grade class. The unit, entitled Economics, requires two weeks, with each individual lesson running from 20 to 25 minutes. Write your terminal objective below. (You might want to consult a textbook for examples or help.)

> ***Terminal Objective (General)***

Now identify the specific enabling objectives that are necessary to meet your terminal objective. Write them below.

> ***Learning Objectives (Specific)***
   1.

   2.

   3.

Self-Check.   When identifying the specific enabling objectives you want the students to achieve, it is helpful to remember exactly what they must do to show you they have met the criteria that you have planned. Do the objectives you have written state clearly what the students must do? Will they be able to understand the performance objective? Have you selected enough specific enabling objectives to meet the terminal objective adequately? Does each objective relate directly to the long-range goal? Can the objectives reasonably be achieved within the given time limits? Discuss this activity with another person in your class. If you have concerns about your choices, consult with your instructor.

Individualizing an Objective

You are teaching a fourth-grade class. One of your students is functioning primarily at the level of concrete formations. It is necessary for you to individualize some lessons for this student so that she can function successfully in the mainstream classroom. Select a topic that is presented in the fourth-grade curriculum and plan for this student. (You may wish to research several textbook manuals before you proceed with this activity.)

Lesson Topic

Terminal Objective

Enabling Objectives

1.

2.

3.

Individualization of the Lessons
Briefly describe your plans for this student.
High Potential:

Poor Reader:

Implementation of the Objectives
What will the student be doing to achieve the objective?
1. (Visual)

2. (Auditory)

3. (Tactile)

Evaluation of the Objective
How will success be measured?
1.

2.

3.

Self-Check. Keeping in mind the stage of development of this student and the grade placement, do your objectives statements meet her learning needs? Are they achievable in the time frame that the unit requires? Have you planned enough activities that will allow her to touch, feel, manipulate, move things around, build, and construct? A typical classroom has a variety of "stages of development" represented in every grade. Provisions must be made to meet all learner needs so every student will experience success.

Identifying Objectives in the Classroom

Make arrangements to visit an elementary classroom. The goal of the visit is to observe a variety of lessons being presented. For this activity to be a valuable learning experience, spend as much time as possible in the classroom. An entire day would be optimum. Your goal is to observe a typical day of an elementary student. As an alternative, your instructor may provide a videotape of a lesson or two for the class to analyze. Specifically, you will be carefully observing the teacher to identify his or her behavioral objective(s) for the students. In addition you will be carefully observing what the students do to meet the objective(s) in each class. Use the format shown in Figure 5–3 to record your observations for the day. Be as specific as you can. Be prepared to share your experience with the class or your instructor.

Continue using this format for the other lessons presented during your visit. Some interesting learning objectives may be observed in art, physical education, music, and science.

Figure 5-3 Record of Classroom Visitation

Grade Level: _____

Lessons Presented:
   1. Social Studies
      a. The objective is _____
      b. I identified the objective when _____
      c. The students did this _____
      d. The evaluation of the objective was _____

   2. Math
      a. The objective is _____
      b. I recognized the objective when _____
      c. The students did this _____
      d. The evaluation of the objective was _____

   3. Reading
      a. The objective is _____
      b. I knew the objective when _____
      c. The students did this _____
      d. The evaluation of the objective was _____

   4. Language Arts
      a. The objective is _____
      b. I knew the objective when _____
      c. The students did this _____
      d. The evaluation of the objective was _____

Self-Check.   At what point did you know exactly what the objective was—at the very beginning of the lessons, after the motivational techniques were presented, or when the students became involved? Did you have the experience of not being able to determine what the objective really was? If you, as an adult, had difficulty with this, think how confusing it probably was for the students to figure it out! This is a very important reason for being clear and specific—the students must know exactly what you want them to learn and do. If possible, obtain a copy of the teacher's lesson plan or discuss your observations with her or him. How does your observation compare to her or his plan?

Concentrate for a moment on the student activities you observed during the visit. Were they directed toward achieving the objective? Were they planned well? Were the directions given clearly and the materials ready? Were the activities appropriate for the age and development levels?

Extension of the Visit: If I were to visit another classroom for the purpose of identifying learning objectives, I would:

1.
2.
3.

This activity was challenging for these reasons:

1.
2.
3.

I had positive feeling for these reasons:

1.
2.
3.

Share your visit with the class or conference with your instructor.

5.2   *Teaching Strategies*

Once you have decided what to teach, you must plan how to teach it. This activity is designed to give you experience in planning a lesson, focusing on teacher and student preparation and behavior. The computer activity provides an opportunity for you to examine some sources of computer programs and to evaluate one or more of the actual programs.

A Lesson Strategy

Preview several current textbooks for the sixth grade and then select a social studies topic. Be a risk taker and choose one you know the least about from personal experience. Do some reading on it and then use the following format to design a lesson strategy.

Lesson Topic:

Grade Level: _____
Objective:

Teacher Input (Planned Behaviors)
The teacher will do these things:

1.

2.

3.

4.

Student Input (Anticipated Behaviors)
The students will do these things:

1.

2.

3.

4.

Teacher Reaction (Planned Behaviors)
If the student reactions/responses are acceptable, then the teacher will:

1.

2.

3.

4.

Teacher-Student Modification (Planned Behaviors)
If the student reactions/responses are unacceptable, then the teacher will:

1.

2.

3.

4.

Self-Check.   The teacher-student modification step in this schema is an important part of the total strategy planning activity. Teachers plan a specific strategy with the idea that the lesson will be successful and the objectives will be met. If the lesson progression does not go smoothly, the alert teacher has a secondary strategy already in mind. This lesson is for sixth graders. These students may be brought into the planning activity by assisting the teacher in the lesson modification process. Brainstorming ideas often give the teacher valuable insights into how students receive and process information.

Designing a Teaching Strategy

This activity gives you the opportunity to design a teaching strategy for a primary- or intermediate-level class. Select a topic for the lesson and think of the various components of an effective teaching strategy. Use the following format. Be specific.

Grade Level: _____

Topic:

Terminal Objective:

Enabling Objectives:

1. The students will

2. The students will

3. The students will

Before-Class Activities

The teacher will do these things:

1.	6.
2.	7.
3.	8.
4.	9.
5.	10.

Some things you need to think about are preparing yourself, getting background information, selecting appropriate materials, planning the entire lesson, and setting the objectives. Your original objectives may be modified after previewing the available materials that are on hand to teach the lesson. List those things that must be done before class. Your list will probably be lengthy!

In-Class Activities

The teacher will do these things:

1. Motivating Techniques (introducing)
   a.

   b.

   c.

2. Presenting Techniques (teaching)
   a.

   b.

   c.

The students will do these things:

1. Receiving Information (listening)
   a.

   b.

   c.

2. Using Information (doing)
   a.

   b.

   c.

Self-Check.   Examine your instructional strategy carefully and evaluate all of the components by using these criteria:

1. The topic I have chosen is appropriate for the grade level and is within an accepted scope and sequence for the designated grade.

2. The learning objectives I wrote are clearly attainable for the average class. I have made provisions for special needs students. (If not, adjust or write an additional objective to meet at least one special need. This may be for a handicapped youngster, a high-potential student, or a limited English-proficiency child.)

3. The before-class activities for the teacher are complete and clearly stated. If I were to do all of these things as stated, I would feel confident to walk into a classroom and present this lesson. (If not, reorganize this component now).

4. The introductory activities I have planned are exciting, stimulate interest, and will motivate the students to want to learn and participate in this lesson. I can utilize these techniques with sincerity. They are not gimmicky or unrealistic.

5. The teaching techniques are realistic and follow sound pedagogical principles.

6. The listening activities for the student include receiving information from

many sources: the textbook, filmstrips, library materials, resource people, and the teacher.

7. The participation activities for the students provide opportunities for them to work alone or in small groups, use a variety of manipulative materials, and utilize their processing skills. (Interacting with peers is an important learning opportunity at this point. Here the students are active learners not passive receptors.)

8. I feel this instructional strategy contains all the necessary components of a good lesson.

9. The lesson can be taught in the time limits available for social studies.

If your comfort level is not reached with any of the above criteria as it applies to your instructional strategy, consult with your instructor. The individual components may need to be modified or adjusted so that you will feel more confident with the content.

Using a Computer Teaching Strategy

Go to the university curriculum materials center or library and get catalogues for social studies and computer education materials that are currently on the market. You are looking for elementary social studies computer programs. Read through the publishers' descriptions of the lessons on each set of programs. With this information in mind, would you purchase these programs for your classroom? Why or why not? How would they fit into an elementary social studies strategy for teaching? Using the following guidelines for a computer teaching strategy, prepare a written or oral report for your class.

Primary Level
Name of program

Format (game, skill builder, or drill):

What does it teach?

Intermediate Level
Name of program

Level of difficulty
easy
moderate
challenging

Lesson sequence
introductory
practice
evaluation

Objective (state it clearly)

Criterion for mastery learning (name criterion)

Reading a publisher's description of a particular computer program gives you some idea of the menu content. A hands-on experience of actually running the entire program yourself gives a very realistic opportunity to judge its appropriateness for children. Make arrangements at the university computer laboratory to run several social studies programs that are written for elementary students. Use these guidelines to evaluate the programs.

Evaluation of a Social Studies Computer Lesson
Title of the program

Could the average elementary student do this lesson independently? If not, why?

Was the reading level appropriate?

Did you like the graphics? Why or why not?

Were terminologies clear or explained?

Are there any factors that you think might interfere with a successful learning experience?

Be prepared to discuss your experience and the data you collected with the instructor.

Self-Check.   Look at your evaluation. Did you find anything else to comment on? Did the documentation with the program provide you with useful information? Did you have any difficulty using the computer or the program? Using the computer to teach is only as effective as the programs you use. There are many good programs and a lot of useless programs. If they are not appropriate for your lesson, they are not usable and are a waste of your time. Choose carefully.

Extension.   Make arrangements to visit a local elementary school that incorporates computer-based instruction into the social studies curriculum. Interview one of the teachers and/or the principal or curriculum chairperson to find out what strategies are used in the classroom instruction. Talking with professionals already in the field will help you formulate your own working philosophy about the most appropriate use of computer-based instruction for elementary students.

If it is possible, plan to preview the social studies programs that are used in the school. Observe a teacher using a computer with her or his class. What observations can you make? Include as much information as possible for your report to the class.

Summary

New teachers are required to teach many content areas other than social studies. There is no question that you are undertaking a major responsibility. There are responsibilities to the parents and the community to teach all that is in the established curriculum and to prepare the students with life skills. There are responsibilities to the students to teach them what they need to function successfully in the school and community environment. You also have a responsibility to yourself to become a professional and to perform all the duties related to classroom teaching.

Planning to perform all these duties successfully is required and necessary. To accomplish these requirements, you must not only have instructional plans, but some strategies to implement them. All of the lesson elements should be directed toward successful teaching and learning experiences. Now is the time to study, observe, and contemplate the various strategies that teachers use. There are strengths and perhaps some weaknesses in each; investigate them. The social aspect of social studies indicates that strategies of an interactive, cooperative nature are good choices. Some content lessons that emphasize factual information may call for a teacher-directed or an individual study approach.

Students are ultimately responsible for learning the social studies material, but teachers are responsible for using strategies that increase the probability that the learning will occur. New teachers must work to develop an expertise—a usable repertoire of strategies that apply particularly to social studies education.

READING RESOURCES

Meier, D. "Learning in Small Moments." *Harvard Educational Review, 56* (August 1986): 298–300.

ENDNOTES

1. Havighurst, Robert J., *Developmental Tasks and Education*, 3rd ed. (New York: David McKay Company, Inc., 1972).

2. Texas Education Agency, Austin, Texas, reprint May 1984.

3. Mager, Robert F., *Preparing Instructional Objectives* (Belmont, CA: Fearon Publishers, Inc., 1962), pp. 2–3.

6
Evaluating
and Questioning

PROJECTIONS

Teachers, curriculum committees, and advisory groups determine exactly what social studies material needs to be taught and then make the necessary provisions to teach and evaluate it. The question will be: Is social studies being evaluated in ways that are compatible to the ways it is being taught? We will have to evaluate the method of evaluation as carefully as we evaluate all other aspects of teaching.

Change in education is inevitable if the school environment is to prepare students adequately with life skills. A significant factor in this change process will revolve around two major items: what schools are teaching and how it is being evaluated. Social studies curriculum content undergoes the updating process at regular intervals, frequently in conjunction with new textbook adoption. Some viable options for evaluating the learning of the new curriculum are clearly needed.

Revision of evaluation and grading systems must accompany changes in school operation, philosophy, instructional practices, and student performance expectations. Schools will continue to find better ways for reporting to parents. What will the report card of the future be?

Business and education planners are predicting some rather drastic changes for our schools. More compacting of curriculum, students spending less time in the school building and being educated in nonacademic settings, students graduating at a much younger age, more fluid movement through the course requirements, and graduation correlating with what the student knows and can do rather than a specific number of years spent in the school system are some of the changes that are foreseen.

The impact on social studies education is important to note. Technology makes it possible to retrieve a multitude of facts, figures, and other data at a moment's notice. Is it a valid use of school time to teach and expect students to retain and reproduce large volumes of this information? Students are capable of learning and reproducing information for particular testing periods; however, a large amount of this information is learned for the short term and unfortunately forgotten or extinguished shortly thereafter. We may choose to use school time to teach and evaluate the social studies life skills the students will need to be functional citizens.

175

Our goal is to educate socially competent citizens who will ultimately become creative producers. These citizens need many competencies to function successfully in the workplace and in their personal lives. Teaching these many competencies will be a challenge; evaluating them will demand some creative and productive teachers, administrators, and community representatives. A benchmark for evaluating the success or failure of the school community to teach these skills is to determine how successful the students are in using them after they leave the school setting. The greatest compliment a school can receive is to graduate students who are productive, competent people in all phases of their lives.

If you don't like the answers you're getting, change your questions—at first glance this may appear to be an oversimplified statement. It does have applications to social studies education now and in the future. Are we satisfied with the learner outcomes we are now realizing from present-day materials, curriculum, teaching strategies, and methods of evaluation? If the answer is yes, will this state of satisfaction continue into the next century and beyond? If the answer is no, then we must begin to change.

Teachers are always asking questions or making statements that elicit student responses. The rapid changes in national and world events make the acquisition of factual information unstable at best. Teachers routinely ask questions that call for a response that is either right or wrong—an efficient way of determining whether or not certain material has been learned. Although this is appropriate for the moment, it does not address the problem of long-term retention. We must learn more about long-term learning and ways to evaluate it. Once we gain this knowledge we will have to change the way we question and evaluate our students.

Evaluation Techniques

Why can't all evaluation be informal? Doesn't formal evaluation cause undue stress, worry, and competition? Why evaluate elementary students at all? Evaluating performance is necessary to determine the rate and degree to which the students are achieving specified objectives. Evaluation is used to determine the appropriateness of objectives, the effectiveness of materials and lesson strategies, and the effectiveness of the teacher. It is finding out what the students already know, what they have learned, and what the teacher has taught. Evaluation is also a very important tool for reporting to parents on the progress of their children.

Evaluating student learning has been a major component of education throughout the history of the formal school and it will continue to be so. Measuring the learning of students, beginning at the kindergarten level, gives the teacher critical insights into the readiness for learning of each child. When the teacher determines that state of readiness, he or she can more effectively plan lessons and experiences students can perform with some degree of success. Early evaluation is critical for effective teaching; without it, subsequent planning is haphazard at best.

Evaluation in terms of grading papers for young learners is a positive reinforcer when done in an encouraging manner. Consider a kindergarten social studies lesson. The objective is to correctly sequence a set of pictures showing safe ways to cross the street. Jackie completes the task correctly. The teacher marks the paper with a star, a smiley face, or a written comment such as ''Good Job'' or ''Very Good.''

Michael completes the task but makes more mistakes than is acceptable. The teacher who thinks positively and wants to convey this attitude to the student marks the paper ''Good Try!'' or ''Thank you for trying so hard!'' Is this evaluating? Yes. The teacher knows who has successfully completed the task and who needs more opportunities to learn it. Does this type of evaluation cause negative feelings for students? Probably not. Jackie feels very good about himself for getting everything correct. Michael has a good feeling about himself because the teacher recognizes his effort, even though mistakes were made. He knows he will get another chance. The parents have a positive feeling when the child brings home the paper with some communication from the teacher. They also know what their child needs to learn. Thus, the evaluation becomes a positive, growth-oriented experience for all three persons involved. The teacher gains insights into the learning needs of the child, the parents get information about the child's progress in a particular unit, and the student gets immediate feedback about what is being learned.

The process of evaluation is two-sided: evaluating the learning of the students and evaluating the instruction of the teacher. Each directly influences the other. If the students are not learning or making acceptable progress, then look very closely at the methods of presentation, the appropriateness of the objectives, and every other element of planning. On the other hand, if the students are consistently learning the material or performing the activities at a high level of accuracy with relative ease, then the performance expectations can be raised. When lessons are too easy they are just as nonproductive as when they are too hard! Teachers evaluate learning to assist in planning productive lessons and to receive feedback regarding the effectiveness of their teaching efforts.

Types of Evaluation

Evaluation may be either formal or informal. Formal evaluation is more structured and verifiable. Usually it requires some type of written or observable performance in response to a specific request. Here are some examples of formal evaluation techniques and applications.

FORMAL EVALUATION

Standardized Tests
Achievement tests
Reading inventories
Statewide subject matter tests
Districtwide assessments
K–6 grade-level assessments

Applications
1. To identify specific strengths of the adopted program
2. To identify weak topic areas
3. To chart individual student's progress from year to year
4. To assist curriculum committees during program selection years
5. To establish a ranking in terms of national standards

Chapter Tests
End-of-chapter questions
Publisher's test booklets
Teacher's manual

Applications
1. To determine the proficiency levels of students on materials presented in the text
2. To determine readiness for succeeding chapters
3. To assist in planning supplemental activities
4. To identify areas that need reteaching

Teacher-Designed Tests
Free response
Multiple choice
Matching items
Yes-no or true-false
Short essay
Fill in the blank

Applications
1. To gain information on skills not included in the text
2. To supplement given chapter tests (more information on particular topics)
3. To more adequately meet the reading levels of lower-performing students
4. To test the upper limits of high-potential students
5. To have some written measurement when none is available with the text

Written Assignments
Matching items
Workbook assignments
Worksheets
Teacher-directed pencil-paper activities
Others?

Applications
1. To determine the ability for following directions
2. To check the transfer of verbal and auditory learning to the written format
3. To provide opportunities for tactile experiences
4. To provide initial reading comprehension opportunities
5. To acquire some paper assignments as samples of the child's work
6. To supplement other informal evaluative measures
7. To show progress to parents at conference time

Other Types
Lessons on the chalkboard
Daily papers
Extra credit assignments
Reports (special and required)
Group projects
Individual self-checks in the textbook
Library research and assignments
Interviews
Others?

Applications
1. To supplement formal book test methods
2. To provide a means for shy students to succeed
3. To provide information to the teacher at regular intervals
4. To give students feedback regarding their progress
5. To make necessary adjustments in planning as needed
6. To establish appropriate work habits
7. To provide opportunities for the different learning styles of students

Physical Performance
Cut-and-paste activities
Matching items
Roleplaying
Do a given task
Construction projects

These future teachers are learning how to evaluate a lesson.

Applications
1. To check coordination
2. To utilize tactile mode for evaluating
3. To evaluate behaviors
4. To evaluate physical development
5. To evaluate nonverbal skills

Informal evaluation is usually based solely on teacher judgment or observations. It is especially valuable in keeping a record on a specific child, checking daily progress, and evaluating the work of a nontraditional-type (special education, handicapped, or gifted) student. The most widely used form of all evaluation is informal teacher judgment, which is an ongoing part of any lesson or activity. Examples of informal evaluation are:

INFORMAL EVALUATION

Anecdotal Records
Index cards (see Figure 6–1 for sample)
Daily diary
Tape recording of a behavior

Figure 6-1 Sample: Index Card Anecdotal Record

Anderson, Jane

8-10-89   Jane correctly sequenced time line dates (process skill)

12-21-89   Completed assigned book report using appropriate format—first time

3-7-90   Tested weak in mapping—check back

3-14-90   Retested mapping—acceptable performance

Applications
1. To record specific notes on a child's progress in certain areas for a period of time
2. To make note of unusual events or happenings, especially in the human relations skills
3. To serve as a reminder of skill areas that need review
4. To note specific strengths or weaknesses
5. To use as a ready reference for conferences
6. To pass on to next year's teacher

Checklists
Teacher-made (see Figure 6–2 for sample)
Textbook lists

Applications
1. To use as a quick check of required skills.
2. To use as an informal check of skills previously learned (a retention tool)
3. To use as a pretest measurement device
4. To measure both process and product skills
5. To test students on an individual basis
6. To obtain a quick overview of class performance in a particular unit
7. To use in conjunction with other formal methods
8. To employ as another method of measuring progress
9. To assess out-of-textbook material and/or information

Narratives
Paragraph form
Short phrases

Figure 6-2   Sample: Teacher-Made Checklist

Process Skills

The student can:	YES	NO
Correctly interpret basic map graphics		
Appropriately use map keys		
Correctly use map symbols ·		
Sequence five events		
Make contributions in group activities		
Use map terms correctly		
Read graph correctly		

Product Skills

The student can:	YES	NO
Tell three things about Abraham Lincoln		
Explain three good rules we have in our school		
Find the four cardinal directions on a map		
Name five products that come from trees		

Applications

1. To supplement the grading system in use

2. To provide additional information not readily understood with letter grades (more specific)

3. To accent a specific subject area

4. To provide detailed supporting information of a problem

5. To give a more personal account of a child's performance

6. To substitute for parent-teacher conferences when needed

7. To use as a tool for reporting in schools that are departmentalized (parents receive a written report from each individual teacher).

Teacher Judgment

Applications

1. To make mental notes about particular students

2. To use as the primary evaluative tool in kindergarten

3. To make a pretest judgment

4. To evaluate verbal activity-oriented lessons

5. To evaluate areas that are not easily testable on paper

6. To use with special students who are unable to perform learning skills in the regular manner

7. To evaluate high-potential students who do not fit the conventional mold

8. To evaluate such skills as the human relations skills

9. To assess the affective domain

10. To assess creative output

11. To assist the overall evaluation process

12. To give parents the teacher's insights into their child's progress

There are other evaluation tools in addition to these. You may want to design your own instrument or use a combination of several of these. Developing your own evaluative procedure is expected. The evaluative measures and applications outlined above can be used as an integral part of your grading system.

Evaluating Primary Students

The process of evaluating young children encompasses several areas of growth and development. Some of them are:

1. The level of performance on written assignments

2. The degree of verbal participation in class

3. The amount of active participation in group situations

4. The understanding of concepts

5. The observable human relations skills

6. The citizenship training

7. The observable processing skills

8. The degree of learning transfer

9. The amount of factual information that is learned

10. The development of acceptable work habits and school behaviors as related to the social studies

Specific social studies skills are readily observable, such as identifying a main idea in a story. Did the student identify it correctly? But a specific human relations skill, such as empathizing, requires very careful, thoughtful observation. Sometimes the teacher must catch the student performing a behavior, and not necessarily during the social studies period.

Evaluating Product Learning

Evaluating product learning focuses on subject-matter content. Some of the topics of current social studies programs are history, geography, famous Americans, government, economics, cities, work, states and regions, and maps and globes. Teachers select the most appropriate evaluative tool and make the necessary adjustments as the knowledge level increases. The method of evaluation must complement the particular subject being taught. Table 6–1 identifies some selected subject matter taught in the primary grades and an appropriate method of evaluation for each.

The following example shows you a sample of product learning followed by possible ways of evaluating the effectiveness of the lesson.

The Product Learning Situation

A third-grade class is beginning a series of lessons that concentrates on informed decision making and making favorable choices. The textbook material presents information on decision making in various situations, which may include the home setting, play group, organizational settings such as school or clubs, and individual situations. Information is offered about tactics students should use when they have opportunities to make choices.

The teacher plans several opportunities, using roleplaying and real-

Table 6-1 Ways of Evaluating Product Learning in the Lower Grades

Grade Level	Product Learning	Method of Evaluating
Kindergarten	You are a unique person What are rules? Accommodation at school Introduction to holidays	Anecdotal notes, narrative, verbal contributions, checklist, teacher judgment, written-artistic, verbal
First	Understand roles in groups How to be a friend Make a simple map	Teacher judgment, narrative, anecdotal notes, group activity
Second	Membership in groups Making decisions Rules and laws A significant current event	Narratives, anecdotal notes (teacher- designed), teacher judgment
Third	Making choices Environmental effects Laws and choices The geography of our city or town Interdependence groups	Teacher judgment, written, checklist

life situations, for the students to practice decision-making skills. The consequences of one choice over another are observed and discussed. The lessons incorporate supplementary materials to expand and enhance the textbook.

The Method of Evaluation.   One method of evaluating this type of learning is teacher judgment. This requires the teacher to become a keen observer in many different situations. When a child uses the skills of effective decision making or is observed making a good choice, the teacher makes a mental note of the event. Special care is taken to observe those choices that affect the group in a positive way. Evaluation occurs almost constantly and in every possible setting.

Skill transfer takes place many times outside of the social studies class. Students make choices in the social studies class, during lunch, on the playground, and in the halls. When a good choice is made, a verbal or visual reinforcer from the teacher increases the possibility that good choices will be made again.

Written evaluation instruments are used to determine the student's level of proficiency in making appropriate choices. A short paragraph describing a situation, followed by multiple-choice questions, is one possible design. Care must be taken to insure that the readability level does not conflict with the product learning that is actually being examined. Here is an example of this format. Read or have the children read the following paragraph then respond by selecting one of the choices.

> Carrie and Lance are in the same class. Lance brought a new tablet to school on Monday morning. At lunch time the tablet was missing. He couldn't find it anywhere, not even in in his locker. Carrie knows right where it is. What should Carrie do?
>
> 1. Go get the tablet and keep it for herself. She needs one anyway.
> 2. Leave the tablet where it is. It's Lance's problem to find it.
> 3. Carrie and Lance are friends and she knows he is upset, so she should tell him where the tablet is and he will feel good again. Friends help each other.
> 4. None of these.

A written or oral evaluation gives the teacher insights into the typical choices students would make or might make in a particular situation. "What if" activities give students safe opportunities to make choices. If choices are made that are not always the best, no one's feelings get hurt and relationships are not damaged. This type of an activity permits the teacher to determine if the students' decision-making skills are progressing. If poor or weak choices are being made, reteaching and reinforcing of particular lessons are needed.

Evaluating Process Skills

Social studies process skills stress doing. Some of the process skills students need to do in social studies are interpreting data, diagramming, sequencing, using the inquiry processes, estimating, and comparing. The process skills lend themselves easily to direct and immediate evaluation. Can the student do it? At the primary level, the beginning process skills give positive, activity-oriented experiences to young learners during their very first social studies lessons. Involvement in the doing aspect of learning is always effective for young children. Table 6–2 shows some process skills that are taught in the primary grades and some methods of evaluation for each.

Here is an example of one of these process skills as an integral part of a social studies lesson.

Table 6-2   Ways to Evaluate Process Skills in the Lower Grades

Grade Level	Process Skill	Method of Evaluation
Kindergarten	To locate north, south, east, and west on a map	Checklist, written (matching exercise)
	To recognize categories	Written (cut-paste), teacher judgment
	To interpret pictures	Teacher judgment, checklist
	To share ideas	Teacher judgment, anecdotal records
First	To identify main ideas	Written (circle, underline), anecdotal records, checklists
	To follow paths	Written, individualized
	To interpret a chart	Teacher judgment
	To use a calendar	Written
Second	To locate context clues	Written, anecdotal records
	To interpret symbols	Teacher judgment
	To classify	Written, checklist
	To sequence	Written
Third	To estimate distance	Written, individualized
	To solve problems	Written
	To use resources	Checklists, anecdotal records
	To make choices	Written, anecdotal records

The Process Skill

A second-grade class is studying the required unit on maps and globes. The textbook gives background information on how to distinguish between the different kinds of maps and globes and their specific uses. It clarifies the globe's representation of the earth. The teacher has maps and globes available for the students to touch, look at, and even write on (the laminated types are very good for young children). Specific skills related to map and globe learning are presented during class time. The process of interpreting symbols is the specific skill the students are to learn in this lesson.

A major portion of the class time is devoted to the recognition and specific functions of many different kinds of map and globe symbols. Some commonly used symbols for beginning map reading are as follows:

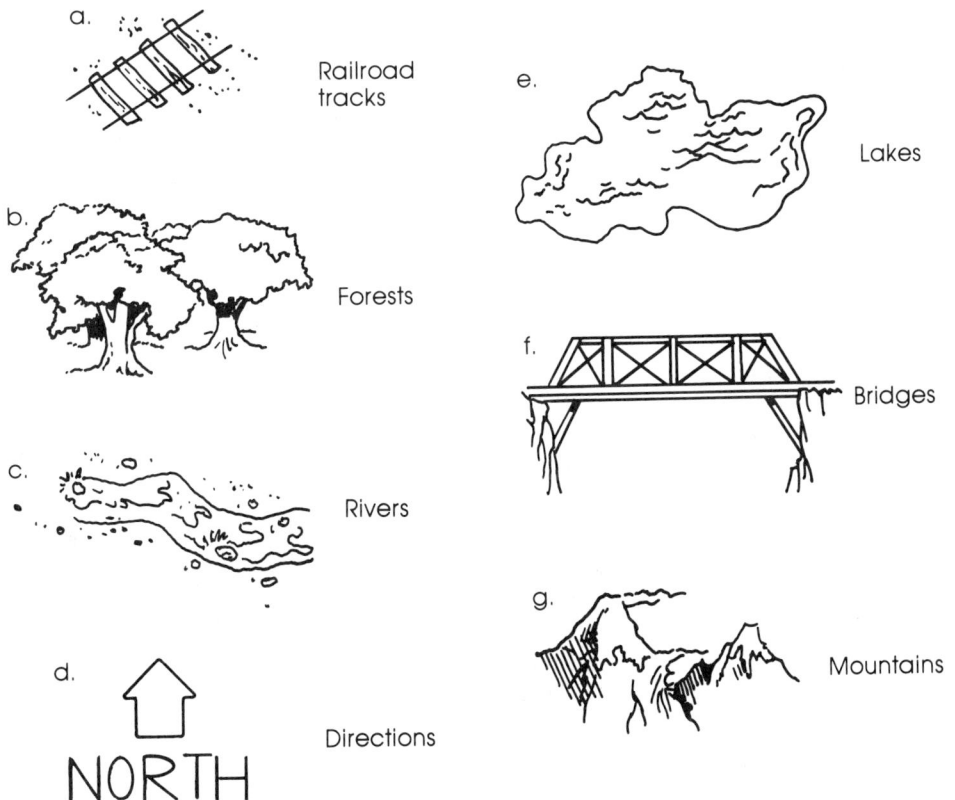

a. Railroad tracks

b. Forests

c. Rivers

d. NORTH Directions

e. Lakes

f. Bridges

g. Mountains

Students have time to examine elementary maps and search for specific symbols and determine how they are used.

The Method of Evaluation.   Teacher judgment is one effective method for determining the student's comprehension of and ability to use symbols. As the class progresses through each phase of the lesson, the teacher notes the degree of success the students display during the doing part of the activities. The teacher watches to see if the student has the ability to explain verbally the use and meaning of particular symbols, the correct placement of symbols on a given map, and the correct location of a specific map symbol when given a verbal command. When students are informally working in a cooperative learning situation examining maps, locating specific symbols, talking and sharing thoughts and ideas, the teacher is available as a facilitator who works on the periphery of each group, noting the conversations that are taking place.

Casual observing is a "must" in a primary classroom. Judgments are made to determine if there is transfer of learning. The creative symbol-making activity shows the teacher, in a matter of moments, which students have grasped the idea that symbols are used for representational purposes.

Another technique for evaluating is to use a checklist. A checklist method requires that the teacher carefully select those process skills that she or he wants to observe the students performing. A copy of the skills list is needed for each student. The teacher works on a one-to-one basis with each student, checking each child through every item on the list. A checklist can also be used as a written verification of teacher judgments that were made previously.

Evaluating Human Relations Skills

The human relations skills in the social studies are those that characterize children as members of our culture, as U.S. citizens, and give them the personal attributes they will need to be successful in these roles. The student's self-identity is recognized and reaffirmed. The socialization processes are strengthened at school. Identifying and exploring the roles of young children in such groups as the family, play groups, learning group, and other similar groups is an important element of school learning. The behavior and adjustment of a particular student is an indicator of his or her individual socialization.

All of the human relations skills are presented at each grade level, not only where listed on Table 6–3.

Here is an example of a human relations skill for the primary level and some procedures for evaluation.

The Human Relations Skill Situation

A kindergarten teacher plans lessons and activities that stress the learning of human relations skills that are needed for entrance into the first grade.

Table 6-3   Ways of Evaluating Human Relations Skills in the Lower Grades

Grade Level	Human Relations Skills	Method of Evaluating
Kindergarten	*Accepting:* I am good at . . . At school I can . . .	Narrative and anecdotal records

First	*Accepting:*
	I like myself . . .
	My group(s) . . .
		Verbal contributions,
		    written (pictorial
		    representation)

Second	*Becoming:* participating showing respect caring	Anecdotal records Anecdotal records, checklists Narratives
Third	*Feeling:* good feelings feeling unsure sadness	Written Anecdotal records Written, verbal discussions

The areas of accepting, becoming, and feeling are very important for young learners to recognize and experience. The skill of accepting has many facets that students will encounter in their early school experience. Among them are:

1. Accepting oneself in different situations
2. Accepting others as they are
3. Accepting strengths and weaknesses
4. Adjusting to new situations
5. Coping with external stresses
6. Accepting security and trust
7. Learning responsibility
8. Accepting structure and order

The specific objective is to show students that each person is accepted as she or he is and each is a valued person. Activities are planned that focus on this idea. Frequent repetition is needed for young children to internalize a concept such as this one. Talking in small groups about such things as ''I am good at . . .'' and ''I want to get better at . . .'' is effective for this age level. Having the children draw all the things they can do well is another good activity.

The Method of Evaluation.   As with many other skills that must be taught at the kindergarten level, written evaluation is almost impossible due to the developmental level of the learner. The drawing lesson suggested is one paper assignment that can be used to determine whether or not the student actually knows what he or she does well. An extension of this activity is to have a mini conference with each student and to ask him or her to tell you about what he or she has drawn. This gives the teacher an opportunity to determine the student's perception of the skills he or she can perform well.

Anecdotal records and narratives are easy to use, convenient, and adaptable for many different skill areas. Having an index card available for each child makes it easy to record particular incidents when the student shows an accepting behavior. This is a concrete way to reinforce teacher judgment, and it provides specific information for the parents at reporting time. The part of the lesson where the students elaborated on the things they want to ''get better at'' gives parents another insight into their child's development and gives them a specific area they can help their child work on at home.

School and home cooperation is always a goal. A simple narrative, in paragraph form, gives parents specific information regarding their child's skill development. It is also perceived as a very personal means of communication from the teacher. Consider the effect of a report such as this:

Skill: Accepting

Michael consistently accepts responsibility for his learning tasks here at school. He makes friends easily and is a friend to others. He makes good contributions in group situations and often tries to help others. He is learning to follow our school rules. He shows evidence of being self-confident and enjoys doing his best. He will need to work on accepting mistakes as a part of learning.

This type of reporting and evaluating clearly states the child's strengths (being responsible, making friends, verbal skills, good work habits) and the areas that need improvement (following rules, accepting mistakes). Evaluation methods that determine what has been learned and what needs to be learned are especially valuable to students and parents. It also gives the teacher information for future planning.

Evaluating Upper-Elementary Students

It is very important to evaluate upper-elementary students for two reasons. One, you need to know what they already know so you do not reteach previously learned material. Two, you need to find out if you are achieving your objectives as you teach. Evaluation of upper-elementary students is more structured and formal than with lower-elementary students because they have better-developed skills in areas such as reading and writing, thinking, coordination, memorization, and problem solving. We test for specific information or behaviors by explicitly asking for the information or for the performance of a task. We have several different evaluation techniques available to us, but we must remember that any evaluation method or instrument that takes too much time or effort for the results produced will not be very useful or usable.

The teacher must be constantly aware of the students' performance on daily learning activities. Participation during group or individual activities, as well as the performance level on written assignments, gives the teacher an ongoing indication of how individuals are grasping the material. A daily grade in the teacher's grade book is not required, however. The observation skills of the teacher play a significant role in evaluation and become more acute with experience.

Some students do not perform well during written test situations. For these individuals, the performance on daily work should be considered as an important factor in their educational growth. Individual circumstances must be considered.

Effective teaching does not require a grade on every paper a student completes. Grading every practice paper or workbook page can be cumbersome. Select those papers that you determine to be the most appropriate for checking the progress toward the specific objective. Spot checking specific items on all papers does give you an idea of the students' performance. Work should have some comment or mark on it so the students and parents know the effort has been evaluated in some way.

The Pretest

Why do teachers administer pretests and how are the results used? Teachers use the pretest before a unit or new task to find out what and how much the students already know about it. The pretest is an efficient, reliable means of determining the degree of retention of the product, process, and human relations skills taught at the previous grade level(s). For a fourth grader, those social studies skills can be rather extensive, and for a sixth grader, even more so. The pretest also serves as a quick check of learned skills for new students who enter in the middle of the year.

An effective, usable pretest does not have to be long and cumbersome. Selecting test items that are to the point and definitive, and that will yield the kind of information you want to know, makes it possible for the entire task to be presented in 25 test items or less. Such a test does not take very long for the students to do nor does it take too long to correct.

How does the teacher use the results of a pretest? If the individual test items are carefully written, the student responses will indicate what is already known and retained about the topic in question. Test results that reveal significant previous knowledge tell the teacher that the learner objectives should be set at a higher level, if presented at all. It is possible the teacher may decide not to present this particular unit, but only review it before moving ahead to another unit. On the other hand, test results that show little retention or weak comprehension tell the teacher that this unit needs to be emphasized. In addition, re-teaching specific skills from previous grades may be necessary.

The results of a well-planned pretest assist the teacher in determining the range of performance in the class. A small differential indicates that a closely organized strategy may be the best choice for teaching the unit. A wide range of scores indicates that performance grouping, individualizing, or some other lesson modification may be required. More teaching time is needed for a unit when the pretest results show a wide range of scores. An analysis of the pretest will show the teacher which specific elements of the unit need the most teaching time, which need the least, and which may be eliminated entirely. In this way the teacher plans to make the best possible use of the time available for teaching and learning. Figure 6–3 shows a sample pretest for a fifth-grade geography unit.

This sample pretest for the geography portion of a unit on the northeastern states gives more than one type of test item. Included are some multiple choice, true-false, free response, and short narratives. The text extension provides an opportunity for the higher-performing students to give their full input and expand upon ideas. A test extension of some type is a good testing technique because all the students have the opportunity to try it. The open format may reduce the test stress of some learners and significant or unexpected information may result. Information is the goal, not perfect punctuation and grammar.

Formative Evaluation

Formative evaluation should tell the teacher how the students are doing at certain points in the unit. The tests are designed to give the teacher information that shows the direction of learning and the rate of achievement for each student. The teacher uses formative evaluation to look carefully at what is being taught, what is being learned, and what to do next. Actually, formative evaluation is an ongoing procedure—the teacher must maintain a constant awareness of what is going on in the classroom so that lessons can be continued, modified, or retaught. Not all formative evaluation is formally structured or in written form. It may be as simple as a look at the students' work or a question-and-answer session, or it may be a structured written test.

A formative test can be one that is a part of the evaluation module of a particular textbook series, or it can be teacher designed. The test that accompanies the textbook evaluates the specific goals and objectives of each unit. Textbook authors use care in the writing of their testing programs so that the tests will correlate with the lessons presented in the text. The teacher who adds out-of-text material to the lesson will have to develop her or his own test materials. A very important point to remember is that formative testing is not used to evaluate goal completion, but rather to determine if the students are moving toward mastery learning of the material.

Figure 6-3 Sample: Pretest

Name: _____   Date: _____
Unit: Geography: The Northeastern States

1. Name the northeastern group of states.

2. Which of the following physical features would you expect to find in this
   region?
   a. forests   e. glaciers
   b. river systems   f. lakes
   c. deserts   g. lowlands
   d. mountains   h. sparse vegetation

3. The northeastern states are located within which of these zones?
   a. the high latitudes   c. the low latitudes
   b. the middle latitudes   d. none of these

4. The natural boundaries of this group of states are which of the following?
   a. Canada   d. the Mississippi River
   b. Mexico   e. the state of New York
   c. the Atlantic Ocean

5. Due to its geological history, the land in this region is:
   a. flat, level plains   c. rough and rocky
   b. wet and swampy   d. dry and desertlike

6. The climate of this region
   a. has four seasons   b. has summer only

7. Some of the natural resources for this area are which of the following:
   a. lumber   e. textiles
   b. farm products   f. mines and quarries
   c. fishing   g. good soil
   d. power sources   h. clean air

8. Honest, hard-working people are considered an important "resource" to a
   region.
        True   False
   Give some reasons for your choice.

9. The nearness of waterways and river systems contributes to a region's
   geographical well-being.
        True   False
   List three reasons why or why not.

10. The soil will always grow our food, no matter what we do to it.
        True   False

11. A clean environment has no effect on the geography of an area.
        True   false

(continued)

Figure 6-3 (*continued*)

12. The wind, rain, snow, and other elements change the physical features of the land.

    True   False

13. The term *geography* means:
    a. the longitude and latitude of a region
    b. the products of a region
    c. the natural aspects and features of a region

14. This represents the distances east and west on the earth's surface and is expressed in hours and minutes or degrees. What is it?
    a. longitude   c. latitude
    b. the equator   d. none of these

15. In your own words, describe the following:
    a. peninsula   c. continent
    b. bay   d. latitude

16. The geography of an area affects the number and variety of animals it can support. List three physical features the northeasern states must have for animals to survive.

17. The ecology of the northeastern states is:
    a. very important
    b. not very important
    c. acceptable the way it is now

18. The geography of this area has some influence on the development of business and industry. Choose one that you know and give your supporting data.

19. The northeastern states are important to the future of our country. List the reasons why this is true.

20. If the ecology of the northeastern states is endangered, then . . . Write your response below.

Test Extension
21. In this space, you may write anything else you know about the northeastern group of states. You may write as much as you wish within the limits of the class.

Summative Evaluation

Summative evaluation is used to determine if long-range goals and terminal objectives have been met. A unit on Cities, for example, may take several weeks to complete. A summative evaluation is administered at the end to evaluate the goal achievement of the students for that entire unit. Quite often, summative evaluation will take the form of a posttest. The posttest is more comprehensive than a pretest that measures prior knowledge, or a formative test that measures sections of learning over a shorter period of time. A summative test for a unit or chapter is designed to evaluate the learning of the factual information presented in the unit, the main ideas and general concepts, and the attainment of the terminal objectives.

The results help to determine the readiness of the individual and class for the next unit or group of skill objectives. The test scores identify the students who require remediation in specific areas. Summative evaluation enables the teacher to determine the appropriateness and effectiveness of the specific lesson. The test results may yield information about particular materials, strategies, and techniques that were particularly effective as well as those that need to be reevaluated and either modified or discarded.

Valuable information on the content taught, the students' learning, and the teacher's planning skills can be obtained. Summative evaluation and the results should be considered within the total schema of curriculum planning for social studies. Successes as well as problem areas should be noted for future planning.

The Teacher-Student Conference

The teacher-student conference is an evaluation technique that has particular benefits for upper-elementary students. The conference format is a personal, one-on-one opportunity for the student to give information to the teacher. Factual learning can be evaluated. Discussing, explaining, paraphrasing, justifying, and other higher-level thinking skills can be verbalized. The conference provides an opportunity for those students who do not test well on written instruments to communicate verbally what they know. The age of upper-elementary students as well as the higher-level verbal skills contribute to the success and appropriateness of this technique.

Using the conference for evaluation requires preparation. Examine some of the elements that contribute to a successful teacher-student conference.

Content.   Exactly what is to be evaluated? A written test determines the learning, the achieving, the internalization of specified objectives. A conference should strive to achieve similar goals. Determining whether or not the student has grasped the main ideas, the important facts, and the skills contained in the unit are the main purposes of the conference. The teacher selects conference topics in each of these categories. All of the conference items should be written in advance so that none are omitted.

Start the conference with the factual data that are being evaluated. This could be in the form of some true-false or multiple-choice questions. Some short-answer items are appropriate. Then give the student a chance to volunteer any information he or she wishes to elaborate upon. Provide some time for the student to tell things he or she did not understand or could not perform during the unit, and make note of these contributions.

The teacher can now move into evaluating the higher-level thinking and processing skills that can be difficult to assess in written form. This is where the student can verbalize ideas, explain, question, and elaborate while interacting with the teacher. Use Bloom's taxonomy to evaluate at different levels. Items may follow along these lines:

1. Tell me everything you remember about the colonists' voyage to the New World.   (Knowledge)

2. What are the possible outcomes of acid rain upon the Great Lakes?   (Comprehension)

3. Use the laws the Pilgrims established for the colonies and explain how they would affect daily life in a space colony.   (Application)

4. Tell the reasons why the laws established by the southern plantation owners were so well adapted to their particular life-style.   (Analysis)

5. Design a set of laws for a space colony.   (Synthesis)

6. Our school has a set of rules that we all try to remember. Explain why you feel they are good or not good for our school.   (Evaluation)

These samples of conference questions cover different subjects. Those actually used during a conference would center on one unit.

The Time.   Conducting a teacher-student conference with an entire class of students requires a time commitment. Daily schedules are already full, but effective teachers somehow find the time to do what they consider necessary and important. Here are some possible ways to find the necessary time for conference with students:

1. Use the morning homeroom time before the scheduled classes begin.

2. Use a study period.

3. Use the library period when no specific assignments are planned.

4. Schedule a part of each social studies period to be used for conferencing when needed.

5. Some parents may be willing to bring their child to school before the required time for the conference. Some students may be willing to stay after school.

6. Use your preparation period.

7. Consider other possible times you might be able to use.

As skilled as a teacher is in finding these blocks of time, it still may not be possible to schedule a conference with every student at the culmination of each unit.

An effective teacher-student conference can easily be conducted in fifteen minutes. Keeping on task is important. Social conversation and other interruptions must be avoided if you are to complete the conference in a reasonable time.

Not every student needs this method of evaluation. Use it for those students who will benefit the most, but plan to provide every student with this learning experience at some time during the year.

Conducting the Conference.   The teacher-student conference should be as nonthreatening as possible for the student. Both teacher and student should be comfortable. (The student will be reasonably comfortable if a good trust level has been established in the classroom.) Being cognizant of body language will add to the atmosphere you want to establish. Relax, look at the student, and try to keep any writing of notes or checkmarks as inconspicuous as possible. Get right to the task at hand and keep the flow of the conference going without rushing the student. Be sure that you give the child a chance to talk, and really listen to what he or she is trying to say.

The major objective of evaluating upper-elementary students is to determine what is being learned and to what degree. The secondary objective is that the results will be used to help the students learn more effectively in the subsequent lessons. Evaluation should always be approached with a positive perspective: to improve learning and to assist in more effective planning. The procedures presented in this section are intended as a guide to examine some methods that can be used in the upper-elementary grades. Teacher judgment, checklists, narratives, and anecdotal records are also appropriate at this level with the criteria adjusted to meet the needs of older students.

Teachers frequently design and implement their own personal methods of evaluation. This process requires a thorough knowledge and understanding of the social studies curriculum for a particular grade. A teacher should identify the content she or he is attempting to evaluate before designing the method to evaluate it. Expected learner outcomes, content, fairness, consistency, and practicality are some of the elements to be considered.

Any evaluative process should be used to help students learn and grow—not to judge or label in a negative way. Schools are the setting in which subjects are taught to children, and the evaluation techniques should reflect this. Evaluation is used to determine if the students are learning what they need to know now and for the future. This pertains to both formal and informal evaluations. Evaluation must be done in some way, so do it in the manner that is the best for students and for your teaching.

Planning a Questioning Strategy

If you visit an elementary classroom and observe the teachers, you will find that they are constantly asking questions. The questions may provoke thought, ask for recall information, or alert the students to important information. They may demand specific answers or allow very general responses. Whatever the type of question, the teacher has a reason for asking it and an expectation of a specific type of an answer. Asking questions is an integral part of teaching and as such requires careful planning. Planning a questioning strategy that enhances the overall lesson plan is an important part of instructional planning.

Questions are statements of inquiry that call for a reply. They may be interrogative such as, "What is the capital of Michigan?" or they may be declarative such as, "Tell the class how you would help Angie learn the rules of our school library." Both statements call for a reply and expect the student to reveal knowledge of the subject under discussion. You may not always get the response you want, especially with younger children, but responses will give you an insight into the child's understanding of the question, the subject, and/or the interest in the lesson.

The questioning part of any lesson is a key factor in gathering information for evaluation. Evaluation allows the teacher to know what to do next. Questioning at the beginning of a lesson serves as a pretest. Questioning during the lesson reinforces material being presented and provides the teacher with a means of determining if the information is being received and if the concepts are being grasped. It allows the teacher to determine which individuals are having trouble understanding the lesson. Questions at the end of the presentation summarize the lesson, reinforce the material taught, and provide the teacher with information about how well his or her objectives were met.

Good questions cause children to perform. Low-level questions that require factual or rote memory answers force the students to demonstrate that they have learned, or at least committed to memory, the factual information that was presented to them. Higher-level questions require them to use the information learned to develop answers that show understanding or insight.

What Is a Questioning Strategy?

Because questions are an integral part of teaching, it stands to reason that teachers should seriously consider the questions they ask. Think of a questioning strategy as being a planned procedure to elicit appropriate responses from an individual or group during a lesson.

Questioning strategies are important because they are one of the ways teachers determine whether or not lesson objectives are being processed and understood. The strategy should be planned along with the other parts of the lesson. It is not possible to write down all of the questions you will ask, but key questions can be formulated in advance. Choose specific questions that are structured to the level of the students and the needs of the lesson.

Most of the questions that teachers ask are not preplanned. Teachers ask key questions and, based on the responses received, ask new questions. Questioning is a constant prodding of the mind. Experience makes the process easier. You know what you are trying to teach and must decide what type of information you want from your students. You cannot plan all of your questions, but you can decide on your strategy with an awareness of the types of questions you want to ask and then formulate them as needed.

As a final note, flexibility is a virtue in questioning, as in all other facets of teaching. If what you are doing is not producing the desired results, do not be afraid to change and try something different. Should you decide that your questions are not getting the responses you want, change strategies. You may have to be inventive, but that is good teaching. An awareness of questioning strategies and the different kinds of questions that you can ask will help you make the adjustment.

Questions . . . and Answers

Writing the perfect question is not enough. You begin the questioning process by asking your question. What is the student's response to your question and what is your response to his or her response? Asking a question does not automatically guarantee that you will get a desired response. High-level questions may generate low-level answers, or students may not be ready to give you the type of answer you want. There is always the possibility that you have not taught your students how to answer your questions. They must know what you want.

This teacher is using a map as her source of questions.

Do you want a long detailed answer or a short concise answer? Familiarity with you and your tactics will help the students know how to answer your questions. At the beginning of the school year you will hear the refrain, "That's not the way we did it in Mrs. Lewis's class." Well, Mrs. Lewis taught her students her way, now they must learn your way. When questioning, tell the students what type of answers you want. Teaching is not a guessing game between students and the teacher.

You have asked a question and the student has answered it. Now what? Your response to the student's response is as important as the question you so carefully constructed. It is important to remember that you make two responses—oral and attitudinal. Your attitudinal response will say much more to the student than your oral response. Students are very adept at "reading the teacher" in an effort to please him or her, and nowhere is this more evident than in answering the teacher's questions.

Your oral response to a student's answer will take one of these forms:

1. *Accepting or rejecting*: Some questions demand only a right or wrong response and the teacher responds, "Yes, that is correct" or "No, that's wrong." This response is usually associated with factual material and memory-recall questions.

2. *Asking for additional information or clarification*: This response is used when trying to get the student to really think about a topic. Follow-up questions such as, "Can you think of anything else?" or "Is there more you want to add to that?" force the student to think deeper about the topic and prevent short, general answers.

3. *Referring the question to another student for more information*: A question designed to initiate discussion or divergent answers can be handled this way. The teacher accepts an answer, without prejudging it, and asks another student to answer the same question. An example of this response might be, "An interesting answer, Jack. How would you answer the question, Martha?" or "Some good points, Bill, but do you agree with him, Jean? How would you change his answer?" When using this type of response, be careful not to prejudice the first answer or you will not get the discussion you want. A response such as, "Great answer, Sue. You really know your material. How would you answer the question, Randy?" will insure the same answer from Randy or any other student in the class: "Same as Sue did." There goes your discussion on that question.

There are many combinations and variations on these three basic responses. The most important thing to remember is that responses must work with the purpose designed into the question. High-level, thought-invoking questions do not always provoke high-level, thoughtful answers, but careful responses to the answers may.

Think Time

Have you ever been asked a question but not allowed to answer it? This happens to many students everyday. Teachers tend to get in a hurry and demand answers immediately. Research, especially that conducted by Mary Budd Rowe,[1] has shown that teachers tend to wait only a very short time, usually three to eight seconds (shorter time for slower students, longer time for faster students), before either going on to another student or giving clues. It seems that teachers really do dislike silence even when students need it.

When questions are asked, it is important to allow sufficient think time. Ask the question then give students time to think about it. This time is necessary for the following reasons:

1. It gives students time to comprehend the question. What is the teacher asking? What does she really want to know?

2. It allows students time to organize their thoughts and eliminate extraneous bits of information that are not germane to the question.

3. It increases the probability of getting a better answer with pertinent elaboration.

4. It reduces student anxiety. Students know they will have time to think about the question and not be forced into immediate, unsure responses.

5. It encourages students to try some risk-taking strategies after having had time to consider the question.

6. It may provide the needed impetus for the reluctant responders to participate more actively in the lesson.

How much think time is enough? Each student or group of students has particular requirements. The teacher may have to experiment to determine the needs of each particular group. The idea is to resist the tendency to ask a question and immediately call on the first student who indicates a willingness to respond. Try counting to ten before you do anything. This may not seem very long until you try it. Ten seconds of silence is an eternity for the teacher, but it is needed think time for the students. Good questioning and answering skills take time, planning, and practice.

Group and Individual Questioning

Posing a question to the entire group of students serves two purposes: it demands a group student response or it gives the group time to think of an answer but only one student (or a few) is called on to respond. This strategy allows all of the students to think about the question, and each to have an opportunity to be the one chosen to respond. It allows the student to mentally compare her or his answer to the one(s) actually given. Suppose a question is asked of an individual: "Kevin, explain the difference between latitude and longitude." Directing the question to one particular student sends a message to all the other students that they do not have to think about or try to answer the question. The spotlight and burden is on Kevin. Everyone waits on him alone while he tries to think of an answer. If he responds correctly, the teacher will either ask another question or move on to another part of the lesson. This is not group questioning.

On the other hand, suppose the teacher says, "Let's all think about latitude and longitude. Who can explain them?" This question is addressed to the entire group. All of the students are asked to consider the question, and each one has an equal chance of being called on for the answer. After sufficient think time has elapsed, a number of individuals indicate their readiness to respond. The teacher may choose to call on one of them or a nonresponder. The key is that everyone is asked to think—even though only one is asked to respond.

Another form of group questioning is the total student response technique. The teacher poses a question and all students respond verbally, en masse, or by displaying individual response cards. This is a valuable reinforcing technique, especially for very young children.

Individual questioning strategies are planned to elicit individual responses. For example, you might say, "Mary, give five reasons why the St. Lawrence Seaway was built." There are numerous reasons to use this strategy:

1. The class is doing a brainstorming activity in which every child is called on and all answers are acceptable.

2. You are attempting to get a nonverbal or unresponsive child to participate. Direct questions do not allow the child to hide.

3. Personal recognition of a student shows that you are interested in the child's knowledge and performance. Care should be exercised to make this a positive experience rather than a threatening one.

4. This is a quick way to check on an individual's comprehension and/or keep her on task.

5. Sometimes you need to change strategies to provide for variety in questioning.

Students need the opportunity to show their own individual talents and knowledge and to be recognized for their efforts. It is important that teachers allow this, but they must be careful not to use individual questioning to humiliate, punish, or catch students in weak moments. It is a teaching tool, not a whip.

Questioning for Divergent and Convergent Thinking

In a questioning strategy, the teacher is trying to elicit particular responses in an effort to direct the students' attention in a specific direction. Divergent and convergent questions direct the gathering, processing, and focusing of information.

Divergent Questioning.   Divergent questions direct students in many directions in search of various possible answers. They are most effectively used in the earlier stages of a lesson when students are developing interest in a topic and are seeking information. Divergent questions are generally open ended, allowing many possible responses with no definite right or wrong answers. They are very effective for brainstorming or creating an interaction of ideas for open discussion. As thought questions, they allow students to listen to or read about different points of view, opinions, and explanations before answering. This requires more gathering and sorting of information and creative thinking is encouraged. Some examples of divergent questions are:

1. How many ways can you send a message to a friend across town?
2. Name some ways that we use transportation to get our food.
3. Design your version of a pioneer cabin.
4. Pretend you are a senator. What is your plan to clear the litter from our highways?

Look at the examples and note they are not restricted to one distinct answer. There are many possibilities and each student can have his or her own answer.

Convergent Questioning.   Convergent questions focus on one answer and tend to be remembering types of questions. For instance, students are called on to remember specific textbook information and responses are verifiable as right or wrong. Convergent questions are designed to converge on the correct answer.

Convergent questions are most often used at the end of a lesson to affect closure. After many possibilities have been examined, convergent questions concentrate on the main points of the lesson. Students then know what the answer is and can relate to what they were supposed to learn. Some examples of convergent questions are:

1. What is the capital of Texas?
2. Show me the picture of an igloo.
3. Who is the president of the United States?
4. Name four tribes of Plains Indians.

All of these questions demand a single answer, even the fourth question. Although there are more than four tribes to choose from, there is no debate or alternate possibilities to the answer. It is either right or wrong.

In convergent and divergent questioning, the key words in the questions are the verbs you select. Using verbs such as *show, produce, diagram, develop, hypothesize,* or *design* determine the thinking processes that are necessary to answer the question. *Show, produce,* and *diagram* are verbs that call for a convergent response. *Develop, hypothesize,* and *design* require a divergent response. Look at Figure 6–4 and decide if the verb would promote a convergent or a divergent response. Also determine if the verb would be more appropriate for primary, upper, or all grade levels. Be sure to think of each verb and the kind of response it will invoke. Try writing a question using the verbs to help you to determine your choice.

There are many other key words that teachers use for composing ques-

Figure 6-4 Some Key Words for Questioning Strategies

Key Verbs	Convergent	Divergent	Primary	Upper	All
describe					
demonstrate					
outline					
change					
build					
make believe					
organize					
model					
design					
compare					
find out					
modify					
reconstruct					
create					
solve					
list					

tions. They could be a motivational, developmental or evaluative type of word. Can you think of any more? You might want to brainstorm some ideas with a group.

Formative and Summative Questioning

Formative questions are those that provide feedback to the teacher regarding the progress of the lesson, or more specifically, the students' comprehension and application of the lesson objectives. Formative questions are asked during the instructional phase and are ongoing. The specific responses the teacher is given indicate the need for lesson modifications and/or adjustments of various kinds.

Summative questions are those used for evaluative purposes. A summative question is cumulative, concise, and is part of the closure procedure. It is convergent in that the teacher is seeking a response that is a result of the learning that has occurred. Therefore, a summative question is most effective at the end of a lesson. Intermittent quiz questions would be formative (evaluating as learning is occurring) and chapter or unit test questions would be summative (evaluating after learning has occurred). The timing for these questions is the key issue, not necessarily the structural form.

Bloom's Questioning Strategy

Teachers ask questions to find out what a learner knows and to encourage thinking. Bloom's taxonomy[2] provides a convenient framework for developing a questioning strategy to help teachers do this. Questions at the lower level require answers based on knowledge, whereas those at a higher level require the application of knowledge. Unfortunately, many teachers tend to ask only low-level questions and never really require students to think about and apply what they have learned. This does not mean that teachers should stop asking low-level questions and ask only high-level ones, however. Plan your questioning strategy so that you ask questions appropriate to your lesson.

Level One—Knowledge

The Level of Simple Recall: Questions ask for factual information and answers are either right or wrong.

Use: To find out if the individual knows, or has memorized, the factual information in the lesson.

Examples:

1. Name the first president of the United States.
2. Who is the president now?
3. Where does he live?
4. Which branch of the government does he head?

Level Two—Comprehension

The Level of Understanding: Questions ask for reasons. Answers are usually right or wrong.

Use: To find out if the knowledge learned has meaning to the individual. Can the student make a personal interpretation of the factual information?

Examples:

1. What do you think the president does?
2. In your own words, explain how the president gets elected.
3. Explain what the title Commander-in-Chief means.

Level Three—Application

The Level of Usage: Questions usually ask for ways to use knowledge and allow for individual creativity. There may be more than one correct answer.

Use: To find out if the learner can transfer knowledge to a new or unique situation. (This is the first chance for the student to use what he or she knows.)

Examples:

1. How can we select a class president?
2. What duties will our president have?
3. Can a woman meet the requirements for president?

Level Four—Analysis

The Level of Relationships and Intent: Questions ask for comparisons to be made or for component parts of an idea. Answers are more divergent and personal.

Use: To find out if the learner can review information logically to determine the intent of the information. Can the student see patterns and relationships in the data?

Examples:

1. How does the role of the Canadian Prime Minister compare to that of the President of the United States?
2. What would have happened if Washington had decided to continue as president after his second term?
3. How are the Republicans and Democrats alike? Different?

Level Five—Synthesis

The Level of Ideas: Questions ask students for ideas for new or different solutions to problems. Answers are creative and divergent; there is no one correct answer.

Use: To find out if students can combine knowledge and ideas into new and creative solutions to problems. Can they use all they know?

Examples:

1. A space habitat has just been built and people are living there. Develop a government for these people.
2. How would you change the Presidency?
3. Plan a campaign for class president.

Level Six—Evaluation

The Level of Judgment: Questions ask students to make value judgments about ideas of their own or others. Answers are very personal, divergent, and sometimes argumentative.

Use: To allow students to express their own position and question the position of others. (This forces students to make and defend value judgments.)

Examples:

1. If you were a voter in 1786, would you be for or against Washington for a third term as president?
2. Who is your favorite president and why?
3. Should we have a woman or a minority president?

As you look at these six levels of questioning, keep in mind that higher is not necessarily better. All levels have a purpose and your task is to select the appropriate level question for your lesson. You may use questions from several levels in the same lesson.

All levels of Bloom's taxonomy can be used in all grade levels. Kindergartners can make value judgments (level 6) as can sixth graders. The same degree of sophistication is not there, but they do have their own values and reasons. You have to tailor your questions to the ability of the students and allow for answers commensurate with their abilities.

Asking a high-level question does not always produce a high-level answer. You may have to repeat the question or ask for more information to get an answer that is equal to your question. Do not be surprised to find that you have to teach children how to answer questions. Until they know what kind of answer you want, children try to give the shortest and easiest answer possible.

Written Questions

This chapter examines questioning strategies as one element of planning for instruction. These questioning strategies are verbal; the teacher asks a question during the instructional phase and the students respond verbally. This verbal interaction between teacher and students is not the total extent of questioning in the elementary social studies lesson. There is also a written questioning process that teachers use. Before proceeding, refer to Figure 6–5 and examine your personal feelings about written evaluations for social studies.

This self-examination highlights some prevalent thoughts regarding written testing for elementary students. It is by no means complete. It is important for you to think about your feelings and attitudes about written evaluations. If your attitude about testing is generally positive (you have low test anxiety), then testing situations in your classroom will probably be positive and supportive. Conversely, if your attitude toward testing is negative (you have high test anxiety) or if you feel insecure about testing children, you will have to work at not allowing those feelings to unduly influence your students.

Examine Figure 6–5 and note how you rated each one. Consider these areas in terms of how you marked each item:

1. Difficulty factors
   Difficult for children to do
   Too difficult for the teacher to design
   Difficulties in interpretation and justification

2. Appropriateness factors
   Ages of the students
   Performance levels of the students
   Content factors
   School-community attitudes

3. Format factors
   Verbal and written questioning
   True-false, essay, multiple choice, others
   Wording and phrasing of the items
   Written for primary or upper elementary

As you proceed through this chapter your positive attitudes and feelings about written evaluation will be strengthened, and your negative or unsure attitudes will be clarified, modified, or changed. With experience and practice, test writing and administering becomes less anxious and stressful.

Constructing Written Questions. Written questions are used in several ways. They are an effective tool for pretesting, to determine what the students already know about a subject before it is taught. Written questions are also used on specific daily assignments for information gathering. In addition, they are used

Figure 6-5   A Self-Examination: Written Questioning for Elementary Students

Item	Agree	Disagree
1. Written questions for primary learners are both unnecessary and inappropriate.		
2. I am unsure exactly how to write good questions for primary children.		
3. Nonreaders are unable to perform on a written activity.		
4. Written assignments tend to be factual in nature.		
5. Written questions in the text are all I will need to teach social studies.		
6. Teacher-made tests are difficult to justify to parents and administrators.		
7. Test-taking skills are unnecessary for primary children.		
8. Informal evaluative measures are adequate.		
9. Readability levels on tests are so difficult to establish that writing test questions becomes overwhelming.		
10. Verbal questioning strategies and written questioning strategies are essentially the same.		
11. Tests are too difficult to write.		
12. Questions for the affective domain are difficult to compose.		
13. Children have difficulty responding to an essay (short-answer) item.		
14. I feel the most comfortable with a multiple-choice test.		
15. For upper-elementary children, an essay item requires upper-level thinking processes.		
16. Primary children can tell me their responses for certain test items and I can record for them individually.		
17. Take-home tests are acceptable for upper-elementary students.		
18. Test results are too difficult to explain to children; they are primarily for my use.		
19. Written questioning strategies are most useful for summative purposes.		
20. Written questioning tends to be more elaborative than verbal questioning.		

for evaluation purposes at the end of a lesson or unit in the culmination activities. Can you think of other ways a teacher might use written questions?

Regardless of when written questions are used in the lesson, the construction of the questions is most important. What are the specific parts of a question that contribute to its effectiveness? Consider these:

Directionality: Is the question directed to an individual or to the group at large? Some questions may be written for a specific student.

Classification: Is the question asking for a convergent or divergent response?

Application: Is the question being used as part of a formative or a summative strategy?

Level of response: Is the question asking for a low-level response (recall) or for a higher level of thinking? (Bloom's taxonomy)

Vocabulary: Are the words within the reading and speaking comprehension levels of the class?

These elements need to be considered when constructing written questions for both primary and upper-elementary students. Look at the following question examples and their particular elements.

Sample Questions

1. "Lance, list at least ten products we get from trees and how you can use each in a new way."

   Explanation: Lance is a high-potential first grader; all of his scores on the Stanford Achievement Test are above the 90th percentile. This question is an individualized item, especially for Lance, on the unit test for Forests. It is used for summative purposes. It calls for a higher-level response; specifically, it is an application type of question. The listing part of the question can rename the products that were presented in the unit, but is not limiting to only those. The student is asked to create a new application for each item he chooses. The wording is appropriate for a high-performing student.

2. "Billy, draw five (5) things that come from trees."

   Explanation: Billy is a low-performing first grader with limited reading and writing skills. This question is designed specifically for him. He can recognize and read his name independently. The words *draw*, *circle*, and *underline* are good choices for low-performing students because they are learned very early in first grade. The number word *five* is followed by the numeral for further clarification. The teacher would give Billy the opportunity to read the item independently, and assist only as needed. This recall question is summative and divergent and the vocabulary is appropriate.

3. "We have been studying the forestry industry in the northeastern states and Canada. Develop a set of criteria to determine the environmental advisability of harvesting a forested region, and assess the value of each item in your set."

Explanation: This question is for an upper-elementary class. It is a group question that calls for a divergent response. This test item is a higher-level thinking question that requires both synthesis and evaluation. It asks the student to devise a set of criteria (synthesis) and to make judgments (evaluation) on each item.

4. "The organization of the logging camp plays an important role in the successful operation of the forestry industry. Project ahead about fifteen years from now. Design a functional logging camp site and include one new machine. This test project is due in three days."

Explanation: This is an example of a take-home test item for the upper grades. It is a group-oriented item; everyone is expected to do the project. This type of project is especially for those students who excel in the creative areas. Their camp site may be drawn in pencil, painted, or represented in a three-dimensional form such as a diorama or a model. Their new machine may be constructed with boxes and cardboard tubes of varying sizes. The project statement is open ended enough for creative interpretations. This is an example of synthesis. The various working elements of the logging camp must be taken into consideration and be workable in the new camp design for the future. The students are asked to invent something new that will be assimilated into the new camp.

These four examples are given to show how appropriate questions can be written for both primary and upper-grade students. Note that an upper-level thinking question does not need to be long. The length of the question has nothing to do with the specific level of thinking that is being addressed, as in the item designed for Lance. Short questions are not necessarily easier to answer either. Billy's question might be very challenging for him if he is to complete it successfully. The topics of forests, forestry, and logging are part of several social studies programs. The subject is highlighted here to show the range of one topic from the first grade to an upper grade. Mary Thomas Farrar poses this idea: "Both reason and recall questions can be phrased to require responses of varying lengths and varying difficulty while still covering the same content."[3] Keep this in mind when you construct questions.

Writing a Social Studies Test

Good questions are worded clearly, call for responses within a specific level of comprehension, focus on the learning objective, and cover both the verbal and nonverbal activities of the lesson.

One use of written questions is for tests. Testing is a part of the elementary program and will continue to be so, whether in its present forms or in new and innovative forms. Prewritten tests for the social studies are available with textbooks, practice books, and other supplementary materials. These tests are convenient, uniform, and easy to correct. They are a valuable teaching tool and should not be underrated. Using a prewritten testing instrument is a good place for new teachers to start.

Standardized tests are an integral part of evaluation in elementary schools. It is a common practice to test various grades to determine academic achievement, usually in the spring of the year. Parents and the school want to know how their children are doing compared with others in the class, in the state, and in the nation. If primary students are to perform well on these very formal tests, they must have opportunities to practice taking written tests. Teacher-made tests provide one method for these practice sessions.

There are times and situations in which a teacher-made test is most appropriate. Constructing your own social studies test requires that you thoroughly understand what you are teaching before you can construct a valid test to evaluate it. Writing a test is an extension of planning and organizing. Here are some advantages to writing your own test:

1. You can test your own objectives.
2. You can meet the specific needs of a particular class (or student).
3. You can adjust the readability level as needed.
4. Once the test is written, you can modify it for use with another class. (Some elementary schools departmentalize for some subjects.)
5. You can make the test as challenging as you think necessary.
6. Your own test can include a variety of question types, learning styles, and formats.
7. You will determine the criteria for success.

You have decided that you are going to write your own test. How do you start? What should you try to avoid? Before you actually write anything, be sure that you are totally familiar with the entire unit or segment you have just completed and that the specific objectives are clearly in mind. Your main ideas and factual data are definite. When thinking of factual data, concentrate on the important facts and concepts, not the isolated or trivial ones. Decide on the levels of responses you want and the format that is most suitable.

What are some things to avoid? Test writing is not easy and there are some traps to keep in mind. Trick questions or ambiguous statements have no place in tests or other written assignments for children. The students are working on successful completion of a task, not at being clever enough to decipher trick questions! Long questions that go on forever are confusing. State each item clearly with no superfluous wording. Avoid using vocabulary that was not used in the lessons or that is not in the speaking and reading vocabulary of the class. Also be careful with formatting the test. A test that is crowded is visually confusing, especially for students who are anxious about testing. Avoid these pitfalls when beginning to write your first test. You will probably find others as you construct tests.

When you are constructing written questions for your class, either as part of a daily assignment, a quiz, or a test, it may be helpful for you to use a labeling system that indicates the level of difficulty for each item. The following symbols are used in the Allyn and Bacon social studies series.[4]

→ Easy to solve

• Harder to solve—more thinking is needed

★ Something extra—maybe for homework

Testing Primary Students: Some Concerns.   Preparing a written social studies test for primary students requires particular attention to the reading and writing abilities of the class. Although younger children, especially kindergarten and first-grade youngsters, are just beginning to read and perform minimal paper-and-pencil tasks, it is not impossible to prepare a written test they can complete successfully. Although most of the social studies for this age group is activity-, listening-, and experiencing-oriented, written activities are introduced at appropriate times. Learning how to do lessons on paper is an important experience for young children and they should have many opportunities to perform them in the classroom.

A functional test for lower-grade (K–2) children is largely teacher-directed. The teacher gives a verbal direction and the students perform a specific task on their papers. A format that works well is visual, with pictured items the students can cut-and-paste, circle, underline, or match. This testing procedure utilizes the three modalities of learning: the auditory (the student must listen and process the verbal command), the visual (the student must recognize or locate the specific item on the paper), and the kinesthetic (the student must manipulate the scissors, paper, pencil, crayons, and paste). Using all three of these modalities, the child is asked to successfully perform the given task.

A test for lower-grade children could reasonably present five or six specific tasks for the student to do under the direction of the teacher, one item to locate and circle, two cut-and-paste items, two matching items, and one to draw. Although children of this age can visually recognize and read some introductory vocabulary words, successful completion of this exercise should not depend totally on reading ability. Is this a reading exercise or a social studies exercise? Test what you are teaching.

Sample Tests

Here are two examples of teacher-made tests. An overview of the lesson will provide the background needed to understand the objective(s). The tests are examples of the type of questions that can be used and the way the teacher will administer and interpret the results.

A Kindergarten Lesson/Unit Test

Kindergarten social studies programs commonly include one or more units of study on the socialization processes of young children. These processes occur in their various social groups such as play groups, school groups, and family groups.

Your kindergarten class is now completing a unit on The Family. You have presented several successful lessons and the students have participated actively and freely. It is the second semester of the school year and the students are learning to perform some paper-and-pencil tasks. A written evaluation will be given for this unit. Here is a sample test for a kindergarten class.

Grade: kindergarten

Topic: The Family

Objective: To identify the roles of family members: mother, father, children, others.

Administering the Test

1. "Boys and girls, find the word *name* at the top of your paper. Print your name on the line next to it."

   (Go to each table to check if each child has written his or her name at the correct spot. Continue . . .)

2. "Find number one and put your finger on it. Look at the pictures of mom and dad. Now listen carefully. In your family, who goes to work in the morning—just mom, just dad, or both? Circle the picture."

   (Kindergartners will visually recognize the words *mom* and *dad* and the drawing provides an additional visual clue for this item. The words *mother* and *father* can be used if they are more appropriate. Check to see if each student has made a choice and circled a response. Continue . . .)

3. "Find number two and put your finger on it. Now listen carefully. Look at the pictures of the kitchen table set with dishes, the bed, the picture of mom and dad, and the picture of you. In your family, whose job is it to set the table for dinner? If mom or dad usually does, draw a line from their pictures to the table. If you set the table, draw a line from your picture to the table." (Repeat and pause.)

Name _____   Social Studies

One Item
to Circle

1.   MOM   DAD

Two Items
to Match

2.   MOM
      or
      DAD   ME

3.   MOM
      or
      DAD   ME

Two Items
to Cut
and Paste

4.   ☐   ME   ☐   MOM
      ☐   ☐   or
                                             DAD

5.   ☐

One Item
to Draw

6.

- -

Cut-outs ⟹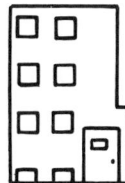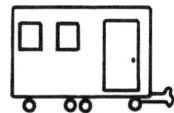

                 MONEY   HOUSE   APARTMENT   MOBILE
                                                         HOME

(Check again for responses. Some children will need an individual repetition of the directions. Continue . . .)

4. "Now look at the bed. Put your finger on it. In your family, who makes your bed: Mom or dad, or you? Find the picture of that person and draw a line from it to the bed."

   (Check for responses. Continue . . .)

5. "Find number three. Put your finger on it. Now listen carefully. Look at the pictures of the garbage can, the toys, mom and dad, and you. At your house, whose job is it to take out the trash: Mom or dad, or you? Find the right picture and draw a line from it to the garbage can. (Repeat and pause.) Look at the picture of the toys. In your family, whose job is it to pick up your toys: Mom or dad, or you? Find the correct picture and draw a line from it to the picture of the toys."

   (Check for responses. Continue . . .)

6. "Find number four. Put your finger on it. Now listen carefully. Look at the bottom of your paper. Do you see the pictures of the money, the house, the apartment building, and the mobile home? With your scissors cut out these pictures and put them in one pile on your table in front of you. Do this now." (Pause)

7. "Find the two pictures of money. Now put your finger on number four again and look at the picture of you and mom or dad. In your family, who decides how to spend your allowance money: You, or mom or dad? Paste one picture of money by that person." (Pause, then continue.)

8. "Take the other picture of money. Listen carefully. In your family, who decides how to spend money for 'needs and wants': Mom or dad? Paste that money picture by that person."

   (Check and continue . . .)

9. "Put your finger on number five. Look at the pictures of the house, the apartment building, and the mobile home. Which one of these looks most like where you live? Paste that picture in the empty box by number five."

   (Check and continue . . .)

10. "Find number six on your paper. There is a big blank space next to number six. Draw a picture of some ways you help someone in your family. Use the back of your paper if you need more space."

    (Check for responses. Give ample time for this.)

Administering any test or written assignment for the kindergarten-aged child necessitates some preliminary instructions. The students should have all the supplies they need to perform the given task. In this case, they need a scissors, paste, pencil, and crayons. When supplies are ready and provided, unnecessary interruptions are eliminated and the thinking process can proceed.

This particular sample test focuses heavily on the modalities of learning. The visual mode is evidenced in each test item. Pictorial representations are used in items one through five, with pictures that are readily recognizable for the average kindergarten child. The written words *name, mom, dad,* and *me* are a reasonable expectation for sight vocabulary. The auditory mode is used for each item with the teacher-given directions. Care is taken to word each direction clearly, to repeat as needed, and to keep the sentences short. The tactile-kinesthetic mode is used in each item when the teacher asks the students to locate a number and put a finger on it. The matching and the cut-and-paste items use the tactile mode to a greater degree. Using the three modalities of learning simultaneously enables each one to be strengthened.

Item number six is a free-response item. Here, the students are asked to use their own family experiences and show how they accept the responsibility of helping. (Good citizens help each other!) Although the artistic development of kindergartners is unpolished at best, they like to draw pictures of themselves, friends, and family in a positive light. A reasonable expectation for this item could be any of these: helping a sibling learn to play a particular game, caring for a sibling, helping mother cook or clean, helping to rake leaves, picking up toys, running the vacuum, or helping mother by "being good." With experience, you will become skilled at interpreting drawings. It is often helpful to ask each child individually what it is he or she has drawn, and then write it down on the paper, "I am helping. . . ." It gives you insights into the developmental stage of the child and it is an effective means of communicating with the parents. They know you have cared enough to talk privately with their child and to write the response. These personal communications are very important to remember.

Also note that each task was explained and completed before going on to the next. At this stage of development, children can remember and do only one task at a time. They cannot remember a sequence of instructions.

Look over the student page and the test directions again. Think about each verbal direction given by the teacher. Using Figure 6–6, categorize each item as a convergent or divergent question and list the process verbs used for each.

Figure 6-6   Analyzing Convergent and Divergent Questions Using Process Verbs

Test Item No.	Convergent	Divergent	Process Verbs
1.			
2.			
3.			
4.			
5.			
6.			

Work with a partner and discuss your answers. Were there differences of opinion regarding convergency and divergency? Which process verbs do you feel are the strongest? The weakest? Take some time to share your thoughts.

A Third-Grade Lesson/Unit Test

The third grade is frequently viewed as a transition year from the primary developmental learning period to the intermediate learning stages. In social studies and other curricular areas, the content and the processes are more challenging and advanced. Students are given more responsibility for their learning. Projects and assignments are more involved and the teacher's role includes more facilitating than is possible with younger children. Examine this third grade unit and sample test.

Your class is now completing a unit on the settlement of the Mississippi Valley and the Old Northwest. This unit examines the rigors of pioneer life as the early American settlers moved steadily westward. The farming economy, the need for and the development of early waterways systems, and the settlement of the Kentucky region are the focal points of this unit. Dealing with the concepts of change and cultural differences with the Indian population are some of the human relations skills that are highlighted. Some map-reading activities are a part of this unit, as well as information gathering from pictorial representations. Here is a sample test for a unit such as this.

> *Grade*:   Third
>
> *Topic*:   Settling the Mississippi Valley
>
> *Objective*:   E = Easy
> H = Harder; More difficult
> EXTRA = Extra credit

An evaluation instrument like this sample should include a variety of item types such as true-false, multiple choice, fill-ins, and free response. This sample shows how to use a labeling system for identifying the level of difficulty of each item. Can you think of other ways? Using this identification system in a testing situation should not be the students' first experience with it. They should be familiar with it before a test, which necessitates some introduction and practice beforehand. Remember that teachers do not try to trick or confuse the students.

The length of this sample test, 10 questions, is not intended to be a standard for third grade. For some groups, it may be just right, for other groups it may be too short or too long. Adjusting and monitoring the length of a test is one of the advantages of writing your own. A set of verbal directions for the teacher is not given for this grade. Students at this level have already taken a variety of tests and can perform the task independently with minimal directions.

Name _____ Social Studies, Part 3, Chapter 2 _____

(E) 1. In the year 1790 the Old Northwest Territory covered a large area available for expansion and growth. Name three states that were eventually organized within these boundaries.
a.
b.
c.

(E) 2. Define these terms:
pioneer
canal
gateway

(E) 3. In your own way, identify the differences between these three types of boats. You can write or draw below.
flatboat
keel boat
steamboat

(E) 4. The Mississippi Valley was heavily forested when the pioneers came to settle the area. The dense forests presented hardships for the people.
True   False

(H)   Give at least four reasons for your choice.
a.
b.
c.
d.

(H) 5. The settlers west of the Appalachian Mountains were farmers. They needed to get their products to market east of the mountain range. How was this done? Circle the correct response(s).
a. Products were taken by horse and cart.
b. The railroads were used.
c. Canals and waterways were built.
d. The eastern markets were of no concern to them.

(H) 6. Name five hardships the pioneers in Kentucky faced and how they were solved.

Problem   Solution
a.
b.
c.
d.
e.

(*continued*)

(H) 7. Daniel Boone was an important frontiersman in Kentucky and Missouri. List two ways he showed leadership in each of these areas.

Explorations

a.

b.

Cultural activities

a.

b.

Indian affairs

a.

b.

Politics

a.

b.

(E) 8. The building of the canals and waterways opened up lines of communication for the pioneers, as well as making trade easier.

    True   False

(E) 9. What were some of the problems involved in building the Erie Canal?

disease	crude tools	too many bosses
dense forest	weather	the Indians
others		

(EXTRA)

10. The American Indians lived in the Old Northwest before the pioneers came to settle. Think of the data we read about in our textbook and the other materials we have used in this chapter. Imagine that you are a ten-year-old Indian child. Write a journal entry for a day when the new people were settling the Kentucky territory.

Scoring this test includes both subjective and objective responses. Some items call for a specific response that is either correct or incorrect. Some items provide parameters that allow a variety of responses and several different answers could be correct. These items allow students to draw on the information they have gathered from the various resources they used during the lessons.

Item number ten is a free-response, creative type of question. This provides an opportunity for the students to project themselves into the unit of study in a very personal way. It can be interpreted as a creative writing exercise, and in some ways it is. In scoring this item, the teacher would specifically look for examples of the social studies cultural conflicts, feelings, fears, points of view, facts about daily life, weather factors, and other peripheral data that a young child would experience during that time. The teacher might also look for various elements pertinent to a creative writing lesson. This question reflects the human relations aspect of teaching the social studies. The teacher examines both the informational and the interpretive aspects of this question.

This section has presented information on questioning strategies that are an integral part of planning for instruction. Skillful questioning techniques and procedures take practice and time to develop. A few well-designed questions are more effective than many questions of lesser quality. Group and individual questions were examined as were some approaches for using each. Convergent and divergent questions were also examined in terms of how they are used for elementary students. Allowing students adequate think time to respond to a specific question is important.

Evaluative questioning in the form of written tests for both primary and upper-elementary students is an integral part of the complete lesson plan. Questioning strategies is the topic of much educational research. Entire books are written on the subject. It is suggested that you investigate some of these books. Test writing is a personal endeavor that is approached with the needs of a specific group in mind. As you design each test item, your goal should be success, not frustration or failure.

ACTIVITIES

These activities will help you to establish a mindset toward evaluating and asking questions in the classroom. The first activity establishes a philosophy about evaluating, the second activity is concerned with specific ways to evaluate, the third activity introduces you to standardized testing, and the last activity will help you learn to identify different types of questions.

6.1   *Why Evaluate?*

Thinking about and establishing a personal philosophy of evaluation and grading is important. Both positive and negative factors enter into a realistic attitude toward evaluating the learning of students. How do you really feel about this teaching responsibility? Try to list ten of your personal thoughts or feelings for each of these factors. (*Note*: Negative factors can be viewed as negative results if that clarifies it for you.)

Positive Factors of Evaluation

1.
2.

3.

4.

5.

6.

7.

8.

9.

10.

Negative Factors of Evaluation

1.

2.

3.

4.

5.

6.

7.

8.

9.

10.

Extension: Refer back to your list of positive factors in the evaluation process. Consider each one carefully. Think in terms of **S** for students, **P** for parents, and **PE** for your personal experience. In the margin, label each of your entries in terms of: "Did I list this because it is positive for the students, positive for the parents, or because I remembered it from my own personal experiences?" Do the same for all the items in your negative factors list.

Self-Check.   Look at the labels you assigned in the two lists. Which category had the most? The least? How many **PE**s did you have? It is helpful to think carefully how your own elementary school experiences truly affect your feelings and attitudes about education. When evaluating, try to remember what effects evaluation and grading have on students. You will become a more empathetic educator if you do.

Look at your list of negatives again. Think of possible ways to turn those negatives into positives, and write down your ideas. Have more than one idea for each negative in case the first one does not work out. With your group or a classmate, discuss all of your solutions. Do you have any items that you could not turn into a positive statement? If so, discuss these with your instructor or solicit ideas from your group or the class.

6.2   *Evaluating a Primary Lesson*

Select a product learning, a process skill, and a human relations skill for the primary level. Think of an informal method for evaluating each of the three. Specifically stress the skills in a lesson that are activity-oriented (nonwritten). Use the following format to write your ideas. Do at least three for each area.

> ### *Evaluating a Primary Lesson*
>
> | *Method of Evaluation* | *Teacher Activities* |
> |---|---|
> | *Product Learning* | |
>
> 1.
> 2.
> 3.
>
> *Process Skill*
>
> 1.
> 2.
> 3.
>
> *Human Relations Skill*
>
> 1.
> 2.
> 3.

Extension: You have selected a process skill, a product learning, and a human relations skill with an appropriate method of evaluation. You have identified exactly what the teacher must do to implement that method with the intended results. Think of how you can communicate this to the parents. Be imaginative and creative without being gimmicky. Discuss your evaluation and reporting plan with a classmate or your group. Are your plans reasonable and usable?

6.3   *Standardized Testing*

Obtain a copy of the Standard Achievement Test (or another multiple-disciplinary achievement test) for fifth or sixth grades. Your instructor will help you find one. Carefully examine the social studies portion of the test. Think about the process skills, the product learnings, and the human relations skills of the social studies curriculum. Identify each of the test items as belonging to one of the categories. Are certain skills tested more heavily than others according to your classification? Which are tested the least? Prepare a presentation for your group or the class and discuss your findings. Focus on the specific skills being tested. Try to identify the rationale for choosing the particular test items that interested you most.

6.4 *Questioning*

This is a short exercise to identify some questions that could be used in a social studies class. Some will be for primary students and others will be for upper-elementary students. Read the question or statement carefully, consider the key words, and then decide if each calls for a convergent or divergent response. After each, write **C** for convergent and **D** for divergent.

1. Why do we have rules at Silver Lake School?
2. Tell the class all the ways we can help a new student make friends in our room.
3. Name the significance of the colors red, white, and blue on the flag of the United States.
4. On your map, draw all the paths from the school to the city park.
5. We have been studying about how to be a responsible citizen. Write (or tell) five good reasons for dialing 911.
6. Design the inside of a covered wagon, as it was used in the Westward Movement, and present the design to the class.
7. Locate the capital cities of the northeast states on the map and recite them for the class.
8. Project yourself into the year 2000. Think of three ways your social groups will change. Be prepared to discuss the good and not-so-good aspects of these changes.
9. Suppose America had been discovered in the area that is now Texas. What effects would this have had on the people in Mexico?

How did you identify these questions? Did you assign more **C**s than **D**s? Go through the questions again and decide if you would use each for summative or formative purposes. Could some be used for either? Talk about your rationale with your group or your instructor.

Summary

This chapter presented a rationale for formal and informal evaluation of both primary and upper-elementary students. Formal and informal types of evaluation, accompanied by some suggested applications for specific grades and learning skills, were suggested. The special needs of primary students were considered with methods and processes that are especially adaptable for beginning learners. This chapter also explained how you can evaluate and recognize the learning process, without advanced written material from the student. The higher-level performance skills of the upper-elementary students were noted and provisions were made for evaluating them in special ways.

The second part of the chapter was concerned with the use of questions in the classroom—why you ask them and how you can plan for better questions and answers. Bloom's taxonomy was used as a basis for developing levels of questions. Equally important is your response to the students' response to a question. Written questions were used to construct tests. The activities were designed to help you reinforce your concept of evaluation and questioning.

READING RESOURCES

Cain, Sandra, and Evans, Jack. *Sciencing,* Part 4, 2nd ed. Columbus, OH: Charles E. Merrill, 1984.

Ciardiello, A. V. "Teacher Questioning and Student Interaction: An Observation of Three Social Studies Classes." *Social Studies*, 77 (May/June 1986): 119–22.

Daines, D. "Are Teachers Asking Higher Level Questions?" *Education*, 106 (Summer 1986): 368–74.

Key, L. H., and Young, J. L. "Socriatic Teaching in Social Studies." *Social Studies*, 77 (July/August 1986): 158–61.

Watson, E. O. "They Won't Think? Then Sharpen Your Questions." *Learning, 86*, no. 15 (September 1986): 68.

ENDNOTES

1. Rowe, Mary Budd, *Teaching Science as Continuous Inquiry* (New York: McGraw-Hill, 1973), Chapter 8.

2. Bloom, Benjamin et al., *Taxonomy of Educational Objectives, Handbook 1: Cognitive Domain* (New York: Longman Inc., 1956).

3. Farrar, Mary Thomas, "Asking Better Questions," *The Reading Teacher, 38*, no. 1 (October 1984): 10–15.

4. "A Note to Boys and Girls," *The Making of Our America*, Learner-Verified Edition II (Boston, MA: Allyn and Bacon, 1974).

7
Planning a Lesson from Beginning to End

PROJECTIONS

Planning social studies lessons for the present or the future requires some basic criteria that are standards for good teaching. Knowing what to teach, defining specific objectives, selecting the most appropriate materials for student use, choosing your teaching methods and strategies, determining an effective evaluation procedure(s), and maintaining a strong commitment are benchmarks of competent planning.

Planning for the new social studies will require a commitment to meet new challenges as they appear in our society and, more specifically, as they impact our educational system. The teacher's role in lesson design includes managing materials and groups of students who are performing various functions simultaneously. The present classroom situation of one teacher with one group of students in a self-contained classroom may or may not continue to exist as we now know it. Trends indicate that teachers will assume the more proactive role of facilitator of experiences and activities for various groups of students. Some of these experiences will occur within the school setting; others will occur outside of the academic environment.

It will be necessary for the teacher to coordinate and use available community resources. One community resource is our growing pool of retired persons. Many schools are already utilizing these resource people very effectively. This practice will surely benefit our younger learners who are preparing to enter the workplace as creative producers.

The social studies teacher's planning responsibilities will include making plans for any auxiliary personnel that will work with her or his students. These plans will incorporate the available technology at all levels, from interactive television to the personal computer to the unknown technology yet to be born. Plans will incorporate cross-age and cross-grade experiences that allow older students to interface with younger learners. Teachers already know that students communicate with each other in special ways. It is sometimes puzzling, but youngsters can and do help each other learn new things. Making specific plans for these cross-age experiences to occur, as well as planning for them to occur incidentally, provides learners with another opportunity to learn academic and social skills.

Figure 7-1   Procedure for Planning

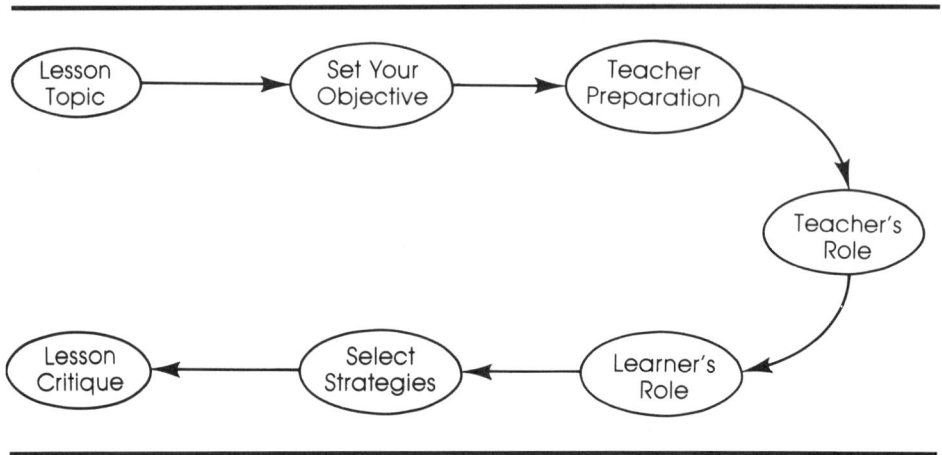

Planning for teaching is a complicated process involving numerous factors that must be carefully considered. Time to teach, content, processes, teachability, the maturity of the students, individual needs or differences, and materials are some of the elements affecting the decisions teachers make for every lesson they teach. Planning a good social studies lesson takes time, talent, and teaching skill. Addressing each of the lesson elements without overemphasizing any single one is an important teaching responsibility.

The task of planning is easier if you have a usable model to follow. There are many available, but examine the one shown in Figure 7–1. The steps are: selecting the lesson topic, setting the objective(s), teacher preparation, teacher's role (What will I do?), learner's role (What will the student do?), selecting the strategies for the lesson, and evaluating the lesson. Use the flowchart in Figure 7–1 to see the relationship and sequence that good planning follows. As you read through this chapter, try to identify each part on the flowchart.

Planning Activities for Learning

One of the major themes of this text is that elementary social studies includes a variety of learning experiences for students and instructional opportunities for teachers. Students learn social studies through many channels: reading textbook material, enjoying creative experiences, using media resources, reading and critiquing other printed materials, participating in large and small group activities, using the senses, and using time to think. Providing interesting social studies lessons and activities is a challenge and a growth opportunity for teachers.

Activities are essential for social studies. How do teachers provide enough quality activities to actively engage a group of 25 students for the duration of a unit? Social studies teacher guides usually include a variety of suggested student activities. These student activities might include using reference materials, vocabulary development, reading skill development, listening skill opportunities, diagramming, and many others. They should be used in conjunction with the lessons. In addition to these textbook activities, social studies teachers plan and design many things for their students to do in and outside of class. Planning for these activities requires creativity, resourcefulness, ingenuity, and commitment to provide students with a variety of social studies experiences.

There are two major types of activities that students perform during social studies: group activities and individual activities. Group activities may be large (the entire class, a group of six) or small (a paired group of two people). Teachers provide experiences that permit students to function in a variety of settings. The following list gives some student activity ideas for a unit on Communities.

Group Activities

1. A group of six will prepare a panel discussion on the topic of "Ways Our Schools Are/Are Not Meeting Student Needs."

2. The teacher directs a brainstorming session on "What are general community needs?"

3. A group of two interview the mayor, chief of police, school superintendent, or the mall manager.

4. Write and conduct a community survey to cover a six-block radius.

5. Construct a model.

6. A group will plan and produce a videotape about the community.

Individual Activities

1. Give an oral book report.

2. Present an impersonation of a historical community figure.

3. Construct a diorama of your community as it appeared 50 years ago.

4. Use a computer program.

5. Compose and send a letter to three mayors of surrounding communities regarding waste disposal.

6. One person is the designated research captain for locating and delivering all pertinent student resources in the library and the learning center.

These suggested activities are representative examples of what elementary students are capable of doing. Each activity requires a certain degree of maturity and responsibility. The readiness of a particular student to perform a given activity is determined by the teacher or by the teacher and the student together. Student activities draw upon the individual student's stage of development, preferred learning styles, informational background, and social and academic skills. Student activities are particularly cogent when they utilize the social studies learning resources, media materials, as well as other materials collected by the teacher. Student activities that investigate and use community resources are also valuable experiences.

Developing Lessons for Primary Grades

Characteristics

Selecting and developing specific lessons for the primary grades require an understanding of the learning needs for this age group. Keep in mind that primary children are in the concrete formation stage of mental development and that the younger individuals can be functioning at the preoperational level. Optimal learning occurs more readily when all three learning modalities—the visual, the auditory, and the tactile—are used.

What are the learning needs of young children? Which learning experiences/activities work well for them? Consider these characteristics:

1. Young children need to learn how to learn. Out-of-school experiences do not necessarily prepare children for the kinds of memory work that in-school learning demands.

2. A series of short lessons, 15 to 20 minutes at the maximum for kindergarten and first graders, is more effective than one long session.

3. It is advisable to tell the students at the beginning what they are expected to learn and remember. This relieves any guesswork on their part. Children need to know if they have to remember everything the teacher says or only specific parts.

4. Find ways to transfer information learned during the day from one lesson to another.

5. Young children are open to new learning situations. Capitalize on their interests and enthusiasm by being energetic and excited yourself.

6. Be careful not to teach what your students already know. Use pretesting to help you decide where to start. Informal methods work well and yield good results.

7. Make adequate provision for "kid talk" in the lesson. Children learn a lot from each other. This is another reason for pretesting.

8. Lessons that employ highly visual and tactile activities and materials are very good. Prepare them carefully with color, texture, and an element of childlike fantasy.

9. Doing, moving, touching, trying out, talking about, exploring, and examining are very appropriate and acceptable for young children.

When developing lessons for teaching primary-grade children, there are other key components to keep in mind. The first and most important factor is the age level of the class and the performance level of the individuals in the class. The chronological ages of the children will probably fall within a few months of the norm, whereas the performance levels may span one or two grade levels in either direction. Chronological ages are a given element that cannot be changed, but performance levels should be considered when selecting methods and materials to meet individual learning needs.

Another key factor is the scope of the curriculum and the supplementary materials available to teach it. If the curriculum is very heavy in factual learning requirements and there are few materials to reinforce the goals, then which strategies would be the most effective? If the curriculum is more activity-based, which methods would that indicate as being the good choices? Another consideration is that some areas of the social studies curriculum are largely informal at the primary level. Although having a certain degree of freedom may seem attractive, it does require as much, if not more, planning of strategies than some formal topics.

The reading and audiovisual materials chosen for a lesson are most effective when they meet stated selection criteria. Here are some pointers to assist in choosing them.

Reading Materials

Supplementary reading materials include such items as worksheets, workbook pages, assignments or information from the chalkboard or overhead projector, library books, pamphlets, computer programs that are primarily reading text, trade books brought from home, and any other teacher-made materials that require reading ability. Reading materials must be selected and/or prepared at the appropriate readability level of the students, which is usually below the class reading level. If it is too difficult to read and comprehend easily, the students will struggle, concentrating so hard on decoding that the real social studies lesson may well be lost.

Reading for content is an important part of any program, especially for a content area such as social studies. Make the sentences short, using vocabulary the students recognize. Preview the books the children will be using. Do not make the mistake of assuming that a book is readable just because it is in the easy section of the library. Previewing is also necessary if the teacher plans to read the book to the children. The vocabulary level must be appropriate and the illustrations well presented.

Audiovisual Materials

Audiovisual materials provide for the auditory and visual modes of learning. Audio materials should be clear and easy to discriminate. Static and poor quality of reproduction are unacceptable for young children for they are still learning to discriminate the sounds in words and of words. A cassette or a record should be of high interest with pleasant voice, tonality, and pitch. Materials that are strictly auditory need careful selection because of the visual dominance of young children. Total auditory learning is not yet a well-developed skill and tends to be somewhat abstract, so keep auditory lessons short.

Visual materials such as filmstrips, charts, pictures, books, articles (realia), snapshots, movies, and other supplementary items should also be carefully selected. You are using them for a reason, so be sure they are doing what they are supposed to do. Visuals are most acceptable when they are up to date, clear, uncluttered, visually attractive both in format and color quality, interesting, and pertinent to the lesson.

Materials that allow listening and seeing to occur simultaneously, possibly even with some touching and manipulating, are by far the best because they incorporate all of the modalities and relate to the natural inclinations of the young child. Always try to use those materials that are best suited to the child's stage of mental development.

In conclusion, selecting and developing a particular lesson for young learners must take into consideration the nature of learning at the primary level. How children learn is of utmost importance. The nature of the specific lesson may strongly indicate the preference for a particular method of presentation and follow-through. Motivation is a high priority in planning to get the students to want to learn and somehow connect that learning to their real world.

Look at these sample lessons and see how they are put together. Try to locate the seven steps in planning that were shown in Figure 7–1 at the beginning of this chapter.

A Sample Lesson (Kindergarten)

Lesson Topic: A Lesson for Mapping

Specified Objective: To recognize and locate the four cardinal directions in the classroom (north, south, east, and west)

Provision for High-Potential Learners: The students may point out the directions when outside the classroom.

Teaching Note: In many current social studies programs, one of the learning goals, beginning at the kindergarten level, is to develop mapping skills. Although the initial lessons may be largely teacher-directed, it is important that the learners become actively involved as soon as possible. Their auditory processing skills are just developing. They cannot follow instructions easily—one verbal command at a time is about all they can handle. The teacher must lead them step-by-step through a given set of instructions. Kindergarten and first-grade children are just starting to learn to think. Keeping attention focused on the immediate task requires constant effort by the primary teacher.

Concepts to Be Developed: The concept of direction may seem simple to an adult, but it can be very hard to teach to five- and six-year-olds. Some basic directional vocabulary for five- and six-year-old children may include:

near	in front of	next to
far	in back of	on top of
under	over	up
down	beside	in between

Can you think of others? Add them to this list.

Teaching Strategy: Incorporating these vocabulary/concept items into an active lesson is exciting for the teacher as well as the students. Here are some methods that are appropriate for kindergarten:

1. Have the directional words *north, south, east,* and *west* written in large letters and posted on the appropriate walls in your room.
2. Place several objects around the room with your location/vocabulary signs on them. Put a teddy bear "on top of" the book case, the scissors box "next to" the sink, and so on. (See Figure 7–2.)
3. Design and construct a bulletin board with directional vocabulary as the focal point. When the students come into the room, call attention to the display. Tell the class they will be learning about this during social studies class today.

Teaching the Concept: Using a total student response technique, walk with the class or a small group through all the areas where you have location words displayed. If your students are operating at the phrase level of language development, use a statement such as, "The teddy bear is *(on top of)* the bookcase."

Figure 7-2   Location and Direction Words in the Classroom

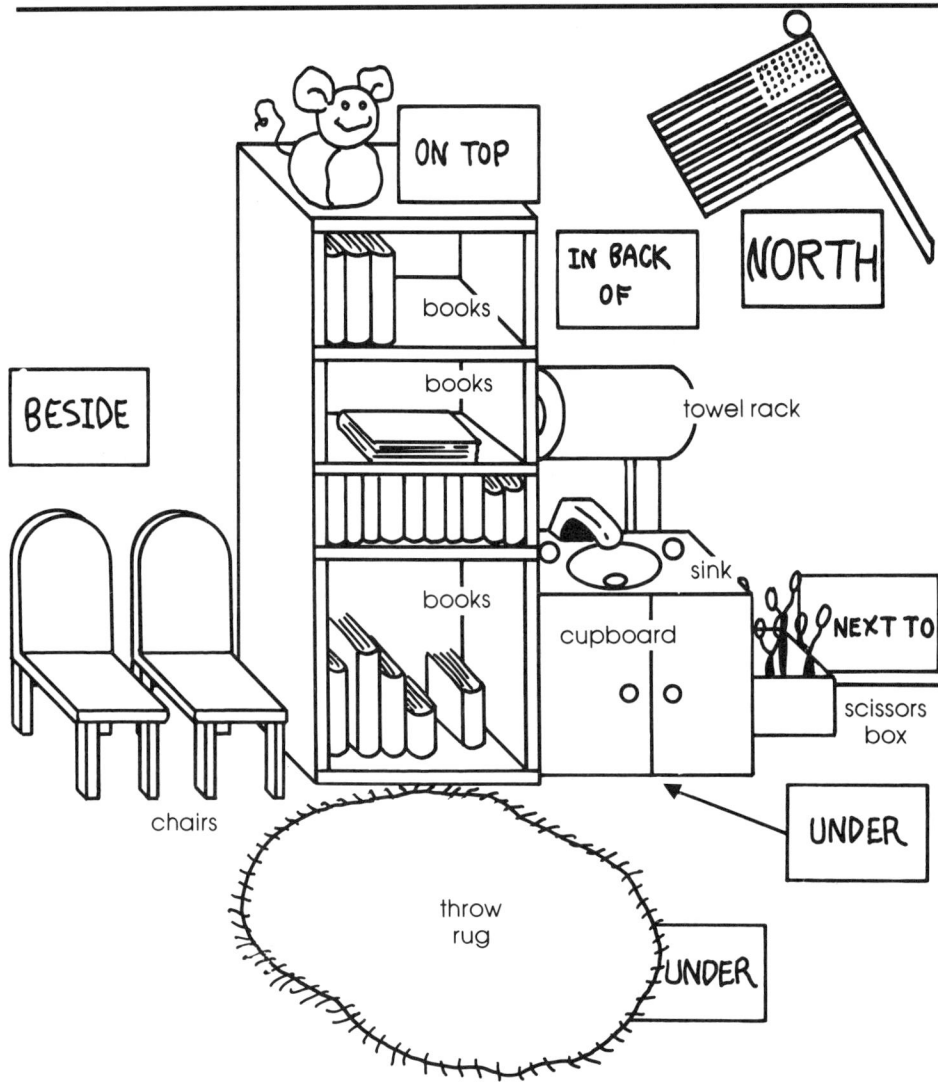

ON TOP

IN BACK OF

NORTH

BESIDE

books

books

towel rack

sink

books

cupboard

NEXT TO

scissors box

chairs

UNDER

throw rug

UNDER

Accept either a group response of "on top of" or solicit individual responses. If your group is at the sentence level of development, you may wish to pose a question, "Where is the teddy bear?" You can anticipate a full sentence response such as, "Our teddy bear is on top of the bookcase" from the whole group or an individual. Knowing the verbal stage of development of the class enables you to formulate your questions appropriately.

Reinforcing and Applying the Concept: While you are moving around the room, challenge the group: "Who can find north?" "Who can point to the south wall?" The more opportunities young children have to practice a skill or a new concept, the more likely that skill will be learned and retained.

Extending the Application: Change your technique. Challenge the students to move the objects around to a different location: "Ben, move the scissors box *in back of* the flannel board." "Susie, place the teddy bear *under* the flag." Here, you are taking the students from an identification skill level to an application skill level.

Closure: The closure procedure you select should bring all the lesson elements together in such a way that some conclusions can be made. The specified objective encompasses two learning behaviors: a visual recognition behavior (visually recognizing the word *north* when it is displayed, or pointing to it when asked to locate the term somewhere in the room) and a physical behavior (relocating an object when given a specific verbal command).

An effective technique to guide the students toward closure is the basic recall of all the tasks the students were asked to perform during the lesson. Begin with a brainstorming question such as, "Who can remember one of the place words (directional vocabulary) we talked about today?" Acknowledge all contributions with a positive comment ("Good thinking today!") and visual contact with the child. After the responses are all given, it will be evident which of the terms have been retained. If some locational terms are volunteered that were not included in the lesson, consider those as a bonus!

Continue the closure procedure with an activity to reinforce the physical behavior part of the objective. During the lesson the students were asked to place an object in a particular location to demonstrate their understanding of a designated place word. To maintain a high interest level that is fun for both teacher and students, try the placement activity yourself and ask the students to tell you if it is done correctly. In this way, you are providing an opportunity for the child to learn to make introductory judgments. Young children enjoy walking from place to place with the teacher and calling out "Right!" or "Wrong!" after each selection is made.

Another idea for closure is to incorporate the directional vocabulary into a lesson using the flannel board or bulletin board. Design the board with several movable pictures and each of the vocabulary terms printed clearly. The board becomes a closure activity when the students manipulate the pictures and/or the word cards in response to a given command, or when they choose to manipulate the cards on their own during free time.

Evaluation: The method for evaluating a particular lesson should reflect both the skills that are being learned and the teacher's guiding role. Does the lesson itself indicate a particular method of evaluation is more appropriate than

These lower-grade children are working on their lessons as they listen to instructions from their teacher.

another? This introductory mapping lesson focuses on vocabulary recognition with active learning as the medium. The active, moving-around aspect of the lesson lends itself to an evaluation strategy in the same mode. Thus, the most practical evaluation is an informal technique. Observing the child during the activity and during closure will provide you with enough information to decide if specific individuals need extra help. Keep in mind the inability of kindergartners to perform written tasks, which mandates an evaluation using a format other than a paper-and-pencil test.

Teacher judgment is an invaluable tool for evaluating the primary grades, especially at the kindergarten level. Skills of observing, listening, guiding, and designing activities are necessary in order to do an informal evaluation. The ability to formulate specific questions to determine previous knowledge of the lesson topic is an evaluative skill that is needed at the start of the lesson. The teacher must observe carefully how many students are responding during the verbal parts of the lesson and how many are not. She or he must also observe which students are utilizing the flannel board or bulletin board during free periods and if it is being used correctly.

Teacher judgment allows the teacher to determine the point at which the majority of the class has grasped the particular concept being presented. At each step of the lesson the teacher must ask himself or herself, "Are they getting it?" If the response is a confident yes, then move on to the next part of the instructional plan. If the response is "I don't think so," then begin an alternate presentation of the concept or make a mental note to come back to the lesson later. Free activity periods can be used to reteach the lesson to a small group of children.

A Sample Lesson (First Grade)

Lesson Topic: A Lesson for Mapping

Specified Objective: To recognize and locate the four cardinal directions on a simple map (north, south, east, and west)

Provision for High-Potential Learners: The students may add three or more items of their own choice on the map.

Teaching Note: At the first-grade level, chances are the students have had some exposure to the cardinal direction vocabulary. If not, some introductory lessons will be needed before asking them to demonstrate their recognition-location ability. Young children delight in having something to take home to show their parents. Care must be taken when assigning a paper-and-pencil lesson. Be sure the following criteria are met:

1. It is at the appropriate level of instruction.
2. The activity really shows the skill they are trying to learn.
3. You are reasonably sure that the lesson can be completed successfully.
4. Provisions are made for the initial written skills level of the children.

This first-grade mapping lesson may require some reteaching of directional vocabulary. Some short motivational or reteaching activities may include:

1. Have the room labeled with the words on the appropriate walls. Use large letters in a bright color, perhaps red, so that the words will catch their eyes often during the day.
2. Carry a small set of the word cards in your pockets, and challenge the class while lining up for dismissal or before going to lunch. Be spontaneous!
3. Prepare another set of the word cards to use with a pocket chart. Have a series of short sentences with the cardinal direction terms left out. The students will correctly identify the term and place it in the sentence. Short, readable sentences such as these work well for first graders:
    a. The flag is _____ of our school.
    b. The playground is _____ of the parking lot.

    c. The school faces _____.

    d. Our classroom faces _____.

Teaching the Concept: A movement activity may involve asking Joey to move his chair to the north side of the room, or asking Maria to hop to the south wall and stand on one foot, or asking Tim to use his walker to go to the west side of the room. Activities such as these not only employ a student's visual recognition of the mapping terminology, but they call upon a student's body to respond physically. The teacher can determine almost immediately the levels of recognition and internalization. Involve even more of the children in the learning process by reviewing the other locational terms: *next to, beside, in between,* and *over.*

Extending the Application: When you have finished some introductory activities such as these, your class may be ready for a paper assignment such as the one on page 239. This mapping lesson is very basic yet at the same time it tests the skill stated in the objective. Using the given format, five or six simple directions will accomplish the goal. They may proceed in this manner:

1. "Put your name on the paper."
2. "Cut out boxes at the bottom of the page." (Pause.) "Put them in a pile on your desk."
3. "Find the word *North.* Paste it on your paper where north is located on the map." (Pause.) Continue in this manner with the remaining terms.
4. "Draw a lake on the north side of your map. Color it blue." (Pause.) "Put a swing set on the west side." (Pause.) "Make a group of trees on the east side." (Pause.) "Draw yourself on the south side."

Extension for High-Potential Students: Give the students an opportunity to be creative and perform the lesson extension by adding items of their own to the map. Accept all efforts. It takes some risking for young learners to do this as they want to please you. Some typical items children frequently select for this kind of activity would be a park bench, butterflies, a rainbow, smiling dogs, and slides.

Teaching Note: A lesson such as this gives children a sense of accomplishment. They can do things on their own and do them successfully. In addition, it gives the teacher an opportunity to determine each child's skill level in processing verbal directions. Another benefit is that parents can see what their children are learning in the social studies and they may be motivated to do some reinforcing activities at home. Give youngsters a real outlet for their learning efforts and make it important.

Closure: Closure strategies unify all the lesson elements to present order for learners. What exactly are the elements of this lesson? They are:

Name _____

Social Studies
Activity Sheet

Student Sheet →

Cut-outs →

North | South
East | West

1. Post the location words in the room for visual recognition.
2. Use common objects to reinforce visual learning.
3. Use the bulletin board display as a motivational strategy.
4. Employ active learning by walking through specific activities.
5. Use all three modalities of learning: visual, auditory, and tactile.
6. Plan lesson transfer into the area of language development.
7. Guide the lesson from the beginning level of simple identification to the application of the skill.

8. Use verbal recall.

9. Provide a written assignment.

10. Make allowances for creative efforts.

A Closure Lesson: The activities outlined in this lesson from the introductory motivators to the cut-and-paste map are planned to lead to successful closure. The specified objective of recognizing and locating the cardinal directions and vocabulary words can now be brought into perspective on a real map. This particular lesson can be used with the entire class, a small group of five or six students, or on an individual basis with special needs children.

Display a primary-level city, state, or United States map. A laminated type of map is ideal so that students can write on the surface and erase easily, or put stick-on labels at appropriate locations. To demonstrate their ability to perform the objective, the students will locate north, south, east, and west on the big map by correctly pointing to a specific direction as stated by the teacher. Another approach is to prepare word cards with adhesive on the back, and direct the student to place each one correctly.

A challenge for the more adept students is to pose this question: "Who can come to the map and find northeast?" Be aware that the "between" directions have not been specifically taught in this lesson. The higher-performing children may be capable of logical thinking in this manner:

I know where north is. (Students will focus on north with the eyes and probably point with fingers.)

I know where east is. (Same procedure.)

Therefore, northeast might be between north and east.

These children can use lesson transfer in situations such as this without specific teacher direction. The transfer strategy used here may have its basis in a math lesson on telling time that was taught earlier. Consider the logical pattern of figuring out where the hands on the clock should be to show 1:10, when the student already knows the locations for 1:00 and 1:15. This closure activity can also be directed into additional learning situations that check the internalization of the concept. Have several different types of maps displayed. Ask the students to locate the cardinal directions on each map. Also ask them to determine which direction a particular physical feature on the map such as a lake or forest range is located in relation to another specific feature.

Evaluation: The level of learning in a lesson that requires active student participation is obvious and immediate. Each time the students are asked to demonstrate a particular skill, such as pointing to or placing something correctly, the teacher recognizes immediately which students can do it and which ones cannot. Making mental notes of such evaluative information is a necessary teaching skill that you need to develop. Students who are progressing at the anticipated rate will be responding and participating readily. The students who are unsure or apprehensive about performing the skill will need additional activities in order to achieve success. These reteaching activities are an important part of total planning.

Is it necessary to design a formal, written evaluative instrument for this lesson? Formal evaluation plays an important role in determining what is being taught by the teacher and learned by the students. Making decisions to test formally or informally requires an understanding of the learning needs of this particular age group.

The reading abilities of first graders are at the beginning stages, as are the writing skills. Unless a paper test (such as the application activity) can be designed to actually test the specific skill, an informal evaluation strategy is probably the better choice. The strategies outlined in the lesson closure can be used in evaluating the students' success in achieving the goal. The students who need more opportunities to reach the goal can continue to practice under teacher direction and at various times during the day. When evaluating student learning of a particular skill, it is important to remember that once the skill is learned students want to move on to something new. This can be an entirely new skill or an activity that is designed to reinforce the skill in a new way. Do not discourage enthusiasm by repeated exposure to things they already know!

Lesson Critique: Upon completion of the lesson, you will want to critique the process that was followed. Begin with the objective you set.

The Objective
1. Was it appropriate for the age group?
2. Was it achievable for the majority of the class?
3. Did any of the students already know the skill before the lesson?
4. Did I pretest informally to determine this?

Teacher Preparation
1. Did I prepare myself well for the lesson?
2. Which resource materials did I use for my preparation?
3. Was the teacher's manual helpful? If so, how much?
4. Did I anticipate any student special needs?

Teacher's Activity
1. Did I give sufficient time to think through what I would do during the lesson?
2. Was there too much "teacher talk"?

3. Did I solicit as many student responses as possible? Too few? Too many?
4. Was my role that of facilitator, sage, or manager of information?
5. Did I show enthusiasm, excitement, and understanding?
6. Did I track the nonverbal cues of the students?

Student Involvement

1. What did I plan for the students to do to facilitate learning?
2. Did I plan for different learning styles so each student could function in the mode most comfortable for him or her?
3. Which responses indicated learning was taking place?
4. Were the students enthused, receptive, bored, or not interested?

Review the Lesson

1. Which areas went really well? Whcih could have been better? How so?
2. What will I change if I teach this again? How?
3. If you wish to add experiences, materials, activities, teacher or student resources, make notes.

Evaluation

1. Was the paper test adequate to test the objective I set?
2. How many students performed the lesson extension? Were the responses appropriate and creative?
3. What percent of the class placed the cardinal direction words appropriately?
4. Am I satisfied with these results, keeping in mind reasonable expectations?
5. At what point did I know the class was ready for the test? Note this.

Planning an effective lesson for the primary grades entails careful decision making beginning with the selection of the lesson topic and extending through the method(s) of evaluating learner outcomes. The young age of the students and the early stage of mental development charges the teacher with the exacting task of planning an activity that can be completed with relative ease, yet be educationally challenging. Creativity is required. The ability to teach to a specific level of learning while maintaining good pedagogy is the mark of a strong primary teacher. Being alert to student needs and flexible enough to change strategies as needed are teaching characteristics that are constantly developing. The process of becoming a master teacher is continual.

Keep in mind that both the kindergarten and the first-grade lessons outlined here are introductory activities. After these initial activities, the classes can progress to experiences such as recognizing the function of simple keys and legends, identifying land and water masses, uses of coloration, and other primary map skills.

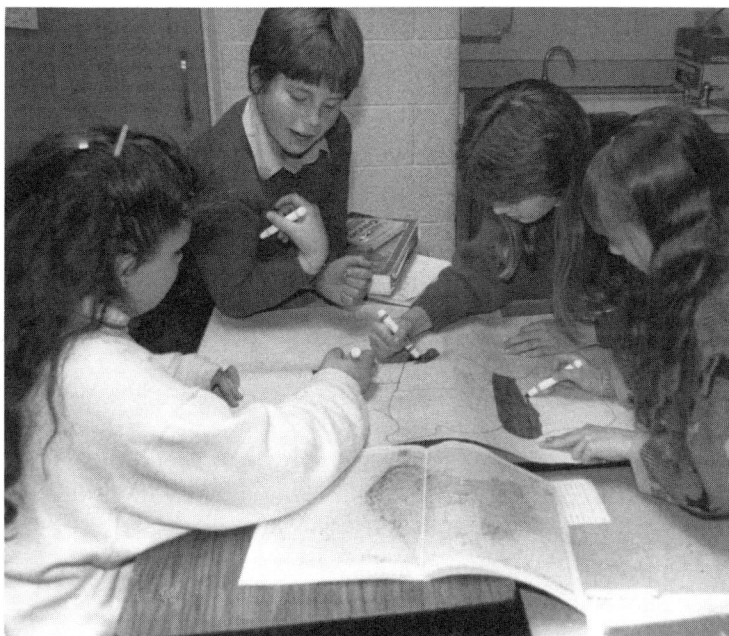

Making a map gives students experience in manipulating materials.

Developing Lessons for Upper-Elementary Grades

Selecting and developing lessons for upper-elementary grades require the same careful planning and understanding of mental development as the planning you do for primary children. As students progress through the early school years into the intermediate grades, the development of all the individuals will not be progressing at the same rate. The intellectual, physical, and social rate of development is highly individualized. You can expect a mixture of Piagetian stages of development to be evident in the upper-elementary grades. Some students may be just into the concrete formation stage whereas others are solidly into more formal operations.

Learning Characteristics

What are the implications for planning strategies to meet the learning needs of everyone in the class? Here are some learning characteristics to consider:

1. Intermediate-age students are more independent workers. They can concentrate for longer periods of time and read directions. They also have

library and other media skills that allow them to locate and use alternate sources of information.

2. Group interaction projects are more easily planned. The group can choose a leader, assign specific tasks, plan strategies for completing a project, and do some preliminary evaluative tasks relating to the effectiveness of the project.

3. Older students can usually read most of the textbook material by themselves out of class. This eliminates using limited class time for reading the book together, and makes more time available for other activities.

4. These students can handle more responsibility. They can work alone in the library or with others without constant supervision.

5. Some out-of-school tasks can be assigned by the teacher. Homework is productive when planned and appropriate.

6. The impact of current events on older students is more visible and concrete. They are more aware and concerned with what is happening in the world.

7. Higher-quality verbal contributions that are on the topic can be expected during discussion periods.

8. Logical thinking, cause-and-effect, probability, and discriminatory strategies are developing.

9. The creativity, artistic skills, and project capabilities can be quite impressive.

Here is a variation on the planning model presented at the beginning of the chapter. We will examine how each part applies to a lesson.

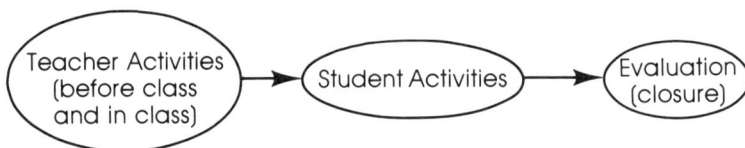

Teacher Activities

One role of the elementary teacher is that of a giver of information. Knowledge of subject matter is even more important in the upper grades. The other role is that of facilitator for learning. Guiding, directing, challenging, stretching, and enabling are important elements of the facilitator role. These two roles work in concert with each other for effective teaching.

The *teacher activities* part of the model establishes the main thrust of the lesson and the effectiveness of it. It may also require the most effort. You will work harder than the students. Your efforts will be divided into *before-class* and *in-class* activities.

Before-Class Activities

Plan and Prepare the Introduction.   Planning and preparing the lesson introduction is one of the most important parts of the lesson. A good introduction sets the stage for all that follows. Careful planning pays dividends throughout the lesson. The techniques selected for the first day or two are very important to create high interest at the outset and to maintain it throughout the duration of the introductory phase. Here are some things to try:

1. Design a bulletin board that captures the major themes of the new unit. It will probably be noticed as soon as the class enters the room. Some students may inspect it at length and anticipate what will happen during class. Begin the lesson by using this bulletin board display as your introduction, stressing the fact that it is an overview of the unit. Space can be provided for the students to write in pieces of information that may or may not be relevant to the learning objectives. Refer to these pieces of information

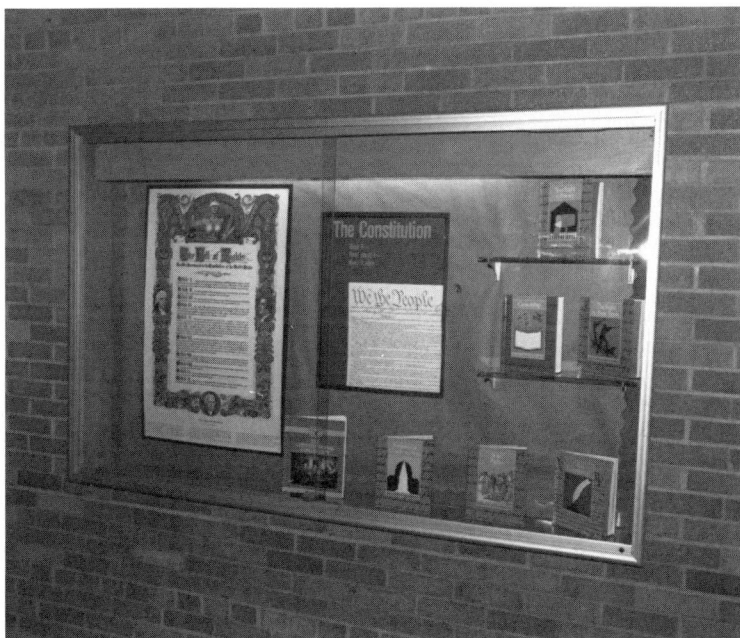

The elementary librarian is an in-school resource for attractive display ideas and materials.

periodically as you proceed. No books need to be used for this. This type of board display is not just room-dressing; it is a teaching tool.

2. For teaching an out-of-text content area, such as local history, begin by presenting the information in a list format. Brainstorm to solicit any and all information the students know. Write down each contribution, even if you are not sure that it is correct. There are no wrong answers. Checking the validity of this information is part of the lesson exploration and research. As a lesson introduction, this approach lends itself to a cooperative teacher-student planning session. Look at what you and your students have cooperatively gathered about your local history and decide where to go from there. Remember that teachers are not expected to know everything.

3. Using a resource person to speak to the class on the very first day can be an effective introduction strategy. Selecting the best person must be done carefully to insure he or she is truly knowledgeable in the field. An effective speaker can set the informational base for the entire unit.

4. Planning a multisensory display using a montage of various audiovisual materials is another possible way to introduce a lesson of this type. Select the materials carefully and set them up in a learning station so the students can move from station to station and get some exposure to each item. With perhaps 25 students in a class, efficient time management will be necessary to utilize this technique.

These are but a few of many introductory strategies that are used to create interest in a lesson. The imaginative, creative teacher spends planning time thinking of new or novel ways to introduce lessons. Flexibility is a characteristic of good planning.

Design a Pretest.   Prepare a short pretest to determine the extent of previous knowledge of your subject. From 20 to 25 test items is sufficient. If the topic was taught the previous year, all pertinent information will not necessarily be retained. It is always good to know the degree of retention and extinction. Plan from that point. Be flexible enough to implement Plan A (the students already know a lot about this) or Plan B (the students know very little about this).

Set the Objective(s).   Having gathered some basic information regarding retention, one or two tentative objectives can be formulated. The objective(s) must be tentative at this point until you actually administer your pretest and interpret the results. Your objective(s) may ultimately need to be adjusted to a more or less challenging level.

Prepare Yourself.   Being prepared as the leader of this learning endeavor is very important. All of the best learning materials available will not teach your children anything; *you* will. The teacher does the teaching, not the material. Be sure that you know your material thoroughly and have everything that you need to teach the lesson. Do this ahead of time! Get ready to teach before you start.

Plan the Lesson.   If you anticipate a lesson will run more than one day, and it frequently will, try to plan for at least the first three days in advance. Look at these plans as tentative. After the first day, you will probably have some indication as to which way the lesson is progressing, and adjustments can be made.

Consider the Need for Auxiliary Arrangements.   Planning ahead for such things as having the Computer Lab available for your social studies period, using the lunch room for group projects, having the filmstrip projector in operating condition, or arranging for a resource person to make a presentation to your class must be done well in advance. What if you need to move furniture? Will the custodian be available on a moment's notice, or do you need to get his services scheduled in advance? There is more to teaching than getting textbooks ready. It can be very disconcerting, both for teacher and students, when you suddenly discover in the middle of the lesson that you forgot to get the projector or to prepare a handout. The lesson momentum is interrupted and it is difficult to regain. Good planning helps you to know what you need.

Select Written Assignments Carefully.   Select the written work you will assign your students very carefully. Written assignments include such items as workbook pages, end-of-chapter study questions, reproduced practice sheets, and original writings. Be discriminating in your selection of written work. Is the time spent in reproducing all of these materials the most effective use of your in-school time?

Select Your Strategy.   Think about and plan all of your strategies in advance. Your method of introduction has already been discussed. Plan other strategies as well. Which questioning strategies will you use? What questions will you ask and what answers will you accept? How about culminating the lesson? How do you plan to evaluate the lesson? Strategies are too important to be left to the last minute.

The before-class teacher activities give a preview of the things that are organized before the students arrive. Being prepared as completely as possible diminishes lesson interruptions and other inefficient uses of learning time. We will now look at what the teacher does when the students arrive.

In-Class Activities

Present the Introduction.   The lesson introduction will be presented on the first day. You have planned this carefully before class, so it should go well. If you have chosen the audiovisual stations as your approach, watch carefully that all the students participate at each station. With 25 students moving about, it is easy for some to get lost in the shuffle.

Administer the Pretest.   If your introduction is completed on the first day, you are ready to give your pretest. To alleviate test stress, remind the students that this test will not be graded but they should do their best. Afterwards, evaluate with the students to find out what they know and what they do not know. This gives you clear indications for your planning and it notifies the *students* of the areas that are weak. The expectation of things to come is set.

Begin the Lesson.   Use your pretest results to help you look at your objective(s) critically. Decide if they are still valid. If not, rewrite them now. Tell the students the objectives they are to meet. Begin the main thrust of your lesson plan. Guide the discussion times and keep the class on the topic. One technique is to present all of your information at the beginning, then begin using the textbook and supplementary materials as needed. Do as much compacting as possible. Always be certain your directions are clearly understood for all assignments.

Assign Group Project.   If you have planned cooperative learning activities, move into this phase while the interest level is high. You must set the expectation for appropriate behaviors, especially if your class has not had this type of responsibility before. When you have organized the group structure and plans for completing the task(s) at hand, then your role becomes one of monitoring both the direction and the progress. Expect the groups to experience some conflicts, as they may be unsure of how to proceed or they may spend too much time on one part of the assignment. Try not to be too quick to help; the group may be able to solve their own problems. Chances are the members of the group will work together and find ways to keep the momentum going. Let them come to you if assistance is necessary.

Monitoring cooperative learning experiences requires keen observational skills. Some things to look for are:

1. Is every member of the group participating?
2. Are all of the materials being used?
3. Are all of the groups progressing into the lesson at a satisfactory rate?
4. Is the group leader doing all the telling and the members doing the work?

Being visible on the periphery of the various groups allows the teacher to listen, observe, float into and out of the individual groups, question or make a contribution, and assist if and when needed.

When the necessary before-class preparations are made in advance, the in-class activities are largely direct contact experiences with the learners. Organizational patterns, planning, appropriate use of time, and other management skills are learned by the students as they observe the teacher using them.

Student Activities

The second element in the model for planning a teaching strategy is student activities. You have planned the activities for the lesson. Now, what will the students do in this lesson?

Lesson Introduction. Planning and executing the lesson introduction is the responsibility of the teacher. During the introduction the student activity is determined somewhat by the particular strategy that is selected. The bulletin board idea indicates that students will offer some ideas to be written into the display. Attentiveness and acceptance of each other's contributions are expected. The audiovisual montage technique requires the students to experience and preview as much of the material as possible within the limits of the available time. Using a resource person for the lesson opener requires listening for information and asking pertinent questions at the appropriate time. The main role here for students is to receive and process information.

Lesson Pretest. Participating in the pretest may be one of the first tasks requiring individual responsibility from the learners. The pretest may be written or oral, and it requires the participation of all. Upon completion, the teacher-student interaction identifies both the strengths and the areas that need to be improved.

Textbook Tasks. The students should be informed right from the start just exactly what their textbook responsibilities are for the lesson. They will read the assigned textbook material outside of class. Textbook-related activities include such things as locating statements that show author bias or point-of-view, finding specific topic sentences, making some generalizations based on given statements in the text, and categorizing the end-of-chapter quizzes or study questions by using Bloom's taxonomy. Students may use the textbook as the primary source for an open-book quiz or test.

Written Tasks. Written tasks may occupy a large portion of class time on some days. Activities such as cooperative report writing, assignments that must be done in the library, or learning outlining skills under the direction of the teacher are examples of written tasks the students will do. It is helpful to remember that each student's writing ability may not be at the same level as his or her thinking ability. Can you think of any other written tasks that may apply here?

Project Tasks. When you are in the middle of the lesson, project tasks may be the major student activity. Projects are done in cooperative learning groups, with pairs of students or with students working alone. Projects are valid learning experiences and must be given adequate time for successful completion. If the students plan a project, they must plan the times, under teacher guidance.

What are some project tasks that your upper-elementary class may possibly perform? Here are some ideas to consider:

1. Construct a diorama to depict a typical home in your neighborhood when the city charter was granted.
2. Design and assemble a three-dimensional time line.
3. Design and construct a model of a small city to be used for a mapping lesson.
4. Write and present a short play.
5. Do research on someone mentioned in the textbook. Write a short speech and give an impersonation of that individual.
6. Choose a biography to read and prepare a creative dramatization. (Several students can work on this together.)
7. Write and assemble easy-to-read books about famous persons in history, and read them to the first graders. Put the books in the school library when the project is finished.
8. Write original study questions for everyone in the class to use. These can be kept for several years at the grade level.
9. Musically talented students can research the library and other sources for musical selections from the particular period they are studying. They can choose some short pieces, learn them, and present a concert to the class.
10. Projects also include those lesson requirements specifically assigned by the teacher that everyone must complete.

These are but a few ideas for projects that can be incorporated into a unit. With a solid foundation of information from the text and other supplemental materials that are available, the student projects provide reinforcement exercises.

Evaluation.   The students are responsible for taking any quizzes or tests that are required. Textbook series have reproducible unit tests available for purchase. Some chapter tests are in the student text. Teacher-made tests may more adequately meet the learning needs of a particular class or lesson.

Nonwritten evaluation is an ongoing process for all elementary grades. The teacher constantly evaluates the progress and direction of learning by noting such things as student verbal responses, the type of questions being asked, and the degree of student participation. Students in the upper grades frequently assist in lesson evaluation by participating in a critique, such as answering: What went really well in this unit? What could have been better? I would like to have spent more time on the _____ phase of the unit. This evaluation by students is very helpful for future planning.

A Sample Lesson

Following a specific procedure for planning enables the teacher to see the logical pattern in a good lesson. Designing a lesson for upper-elementary students follows the same sequential format as that used for primary-aged students.

Refer back to the implications for planning strategies for upper-elementary grades. Keep in mind the aspects of the teacher activities (before class and in class) and the student activities in the overall strategy selection process. Consider the stages of mental development of the individual students in an average fourth-grade class. Now examine a mapping lesson for this grade.

A Sample Lesson (Fourth Grade)

Lesson Topic: A Lesson for Mapping

Specified Objective: To identify and demonstrate characteristics and uses of graphic-relief and political maps.

Provision for High-Potential Learners: The students will demonstrate five distinguishing characteristics and uses of a given map and globe.

Rationale: Successful teaching of intermediate map and globe skills is based upon a solid foundation of initial skills learned previously. Establishing and maintaining a particular ability level with various map and globe activities provides a basic foundation that can be extended and enriched each succeeding year. Following the specific scope and sequence in the adopted textbook series can facilitate building that foundation. However, it is always a good idea to be sure that the foundation is intact before introducing new upper-level skills.

Concepts to Be Developed to Achieve the Objective: Here are some primary-level map and globe skills that should be established before attempting to teach this particular lesson.

1. To recognize that the globe is a model of the earth
2. To use map scales, legends, and keys
3. To know and use the cardinal and in-between directions appropriately
4. To locate the North and South Pole
5. To construct a simple map using the above skills
6. To use various units of measurement, both formal (inches and centimeters) and informal (paper-clip units, finger units, bead units)

Can you name some other introductory map skills the students should know at this time? If so, add them to the list above.

Teaching Strategy: The objective for this lesson is to identify and demonstrate the characteristics and uses of two different types of maps. The students are at varying levels of mental and physical development. Select a strategy that provides opportunities for the students to be more self-directing and the teacher to be less of a giver of information.

Motivators: Lesson motivators create interest in the lesson and encourage the learners to seek information. Motivators that are readily available, easy to interpret, and concrete work best. Here are some that can be implemented for this lesson:

1. Make two large signs to put up in the room, each displaying a working definition of a graphic-relief and a political map that will be highlighted during the lesson.

2. Have a display table or shelf with several different kinds of maps for the students to manipulate and study. Be sure there are several of the political and graphic-relief maps, as they are the purpose of the lesson.

3. Design a map and globe vocabulary chart with the specific terminology contained in the lesson. Some of those terms could include:

pole	continent
axis	sphere
diagram	equator
cartography	hemisphere
plateau	key
interpret	approximate distance
scale	symbols

4. Display a variety of different charts and graphs for the students to practice gathering information and making inferences. If they can correctly gather information from one source, that increases the probability of success in using another source (transfer).

Teaching the Concept: Teaching factual information about the characteristics and uses of political and graphic-relief maps can begin by using the textbook. Prior to class, examine the material to determine how much of it to use. If there is a large amount of reading material, it can be assigned as an out-of-class responsibility. The graphics, charts, tables, and other visuals in the text should be investigated together so that you are sure the students are interpreting and understanding them correctly.

Supplement the textbooks with additional resources. A quick check of the students' comprehension and recall of specific facts can be accomplished by using a variation of the total student response technique. At various times during the day ask different students to come to the chalkboard and write down at least two things they can remember about a political or a graphic-relief map. Another technique is to ask the students to write down their responses and put them into a box or large brown envelope. Either way, the teacher can determine the recall level of the class in a relatively short time.

Reinforcing the Concept: There are many computer programs that reinforce map and globe skills at all levels beginning with primary-level introductory programs. Consider using a computer program to reinforce the characteristics of the political and graphic-relief maps you are teaching. Carefully preview the program to determine if it meets the learning objective adequately and if the information is understandable and readable. An effective computer-based program can provide the needed stimulus for some students to process information that might otherwise remain unlearned.

Extending the Application: Making a lesson important to the students is critical, especially if the content is not part of their everyday experience. Finding out why these kinds of maps are needed and who uses them can be an investigation activity at the school library or other resource centers. A career investigatory module may be used to examine map usage in such areas as construction, politics, forestry, parks and recreation planning, real estate, land development, mining, municipal planning, and intercommunity relations. A cooperative learning plan can be devised for small groups of students to research the practical application of these maps.

The computer is a valuable tool for teaching and reviewing a lesson.

Another option is to assign a particular application project to each student, or to allow each student to choose one. An additional lesson extension is for the class to construct a graphic-relief map of their immediate community. Constructing such a map can reinforce the planning that was used for the development of certain areas in their locale.

Remember the provision that was set for the high-potential students? Providing for individual differences can occur at almost any point in the lesson. If a pretest is administered and these students "test out" on all of the criteria, then it is appropriate for them to begin the project as stated in the objective. Assignments, projects, goals, or individualized instructional programs for higher-achieving students are most successful when they are achievable within the organizational structure of the class and when there is a sense of productivity and achievement for the individual. If assignments are given that are totally separated from what others are doing, a sense of isolation and being different pervades. The ideal is to give challenging projects that meet specific learning capabilities and include all individuals in the large group.

Closure: The elements of closure for this lesson should include:

1. The beginning map skills that were taught the previous years
2. The ability to name the identifying characteristics of the two types of maps being investigated
3. The ability to demonstrate practical uses for the maps
4. The recognition of map usage in certain career fields
5. The utilization of the two kinds of maps for information gathering
6. The use of the library, the instructional media center, and community centers as sources of information

Lesson closure for fourth grade can be activity-oriented, a written assignment, or some of each. If the lesson has proceeded satisfactorily, the majority of the students will be comfortable with either closure plan. The students with strong reading and writing skills will do well on a written assignment. Students with lower reading and writing skills may need an individualized assignment. The same skill lesson can be presented to these students by choosing appropriate reading vocabulary.

<u>*A Closure Lesson:*</u>   Examine this written closure plan. The format is an informal quiz with items that require free-response answers. Extension is available for those who choose to do it. Here are some possible quiz items that will address the lesson objectives.

1. List five mapping skills that you knew before this lesson. (*Note:* Getting this information from the students now will assist in the planning strategy

for the next time you teach this lesson. Some probable responses might be: "I knew where north, east, south, and west are on a map. I knew the blue color is for water. I thought the triangle shapes on a map were for mountains."

2. Give three instances when you could use a graphic-relief map on a family vacation.

3. Why would a mining firm need and use a political map? List many reasons.

4. State one reason why a pilot needs to be familiar with land formations.

5. On the map of the United States, put in at least five physical features that you have investigated during this lesson.

6. You own a construction company and are considering building a shopping center for a certain area. How would you use a political map? List all the ways you know. You may use any library materials to help with this activity.

Doing one of the following optional activities affords an opportunity for the students to become involved in a project that is largely self-motivating and requires a time commitment. Establish a due date so the students know how much time they have to complete the project.

7. Make a three-dimensional graphic-relief map for your state. Use appropriate coloration. Bring it to class when you are finished.

8. Make a political map for your region of states showing the appropriate divisions. Be ready to give a short explanation of what you did to complete your project.

9. Select a career field that requires the use of maps. Investigate the job requirements, training, and any other specific information you can gather. Prepare a report to be given for the class.

10. Choose a friend to work with you. Prepare a "Concentration" type of game for your class. Try to include as much information as you can from all the resources that were used in class.

Evaluation: The evaluation strategy should correlate with the objectives of the lesson. In this example, the objective is the identification and use of graphic-relief and political maps. The degree to which the students can identify and use the particular map skills indicate the success of the lesson. A written paper-and-pencil test can be designed to evaluate recall of specific lesson elements. The test can be true-false, multiple choice, fill-in-the-blank, free response, or a combination. Each of these formats can be used to test what the teacher wants to find out.

Evaluation is a constant ongoing responsibility. The elementary teacher continually makes mental notes of student responses, monitors the questions that are asked, and observes how problem-solving activities are approached by individual students. These and other occurrences during a lesson give information to the teacher regarding where the lesson is going. With experience, these perceptions become more acute.

Consider the closure activities to be evaluative instruments. Each activity requires a certain understanding of factual data in order to be completed successfully. Look at each project or presentation as a personal extension of the student. Judge the presentation in terms of effort, time, resources, organization, and processes of learning. A letter grade is not always required in this type of situation.

Lesson Critique: At the conclusion of any lesson or learning activity, look closely at the various elements and try to determine the particular strengths as well as the areas that need improvement. Begin with the objective. Write notes to yourself in the space provided.

The Objective   *Notes*

1. Appropriate for the age group

2. Achievable

3. Previous knowledge

4. Pretest strategy

Teacher Preparation   *Notes*

1. I did this

2. Specific resources used

3. The teacher's manual was

4. Anticipating special needs

5. I already knew
   I did not know

6. My motivation activity was

Teacher's Activity   *Notes*

1. Time for planning

2. Teacher-student interaction

3. Specific teacher role was
   (facilitator, resource, sage)

4. Lesson atmosphere

5. Questioning strategy used

6. Provisions for special needs

Student Involvement   *Notes*

1. Student tasks

2. Learning styles exhibited

3. Level of verbal response

4. Student motivation

5. Examples of creativity, forethought,
   higher levels of thinking

Lesson Procedures   *Notes*

1. These areas went very well

2. These areas need revision

3. These areas are uncertain

4. Use of materials
   Textbook
   Manipulatives selected
   Audiovisuals
   Others

Evaluation   *Notes*

1. The written activity

2. In-class verbal responses

3. In-class nonverbal responses

4. Level of expectation

5. The group project(s)

6. The individual lesson extension

7. Level of primary skills

8. Role of the motivators

9. Role of the textbook
   Role of the manual

10. Others

Planning for the upper-elementary grades involves more complex factual information, relationships, and causes and effects, and provides for more independence and self-direction. The fourth grade in particular is viewed as the stepping stone from the primary learning stages to the intermediate learning stages. Creative abilities are emerging in a more visible way. Planning projects for groups and individuals add a new dimension to the lesson. Written skills are at the point where significant writing and research tasks can be accomplished successfully. As students move through the grades the span of performance levels widens, and the specific task of planning to meet those needs must be more realistic and within the boundaries of achievable expectations.

ACTIVITIES

These activities are designed to give you an opportunity to do some planning on your own. As you work through them, always be aware of the teacher's role and the students' role in the classroom. There are several activities available to you. Try to do as many as possible.

7.1   *Outlining a Lesson (Primary Grades)*

You have just read and examined a schematic layout of an elementary social studies lesson. Beginning with the selection of a topic and setting an objective, then moving through what the teacher and students do, to the culmination and evaluation, you can appreciate the true scope of effective planning. Now it is your turn.

Outline a lesson for an intermediate grade. Which topic will you choose—geography, trade, economics, U.S. presidents, pollution, or consumer concerns? Your instructor may provide a specific topic or give you a list. Think about your topic, then begin to plan your lesson using the following outline:

Topic:
Grade Level:
Objective(s):

Background Materials:
    1. For the teacher
    2. For the students
Teacher Role:
    I will. . . .

(Have I provided for three modalities of learning?)
Student Role:
    The students will. . . .

Evaluative Procedures:

Lesson Critique:
    1. The teacher's input
    2. The students' input

Self-Check.   Now examine this lesson outline in terms of the specific things that will happen and are observable during the lesson. The learning objective should be stated in such a way that you and the students know exactly what the lesson outcome is intended to be. Is it very clear? The background materials you select should provide necessary information or reference sources for introducing the lesson or for using during the lesson. What did you select for the teacher to do? Is the students' role to receive information only? Plan some diversity.

The evaluation procedures should include provisions for determining the degree of success for both the factual and behavioral learning that is planned.

Get together with some other people and share your outline. Where do you see your strengths and/or weaknesses? Which part of the outline did you enjoy doing the most? The least? Do you see your plan as being book-oriented or activity-oriented? Would an elementary student enjoy doing this lesson? Would she or he learn? Why or why not?

7.2   *The Lesson Plan*

Using the lesson outline in Activity 7.1 as a basis, extend it into a lesson plan using the sample lesson as a guide. Some of the items in Activity 7.1 can be used "as is"; some will have to be revised and restated.

Title of Lesson:
Specific Objective(s):

Provision(s) for High Potentials:

Rationale:

Concepts to Be Developed to Achieve the Objectives:

Teaching Strategy: Motivation

Teaching Strategy: Teaching the Concept

Teaching Strategy: Reinforcing and Applying the Concept

Extending the Application:

Closure:

Evaluation:

These activities are designed to give you an opportunity to practice initial lesson outlining and planning under the supervision of the instructor. They provide a chance to address the ways children learn, as well as an opportunity to look at planning in a step-by-step manner. Effective planning is more than opening a manual and beginning to teach. Performing these tasks with peers can help you learn with each other.

7.3   *Objectives and Evaluation (Upper Grades)*

Flexible, child-oriented activities lead directly to effective lessons and the building of a solid foundation for future learning.

Examine the mapping lesson again, specifically the stated objective. The general lesson revolves around graphic-relief and political map skills. Write three or four other learning objectives that would be acceptable for this lesson. Be specific. Is your objective measurable?

Specified Objectives
1.

2.

3.

4.

Examine the motivators used in this lesson. Keep in mind the age of the students. Design three or four additional motivators—you never know when you might need them. Be prepared to explain why you chose these particular motivators.

Motivators
1.

2.

3.

4.

Consider the methods of evaluation used for elementary students. Which do you think are the most valuable for you? Which evaluation instruments are the most valuable for the learners? What is the evaluation strategy that you will use in your lesson? Write at least three reasons for each of the methods you list below.

Evaluation

Formal	*Informal*
1.	1.
2. (for the teacher)	2.
3. (for the teacher)	3.
1.	1.
2. (for the student)	2.
3. (for the student)	3.

When you are finished, share this activity with your instructor. Share with others and get some varying perspectives. You are all in the process of becoming ready to teach.

7.4   *Planning for the Special Student*

An average fourth-grade class will have a wide range of academic abilities. Some children will probably be performing above grade level; a larger number will be solid, average fourth graders; and some will be performing below grade level. There may be special needs children in your classroom for whom you must provide appropriate instruction.

Assume that one of your students is a physically handicapped youngster who has very limited use of her hands and fingers. Her mental development is slightly above grade level and she functions well in smaller group settings with two or three other children. What specific plans can you make for her in the lesson? Write out a workable plan for this student. If you think that you need more information on teaching the physically disabled, do some reading in the field and then bring this activity to your instructor.

A PLAN FOR A PHYSICALLY HANDICAPPED STUDENT
(Limited use of the hands)

Teacher's Activities

1.
2.
3.
4.

Student's Activities

1.

2.

3.

4.

Extension: Choose another type of special needs child and plan for him.

Summary

These activities are designed to give you practice in meeting practical realities that confront every teacher. Thinking about and planning for good lessons that will excite students and arouse their interest is a constant process. Meeting specific learner needs challenges the creativity of even the most experienced educators.

READING RESOURCES

Cohen, H. G., and Kniep, W. M. "First Lessons in Map Use: The Primary Grader." *Social Studies,* 77 (July/August 1986): 162–64.

Common, D. H. "Students, Stories, and the Social Studies." *Social Studies,* 77 (November/December 1986): 246–48.

Neely, A. M. "Planning and Problem Solving in Teacher Education." *Journal of Teacher Education, 29* (May/June 1986): 29–33.

Neely, A. M. "Teacher Planning: Where Has It Been? Where Is It Now? Where Is It Going?" *Action in Teacher Education,* 7 (Fall 1985): 25–29.

Ohanian, S. "Planning Ahead." *Learning, 14* (1985): 14.

Pigford, A. P. "Why Do Principals Collect Lesson Plans?" *Principal, 66* (March 1987): 50–51.

8
Social Studies Textbooks

PROJECTIONS

The social studies textbook is the mainstay of the curriculum. Will it continue to be so? What is the role of textbooks in the future? It is reasonable to expect that textbooks will continue to maintain a prominent place in the elementary curriculum? A textbook helps teachers, curriculum coordinators, and administrators to identify the skills that need to be taught. The textbook helps individual teachers focus on skill development in a sequential organized manner. Without a textbook series for reference, teachers may do a thorough job of teaching a number of skills yet inadvertently omit some others. The textbook coordinates a complete skill development program.

It is anticipated that individual social studies topics (as presented in the basic textbook) will be supplemented with specific reading materials on a regular basis. Using other materials to more completely explore a particular topic is not a new idea. However, trends indicate that this practice is an integral, planned component of curriculum development. It is logical that students can learn a great deal about political conventions, for example, by reading trade books and newspaper articles written specifically on that general theme. The textbook provides the basic information; supplemental materials provide clarification and enrichment.

An exciting development in education is the practice of using specialists and practitioners to teach particular topics in the classroom. These individuals are primarily used as guest speakers. For example, a representative from the Better Business Bureau might speak on the topic of consumer rights and responsibilities. It is possible, even advisable, that specialists will collaborate with educators in the writing of textbooks and other educational materials.

The cost of textbooks is a significant budget item for school districts. The increasing cost is one reason why classrooms share a set of books. Will technology affect the future of our traditional hardcover textbook? It is possible that textbooks will eventually be a computer disk. The technological capability is available. Consumer demands and publishing priorities will eventually determine the format of future textbooks.

The social studies textbook can be the foundation of a comprehensive program. It provides the basic social studies concepts and principles, as well as factual information. The basic text is the source of materials to be presented to students in group and individualized programs.

The social studies textbook is not all-inclusive, nor should it be. If the basic text contained everything the students needed to learn, a typical social studies lesson would probably be nothing more than an exercise in reading. The science of teaching would be nothing more than guiding the students through the pages of written material, and the art of teaching would be nonexistent. The best-designed textbooks have broad parameters to accommodate both the art (creative extensions, personalized and individualized activities, incidental teaching, integrating lessons) and the science (sound instructional strategies, evaluative procedures, adhering to the principles of educational psychology) of teaching.

This chapter examines the use of textbooks as the primary source for an effective social studies program. Knowing how to use the textbook effectively adds significantly to well-planned lessons and learning experiences. Specific textbook organizational strategies will be examined, which are important for the beginning teacher. Using the textbook facilitates a smooth progression toward the expected learner outcomes. Some current elementary textbooks will be reviewed to present insights into social studies materials, philosophies, scope and

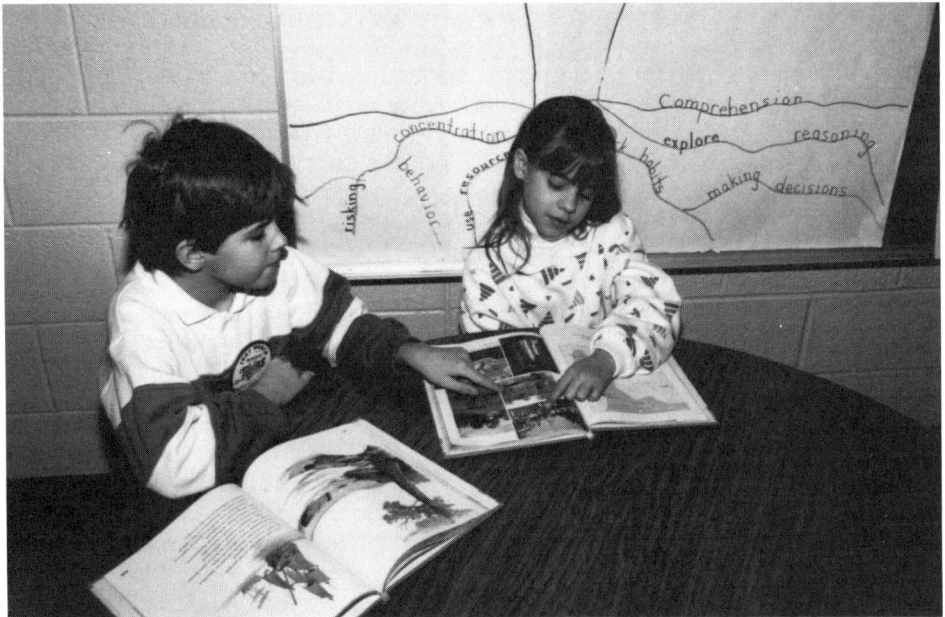

Pairing students to work together from the textbook is one way to meet individual needs.

sequences, and patterns for instruction and learning. Some criteria for selecting and evaluating textbooks (and their supplementary materials) will be given. Examining textbooks is necessary to insure the best selection of materials for students.

Why Use Textbooks?

Advantages

An Instructional Tool.   A good up-to-date textbook is an excellent instructional tool for teachers. For the student, the textbook provides needed data and is their primary source for information-gathering activities. For the teacher, the textbook provides the factual information needed as well as suggestions for teaching the lessons. The textbook usually contains all the information necessary to teach the lessons without having to use any supplementary materials. Supplementary materials should be used, but if none are available, you can teach the lesson adequately by using materials in the textbook. The textbook also provides suggestions for enrichment, individualized activities, special needs students, hands-on activities and projects, and other out-of-text activities. It is your primary teaching aid. You must adapt your textbook to fit the needs of your students; do not try to adapt your students to the textbook.

Curriculum Continuity.   Every school system must have a curricular plan that specifies what is to be taught in each grade level. In most schools, the curriculum is set by the textbooks that are in use. Adopting and using a social studies textbook assures local curriculum directors, administrators, and school boards that the students are presented with basically similar data and learning experiences. Every teacher knows what she or he is supposed to teach, what the students have covered before, and what they will learn when they enter the next grade level. The textbook approach facilitates cooperation among the instructional staff to work together to achieve specific learning goals.

Convenience. A good textbook presents information on a wide variety of social studies topics. It is a convenient source from which the teacher builds and plans lessons. The text, as a basic sourcebook, eliminates the need for searching out many different trade books and supplementary materials that may or may not coordinate effectively. With a basic text, the best supplementary materials are more easily identified for each lesson or unit.

Management. A well-balanced textbook offers planning strategies and learning activities for whole class lessons, individualized lessons for the special needs students, and enrichment activities for the advanced learners. Whereas a large part of lesson planning must be a personalized effort on the part of the teacher, a good textbook provides the format and parameters for this process. Using a textbook for classroom instruction eases the logical, timely transition from one major instructional mode to another. It keeps the progression of teaching and learning on track and within specified time frames.

Evaluation. The textbook provides a basis for evaluation. Evaluation procedures that are established in the school system or region are more applicable when the teaching materials and strategies are complementary. It is difficult, if not impossible, to evaluate the learning of individual students or groups of students (at particular grade levels or within buildings) when there is little or no organization to the teaching of social studies. A common textbook provides the core of knowledge that all are expected to master.

Disadvantages

Overdependence. A teacher is overly dependent on the textbook when it is used primarily as a social studies reader. A text that is used only to read about certain topics of interest and to answer questions at the end of the chapter is not being used appropriately. A person who is uncertain or insecure about teaching social studies may rigidly follow a step-by-step lesson outline as presented in the teacher's guide, ask each question as it is printed, and attempt to present every learning activity as suggested. This type of textbook usage is limiting for the teacher in the sense that it leaves little space for instructional creativity or professional growth. It is unnecessary to do every activity or follow every suggestion that is in the book for a lesson to be successful. The materials in the teacher's guide are given as *aids* for planning. The teacher should read and consider all of them and then select those that most adequately meet the learning needs of his or her students. The children should not be penalized for having a weak and poorly prepared teacher. The textbook cannot teach by itself.

Unrealistic Expectations. A textbook is limiting for a teacher when she or he has unrealistic expectations for the text that is being used. One common expectation is the belief that the book should contain everything that is needed to carry out the entire social studies program. "Give me a book and let me teach" is a poor attitude toward the teaching of social studies. A text will contain a large portion of the data or content and many skill-building activities that are needed, but no text can possibly have everything a teacher needs to motivate and properly teach social studies. Supplementary material such as audiovisuals, library books, trade books, community resource persons, group learning activities, out-of-building experiences, and all other available sources are integral parts of an effective social studies program. It is unreasonable and undesirable for the teacher to think of the textbook as being all-inclusive.

Readability Levels. Social studies textbooks are intended to be read by the students. A text for the fourth grade, for example, is written for the average fourth grader to read independently with relative ease. A textbook that is too difficult to read is a stumbling block for students who read significantly below grade level. If the teacher must read the text to the class a large portion of the time, that particular text is inappropriate for the class. If the teacher reads the text to the class on a regular basis, it is time-consuming and results in a largely auditory-based lesson. However, it is beneficial for the teacher to read to the class for a specific purpose. She or he may choose to read a passage from the text to model a point of view, an attitude, or a personal point of reference. Reading a diary selection or a cartographer's report is a learning experience that is best performed by the teacher for proper emphasis or feeling.

Readability formulas such as those developed by Dale-Chall, Spache, and Washburne can be applied to various textbooks to determine the readability level of written material. What can the individual teacher do if the book is too difficult? Some major adaptations will be necessary to conduct a successful lesson. The student who cannot successfully read the material independently can be paired with another student who will read aloud to the group and perhaps function as a discussion leader to assist in clarifying the data and concepts. A special needs student may be paired with the teacher or a peer. Continual usage of a text that is above the comprehension level of the class is stressful for both the teacher and the students. Obtaining a text that more adequately meets the developmetal needs of the class should be a top priority.

Current Events Issues. A textbook is limited in its treatment of current events issues. A major world, national, or local event may appear on the scene literally overnight. No text can possibly keep current with matters such as these. Events such as a famine or drought, changes in governments, breakthroughs in science or technology, and other timely happenings must be handled as they happen. Some background information and data that correlate in a general way may be found in the social studies textbook or in the library. Information on a newly formed country, on the other hand, will not be available except perhaps in the newspapers, national magazines, or on television news broadcasts. A good textbook will contain the appropriate process skills that are needed to investigate current events in an organized, goal-oriented manner. The techniques of teaching current events should be an integral part of the organizational structure in a good social studies text.

Inflexible Format. A textbook is limiting if the format and the structure are restrictive and inflexible. An effective, usable text gives the teacher a solid basis for instruction in the product, process, and human relations skills. It is also open and flexible enough for the teacher to exercise judgment in terms of scheduling, timing, decision making, monitoring and adjusting the scope or sequence, and selecting supplemental materials for enrichment. A textbook that must be followed in a rigid, page-by-page manner is exclusionary and even boring to use after a period of time.

A textbook is inflexible if there are few or no provisions for crosscurriculur lesson integrations. The teaching of social studies as an isolated subject is limiting. Social studies is one subject that readily lends itself to lesson integration. The creative teacher integrates the music, art, customs, games, labor, scientific accomplishments, folk tales, and other aspects into the planning of particular units. Even math can be included—for example, coinage, barter, and weights and measures.

A textbook format is inflexible if the lesson designs are for large group instruction only and if provisions for individualization are incidental or infrequent. A good text must meet the needs of a variety of learning styles and modes. A flexible textbook includes many hands-on learning experiences for students in both large and small group settings. Out-of-text experiences reinforce learning and provide another opportunity to internalize material presented in the book. Usable textbooks provide and encourage the use of teacher-student interaction activities. A text that gives all the answers leaves little room for problem solving, research, logical reasoning, or other activities that require cooperative research or the consideration of varying opinions. If the textbook is inflexible, it is not an appropriate tool for quality teaching and learning.

Other Limitations. A textbook limits quality teaching and learning if it is blatantly stereotypical, sexist, or dated. Propagating such stereotypes as Eskimo families living in igloos or African families occupying only cone-shaped mud huts is inappropriate and prejudicial. Keeping the material current is an important responsibility of textbook authors and publishers.

Ineffective, unattractive, or confusing illustrations and graphics limit the effectiveness of a textbook. Colorations, size of type, clarity, legibility, and contrast affect the usefulness to students. An attractive, colorful, varied textbook adds interest to the prospect of using a book. Examine some elementary textbooks and ask yourself if you would enjoy using this book if you were in the fifth grade.

A textbook is limiting if the questioning strategies are largely recall. These questions are most appropriate for introductory purposes. Questioning strategies in the student text and the teacher's guide should include items that challenge the learners toward the higher-level thinking skills. Thought-provoking questions that give students the opportunity to respond at a level beyond that of memory recall should be included in the text.

Social studies textbooks are widely used by teachers because they offer an organized, systematic approach for presenting lessons to students. The basic text is a convenient source for planning and information gathering. New teachers follow the textbook outlines and lesson planning schemes very closely for the first year or so as they are learning effective teaching strategies and establishing a personal teaching expertise. A good textbook is an effective tool for teaching and learning and it becomes even more important when the individual teacher expands its horizons and invests her or his creative abilities. A textbook is only as effective as the teacher who uses it.

Current Textbooks

What textbook should you use? This is not really a valid question because you will use the textbook selected by your school system. There are good texts available but the selection is diminishing. Several publishers have merged and dropped some of the series and combined others. Some of the available textbook series are listed below.

Publisher	Title	Copyright
Harcourt Brace Jovanovich, Publishers	*HBJ Social Studies* (K–6)	1988
Webster Division, McGraw-Hill Book Co.	*Our Nation, Our World* (K–6)	1986
Riverside Publishing Company	*Riverside Social Studies Program* (K–6)	1982
Silver, Burdett and Ginn, Inc.	*Social Studies* (K–8)	1988

As you review social studies textbooks, you will find that they follow a similar content format. Social studies is usually taught by starting with the child and his or her immediate surroundings, then expanding outward to the community, state, nation, and world. By examining Table 8–1 you can see the pattern that is generally followed.

Even though similar material is taught in each grade level, there is a difference in how each textbook approaches the material. There is also a difference in which skills are taught and the approaches that are used. A review of a text and a teacher's manual will show you these differences.

Textbook Organization

Teachers enjoy using textbooks and teacher guides that are well organized and easy to use. Such textbooks enhance rather than detract from the organizational structures that teachers strive to develop. Consequently, a well-organized textbook will be used more effectively than one that is confusing.

Table 8-1 Textbook Content by Grade Level

				Publishers				
Grade	Harcourt, Brace Jovanovich[1]	Riverside Publishing[2]	Silver, Burdett and Ginn[3]	Webster Division, McGraw Hill Book Company[4]
K	Title: *Friends* (Covers: Home and school; Why we need rules)			Title: *Looking at Me* (Covers: Who am I?; My world)
1	Title: *Families* (Covers: Family life, past and present; Citizenship)	Title: *You and Me* (Covers: Likenesses and differences; Relationships to others)	Title: *Families and Their Needs* (Covers: Food, clothing, and shelter; Government; Basic concepts)	Title: *Meeting People* (Covers: School, self, families, neighborhood, and country)
2	Title: *Neighborhoods* (Covers: How people live and work in the neighborhood; Citizenship)	Title: *Here We Are* (Covers: Communities from historic, economic, geographic, social, political points of view)	Title: *Communities and Their Needs* (Covers: Needs of communities; Responsibilities of individuals)	Title: *Going Places* (Covers: People in groups; Needs of community; Farms)
3	Title: *Communities* (Covers: How people live and work in communities, past and present; How people change)	Title: *Our Land* (Covers: Environments of North America; Communities and their resources)	Title: *Our Country's Communities* (Covers: Different kinds of communities; Diversity of people)	Title: *Communities* (Covers: Geography and history of US, Canada, and Mexico)

4	Title: *States and Regions*	Title: *Where on Earth*	Title: *Geography of States and Regions*	Title: *Earth's Regions*
	(Covers: Geography, history and economics of the US; Citizenship)	(Covers: Life on this planet; Diversity of uses of the environment; Role of citizens)	(Covers: Geography, culture, and economics of regions of US and the world)	(Covers: Geography; Living on 5 continents; The 50 states)
5	Title: *The United States: Its History and Neighbors*	Title: *The Americans*	Title: *United States: Yesterday and Today*	Title: *United States: Our Nation and Neighbors*
	(Covers: Geography, history, and economics; Our political system)	(Covers: Life in the Americas; Contributions of earlier settlers)	(Covers: History and geography of the US; Our heritage)	(Covers: History and geography of the US; Our North American neighbors)
6	Title: *The World: Past and Present*	Title: *The World— Now and Then*	Title: *The World: Yesterday and Today*	Title: *The World*
	(Covers: Geography, culture, history, and economics of regions of the world; World citizenship)	(Covers: Cultural change; Relationships)	(Covers: History and geography of the world)	(Covers: World history; Ancient civilizations; Important nations)

[1] *HBJ Social Studies* (Orlando, FL: Harcourt, Brace, Jovanovich, 1988).
[2] *Riverside Social Studies* (Chicago: Riverside Publishing Company, 1982).
[3] *Social Studies* (Lexington, MA: Silver, Burdett and Ginn, Inc., 1985).
[4] *Our Nation, Our World* (New York: Webster Division, McGraw Hill Book Company, 1986).

Student Text

Publishers take great care in the layout of their texts so students will enjoy using them. A textbook that is pleasant to use is a more effective learning tool than one that is not. If the organizational structure is confusing or unclear to the student, it will not enhance learning. A weak or loosely organized text reflects throughout the entire program. We will now examine some organizational features of student textbooks.

Physical Features. A student text must be sturdy and well constructed to endure constant use. Quite frequently one set of texts is shared by several classrooms, so the construction of the book becomes even more important. Purchasing textbooks is a large budget item for school districts, so it is important that the text will last more than one year. A spiral-bound text does not stand up to heavy use very well. Although the spiral design lays open on the student's desk very nicely, the daily page turning tends to encourage tears along the spirals. Pages tear out and get lost. The spiral design is more adaptable for the student workbook.

A hard-cover text is probably the best choice for elementary students. These books are sturdy, well bound, and more adaptable for heavy use. The weight and strength of the paper in a student text is also an important feature. Good quality paper will not soil or tear easily.

Appearance. Students enjoy using a text that is esthetically appealing. A book that is well designed, clear, and spatially balanced will appeal to the child more than a childish or gimmicky text.

The physical size of the book should be appropriate for the age and general size of children using it. The book should be well balanced and feel comfortable to use. The illustrations, photographs, and other grapics must be clear and easily identifiable. Illustrations and photographs are used to reinforce and clarify the printed material. Children who may have trouble reading the print can get meaning by reading the pictures. Photographs should be in focus, true to life, and appealing. Illustrations in the student text should add to the general appearance of the book.

The size of type and page layout are also important to students. Younger children can decode more easily when the type size is larger; older children can read type that is smaller. The spacing between words should be at appropriate intervals. The amount of written material on each page is also important. A first-grade book may have only one or two sentences on each page, whereas an upper-grade book will have full pages of print. Students enjoy using their text when the amount of written material is not too overwhelming and if it is in proportion to other items on each page. Students have positive attitudes toward their texts when the reading material is clear, concise, and relatively easy to read.

Content. The content of the student text determines to a large degree the strength of the entire social studies curriculum. A strong social studies program has good student materials to aid in achieving its goals and objectives. If the content does not come across very clearly in the materials the students use, it is very likely that it may not come across at all. An effective teacher's guide must correlate with the content in the student's book. Here are some organizational content items to examine in a student textbook.

Table of Contents: The table of contents lists the chapters, units, or learning modules that are presented in the book. Reading this gives the students an idea of what they will be studying during the year.

Introduction: The introduction welcomes the students to the textbook and the social studies program and gives a brief account of the topics that will be studied during the year as well as the new skills that will be introduced. It might also give one or two high-interest motivators such as: "Have you ever constructed a real thatched roof hut? You will when we study the people of the South Seas in Chapter Six." The introduction serves to orient the students to the core curriculum for the year.

Chapter-Unit Organization: A good textbook is well organized at the chapter or unit level. Each chapter emphasizes specific goals and objectives as well as provides activities, assignments, questions, and other learning experiences. The specific objectives of each individual lesson and the overall chapter itself must be clear and definite.

   Learning activities that relate directly to the objectives insure the achievement of the objectives. Each lesson is designed with learner needs in mind. The questions that are to be answered must be clearly stated and should relate directly to the main lesson objective and all supplementary objectives. Lesson questions should include some opportunities for practice in the higher-level thinking skills.

Lesson Design: The lesson design is important if the students are to follow it in some semblance of order. A lesson that is largely reading about social studies is just a reading lesson. An effective social studies lesson includes these processes:

   Reading: The students read the text material independently. (Special needs children will receive assistance.) The students read selected supplementary materials that enhance the textbook presentation (library books, pamphlets, reports, magazine articles, trade books, encyclopedias, and other written material). The teacher reads selected materials to the class.

   Thinking: The students are given time to think about the materials they have read. Thinking time can include sharing thoughts and ideas with a friend or small group. Talking it over results in exposure to ideas and specific points one person may have overlooked during the reading process.

Doing: The students are given opportunities to do activities that help them experience the lesson. Doing the lesson includes projects, hands-on activities, creative experiences, lesson extensions, group projects, individualized activities, and other things that get the students actively involved.

Evaluating: The students are given the opportunity to make some judgments about what they have learned and how they have learned it. The students will give ideas and thoughts about particular materials they have used to help them learn: Which ones are the best? Which ones did not help very much? Why or why not? What would have worked better? Students are given an opportunity to project: How will learning about this particular topic help me? Why should I know about this? Can we see any relationships here?

Glossary.   Current student textbooks usually include a glossary of specialized social studies terms and the vocabulary words that are introduced in the book. A glossary that defines terms as they are used in the book is a more effective tool than a regular dictionary, especially for young learners.

It is important to discuss student workbooks and practice books. Many publishers provide a workbook to accompany the student texts. These are usually a consumable, soft-cover book with perforated pages. The lesson content of workbooks has been improving steadily in recent years. The tasks students are expected to perform in their workbooks are application-oriented, designed to apply what they are studying in the text. A workbook is a valuable learning tool for students if it is used to enhance the concepts that are presented in the textbook. Using the workbook as a time filler or as busy work is a misuse of an otherwise effective learning tool.

Teachers who use a well-organized textbook that follows established guidelines of how children think will help children experience the social studies in positive ways. The organizational patterns of the texbook should be clear and easy to follow. A textbook that shows obvious well-organized lessons and activities assists in the learning process.

Teacher's Guide

The teacher's guide (manual) strengthens the total social studies program when it is well organized and substantial. Effective lessons are enhanced by the material that is available in the guide. We will now examine the components of a teacher's guide.

Format.   Like the student's textbook, a book the teacher will be using all year should be appealing to look at and comfortable to hold. Sturdy construction is an important feature for a book that must endure constant use. A spiral-bound guide lays flat so the teacher can scan the pages while teaching a lesson. The lesson goals and objectives, questioning procedures, and other lesson elements can be seen at a glance. Most current teacher guides present the student text pages in reduced size directly on the pages the teacher uses.

Scope and Sequence.   The scope (what you will teach) and sequence (the order in which you will teach it) of a social studies program encompasses the content and concepts that are to be taught, the expected learner outcomes, and the lesson presentations. The teacher's guide presents the scope of the program so that teachers know exactly what content is to be taught during the year and at what level. For example, some guides and programs organize their material in a three-step pattern:

> *Introduce:*   A skill (topic, lesson, or activity) is introduced. This is usually the student's first exposure to it.
>
> *Emphasize:*   The skill is explored or emphasized in depth. This covers more than one lesson.
>
> *Master:*   The skill is mastered or learned at this level. Long-range retention of the skill is expected. (Evaluation is done here.)

The guide shows individual lessons as geared toward one of these three levels of instruction. A lesson that is *introductory* is highly motivational, interest provoking, and stimulating. Introductory-level lessons usually do not demand extensive periods of time.

Lessons that are at the *emphasis* level are the core of the unit. These require considerable teacher effort and longer instructional periods as the major learning objectives and reinforcing activities are stressed heavily. A variety of learning experiences, materials, and teaching strategies are necessary for these lessons.

Mastery-level lessons are designed for long-range retention. This level is preceded by effective introductory lessons and solid emphasis level lessons. Without these two foundation-building levels of learning, true mastery level is very difficult if not impossible to achieve. Checking for retention of these mastery skills is an integral part of units that follow.

Teacher guides present the sequence of the social studies program and address the order in which units and skills are taught and learned. Can the students at a given grade level understand, accept, relate to, learn about, and experience a given topic? Lessons, ideas, and experiences that are out of sequence from a developmental point of view are difficult to teach and even more difficult for students to learn. Looking at the sequence of lessons in the guide gives a general idea of program expectations. The sequence of a program is very often given in a flowchart format in the teacher's guide and is relatively easy to interpret.

Goals and Objectives.   A well-organized teacher's guide states goals and objectives in a clear, forthright manner. Specific objectives are both achievable (the students can do this) and sequential (objectives progress from relatively easy to

Reviewing textbooks in class helps these future teachers prepare to teach a social studies lesson.

slightly more challenging at each level of instruction). The goals and objectives reflect a commitment to a well-balanced social studies experience for students. The product, process, and human relations skills of the social studies are kept in immediate focus.

Examination of the teacher's guide reveals the program goals. The goals may be product-oriented (students learning a variety of process skills that apply to many situations) or may emphasize the human relations skills (students experience the becoming, valuing, caring, empathizing skills). Individual lessons and units should correlate directly with the primary program goals.

Lesson Design. The organizational structure of the teacher's guide includes complete lesson designs from motivational techniques to evaluative procedures. A good, usable lesson strategy has a direct correlation to the specific objectives of the individual lesson as well as to the unit objectives. Stating a clear, definite objective for a lesson is one thing, designing and planning the entire lesson to implement that objective is quite another matter.

A complete lesson design clearly shows all of the necessary elements of a lesson that is ready to be used in the classroom. The lesson presentations in the teacher's guide should include these elements:

Objective(s):   The lesson objective states clearly what the students are expected to do at the completion of a lesson. Accomplishing the objectives pervades all phases of the lesson.

Motivational Techniques: The lesson motivators are the activities that create interest in the lesson. Motivational activities are teacher-directed.

Introduction: The introduction to the lesson should prepare the students for the material that will be presented in the entire lesson. The introduction can encourage or discourage further interest in the lesson.

Lesson Development: This is the main body of the lesson and includes both teacher activities and student activities. Student activities include opportunities for concrete hands-on experiences, exposure to various learning materials, and many opportunities to learn. Lesson development provides activities for the teacher to model the skill, the students to practice the skill, and the teacher and students to work together. Provisions are made for the various preferred learning styles of students and adequate lesson extensions are provided. The lesson development component includes a large variety of supplementary materials for student use and for reinforcing the textbook presentation.

Evaluation: The evaluation techniques and strategies are designed to determine the level of objective mastery. Evaluation strategies are clear, usable, and unencumbered, and are appropriate to the objective and the stage of development of the students.

Special Needs Students: Provisions are made to address the needs of the high-potential, special education, physically disabled, and limited-English-speaking students.

A Special Notation: Educators at all levels recognize the need for teaching students how to think. Teaching students how to develop and use the logical reasoning and thinking processes is an integral component of many elementary programs. Teaching the thinking skills is part of reading, math, science, language arts, and the social studies. Teaching factual data alone is not an acceptable strategy. Beginning in the primary grades, students are learning decision-making strategies, cause and effect, procedures for effective planning, projecting, analyzing, comparing and contrasting, and other upper-level thinking skills.

Textbooks are addressing the students' need to learn these thinking skills, and educators are demanding their inclusion in the materials they use. Current teacher's guides and supplementary materials are including activities that challenge students to stretch their thinking processes beyond the memory level. A social studies program that works toward establishing some upper-level thinking skills will be evident in the questioning strategies presented in the guides.

Questions that accompany the lessons in the teacher's guide should contain items directed toward the cognitive and affective domains. Questioning strategies that address the cognitive domain require a knowledge-type response. Questioning strategies that address the affective domain require responses that draw on a student's values, emotions, feelings, and experiences. Both types of questions are necessary for integrated learning to occur.

Supplemental Materials.   The teacher's guide includes a listing of the supplementary materials that may be used to teach a lesson. These supplementary materials can include such things as books, filmstrips, computer programs, skills kits, and other hands-on materials for both the teacher and the students.

A guide that is complete, clearly defined, and written with the classroom teacher's needs in mind will be used regularly and effectively. An organized teacher's guide is especially important for beginning teachers and experienced teachers who are using a program for the first time. You will probably use the teacher's guide extensively until you become familiar with the social studies program you are using.

Using a Social Studies Textbook

The textbook is a teaching aid designed to help the teacher do a more effective job. As the teacher, you will determine what your students will learn, the teaching strategy to be employed, and the resources you will use. The textbook provides the content information for the students.

The Teacher's Guide

The teacher's guide is one of the most useful aids that a teacher can have and there are good reasons for the beginning teacher to rely heavily on it. The most important reasons are that it tells you what you are to teach and it provides a base to work from until you get to know your students. Then you can tailor your program to fit their needs and learning styles, as well as your own teaching style. As you become more experienced, you will rely less on the teacher's guide and more on your perception of students needs.

The first step in using a teacher's guide is to examine it carefully. There is usually an introductory section on how to use the guide. It explains the format and teaching strategy. Look at the objectives and skills to be developed. Then read the textbook material to see if the objectives fit the content. You will find that a lot of your planning has already been done for you in the teacher's guide.

As you become familiar with the material, look for ways to modify the teaching strategy. You can try different motivational schemes or data-processing activities. If needed, you may change the level of difficulty to a more appropriate level for your students.

Supplementing the Text

The teacher's guide will supply a list of resources that can be used with the textbook. These resources may be background information for the teacher, additional reading materials for the students, audiovisual materials, and even computer software. Because these resources are not always available, you should develop your own resource collection.

Trade books are excellent supplemental reading materials. You may obtain books from the school library or you may purchase several to keep and use in the classroom. One of the best sources is to ask your students to bring in books they have at home and are willing to share with the class. Children who do not read well should not be penalized for not reading, but all children should be exposed to books that relate to the topic under discussion. This allows the student to know that there is much more information outside of the textbook than there is in it. It also shows the slow or nonreader the importance of reading to obtain information.

A collection of pictures is a good way to enhance a lesson. Children who cannot read the textbook can read pictures. Colorful pictures provide a more concrete dimension to the lesson.

Artifacts and realia bring the lesson to life. Collect real things or replicas that go with the lesson. Such things as coins, clothing, art work, and tools allow the student to touch and examine real items, providing experiences that make the lesson more concrete. They add the visual and kinesthetic modes to the lesson.

Bring art and music into the lesson. Creating murals, making models, and drawing pictures are other concrete activities that relate directly to the topic. Art activities allow students to be creative and at the same time express their conception of the topic. Music involves physical participation in the lesson. As children listen to people sing about their homes, families, and occupations, they can understand that there are people just like themselves in other areas of the world. They can sing songs of other cultures and pretend to be a part of that culture. The true character of a people can most easily be found in their art and music.

Bring in resource people. A resource person with pictures, slides, and/or authentic objects is exciting and informative. You may know a lot about a topic, but not as much as a resource person who can share information not found in books. The personal touch cannot be duplicated in a book. Would you rather read a book about Egypt, talk to someone from Egypt, or listen to someone who has been there?

The textbook is designed to have enough information for the students without having to use any other resource. Recognize that any supplementary materials you add will ultimately enhance the program. This is why lists of supplementary materials are available. You can and should enhance your social studies lesson by supplementing in every possible way.

Personalizing the Textbook

The ultimate goal is to use the textbook to fit your teaching style and your students' needs. This comes with experience. After you become familiar with the material you are to teach, you will develop your own version of the lessons. You will use some materials from the textbook but you will also develop appropriate activities, use supplementary materials, and rearrange your time allotments. When you can teach what is in the textbook without having to rely on the teacher's guide, the program is in your control. You can truly say that you have made the content of the textbook learnable for your students.

ACTIVITIES

The following activities give you the opportunity to examine a textbook and a teacher's guide. Select a social studies textbook and the accompanying teacher's guide. Check with your media center or your instructor for copies.

8.1 *Reviewing a Textbook*

Examine a student textbook to get an idea of how the students will perceive the text. Use the following criteria as a guide. Do not answer with a simple yes or no; explain your answer. Make comments that you can share with your instructor or group.

Title of the Textbook:

Publisher:

Grade Level:

Appearance
   Cover:

   Print:

   Illustrations:

   Size:

   Comments:

Content
Content covered:

Readability:

Vocabulary:

Glossary:

Up-to-date materials:

Stereotypes:

Index and Table of Contents:

Others:

Comments:

Will this book grab the students' interest? Why or why not?

8.2   *Reviewing a Teacher's Guide*

To use a teacher's guide effectively, you must know what it contains. This activity requires that you examine a teacher's guide. You will learn what it contains and how lessons are organized. Describe the features as you examine them. Make comments to relate what you think.

Title:
Publisher:
Grade Level:
Appearance
Print:

Size:

Cover:

Binding:

Comments:

Organization
   Teacher's guide and Student Text (separate or together):

   Can you find what you need?

   Comments:

Contents
   Objectives:

   Skill development:

   Vocabulary:

   Strategies:

   Activities:

   Others:

   Comments:

Resources
   Suggestions for
   Gifted:

   Slow learners:

   Remediation:

   Nonreaders:

   Others:

   Comments:

What was your overall opinion of the guide?

Now meet with your group and compare your evaluation. Did you like your textbook and teacher's guide? What do you consider to be the best features? The weakest? Would you be able to plan and teach a lesson using this textbook and teacher's guide?

Summary

This chapter overviewed social studies textbooks. Advantages and disadvantages of textbook programs were discussed. Some current textbooks were listed and the content taught at each grade level was compared. The organization of the textbook and teacher's guide were detailed, showing you what type of information you could expect to find. A section on how to use a teacher's guide and textbook was followed by activities that required the examination of a textbook and a teacher's guide.

READING RESOURCES

Cain, Sandra, and Evans, Jack. *Sciencing,* 2nd ed. Columbus, OH: Charles E. Merrill, 1984.

Savage, Tom, and Armstrong, David. *Effective Teaching in Elementary Social Studies.* New York: Macmillan, 1987.

Schug, Mark, and Berry, R. *Teaching Social Studies in the Elementary School.* Glenview, IL: Scott, Foresman and Company, 1987.

Skeel, Dorothy. *The Challenge of Teaching Social Studies in the Elementary School,* 2nd ed. Santa Monica, CA: Goodyear Publishing Company, 1979.

Woolover, Roberta, and Scott, Katherine. *Active Learning in Social Studies.* Glenview, IL: Scott, Foresman and Company, 1988.

9
Classroom Management

PROJECTIONS

Managing the elementary classroom of the 1990s and beyond will continue to be the challenge and the responsibility of you and your colleagues. It will be demanding and precise at times, but always exciting. The management of materials (all the curriculum responsibilities) and behaviors (all the diverse personalities and learning capabilities) is a major skill that teachers must develop. A repertoire of various skills is a necessary part of your professional portfolio.

The business community actively pursues a variety of management styles for persons in supervisory roles. Open communication, cooperative planning, and goal setting involve persons from all levels of the organization. Teachers can adapt some of these strategies for their classrooms.

Teachers who enlist the ideas, thoughts, comments, and views of their students will experience positive changes in the classroom environment. Cooperation, trust, behavior, work production, humor, less tension, freedom with responsibility, and other aspects of classroom management can dramatically change. Working with students to analyze, discuss, plan, and evaluate classroom needs is a rewarding experience. Elementary students are very aware of adult expectations and usually try to meet them. Establishing a positive working relationship with students will become more important. Students are ready to become partners with the teacher in this adventure called education and are already demanding a voice in their curriculum.

Classroom management in the 1990s may very well be significantly different than it was in the 1960s, 70s, and even the 80s. Research and technology demand that schools adapt and change to meet future needs. Indeed, teachers' skills and expertise must adapt also. One teacher with one group of students is probably not relevant for all academic situations. Elementary school restructuring is on the near horizon. Organizing large and small groups of students for learning activities is one of the professional responsibilities that teachers will perform. New and creative ways to do this, within the parameters of sound pedagogy, is the challenge and the focus. The issues of whole group instruction, individualization, performance groups, ability groups, and various combinations of these are matters of much concern. The academic community will continue to debate and try new approaches to these organizational patterns.

Classroom management—what is it? And what is the connection to social studies? Classroom management covers a wide range of instructional, human relations, and organizational skills that must be developed to a high degree of proficiency. Managing a classroom of active children for six or seven hours a day demands a skill level not present in other careers. Not only must you manage from a discipline standpoint, but you must manage to teach the required curriculum. The social studies connection is this: Social studies teaching requires a variety of materials, strategies, methods, and techniques. Classroom management skills help you to use them more effectively.

Classroom management skills are those talents, responsibilities, job requirements, and abilities that distinguish you from other people who work with children in the school. The instructional side of classroom management includes such things as studying your curriculum thoroughly, as well as developing and practicing various methods and strategies for lesson presentation. Keeping current regarding new research and practices in your field increases your repertoire of instructional skills. The organizational skills that affect positive classroom management include such things as efficient time structuring, making informed decisions, staying on task with smooth transitions from one activity/lesson to another, and thorough planning. Knowing, understanding, caring, empathizing, and just being there for students are some of the many qualities that excellent teachers project in the area of human relations skills. Although the educator's job is to teach children, the importance of the teacher-student relationship cannot be ignored. For many children, the accepting, loving, trust-building qualities must be secured before they learn content.

These characteristics by no means comprise a complete list of all the necessary skills that affect classroom management. Classroom management is a multi-faceted area that affects almost everything you do in the classroom, as well as the student responses and behaviors you will observe. This chapter addresses two major topics that affect classroom management: organizing your classroom for teaching and organizing the students for learning.

Organizing the Classroom for Teaching

Classroom Furniture

It is the first day of teacher workshop in September and you arrive at your classroom full of excitement and anticipation. You open the door to a room full of various pieces of classroom furniture stacked one upon the other and pushed to one side of the room. One of your initial thoughts may be, "With all of this, is there any room for the students?" This is your classroom. Here is your furniture. Now, what will you do with it? How you arrange it, from the very beginning of the year, is critical for good teaching. Make your furniture usable.

The Placement of Furniture (Where Things Go).   The particular classroom arrangement you select must fit your teaching style. If your style is primarily in the lecture mode, then the classic rows of desks would probably be effective. If your style is largely group-oriented, then a different arrangement would be in order. There may be no particular place for the teacher, but several places for small groups at various locations in the room. Whichever teaching style(s) you plan to use, the classroom arrangement must be compatible.

Team teaching, departmentalization, pairing, open schools, and the traditional self-contained classroom are some of the more prevalent organizational structures that are used in elementary schools. Which type of setting will you be in? There are classroom arrangements that work better for a particular structure and not so well for another. Whichever setting you are in, some decisions will have to be made regarding where things will go. In a self-contained room, the decisions will probably be yours alone. A team teaching or pairing situation requires a joint effort. Let the more experienced staff members assist you in this matter. They have probably worked together before and know what works best.

A departmentalized situation has some unique advantages. As the social studies teacher, you will be teaching social studies to a different group of students each period. You do not have to concern yourself with such problems as trying to arrange the room so it is also suitable for art or wondering how to rearrange the furniture when the reading groups meet. You can select the classroom arrangement that adapts easily to the teaching of social studies and the age levels you will teach.

An open-school setting presents special considerations for classroom arrangements. The very openness of it demands that each teacher be especially cognizant of the needs and requirements of every other teacher in the area. The movement of students from one area to another, the noise level, the movable walls, the large and small group instructional areas, and other characteristics of this type of school make furniture arrangement an important responsibility. For example, your audiovisual area cannot be where the science teacher has experiments in progress! Planning with the other teachers in your section results in an arrangement that is suitable for everyone.

The self-contained classroom is probably the most popular arrangement for elementary schools. Students frequently move to another area for special projects, to view a holiday movie, or for some other activity, but for the most part the students are with you all day. The arrangement of furniture you select must accommodate all of the instructional activities that occur everyday and with a minimal amount of moving things around. Before you start arranging and rearranging the classroom furniture, it is helpful to stop and consider the things that affect what you will do. Here are some items to consider before you begin:

1. Do you have map hooks? Where are they located? Are they fixed permanently to the wall or are they on a sliding track?

2. Where is the movie screen? Is it permanent or movable?

3. Where are the electrical outlets? How many are there? Will extension cords be needed?

4. Note the location of the windows. Are there draperies or shades to darken the room for films? Do the windows allow enough light? Is it too bright?

5. Notice the location and size of the chalkboards. Will students have access to them? If they are portable, where will they be placed?

6. If the student coat hooks or lockers are inside the room, that wall is dead space for instructional use.

7. Is the room carpeted or tiled? Carpeted areas are good for floor activities for both primary and upper-grade students. (Note: Carpet square samples are frequently available from local merchants.)

8. Where are the heat vents? Placing desks too close to that area is not advisable.

9. Are the bookcases movable or built-in?

10. Where is the pencil sharpener? Wastebasket? Sink? Water fountain?

Can you think of any other items to consider?

An elementary classroom will probably have some of the following furniture for you to use.

teacher's desk	round table
students' desks and chairs	long rectangular table
bookcase(s)	study carrel or two
lectern	computer stand
room dividers	chart stand
movable storage bin	audiovisual cart

Kindergartens have some special considerations, such as:

1. The area of the room will be larger than other classrooms.

2. A large-muscle central area may be adjacent to the kindergarten wing for physical education and other large group activities.

3. Small tables and chairs are used instead of desks.

4. More storage bins, shelves, racks, and cupboards are provided.

5. Paint easels, playhouse furniture, art corner materials, a sandbox table, rocking or stuffed chairs, and other pieces unique to kindergarten will be available.

6. Kindergarten furniture is smaller in size and easier to move when necessary.

This kindergarten central area is used for large group instruction, demonstrations, and creative play activities.

An average primary classroom is 24 × 30 feet; an intermediate classroom is slightly larger. Using these dimensions as examples, you will now have an opportunity to practice arranging a classroom. Use the classroom and furniture shown in Figure 9–1.

Try several different arrangements. Move things around—you are now using the visual and tactile modalities of learning! Which arrangements do you like the best? What are your reasons? Did one of your arrangements seem not quite right at the beginning? Why not?

What did you do with the teacher's desk? It should be in a usable position, but out of the way. The back of the room is usually a good place for it. You can get to it easily but it does not dominate your teaching space. You may want it at one side as a central place for individual instruction, conferences, or to check work.

The Traffic Patterns (Movement of Students).   Getting everything placed exactly where you want it is a complex task. It is easy to simply put all the student desks in traditional rows with the teacher's desk in the front—a good arrangement for a lot of expository teaching. But is this what you want for your contemporary social studies teaching?

Figure 9-1   Outline of Classroom

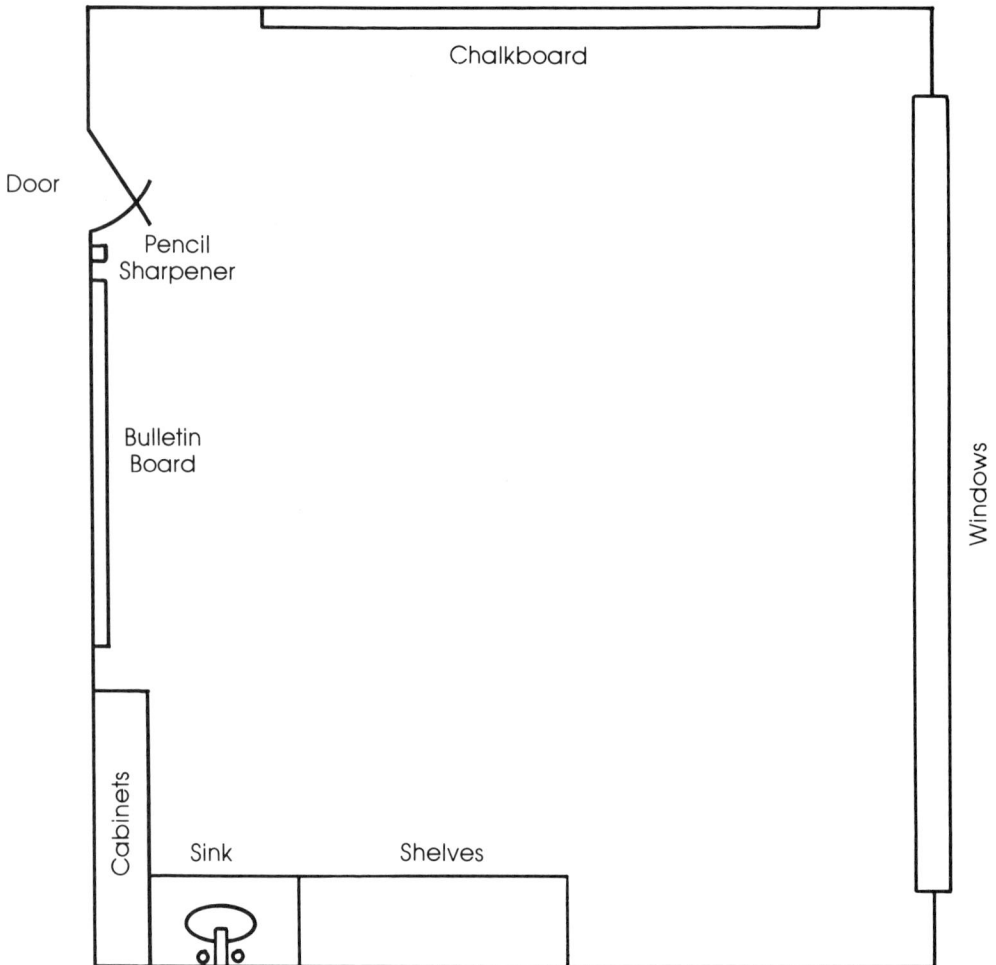

FURNITURE FOR YOUR ROOM

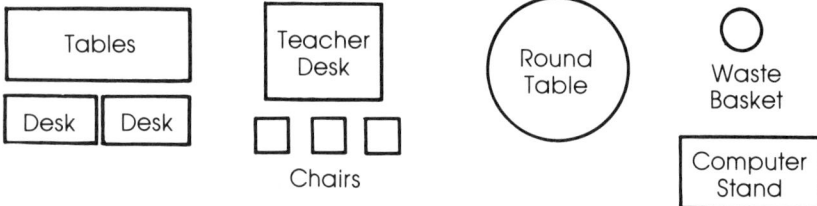

Draw your own if you think of additional needs

Elementary social studies accommodates a variety of teaching and learning methods and strategies. For some lessons, a large amount of teacher talk is needed. For other lessons, the students are in cooperative learning groups and independent activities. Classroom arrangements reflect particular types of student involvement. Elementary students are up and around the room several times every day. Going to the sink to wash hands or clean supplies, getting drinks, getting books and materials from cupboards and shelves, getting things from book bags in the lockers—all these and more give students reasons for being out of the desk. Arranging themselves into activity groups of various kinds can be a big problem for students (Where do we go?) and for you (How can I manage the movement to minimize the confusion and noise?).

Moving from place to place in an acceptable manner is a behavior that students must learn. If you give the direction "Get into line to go to lunch" to first graders without first teaching and modeling your standards, chances are they will all hop out of their chairs and race for the door to be first in line, knocking into each other, bumping into desks, and tripping over their own feet! Humorous as this may seem, it is the way youngsters react. The point is, how does your room arrangement provide for a smooth flow of traffic? Where are the patterns from the desks to: the door, the sink and cupboards, the chalkboards, the carpet area, the pencil sharpener, and your desk? Go to your room arrangement in Figure 9-1 and draw arrows to show how students will move around the room. You may need to do some rearranging so traffic can move smoothly with fewer obstacles.

There are some special considerations you must remember when arranging your classroom. Fire drills, tornado warnings, and other emergency situations demand immediate attention. Your classroom arrangements must not impede students from efficiently and quickly leaving your room in the event of an emergency. Some schools have specific guidelines directly from the fire marshal. Be aware of in-class provisions that are required for other emergency situations. Check them out and know what you are supposed to do.

Meeting Student Needs (Primary Grades).   An important part of physical management is how you provide for the needs of your students. Management skills are enhanced when student needs are clearly met. Primary-level students have many needs—some personal, some maturational, and some educational. The physical aspects of the classroom must be directed toward accommodation of these needs.

Primary-aged students need space to move. When watching young children it is easy to see that they have a lot of energy. Actually, they are quite busy growing. It is very hard for them to stay in a desk for long periods of time. Muscles are developing and need strengthening. Physical growth is occurring and does not stop because the teacher wants the child to sit still. Youngsters need to be up and about to get out the "wiggles." This is especially critical for kindergartners and first graders. Primary teachers must provide space in their rooms for out-of-desk experiences and activities. Learning stations on tables, on the bulletin boards, or even on windowsills give children opportunities to get up and move while engaging in social studies experiences. Arranging for these individualized or small group functions is part of the classroom management you are developing.

If students must be at a desk, then it is important that each child's desk fit him or her properly. If you do not believe this, you try to get comfortable in a kindergarten chair and do your work. The height of the chair should be at the point where the child's feet reach comfortably to the floor and the knees or legs do not touch the underside of the desk. The desk height should allow for a restful, comfortable sitting position for writing and other paper-and-pencil activities. Not all seven-year-old children are the same size, so check each one individually to see if the desk fits properly. If not, ask the custodian to make the needed adjustment.

Young children need to be close to the teacher. Part of this need is that they are bonding to you emotionally. At home, mom and dad are their models; at school, you are the model. Being physically close to you, touching, and holding your hand are typical behaviors of young children. Another part of this closeness is their need to be very near the teacher in order to learn. They need to be close to see what you are doing, to hear what you are saying, and to stay on task during the instructional sequence. This is why many primary teachers call the children away from their desks to come sit on the floor in a group. Being close to the teacher is critical.

With these special primary needs in mind, the physical layout of your room should be accommodating to some degree. Make provisions for those activities that will be on the floor, at tables, or near the chalkboards. The room is yours to teach in but it is the students' room to learn in, so make it usable and practical for everyone.

Meeting Student Needs (Upper Grades). Upper-elementary students have many of the same needs as primary students, only they are at a more sophisticated level of development. Classrooms for the upper grades are designed larger than rooms for primary grades in many schools. As with primary students, the teacher should check to see if each desk fits each student. At this stage of development, there will be some students who are near adult size and others who are quite small. The average fifth-grade desk will not be appropriate for everyone.

Older students can concentrate and attend for longer periods of time. When engaged in stimulating lessons or projects, they can work productively for an hour or longer. They are learning to be more independent and responsible and they can go to the library or media centers to conduct research or use materials. While some students are actively engaged at another location, additional classroom space is available for others to use. Fifth and sixth graders can practice their responsibility and independence skills by using the hall outside the classroom for activities such as putting up displays or murals, working one-to-one with someone, using the floor for assignments that need large work space, inter-viewing, and other things. Using the halls for such activities as these should be cleared with the principal and other colleagues in the area.

Upper-elementary students need the positive role model you project. Guid-ing and directing their educational progress and facilitating their social growth from the elementary toward the secondary level is an important responsibility. A number of social studies skills are taught by example at this age. The increased maturity of these students enables the classroom conversational level to be more adultlike. The formal operations skills are more noticeable. The physical aspects of your classroom must meet the needs of these students.

Desk arrangements can be informal. Tables, study carrels, and other work areas must be accessible. A larger space for project groups and research groups, as well as isolated space for individualized study are necessary. The number of trade books upper-elementary students use can be considerable; where will these materials go? Remember all the other resource materials that will be used for social studies. Will they be placed for easy access? Special needs of older elemen-tary students must be addressed within the physical limitations of your room. How and if materials will actually be used is determined to a large extent by how they are organized.

Meeting Student Needs (Special Needs).   It is imperative that the organiza-tional aspects of your classroom meet the special needs of particular students. Special needs include such things as a physical handicap, a hearing impairment, a visual problem, an emotional disorder, a behavior problem, or any other need that requires special consideration. The physical arrangement of the classroom has an important role in the quality of learning that will (or will not) occur for students with special needs.

It is not difficult to meet these physical needs. A wheelchair student must have more space to get in and out of certain areas in the room. Backing up and turning around requires space. This student may have a special desk or a lap desk. Are the group activities areas accessible? Are the aisles between desks and other areas wide enough? Classroom mobility is an important factor for the phys-ically disabled.

The visually or hearing-impaired child must be close to the front of the room to see or hear. In most cases, that is all the child needs from a placement standpoint. During instructional periods, you should be aware of such things as proper lighting, sound adjustments for recordings and movies, speaking clearly, and writing distinctly on the chalkboards, but you should be doing these things for *all* your students.

Classroom management for a severe behavior or an emotionally disturbed child requires very careful consideration. Although these students are usually serviced through the special education department, they are mainstreamed into the regular classroom and their special needs must be met. Where a particular student is located in the room could be critical for his or her performance. One

A second grader participates in an environmental field trip. He is making bark rubbings.

child may need to be very close to the teacher, whereas another may need to be alone in an individualized study carrel area for written assignments. The learning and social needs of these children are very personal and must be carefully handled. Be aware of the physical arrangement you can make for them in the classroom. Consult with the student's case manager or special education teacher to plan the physical arrangements she or he will need to function successfully in your room. Additional reading in this field is highly recommended.

Making the physical arrangements in the classroom involves decision-making skills that directly affect the students and the teacher. Deciding where things will be affects to some degree the manner in which they will be used, and perhaps in some cases if they will be used. Convenience, availability, and accessibility are the key elements.

The Behavioral Aspects

Classroom management has a behavioral component. It determines how students act and react in different situations. What you do—or fail to do—affects your students' behavior in positive and negative ways.

Class Control.   This textbook is not designed to teach a course on the various aspects of classroom discipline. However, it is helpful to know some of the techniques teachers use to establish and maintain good class control. Good classroom control does not mean that all students are always at their desks and the room is quiet, although this may be the case some of the time. There are several workable classroom management (discipline) plans available, and we recommend that you become familiar with them. If you wish to use one of them, you must do additional reading and research and perhaps even attend a workshop before you can be effective.

You should also read some information about behavior and behavior modification in a good educational psychology textbook. Several are listed in the suggested readings at the end of this chapter. You will learn about the use of rewards, contracts, time out, and positive and negative reinforcement. Several discipline programs such as Lee Cantor's Assertive Discipline and J. Kounin's Classroom Management have been developed for classroom use. The underlying philosophy of Assertive Discipline is that I (the teacher) am going to teach and you (the student) are not going to keep me from it. This is a good attitude to develop.

There are several steps that you can take to better your chances for having a well-disciplined classroom. First and foremost, good teachers plan well. The teacher who enters a classroom with a strong lesson plan increases the probability that the lesson will be successful. The teacher knows exactly what he or she will do and what the students are expected to do. In classrooms where there is good control, the students know what their job is. The teacher will tell them explicitly. This technique of knowing what to do and doing it does not occur overnight. It takes time to develop; experienced teachers continually work to achieve and maintain it. It is not uncommon for a supervisor to say, "Let's look at your lesson plans" when a new or experienced teacher is having trouble with class control. Supervisors know that being prepared to teach—having a good plan—is a good place to begin evaluating the situation.

Teachers who establish and maintain good control also have a plan for discipline, or behavior management. Over the years classroom discipline has had a negative connotation; however, there are many ways to make classroom discipline very positive. Here are some ideas to help with class control:

1. If the school has an established discipline policy, follow it carefully all the time.

2. Establish the rules for your room. When students are doing the right thing, recognize and reward them in some way. Everyone likes to be recognized for doing things correctly.

3. When your rules are disobeyed, deal with the situation immediately. Your

reaction and the consequence for the student should be planned ahead of time so you will know what to do.

4. Recognizing the students who are following your rules, doing the right thing, will give a clear message to those who are not.

5. Be positive and supportive at all times. A positive attitude is more effective than a negative one.

6. When persistent severe behavior continues, seek help from your supervisor.

7. Make adjustments in your discipline plan as needed. Set clear expectations. Expect the students to behave.

8. Be consistent. Students cannot be expected to follow the rules if they are constantly changing.

A discipline plan or policy is only as effective as you make it. As stated earlier, there are many excellent plans available. Some are very complex with rigid behavior modification components; others seem very simple by comparison. Investigate and select the ideas that you think are realistic and usable for your classroom. Start the year with a plan. It can always be modified as the year progresses.

Teachers who demonstrate good classroom management expect their students to achieve academically. If students are to achieve academic goals, they must participate in class activities and complete their assignments. Planning and preparing an adequate work load for the students is another part of management. When students are not kept busy with meaningful, productive activities, class control is affected in negative ways. The students are off task, the noise level increases, and children with behavior problems experience more stress. Keeping the students actively engaged is critical. Students achieve more when teachers set high expectations than when teachers set low expectations. If you expect students to do their work, they probably will!

The Learning Atmosphere.   An important part of classroom management is the establishment of a positive learning atmosphere for students. Having a physical arrangement that meets the needs of your students is a part of the learning environment. Meeting individual needs gives students the clear message that you care. Defining the learning atmosphere you want can be a difficult task. You have to know what you want before you can convey it to your students. As you observe in different classrooms, it will become evident which rooms have it and which ones do not.

There are personal characteristics that good teachers show to enhance this positive environment. Here are some things that affect the comfort level in classrooms:

1. Tone of voice (too loud, too soft, strident, condescending)
2. Attitude (interest, positive or negative)
3. Perspective (what is really important right now)
4. Sense of humor (enjoy funny things that happen!)
5. Posturing-body language (gesturing, stance, facial expressions)
6. Love and caring (show that you care)
7. Professionalism (serious, businesslike, do the job)
8. Cooperation (a team player, helpful)
9. Patience (self-control, calm, relaxed)
10. Consistency (always the same in enforcement and punishment)

Can you think of some others?

A positive learning environment is one in which students and teachers feel comfortable with a visible respect for each other clearly evident. Students feel free to ask the teacher for help and direction, and the teacher is approachable. Working to establish and maintain this relationship is ongoing.

The Physical Environment.   It is important for students and the teacher to be physically comfortable if they are to be productive. Behaviors are affected by such things as temperature, air movement, and light. The temperature in the room should be neither too hot nor too cold. When it is too hot students become sluggish. When it is too cold their minds are on their discomfort instead of on the tasks at hand. What is comfortable is a personal matter in many ways, so take your cues from your students. They will tell you their needs.

Classrooms need proper lighting. For some activities you will want all of the lights turned on; for others a dimmer light is needed. On very sunny days, the outdoor light may be adequate. If your room has study carrels or large area dividers, check to be sure there is adequate light for those spaces. When assignments are to be copied off the chalkboard, check for light reflections that make it impossible to see what is written. The same is true for desks or tables near the windows. You also need to be aware of any special lighting requirements for a visually handicapped student.

The Learning Aspects

Students do most of their in-school learning in one classroom. Every effort should be made to make the students and the classroom learning compatible. This is a high priority for teachers. It is not the only consideration, however; the teacher must work there too. She or he must be able to function comfortably in a given setting. The organizational structure of the classroom must be suitable for instructing.

Teaching Styles and Methodologies.   Teachers organize and plan to accommodate the instructional styles and methodologies they will use during a given year. Sometimes the classroom setting reflects large group instruction with some individualization as the primary instructional method. Another time it might be performance grouping with a heavy emphasis on computer-based instruction. It does not have to be the same all the time. Teachers grow professionally as they try different strategies. If something new or different is successful, both the teacher and the students will benefit. If something does not work as planned, the teacher will try a different approach.

Elementary social studies lends itself readily to various teaching styles and methods. The ones you select will be modified somewhat by the grade you teach. The expository method works well for the sixth grade, but not for six-year-olds. Teachers tend to present lessons in ways that are most comfortable to them. If they do something well, the students will learn.

The organization of your classroom must be flexible (see Figures 9-2 and 9-3). It must easily fit the way you will be teaching. If you are lecturing, the desks or tables must be situated so the students can easily see and hear you. If small instructional groups fit into your style, then you will need space for five or ten desks to cluster together, or space for sitting on the floor. Flexibility is critical if you combine more than one style. For example, an upper-elementary teacher may present the first two or three lessons of a unit in a lecture mode, and then move into small instructional groups. Some movement of furniture is necessary in this instance, but it should be kept at a minimum with the least amount of confusion. Time spent off task moving furniture is wasted time unless the move is relevant and accomplished quickly. Think of some ways this could be done.

Adapting to Learning Modalities.   The organizational structure should make provisions for the visual, auditory, and manipulative activities that are characteristic of how children learn. One way to provide these in the classroom is to organize learning stations. Set aside one area for visual activities, one for listening, and one for hands-on (tactile) activities. During a particular lesson the students rotate through the three stations at appropriate intervals to experience all three modalities. Some students may need more time at one station than another. Primary-aged students especially enjoy and benefit from this procedure.

The management of the classroom is easily modified to allow students to use the modalities. If the learning station approach is used, the students will work independently and the teacher's role is to oversee and keep them on task. If the modalities are addressed in some other way as a supplemental activity, an introductory motivator, a closure activity, or only for those who need it, the

Figure 9-2 Traditional Classroom Arrangement

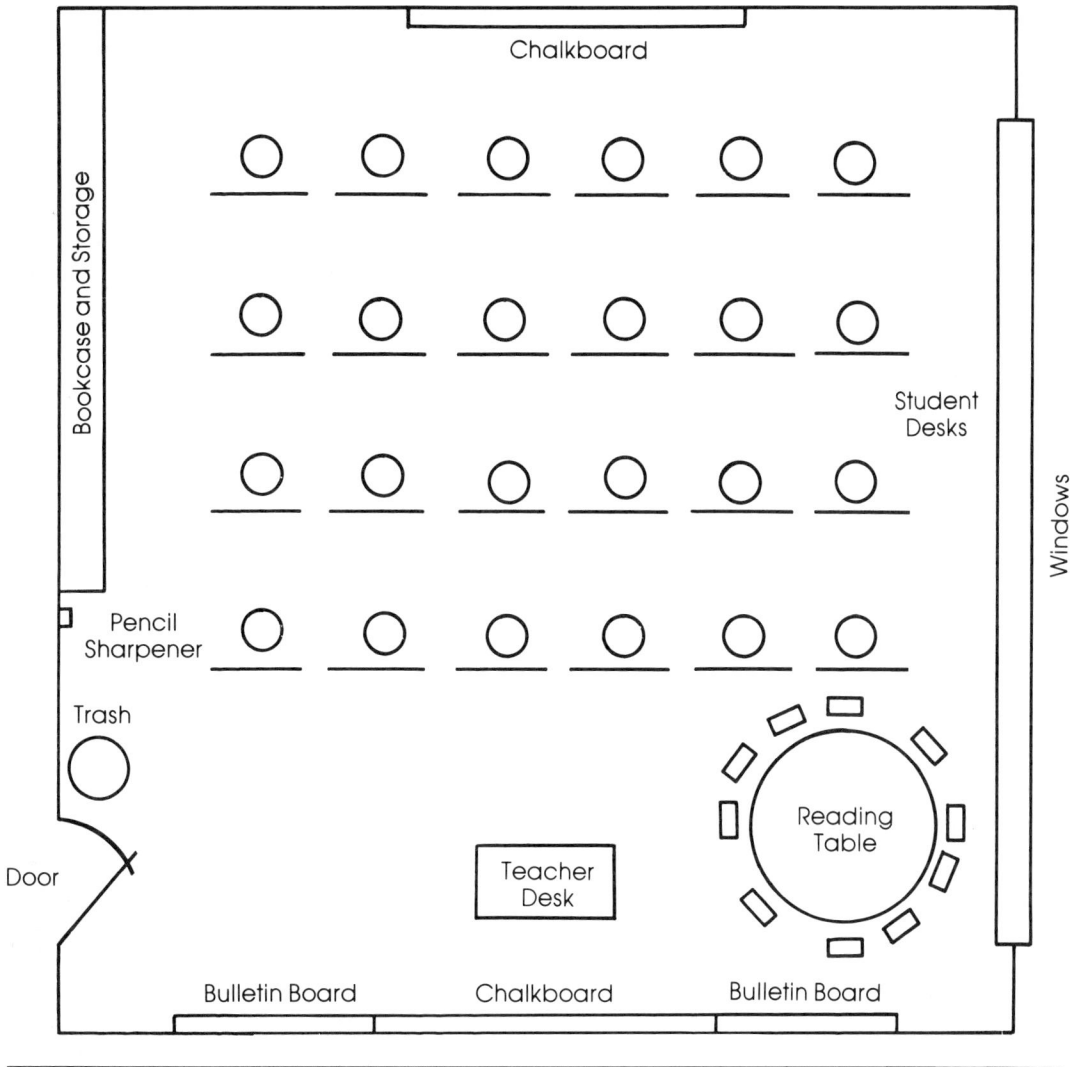

teacher's role will be different. Social studies lessons are particularly adaptable. Some items used in social studies that accommodate the modalities are:

For the Visual Mode

movies   maps and globes
filmstrips   film loops

Figure 9-3 Imaginative Classroom Arrangement

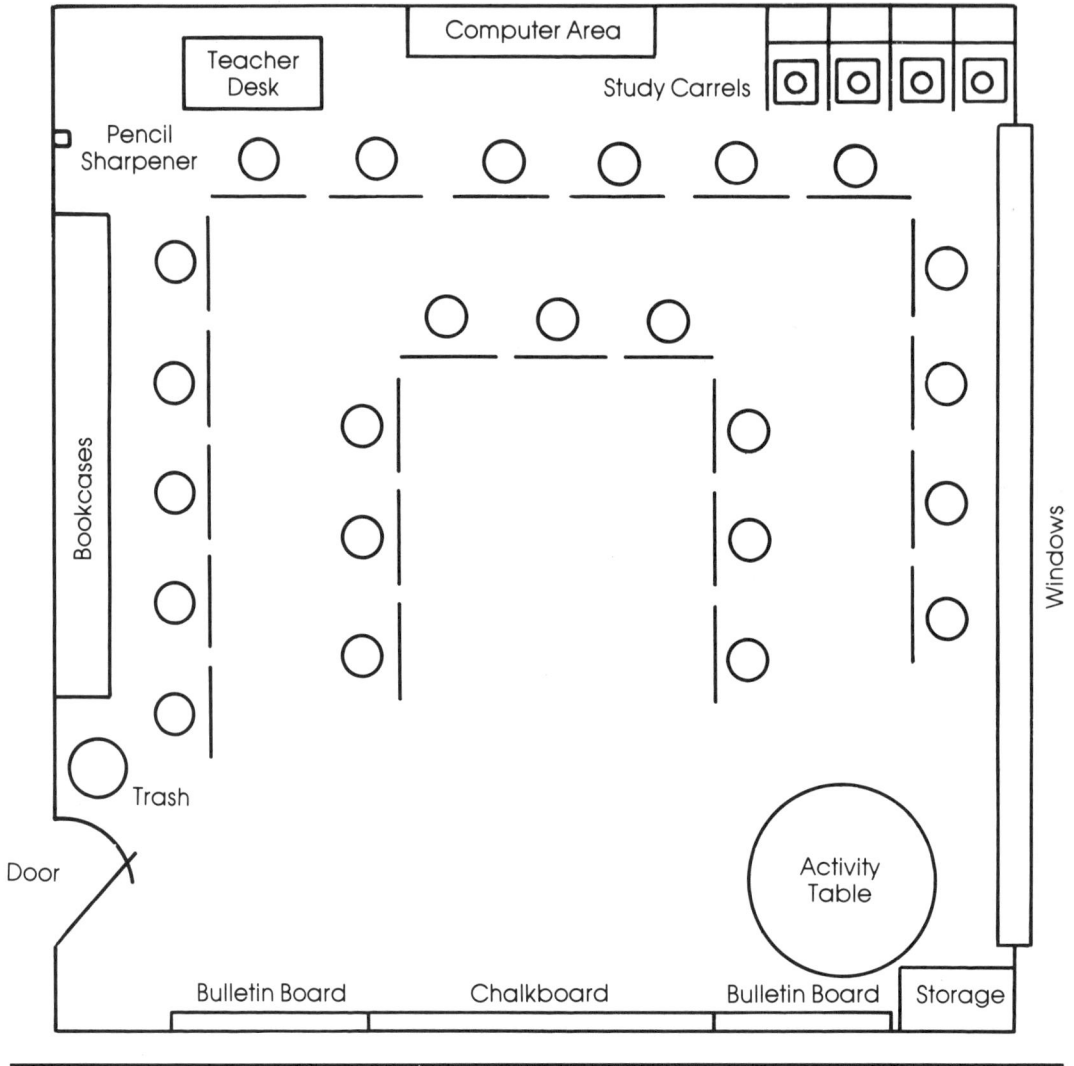

picture books	computer programs
newspapers	magazines
drawings	family albums
puppets	charts, graphs, pictures

For the Auditory Mode

records	radio programs
tapes	cassettes

television, videos   student-made recordings
oral history, stories   oral readings
reports

For the Tactile Mode

tools   building activities
clothing items   collections
relics, realia   furniture
museum displays   toys and games

This brief list is by no means complete. It gives some ideas for things the teacher can select and collect for social studies. A reminder: Tell the students (the auditory mode); show the students (the visual mode); and involve the students (the tactile mode).

Adapting to the Left-Right Brain Learning Styles.

Each hemisphere of the brain processes information in special ways. A person's preferred learning style is related to how the brain most efficiently and effectively processes information. Knowing how the brain functions is useful information for teachers. All the programs and materials you use will have more lasting effects if they are used in ways that exercise the preferred learning styles of students.

When strong right-brain learners are actively engaged in improvising, experimenting, moving around, and working on several things at once, they are likely to succeed or even excel in their assignments. Likewise, the strong left-brain students may choose to read, study, listen attentively to lectures, and approach things in a very logical way (logical for them). They, too, will do well in completing assignments. Students will have the opportunity to learn using activities that allow them to function with the least amount of stress.

Disruptive behavior decreases when students can learn in ways that meet their needs. Many students become behavior-discipline problems because (in part, at least) they are continually expected to perform in ways that are directly in opposition to their own personal "best way." A strong left-brain student may intensely dislike experiments, group work, or improvisation. Make plans for that person to read and do research in the library. When you accommodate students' preferred learning styles they will be happier and more productive, and so will you.

It is interesting to plan an identical lesson (in terms of observable objectives) with very distinct left- and right-brain activities, and then allow the students to choose which ones they want to do. What percent of the class do you think would select each kind? Would there be a significant differential for primary and upper-grade students? It is also beneficial to observe in different classrooms and watch children. Which ones are deeply engrossed in certain kinds of activities, and which ones are busy with entirely different tasks? Which individuals are "reading about it" and which ones are "doing it"?

Be aware of an additional benefit you may not think of at the time. Teachers who go beyond the established routine to help children progress earn the gratitude and respect of the parents as individuals and the community as a whole. Parents know their children. They may be unaware of the educational jargon we use to label things, but they know how their children approach projects at home. Ask specific questions at conference time, or make that special phone call to find out what you want to know. When you communicate your willingness to adapt and accommodate, to try new things, to help their child learn, your professionalism takes a quantum leap forward. Enhancing the home and school relationship is always a good idea!

Review.   This section of the chapter has given some points to examine when preparing a classroom for teaching. It is unreasonable to expect to enter a room and just teach. There are many things that need to be done before the students arrive. Teachers organize and manage in different ways. When you are visiting and observing classrooms, ask teachers why certain things are located in particular places. It is entirely possible that the computer stand is by the exit door simply because "there is no other place for it!" Be aware of room patterns that are strikingly different than most others. Those teachers will probably have some insightful ideas to share.

A classroom must be organized and managed so teachers can teach effectively. A well-organized classroom correlates the physical, behavioral, and learning aspects of management directly to the teaching that occurs there. Having a classroom that looks nice is important, of course. Merely being appealing to the casual observer is not justifiable if learning is encumbered by it, however. If active dynamic teaching and learning cannot take place there, that particular classroom is not functional. Another arrangement is needed to make it usable.

Organizing the Students for Learning

Organizing the students for learning is the second major factor in classroom management. Getting the students ready to learn is part of the teacher's job. In this section three main areas will be examined: grouping students for instruction, individualizing for instruction, and whole group instruction. Each will present special considerations for both primary and upper grades.

Grouping for Instruction

Social studies can be learned and experienced in many ways. Some lessons of a unit are best learned in small groups of two or three students, whereas other lessons require the broader input of perhaps ten students. Some lessons are best taught in a total class situation. We will now examine some groups that are used in teaching elementary social studies.

Panels.   A panel is a group of people (five or six members is ideal) who work together to hold a discussion or debate a given topic. The term *panel discussion* is frequently used. The members of a panel have the job of researching a topic and presenting their information to an audience, which could be their fellow classmates, the other classes at their grade level, or the entire school.

A panel discussion is an especially effective group strategy for social studies. Being on a panel gives students the opportunity to do research, to speak in front of a group, to present data and personal opinions, and to field questions from the audience. Assign as many panels as needed so that every student can be a panel member.

Panel members can be selected alphabetically, randomly, for specific strengths or skills, or through volunteering. The teacher may assume the job of choosing panel members because she or he may want a homogeneous or heterogeneous group for particular topics, or the teacher may need to separate one person from another for behavior reasons. The panel can be used as an introductory, a mid-unit, or a closure activity.

The Research Group.   The research group works together to gather data. This research can be centered in the school library, which is particularly effective for primary grades and those who have not experienced this activity previously, or in the media center. An active research group can also gather data in other classrooms from both students and teachers, from other adults who work in the school, and from each other. It is fun as well as informational for research groups to design questionnaires and ask everyone in the school to respond. This is a good introductory research project. A research group may be responsible for getting background information for the entire class, or it may be responsible for gathering materials or doing research to prepare for oral or written reports. Research groups can meet after school to visit the community library, museums, and other public facilities to gather material.

The members of a research group are chosen in various ways similar to those for a panel. The teacher may wish to group some high-performing individuals with students who could benefit from their expertise. It is important that the students stay on task while they are together. Although their research may be conducted largely out of the classroom and in the library, media center, or other location, the group must conduct themselves appropriately. One strong personality can easily dominate a research group by telling them all what to do and thereby managing to do little or nothing personally! On the other hand, each group needs a strong leader to keep everyone on task.

The Project Group.   The project group is organized to work on projects of various kinds. Although all students should have the opportunity to work in a project group, certain students excel in this setting. A project group whose task is to build or construct something benefits from working with someone who shows a particular talent for designing and building. You may find some of your less academically talented students doing quite well in this type of group. Perhaps all the members in this group will have this talent. Helping to build, paint, pound nails, and do things with the whole body may be perfect for a child who needs to be doing active up-and-about things. A retired person, a volunteer, or the building custodian may serve as the resource person for this group. Use community resources whenever you can.

The project group is a setting wherein some special needs students can function successfully. Including them in a special project where they can make a contribution and be part of the group is the concept of mainstreaming.

The project group is flexible in terms of duration, membership, and specific tasks. The group works together for a few days or for the duration of a particular unit of instruction. Teachers use project grouping for different reasons. A project group may not involve a lot of reading. Those who read poorly can opt to work in this setting. Likewise, the student who wants to read constantly may be placed in a project group for "experiencing and doing." A student who needs to improve in the coping skills may be placed in a project group to practice these.

The Skills Group.   The skills group is organized to practice and learn a particular social studies skill. The group may work on a product skill, a process skill, or a human relations skill. Successfully running three skills groups at the same time is not unusual. The members of a skills group should be selected by the teacher based on student needs. Given a choice, students invariably choose a skill they are good at, not one they really need to improve!

Using skills groups demands preparation by the teacher. For example, if a group is working on the process skills of social studies, it must be clear which specific skills will be practiced and which activities will be at the introductory, the guided practice, or the evaluation level. A skills group can be organized to function at a learning station while the teacher is instructing others. A teacher may decide to initiate a skills group that tackles Bloom's levels of thinking. Organizing a group such as this would clearly address the needs and developmental stages of all the students.

Team Learning.   Grouping for team or cooperative learning differs from the previous groups in that it is usually done at the beginning of a semester or school year. The team (group) remains together for the year. Usually the team is a small group of mixed-ability students who work together on all learning tasks and help each other to learn. There are two considerations that must be in effect for team learning to work. A group goal must be defined and success will depend on the individual learning of all members of the team. The team must work as a group and are evaluated as a group.

Team learning has been very effective. Team members help each other, share information and experiences, and learn from each other. The assumption is that the group is greater than the sum of its parts. Before trying team learning, you should read more on the subject. A good place to start is by reading *Student Team Learning* by Robert Slavin.[1]

Grouping children for instruction requires very careful perceptions of the performance abilities of a particular class and the general maturity level of the individual students. Before assigning students to a particular group, or even before deciding to use grouping at all, here are some special points to examine:

1. Why do you want to use grouping? Will it enhance your teaching skill and the learning of the students? If so, in which ways?

2. When will the groups function? Will it be at the beginning of the lesson, at mid-lesson, during closure, or throughout the lesson?

3. How will you teach the students to be a functioning member of a group? (They do not automatically know this skill.)

4. How much time will it take to get the groups to really work together effectively? Do you have that much time available?

5. Is grouping feasible for this age? Have you observed successful groups in any primary classes?

6. Are you willing to spend the necessary planning and preparation time that is needed for this process to work?

Effective group work does not automatically come with selection of group members and the assignment of the task. You must teach the students how to function as a group and what is expected of each group member. Your first attempt at group work may be less than successful, but it will lay the groundwork for future successes. You might use the following suggestions to start.

Procedures for Grouping

1. Have a clear objective in mind.

2. Choose the group leader. Be specific what the leader's job will be; for example:
   a. assign jobs to the group members
   b. keep everyone on task
   c. try to solve conflicts or problems
   d. ask for help when it is needed
   e. watch the clock—observe time limits
   f. others as needed

3. Place each student in the group where he or she will be the most productive. Define the responsibilities of group members.

4. Discuss expected behaviors for working in a group; it's different than working alone. Be specific.

5. Begin with a familiar activity or assignment that will insure success. Working on a mural or art project is a good idea.

6. Allow the groups to work together a few times (the same members and leader).

7. Gradually increase group responsibilities.

8. Praise proper group behavior when you see it.
9. Set a reasonable time limit. For a first experience, 15 to 20 minutes is adequate.
10. Be available to give assistance when needed.
11. Provide for evaluation.

Primary-Grade Considerations. From a very practical standpoint, kindergartners and first graders are preparing to work in a group. Standing in front of the class and sharing one reason for having safety rules, for example, is a first step in the process of making an oral report. Coloring together with another person is a beginning step for working in a project group later on. Cooperating, sharing, letting someone else be first, and other social skills are necessary before a child can function well in any group.

Primary teachers give their students many opportunities to practice these skills informally. Many first-grade students are socially and maturationally ready to start working in a group. Forming project groups is a good way to begin. Three groups is a reasonable number that you can supervise simultaneously. Examine the following classroom scenario for a project group.

In a small group, each member can contribute to the completion of a project by using individual talents.

A Primary Grade Project Group

Your primary grade is learning about neighborhoods and communities. This is a general topic in most social studies series. As a culminating activity you plan three project groups of eight members each to make a large mural of a neighborhood. It is around Valentine's Day, so for added interest the mural theme is "Valentine Land." To prepare for the group project, you have taught the necessary skills, reviewed them, and asked if anyone does not understand the expectations. Everyone understands.

You meet with the three leaders to clarify their roles. The necessary materials are ready for a group member to distribute. The objective is clear to everyone in the group. Each mural will show buildings, people, nature, and anything else the group decides is appropriate. The group has 25 minutes to work. Each group decides where they will work and they begin.

As the children work, you observe the way each group approaches the task and you permit the individuals to work through some problem solving on their own. You walk from group to group, recognizing and praising appropriate behaviors and those children who get to work right away, and you assist when asked.

At the end of the given time, the groups stop working. If the project is not complete that is okay. The groups can assemble the next day with more fresh ideas. Again, you praise all of the good workers. Set the expectation for the next work period. Conduct a brief evaluation with each group: what was very good in your group, what do you need to work on tomorrow, and so on. The groups are then dismissed.

Upper-Grade Considerations. Grouping upper-grade students for social studies requires special considerations to meet their particular needs. They need more opportunities to work independently and learn responsibility. They should experience pairing with another person as well as being a contributing member of a group.

To use learning materials other than the textbook effectively is a major goal for older students. The social studies requires students to develop and use library skills to gather information. A skills group or a research group could be formed to accomplish that goal. Project groups are very effective for upper-grade students. The project objective could be to design a large bulletin board that shows the major events of the Revolutionary War, or constructing models, or doing a choral reading of poems from a particular area of study. Project groups become particularly active if there is going to be a social studies fair or open house at the school.

Selection of group members is done in one of two ways: they are selected by the teacher or the students choose their groups. When the teacher does the selecting, he or she thinks carefully about things such as ability, performance, personalities, special needs students, ability to stay on task, and left brain-right brain needs. Establishing a group that will function well and accomplish the task at hand is not always easy. Personalities and emotions can be volatile.

When the students decide which group they will be in, several things can happen. At best, every student will flow naturally into one group or another and things will go smoothly. On the other hand, different scenarios may evolve: (1) all the high-performing students will join together, (2) all the leaders will go to one group, (3) the boys won't join the girls and vice versa, (4) the lower-performing students will be left out, (5) one group will not let anyone else join them, or (6) other equally undesirable combinations. To avoid this, it is suggested the teacher approach the ''let them do it on their own'' philosophy very carefully. Learning groups and social groups require a very different amount of teacher input and involvement.

Grouping with upper-grade students can proceed by using the same criteria as you would use for younger children. The expectations and standards are monitored and adjusted for their ages and higher performance levels. Evaluation sessions can be quite enlightening for the teacher. Older students are very frank in expressing what needs to improve in their particular group or what they needed from the teacher. Accept these comments and try to meet the needs more effectively next time.

Panels, skills groups, project groups, team learning, and other grouping schemes are used at different times. A panel may be most effective at the lesson midpoint, whereas a skills group would be necessary shortly after the introduction. Neither is limited to these times, however. Reexamine the reasons for grouping. Which ones are more applicable to the upper grades?

Individualizing for Instruction

Individualization has been a vital part of education for many years. Early promotions, working in a textbook that is a grade or two ahead, contracts, PEPs (Personalized Education Plans), and other specialized programs have been a part of this process. Individualizing is used to meet the needs of high-performing students and is an integral part of special education programs. It is helpful to individualize as part of an organizational strategy for social studies classroom management.

Strategies for Individualization. The content of social studies is very diverse and the topics enable teachers to use many methods and strategies. Under what circumstances might you consider individualizing for social studies? Here are some situations to examine:

1. A particular student achieves a perfect score on all the skills given in a chapter pretest.

2. The school has an individualized program already in place (frequently a pull-out situation).

3. A student demonstrates unusual knowledge of a particular topic; following the general classroom plans would be repetitive.

4. An identified high-potential student is in the class.

5. A special education student is mainstreamed into your class for social studies.

6. You decide to try some individualizing to expand your management and teaching skills.

Individualizing requires significant planning, time, and teacher effort. It is not letting students go off somewhere to do whatever they want. Individualizing for a student or a class is easier to introduce when a complete program is already available. In many situations, however, the teacher must develop and plan a program or lesson herself or himself. To do this successfully, the teacher must know the student's ability (Can he do the work?) and maturity level (Can she work independently?).

One way to individualize is to use a contract or agreement between the student and the teacher that states specific performances, as shown in Figure 9-4. The teacher can design an excellent contract, but if the student is unwilling to perform the tasks for whatever reason, the contract approach will not be successful. Designing contracts (guided investigations, work plan, and other labels are frequently used) requires careful planning for what the student is to do and which materials he or she will need to carry out the planned activity. A specific time should be given to complete the activity, as well as an evaluation method. A procedure for getting help when needed should be clearly stated. The format for contracts is flexible and several different designs are available.

Another way to individualize is to set up a learning station/center on a table or in a study carrel. Self-contained, programmed social studies kits are available for classroom use. A kit may contain activities on one topic only, such as maps and globes, or it may have graduated activities covering a variety of topics. These kits are sometimes available as a supplementary item for a given textbook series or they can be purchased independently. If the program is well organized, it is easy to have individual students go to the learning center and work through the assigned activities. A lesson using the learning kit format can also be designed and prepared by the teacher to meet specific objectives for her or his class.

Teachers use individualizing to highlight the special talents and interests of particular students. A student who is musically talented is an immediate resource person for performing, planning, or composing music for programs, plays, puppet shows, or other activities in social studies. The artist in the class can be highlighted in a similar fashion. Again, these students have a clear objective, a plan, and an expected outcome for their assignments. There are many avenues to pursue when individualizing for social studies.

Figure 9-4 Sample Contract

Name _____

Grade _____

Unit Title _____

Starting Date _____

Due Date _____

My Objective is _____
_____

I will _____

My teacher will _____

Materials I will need: _____
_____

Resource Person(s): _____

My Sharing Plan: _____

Creative Extensions:

     1. _____

     2. _____

     3. _____

Closure Activity:

Evaluation Procedure:

Primary-Grade Considerations. Deciding to use individualization in a primary grade is a major decision. The school community may be unsure of what you are doing, so clear communication is necessary. The chronological age of the primary student is of concern here. Other points to consider are the student's ability to concentrate, interest level (Can the child stay on task until completion?), work habits, writing ability, comprehension, and possession of needed skills. A few first graders may possess all the needed skills to successfully complete some individualized lessons or activities. The teacher should be sure the students have mastered the stated objectives of a given unit before placing them in an individualized activity. Young children need to experience group instruction and interaction with the many benefits they provide. From a practical standpoint, individualization is best used in the primary grades as a supplemental strategy for selected students.

Upper-Grade Considerations. Individualizing for upper-grade students is an option both for supplementary activities and instructional purposes. Supplementary activities are used in coordination with textbook lessons and lessons designed by the teacher for reteaching or enrichment. Some individualized programs are designed to be self-teaching. Many computer programs are individualized from the standpoint that each student in the computer lab runs through the program individually. An entire class may work on the same program. Some students will be in the introductory phase, some will be at the intermediate level, and others may be in the advanced-users level.

Individualizing for older students has advantages that complement classroom management. Their stage of development enables them to work independently and they are mature enough to understand what the lesson or activity is, to complete the lesson, and to accomplish this while the rest of the class is doing other things. Students who are performing significantly higher than their peers can be placed into an individualized program. It gives the advanced students something worthwhile and challenging to do. Be sure that you do not give these students busy work or just more of the same lessons the other students have. Preparing materials for an individualized lesson takes time, thought, and commitment.

A good individualized program is complete, specific, challenging, and self-motivating. It is complete with objectives, directions, procedures, and plans. It is challenging and provides the student with real as well as contrived situations to investigate. Individualized activities provide a favorable format for incorporating Bloom's taxonomy of educational objectives. Develop themes with lessons built around each level of the hierarchy from comprehension to evaluation. One possible approach is to use colored folders, each labelled with a level of the taxonomy and filled with a variety of lessons, activities, or questions. In this way, the student can have many opportunities to practice the thinking skills she or he needs to develop. You can add more lessons and activities to the folders as you develop them during the year.

Whole Group Instruction

Whole group instruction is a very traditional way of teaching. This structure works well in classrooms that are homogeneous. (Note: Some schools group the classrooms by performance levels when there are several classes at each grade.)

Whole group instruction enables the teacher to gear the lesson presentations and student performance expectations at a specific level. Giving one lesson presentation and one assignment to everyone in the class is an example of whole group instruction.

Strategies and Uses.   In situations where students are performing at a similar level, whole group instruction is an effective strategy. Teacher preparation is simplified and the learning needs of the group are adequately addressed. A group that is performing within grade-level expectations benefits from activities that are designed for the average fourth grade, for example. A group that is performing significantly lower than grade-level expectations will benefit from a slower pace of instruction and many diverse experiences. On the other hand, a group of high-performing students is ready for individualized activity, a research group, or a panel shortly after the lesson introduction.

Whole group instruction is frequently used by teachers for introductory lessons. Some units with particularly difficult skills may require more large group instruction than others. Deciding when this is most beneficial is part of classroom management.

Primary-Grade Considerations.   Teachers in the primary grades use whole group instruction to a great extent. It is an efficient way to teach the skills everyone needs to learn. It gets information to large groups in a short period of instructional time. Primary-aged children need to learn both social studies skills and general learning skills. Kindergarten and first-grade children must learn how to learn before they can focus on content. They must learn how to do such things as listen, think, follow directions, keep their bodies under control, work independently, complete assignments, cope with school in general, and many other skills. These skills are not easy for teachers to teach, nor for the students to learn.

Large group instruction for some of these skills is best organized and presented with the students at their desks; others can be learned on the floor or in other places. For instance, teaching the class how to locate north on a large map can begin with everyone on the floor or standing near a large map (provide many opportunities to do this with various maps), then proceed by instructing the students to find north on their own map outlines at their desks. Primary teachers teach many kinds of skills to the whole class and continue with guided practices.

Upper-Grade Considerations.   Whole group instruction in the upper-elementary grades frequently takes the form of expository or lecture teaching. The content of the social studies in the sixth grade, for example, makes some teachers think it is necessary to present needed information by simply telling the students what they need to know. Learning how to listen to a lecture-style lesson prepares students for the transition into the middle-school years. The lecture method provides opportunities to do selective listening and to take notes. It provides opportunities for the auditory learners to use their preferred modality.

In some areas the large group instruction strategy is used by teachers who team teach or pair for the social studies. Mrs. Anderson presents the informational data to her class and Mr. Brown's class. After this, Mr. Brown organizes and supervises both classes in smaller group activities of various kinds. This type of arrangement allows students to listen to (the lecture format) and use (the activity format) information.

Whole group instruction might be used very effectively for a unit that is particularly difficult to learn. The teacher decides the skills and information will be most effectively processed if the entire class proceeds through the chapter(s) together. It may be necessary for the teacher to read some portions aloud to the class while they either follow the text visually or listen to her or him read. Listening to a positive reading model has merit for students of all ages. This strategy enables the teacher to read a selection and then pause to expand and elaborate on the particular passage. Reading through the text may be followed by answering questions or performing end-of-chapter activities together. Intense teacher guidance such as this may be needed for groups with lower reading performance skills. There are many specific situations where whole group instruction is a proper choice.

ACTIVITIES

Class control, behavior management, good discipline, and other terms are frequently used to describe one thing: civilized behavior. Behaving and working are not unreasonable expectations. Students come to school to learn. That is their work, and they will have greater success when they follow the rules. The following activities will give you the opportunity to employ some strategies in this area.

9.1 *Classroom Control*

This activity gives you the chance to plan for your classroom. Establishing and maintaining good discipline is one of your responsibilities, and all teachers must address the issue in one way or another. Knowing specifically what you want the students to do is a big step toward getting them to do it. You are approaching the time when you will be teaching. What kind of behavior do you want? How will you get it? Let's begin to plan for it. List five rules you want for your classroom. Be specific and phrase the rules in a positive manner, for example: Walk into the room and go directly to the desk.

1.

2.

3.

4.

5.

Students want to know what adults expect them to do. They are learning how to act in different situations, and when they know what the acceptable standards of behavior are, they can work to achieve them. Everyone wants to be recognized for doing things correctly—even adults. It is important that you take the time to positively reinforce the behavior you want. Rewarding good behavior increases the probability that the behavior you want will occur again. Rewarding negative behavior does the same thing. It increases the chance of continued negative behavior. Rewards can be verbal, tangible, or experiential.

Look at your classroom rules. Are they practical? Can they be maintained for the whole year? What grade level are they planned for? Are they written in positive language? Share your plan with a classmate or your group for discussion.

9.2 *Meeting Student Needs*

Meeting student needs is an important responsibility of teachers. How well you do this will largely determine how much your students will learn and how successful their year will be under your guidance. It is helpful to have some ideas for approaching this obligation. This activity gives you the opportunity to look at two student profiles and to list some ways to meet their needs.

Student A

Ricky is a high-potential fifth grader. He particularly enjoys social studies and likes to be involved in several different things simultaneously. He has leadership qualities that are ripe for development, but he needs organizational skills.

I would organize and manage for Ricky in these ways:

Physical Plans

1.

2.

3.

Behavioral Plans

1.

2.

3.

Learning Plans

1.

2.

3.

Student B

Christopher is a physically handicapped first grader. He is using a walker and has very limited use of his hands. His vision is poor. Academically, Christopher functions above grade level, so he is in the mainstream all day except for his physical therapy session. His strong point is his determination not to be handicapped.

I would organize and plan for Christopher in these ways:

Physical Plans

1.

2.

3.

Behavioral Plans

1.

2.

3.

Learning Plans

1.

2.

3.

There are no easy answers or solutions to learning needs, but it does help to think about and plan for some of them in advance. Problem solving is a continual process for teachers. What plans did you make for Christopher? Get into a group with some other people and share your plans. Add other ideas and plans to your list—the more, the better. As an extension of this activity, identify your ideas in each section from "most preferred" to "least preferred." Give some reasons for your decisions. Do the same for Ricky.

Summary

This chapter gives some suggestions for organizing and managing the elementary classroom for teaching and learning the social studies. Certain things teachers do and the decisions they make are part of the teaching responsibilities they assume everyday. Teachers and students share the classroom for long periods of time, and the organizational strategies affect everyone in positive or negative ways.

Teachers who are equipped with management ideas can prepare for some eventualities before they happen. Being prepared to organize and plan for a variety of learning needs and teaching requirements makes adjustments and adaptations easier to handle. Managing a classroom of lively youngsters is not easy and to do it successfully takes time, effort, and experience. Preparing lessons and meeting the learning needs of high-performing students, special education students, and average students requires determination and dedication.

READING RESOURCES

Arends, Richard I. *Learning to Teach.* New York: Random House, 1988.
Biehler, Robert F. *Psychology Applied to Teaching,* 5th ed. Boston: Houghton Mifflin Company, 1986.
Duke, Daniel, and Meckel, Adrienne. *Teacher's Guide to Classroom Management.* New York: Random House, 1984.
Glover, John A.; Bruning, Roger H.; and Filbeck, Robert W. *Educational Psychology Principles and Applications.* Boston: Little, Brown and Company, 1983.
Slavin, Robert. *Educational Psychology,* 2nd ed. Englewood Cliffs, NJ: Prentice-Hall, 1988.
Stipek, Deborah. *Motivation to Learn.* Englewood Cliffs, NJ: Prentice-Hall, 1988.

ENDNOTE

1. Slavin, Robert. *Student Team Learning* (Washington, D.C.: National Education Association, 1983).

10
Learning Resources

PROJECTIONS

The elementary social studies teacher needs and uses a myriad of materials to teach every lesson. These various materials are used to initiate, clarify, and reinforce particular social studies concepts. Without the necessary instructional materials, the teaching of social studies can easily become centered around what the teacher does rather than what the students are doing.

Planning, designing, developing, and preparing social studies materials is part of the classroom teacher's responsibility. These learning resources are for her or his personal use, as well as for the other teachers at the grade level or department. There is a need for students to participate in enjoyable activities in all grades, kindergarten through sixth. Merely reading the social studies textbook is not sufficient. It is necessary to provide students with more effective and meaningful concrete experiences. These experiences are not particularly easy to plan, organize, and fulfill; they take time. However, working alone or with colleagues, it is highly recommended that new teachers make every effort to actively engage their students in concrete experiences.

It is increasingly important for students (and adults) to know how and where to get needed information, and it is reasonable to assume that this need will continue to exist in the next decade. Teaching these research skills is incumbent upon every teacher. Teachers agree that certain information must be committed to long-term memory, but other information can be researched as needed. Social studies teachers teach students how to read and research social studies materials in efficient, effective ways.

All of the resources teachers use are noteworthy to the degree that they assist in the learning process. While new teachers may become engrossed in the preparation of physical resources (daily lessons, charts, games, tests) it is easy to ignore the most important, immediately available learning resource—you, the social studies teacher. Developing the physical, hands-on resources is important, of course, but it is equally important to develop and expand your own personal knowledge and attributes. A particular resource may not be readily available for classroom use, but you are. The more you know about your curriculum area, the more knowledge you can communicate to your learners. The teacher is a primary resource for students!

Teachers use a variety of tools and materials to teach social studies. The textbook usually forms the core of a social studies program because it contains the high-priority content areas of the curriculum. But the textbook does not contain everything that you need to teach your social studies lesson. You will need other learning resources.

Learning resources are the materials teachers use to present, reinforce, or evaluate social studies lessons. These specially selected materials enable the teacher to enrich the suggested activities found in the teacher's guide or the activities that the teacher personally develops for the lesson. The specific learning resources that are used to complement the lesson are limited only by the teacher's creativity and time commitment.

Good learning resources actively involve the students and give them experiences. Effective learning resources provide opportunities for students to engage the three modalities of learning: seeing it (visual), hearing about it (auditory), and experiencing it (kinesthetic). In this chapter you will examine some of the learning resources commonly used in elementary classrooms. Some are particularly appropriate for primary children and others are more effective when used with intermediate students.

Some background information will help you select the most appropriate resources. You need to become familiar with Bruner's "Ways of Knowing" so that you can classify your resources. This will allow you to select activities that are appropriate to the development stages of your students. Most kindergarten through sixth-grade students are in Piaget's concrete operational stage and should learn best by using concrete materials. This does not preclude using some abstract materials, however. Elementary students are capable of some abstractions and are moving toward the formal operational stage that requires the child to operate with nonconcrete materials.

Bruner: Ways of Knowing

The learning resources that teachers select for lesson presentation must be appropriate to the students' stages of development. Jerome Bruner[1] proposes three modes of presentation and learning that parallel growth and developmental periods. These "Ways of Knowing" are enactive, iconic, and symbolic.

Enactive

The enactive mode is action-oriented. The student has real experiences with real objects. *Doing* is an important part of enactive learning. Physical involvement in actually doing something (making bread, holding an arrow, sitting on a saddle) is very concrete. Real objects are as important as the physical involvement. Primary-aged children are very successful when presented with learning experiences in this mode. It is especially important to use enactive materials to build an experiential background for students. Encounters with real things prepare the child for experiences with the more abstract form of learning. Some examples that you might use are:

1. Prepare a shopping list and go to a store to purchase ingredients for an ethnic meal.
2. Have a police officer come to the school and bring a police car for the children to see. They can listen to the radio, look at the equipment, and maybe even turn on the lights and siren. (Variations: ambulance, fire truck, garbage truck, tractor-trailer truck)
3. Prepare and eat an ethnic meal.
4. Arrange with a pet store owner, local veterinarian, zookeeper, or other source to bring animals into the classroom. (This must be supervised to prevent accidents or injuries.)
5. Invite an antique dealer or collector to bring in or loan to you items from the period of study. Tools are especially good if you or a guest can demonstrate them.

Iconic

The iconic mode is characterized by images. This is a large category that includes everything from almost real to almost abstract. A model of a train is not a real train, but it is real enough to teach the concept of a train. A video or film that shows a cattle drive may be as close to the real thing as you can get. The iconic mode is widely used to help children learn from materials other than the real item. They also learn how to use representations of real items. As they do this, they are building a foundation for symbolic learning.

Some iconic activities that you might use are:

1. Show films, filmstrips, or videotapes that relate to your topic.
2. Assign a specific television show to be viewed. (Send notes home to parents explaining why the child is to watch the show.) Ask parents and child to take notes.
3. Use a game such as Monopoly to teach economics.

The globe is a model of the earth and its surface.

4. Roleplay a historical event such as the signing of the Declaration of Independence.
5. Hold a mock presidential election, complete with speeches.

Symbolic

The symbolic mode has language as its main focus. The child with facility in iconic learning can proceed toward the symbolic with confidence. The symbolic mode is the most difficult of the three modes because it is the most abstract. Many children are not really ready for this stage until they have had many experiences in the enactive and iconic modes. This is not to say that they cannot learn in the symbolic mode at an early age, however. Witness how much they learn by listening to parents and teachers. We start reading, a symbolic process, at the beginning of the school experience. Have you ever thought about what must occur to read for information? You must visually recognize a printed shape, combine it with others, internalize it in your brain, label it, then combine it with other groups of shapes (words), and make sense of the combinations. Is oral language any easier? Some symbolic activities are:

1. Read the textbook for information.

2. Write your own version of an historical event. This can be a first-person narrative.

3. Make a speech describing an event or an object (a bow and arrow, a plow, the first time you saw a prairie or ocean) to a person who has never experienced it.

4. Have two people work together. One will close his or her eyes while the other describes an object and draws a picture of it. A variation is to let the blindfolded person draw a picture of an object by using the verbal guidance of the partner.

Becoming familiar with the enactive, iconic, and symbolic modes is important for teachers (see Table 10–1). It is easy to fall into the trap of introducing, even pushing, children into symbolic learning too soon. Although some youngsters may outwardly appear ready for it, their command of enactive and iconic experiences may be particularly weak. Upper-elementary teachers should look for specific students that need more experiences at these two levels before pushing them into symbolic learning.

George Maxim[2] developed a Ladder of Experience that shows the various learning experiences (see Figure 10–1). Bruner's modes have been added.

Developing Concrete Experiences

Concrete experiences are those activities that physically involve the students in learning. It is the direct opposite of passive reception. Receptive activities are not negative, nor should they be avoided. For example, reading about or viewing a filmstrip on the locks system of the Mississippi River would be a passive activ-

Table 10-1 Three Modes of Learning

Enactive	Iconic	Symbolic
Very Concrete	Semi-Concrete to Semi-Abstract	Very Abstract

Examples:
  Doing something
  Resource people
  Field trips
  Real things
  Making models
	Examples:
	  Making dioramas
	  Viewing films and
	    videotapes
	  Roleplaying
	  Pictures
	  Maps and globes
		Examples:
		  Reading
		  Listening

Figure 10-1 Ladder of Experience

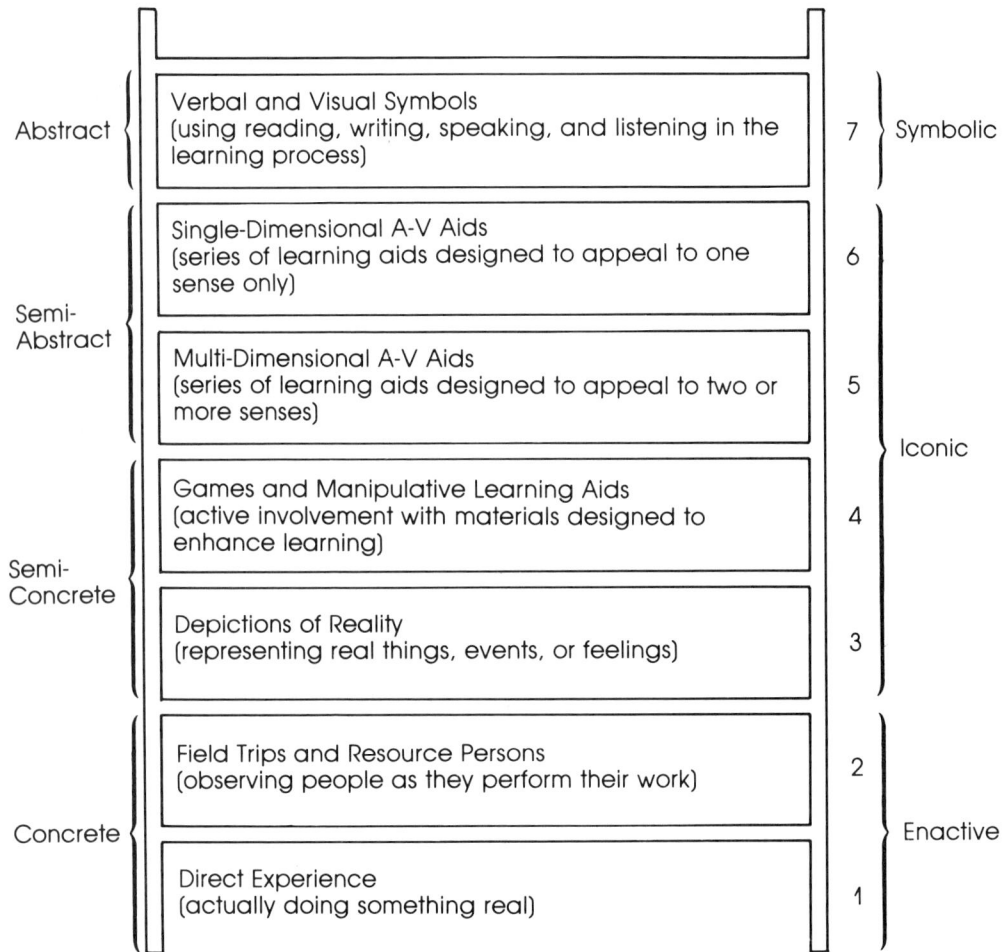

ity. Gathering materials and constructing a model of the locks system would be an example of an active experience. Both are valid experiences. Developing appropriate concrete experiences for social studies requires the teacher to utilize both diagnostic and prescriptive skills.

Concrete experiences are planned for large group and small group instruction. The main goal of concrete experiences is to provide opportunities for students to engage actively in the doing of a lesson. For example, Miss Smith has a diorama she made to demonstrate the concept of life in a pioneer cabin. She explains at great length the finer points of space utilization, available building

Bruner's 3 modes pg 321

to Teach Soc. Studies
HOW – SQ3R
Reason for
E Opportunity

Chapter 10   (Evans and Bruekner)

Key Concepts and Terms

1 pg 319 enactive mode
2 pg 321 concrete experience
3 pg 325 location skills
4 pg 325 interpretive skills
5 pg 321 abstractions
6 learning games pg 331

7 pg 317 iconic mode
8 pg 330-331 role play pg for study, decisions
9 pg 325 directional skills
10 pg 328 research skill
11 pg 321 receptive

Pg 320 12 symbolic mode
Pg 331 13 simulation
artifacts pg 33 14
models 15
SQ3R 16 Pg 326
17 special purpose

activities   map definitions

According to Evans & Brueckner:

Games, as with any tool, are important but must
be used for a purpose (or purposes) of justifiable activity.
Learning games are effective
in reinforcing facts & concepts in both cognitive
and affective areas. Games are a natural
medium in which youngsters learn social and
behavioral skills

materials, and other factual information. The students are listening attentively. In the next classroom, Miss Pichette has several samples of dioramas on display with many building materials available for the students to use. They are directed to construct a diorama of a typical pioneer cabin. Miss Smith does an exemplary job of describing, telling, and clarifying, and the students are receiving information. Miss Pichette, on the other hand, provides the opportunity for the students to actually make the lesson object while incorporating all the finer factual points directly into the project. The students in Miss Pichette's room are participating in a concrete experience.

Here is a limited sampling of lesson topics with suggested concrete experiences to accompany them.

Maps and Globes

1. Direct students to find and mark particular points of longitude and latitude on large room maps or in their student atlases.

2. Make relief maps of a particular region. A large map on a 4×8 sheet of plywood is an excellent class project.

3. Construct a bulletin board showing all the by-products of the lumber industry. Students will collect or make all of the objects that go on the board.

4. Make globes by using balloons, papier-mache, paints, and markers. As an extension, students can create their own planet, including physical features and place names.

Rules and Laws

1. Interview adults and record all the rules they must follow at their places of employment.

2. In small groups, students make three rules for lunchroom behavior (primary-grade idea).

3. Plan a brainstorming activity for this proposition: "If there were no rules in our school, then . . . " List all possible consequences.

Communities

1. Make a diorama of a futuristic shopping mall.

2. Construct a model of a community. Use milk cartons, construction paper, and masking tape. Each child will make a model of her or his home and put it on the big model.

3. Brainstorm in small groups to list many different community needs.

4. Organize a panel to debate the issue of a new freeway to be constructed through the downtown area.

Play Groups

1. Discuss the various qualities of a good leader. Give students opportunities to be the leader in play-group situations.

2. Examine the roles of play-group members. Give students opportunities to practice these roles in various settings.

3. Use the total student response technique. Read statements about fictional play-group members and leaders. The students respond with an appropriate values card.

Concrete experiences are not limited to primary children. Students at all levels enjoy learning with concrete experiences that allow them to actively participate and do things.

Using Maps and Globes

Map and globe skills—for many people these words bring forth memories of complicated procedures, odd-looking symbols, strange terminology, and frustrating attempts to decipher degrees of latitude and longitude. With a little effort you can turn these laborious tasks into challenging and even enjoyable experiences for students.

Historically, map and globe skills are major topics in elementary social studies along with citizenship and geography. We teach map and globe skills because children will need these particular skills to function successfully as adults. Our highly mobile society and fast communications systems require a person to know one place from another with relative accuracy, frequently with little or no help from others. The heavy dependence on private automobiles for transportation makes it mandatory for people to rely on their own devices to carry out everyday errands on increasingly complicated highway systems. The emergence of the Third World nations has created intense interest in that part of the world. Adults talk about places they have been or where they want to go. The news media cannot be underestimated as a motivator, with constant emphasis on various events throughout the world. Children become curious and want to know where these locations are. Studying maps and globes in school helps to answer their questions.

There are many different kinds of maps and globes that are used to accentuate and reinforce specific skills. Some special-purpose maps include:

Road	Product
World	Transit
State and city	Time zone
Historical	Cultural
Political	Population
Landform	Relief
Climate	Wind and ocean current

Among the most useful tools to come into our hands are the individual atlases that most major companies supply at low cost to accompany their textbooks. They contain a good selection of maps and information about them, and are designed for the appropriate grade level. This leads us to another important point. In selecting a map or globe, you must select the right map or globe for your age and grade level and for the purpose of your lesson. The wrong map or globe may be worse than none at all. (Compare it to wearing high-heeled dress shoes on a hike in the mountains—you would probably be better off barefoot.)

Maps and globes are a basic part of any comprehensive social studies program. Map and globe skills fall into three major categories: location skills, directional skills, and interpretive skills.

Location Skills
1. Using map grids
2. Recognizing political features, land masses, and nations
3. Identifying oceans, straits, gulfs, and other bodies of water
4. Identifying continents and hemispheres
5. Using parallels and meridians
6. Finding world trade and travel routes

Directional Skills
1. Finding cardinal and intermediate directions
2. Locating the equator, the poles, land masses, and the prime meridian

Interpretive Skills
1. Identifying symbols on maps
2. Finding guidelines on the earth
3. Using relief maps
4. Using map scales to find distances
5. Using special-purpose maps

(Note: Take special notice of the process verbs used to state the skill objectives.)

You will find that some programs present map and globe skills as one inclusive unit or chapter, whereas others present them as a continuous strand throughout the entire instructional sequence.

Maps and globes provide hands-on experiences and activities for children. Project groups are especially easily organized to work with maps and globes. The textbook gives much of the factual information needed to build a good foundation. The activities and projects the teacher plans develop the skills necessary to use a map or globe.

Teachers use maps and globes in several different ways. At the kindergarten level, the activities provide many opportunities to investigate, look at, discuss, and feel different kinds of primary projections. The teacher leads the children to discover the different colorations for land and water, to name some likenesses and differences between maps and globes, to locate the cardinal directions, and other skills at the introductory level. For reinforcement, the children can trace over the various shapes on a map with their fingers or they might decide to draw their own maps on the chalkboard. The finished products may not resemble any known map, but to the children they are real maps. All of these activities are good beginning map experiences for young children.

Give older students opportunities to plan and organize their own activities in ways that are meaningful to them. Cooperative planning sessions with the teacher often result in fairly sophisticated lessons. Given a chance, many students will experiment with and use learning resources in a qualitative manner.

Reading and Researching Social Studies Materials

Reading the textbook is a minimal requirement for becoming educated in the social studies. A good textbook serves as a springboard toward other sources of information. A comprehensive program requires other reading resources. Such things as newspapers, pamphlets, brochures, advertisements, books, magazines, diaries, letters, and other printed material give vital information. Careful selection by the teacher is necessary, of course.

Reading Social Studies Materials

There are three important areas that you must be concerned with if children are to use supplementary reading materials successfully: (1) how to read social studies material, (2) opportunities to read it, and (3) a reason to read it.

How to read social studies material is very important. Our regular reading program teaches the child word attack skills, sight vocabulary, and comprehension. They can "read"—but can they read social studies? Reading in the content areas should be a major concern of all teachers, especially upper-grade teachers who are more content-oriented. One of the more reliable methods of teaching a child to read for content is the SQ3R technique.

1. *Survey:*   Look over the material to establish a mindset. See what is there and how it relates to what you are looking for. Look at the headings.

2. *Question:*   Formulate some questions that you want to answer. Turn the headings into questions. This will create a focus for your reading.

3. *Read:*   Read the material, specifically looking for answers to your questions.

4. *Recite:*   Orally answer the questions that you posed earlier. Also note any other information that you came across that was not in your questions.

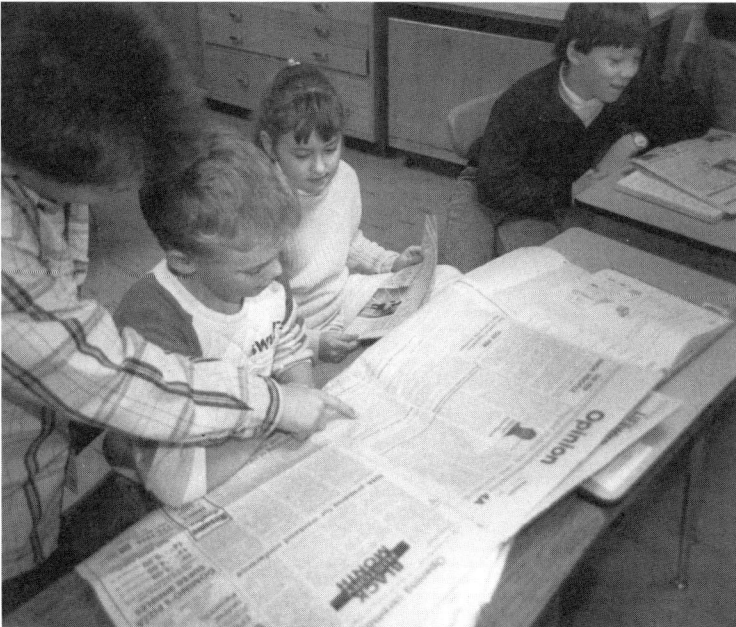

*There are many sources other than a textbook that children
can read.*

5. *Review:*   Reread the material to answer any unanswered questions and to
   reinforce the answers of the previous question.

This is a simplistic overview of a very important skill. Learning how to
teach reading in the content areas should be a component of any reading methods
course.

The second area of concern is the opportunities to read social studies material. You will want to encourage outside reading as much as possible so that the
students are aware of the multitude of informational sources that are available
to them. But you must also be aware that many students do not have access to
outside reading material. They may not go to the public library, or newspapers and magazines may not be available in the home.

If you do not provide an opportunity for the child to read these supplementary materials at school, it may not be provided at all. Your school library should
be included as an invaluable teaching and learning resource. A newspaper sub-
scription is well worth the nominal cost. And begin now to collect trade books,
catalogues, and magazines that will be kept in your room. Selecting appropriate
reading material for your lesson is an integral part of planning and preparation.
This is not enough, however; you must also find time for each child to read the
materials.

The third area of concern is that children must have a reason to read social studies materials. The reason may be to find more information on a specific topic, to gather supporting data, to read a different point of view, to correlate fiction with historical facts, or for enjoyment. Whatever the reason, you must let the children know why they are to read the material. There are those children who really do not see reading as important. If you can give them good reasons and show them why reading is important, maybe they will be more receptive to basic reading instruction.

Research in the Social Studies

Whenever students read social studies materials or collect information, they are doing research. Any learning resource they use is a source of research material. When students learn to use the card catalogue or when they are capable of running a computer program independently, they are doing research. Research means to investigate, examine, or seek out factual information. Most of the activities students perform with library or media materials can be classified as research. It is a big step for a third grader to seek out a book with information on Abraham Lincoln, to read it independently, and to use the data in a lesson. Research for a first grader may be as simple as asking her or his parents "Where was I born?" and remembering to report it to the class the next day. The child asked a question to gather information and used the information to make a report. This activity is an introductory component of research.

Upper-grade students are capable of planning and carrying out more complex projects. A fifth or sixth grader can choose a lesson topic, set some objectives, identify some procedural steps, locate materials, and then proceed to complete an entire research project. The research may include such things as locating appropriate reading materials (using the card catalogue, indexes, encyclopedias, trade books, magazines), designing a brief questionnaire and implementing it, interviewing resource people, and other tasks. The research technique works quite well in the upper grades when done individually, in pairs, or in small project groups.

Direct Observations

Direct observation is a learning resource that allows students to see, hear, taste, smell, and touch an event or a process in action. An observation is what we know based on information gathered through the use of one or more of our five senses. The class goes to an Indian powwow. They see real Indians in real regalia performing some of their cultural rituals. The colorful costumes, the visual experience of the dances, the sounds of the music, the smells, and tastes of Indian cooking, and maybe even the feel of being included in a dance are real. Can any reading materials, films, or oral description come close to matching this learning experience? You may not be able to go to a powwow, but in many areas there are members of local racial or ethnic groups that will come to your class and provide a similar experience.

Students can learn and benefit in several ways from actually observing things firsthand. Certainly, reading is valuable, but would you rather learn about Eskimos by reading a story or by talking to or corresponding with an Eskimo?

An involvement activity you may want to try is a variation of ''Pen Pals.'' Select a school or a person compatible with your students and your topic and make contact. This in itself may be a good research project for your students. Write pen-pal letters to individuals in the class, or at least send the names of your students who want to correspond individually. The students then prepare a tape recording telling about themselves and asking specific questions of concern. Mail it and wait for an answer. This can develop into a long-term friendship between the two schools and between individuals. Variations may include sending slides, pictures, or even videotapes. (I had the experience of having one of the students we were corresponding with come to our school to spend the day with us. Many years and several jobs later, the teacher and I still correspond regularly. JME)

If students are to participate in and learn from a direct observation experience, they must be taught how to observe, what to observe, how to record the data, and what to do with the data afterwards.

What you expect the students to observe will depend on the lesson topic and other related factors. The observation may focus on *people* and what they are doing, or on a *process* (all the steps in processing dairy products, for example), or on particular *environmental elements* (noise levels, sanitation, lighting, atmosphere) that are readily observable. An observation exercise should focus on the collection of facts. What did you see? Hear? Smell? Taste? Touch? Obviously, all of the senses will not be used every time, but try to get the children to use senses other than vision.

Recording the information can be done in many ways. Written notes are still used and will remain a popular method or recording observations. Paper and pencil are easily obtainable and portable. However, written notes are limiting because they must be made while observing and then later interpreted. Trying to remember what you meant when you wrote the note can be frustrating.

Technology has freed us from written notes. The tape recorder is a common tool, small in size, and easily used. With the recorder in your pocket and a microphone in your hand or clipped to your shirt, you are ready to record. It can record exact words and sounds for later analysis, or it can record the observer's comments and impressions. The tape recorder is fast being replaced by the small, easily handled, self-contained camcorder. These are affordable for most elementary schools. Students can now videotape an experience for later playback and analysis. This is a tool with which you should become familiar.

You should decide how the data will be used before they are collected. This may influence how the observations are made and your choice of recording them.

You have a reason for planning the observation, and how the results are used will correlate directly with that reason. Some possible uses could be: to learn new information, to validate information in the textbook, to compare and contrast, to chart or graph particular data, to assist in some project, or to make generalizations.

Some unit topics and ideas to use during an observation are:

1. *Groups:*   Watch a group at work. Who is participating? What are the leaders doing?
2. *Careers:*   Select an occupation then observe a person doing that job. What are some of the tasks involved in the job?
3. *Communications:*   Visit a newspaper office or television or radio station. Which communications skills can you see in use?
4. *Laws and Government:*   Visit a courtroom trial and list the specific procedures used.
5. *Agriculture:*   Visit a farm or a processing plant. How is food grown and processed?
6. *Transportation:*   Visit a trucking firm. What does the dispatcher do? How is the product moved? What happens at the docks?
7. *Environment:*   Visit a water purification plant, a garbage disposal site, or a power plant. Describe the process involved.

Use a format such as this for recording student observations.

People	Tools	Activities	Outcomes

Roleplaying and Simulation

Roleplaying and simulations are learning resources that give students additional active experiences. A roleplaying activity allows children to assume the role of another person. It is an attempt to identify with another human being in a very personal way, to share their feelings, responsibilities, reactions, and everyday activities. For primary-aged children, roleplaying is a vehicle for transcending time and space. It is an opportunity to move into a different experiential set. Playing the roles of significant other persons is an important part of early childhood.

Roleplaying gives students opportunities to practice decision-making skills in a relatively safe environment. Roleplaying is a particularly effective choice for practicing the affective skills. It is an opportunity to experience success for students who are reluctant responders. In the role of another person, they frequently open up and verbalize freely. An interesting roleplay activity for a primary class is to have each student make a puppet of a community helper the class has studied. The child assumes the role of that person in a puppet show. The teacher may design particular situations for the puppets to act out or the action may be spontaneous. The concepts that are practiced may be any of the following: power, responsibility, self-identity, or choices.

Some roleplay activities for fifth and sixth graders are:

1. Write and produce puppet shows representing historical persons.
2. Act out various famous events.
3. State a mock television news program.
4. Write short skits on specific subjects.
5. Roleplay an interview with a U.S. hero.
6. Write and present impersonations of famous people.

Simulations are effective learning resources for upper-grade students. A simulation is an activity designed to represent certain real-life conditions, forms, or appearances without the reality. It serves as a training or guided practice aid without the risk of real failure or embarrassment. The real strength of a simulation is in providing opportunities for decision making with the consequences of the decision an integral part of the simulation. In the book *Practical Approaches to Individualizing Instruction,* Dunn and Dunn propose this clarification: "Simulations . . . are structured, defined in advance, game-like rather than essentially dramatic and designed to develop decision-making ability and problem solving skills."[3]

Simulations give students opportunities to recognize and practice the acceptable behaviors they will need to function successfully in the world. Simulations may be individual or group activities that enable students to practice skills with others, whereas roleplaying seeks solutions or outcomes for individuals.

Learning Games

Games are an important teaching tool but, as with any other tool, they must be properly used. If games are used to fill the social studies time period or merely to keep students occupied, then using games is not a justifiable activity. On the other hand, if a specific skill is being reinforced or practiced with teacher supervision, then it is an acceptable student activity and should be encouraged. A simple rule to follow is: If you can justify an activity, use it; if you can't, don't.

Learning games are effective in reinforcing facts and concepts in both the cognitive and the affective areas. They reinforce learning objectives in a less formal and nonthreatening manner, and they give everyone in the class a chance to participate in the skill objective. The effectiveness of a game is strengthened when one or more of the learning modalities are an integral part of the game.

Students enjoy playing all kinds of games such as word games, map games, physical games, board games, and brain teasers. Games are a natural medium in which youngsters learn social and behavioral skills. The game format is a fun, challenging way to practice group membership skills, taking turns, following directions, and comprehension. A variety of learning games are available through school supply catalogs and stores.

The classroom teacher can design and construct games that will focus on specific objectives, insuring that the game teaches what she or he wants to teach, drill, or practice. Preparing learning games for a specific group of children is a challenge. It forces you to identify specifically which skill(s) the game will stress, and to creatively incorporate those skills into a format that is both appealing and challenging. Knowing the students and their likes and dislikes is a great help. You might spend many hours designing and constructing a very educationally sound game for reinforcing a map skill, but if the students do not like it, or if they use it only to please you, then it probably is not a valuable learning resource.

Primary Grades

Assembling a game for the primary grades can be done rather easily by using colored folders. Folders are readily available, inexpensive, and easy to store and retrieve. For example, a folder game to reinforce the map skill of "locating the forty-eight contiguous states on a map," is assembled this way:

1. Label the tab appropriately (U.S. map, matching).
2. Draw the outline of the United States in black.
3. Outline each of the states clearly.
4. Make a puzzle piece for each state.
5. Print the name of the state on each puzzle piece.
6. Laminate the folder and the states.
7. Insert the states into the folder pocket.
8. Your game is now ready to use.

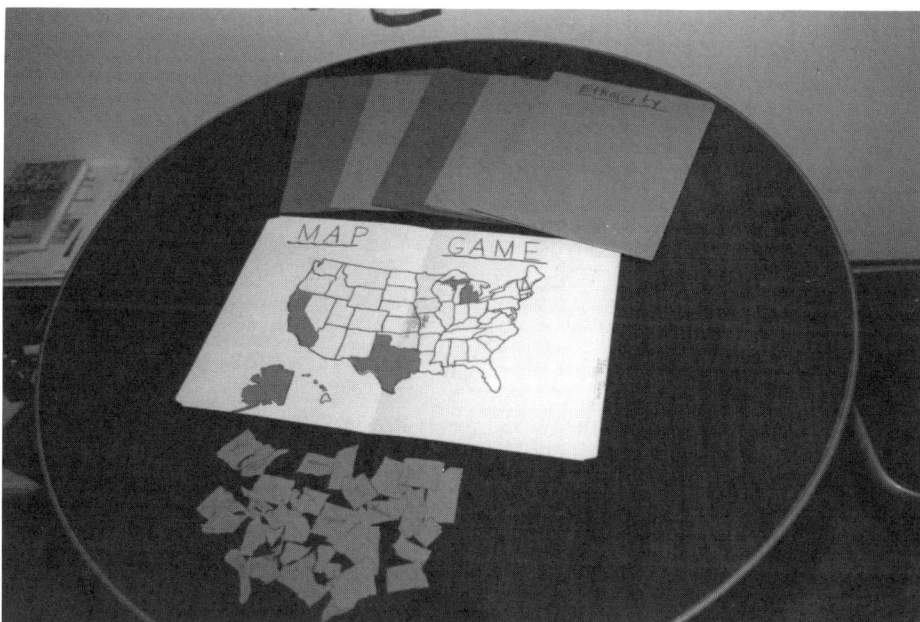

Map games are a good way to learn and practice map skills.

A folder game such as this employs the tactile modality (holding the pieces, touching the outlines), the auditory modality (working in pairs calling out the name of each state, talking to oneself if working alone), and the visual modality (visually examining each piece, visually making choices, discrimination). Folder games are appropriate for teaching objectives that incorporate these processes: locating, matching, identifying, selecting, separating, and labeling. They are effective at the picture level, the word level, and the phrase level of reading abilities. Remember, too, that youngsters enjoy games that are easy to use. Trying to decipher rules slows down the game.

Upper Grades

Games for the upper-elementary grades tend to be more competitive and focus on earning points, although this is not a requirement. Board games and card games are popular formats. They are an alternative for getting students actively involved. Consider a sixth-grade economics unit. The teacher has a board game with ''international trade'' as the central theme. Some of the topic skills might include: an understanding of special-interest groups, monetary systems, banking, political elections, price wars, global relations, nationalism, developing nations, and other factors that affect decision making at the international level. Games are also a practical, useful resource for teachers. Some commercially produced games are listed below, and may be purchased at most school supply stores or through school supply catalogs.

Name of Game	Grade Level
Global Flash Cards	Grades 4–6
Hemisphere Hunt	Grades 4–7
World Wiz	Grades 4–7
Bike Route	Primary
U.S. Bingo	Age 9 and older
The Economy Game	Grade 5 and older
Persuade	Age 12 and older
Can of Squirms	Primary and Intermediate
Role Play Game	Primary and Intermediate
Beginning Social Studies	Kindergarten–2

People, Places, and Things

Resource People

There are times when teachers decide that extra help is clearly needed for a particular activity. A good resource person is a valuable asset to any classroom teacher, and we teachers must begin to use them more. Resource people may be asked to share experiences, show slides, make presentations, organize activities, and bring things to class. Many resource people are already in the school. The school custodian, secretary, and lunch-room personnel are often overlooked. You may be surprised at the experiences they may be able to share. Perhaps your custodian also works as a fur trapper or perhaps the secretary collects political campaign buttons.

Other teachers in the building are possible resources. Many teachers enjoy travel and there may be a wealth of information and photos just down the hall. If, for example, you are studying the Middle East, someone on the staff may have been there and may be willing to serve as a resource. Some sources of resource people are:

1. *Parents, grandparents, and other members of the local community.* Almost any area of expertise, such as hobbies, collections, artifacts, experiences, and photos, can be found here. One father brought his truck, a big semi-tractor, to school so that the children could climb all over it and then ride in it.

2. *Retired teacher groups.* Former teachers have lots of experiences to share and often look for opportunities to return to the classroom.

3. *The Chamber of Commerce.*   Your local community organizations usually have a list of individuals who are available as resource people. If not they can help you locate someone who can help you.

4. *Professional people.*   Doctors, dentists, attorneys, store owners or managers, and farmers are all specialists who want children to know what they do.

5. *Travel agencies.*   Travel agents often have a lot of videotapes as well as travel brochures.

6. *Airports, railroads, and highway departments.*   These are transportation specialists.

7. *Private corporations.*   Large corporations usually have personnel who are available as resource people. Their expertise may be limited to their product or it may encompass almost any area.

If you decide to invite a resource person to make a presentation to the class, prepare your guest so that she or he knows what the children want to know. Prepare your children so that they know what to expect and what to look for. A preview of the material is in order. When you know the material in advance, a proper orientation can be given ahead of time. A thorough interview with all presenters is part of planning.

Out-of-School Experiences (Field Trips)

The school and the individual classrooms are essential elements for the presentation of informational learning. If the learning is confined to a given building or classroom, it can easily become ritualistic and inclusive. Learning resources that are outside of the school environment add meaning, relativity, and reality to classroom experiences. Outside experiences serve as ''connectors'' to classroom learning.

Arranging pertinent out-of-school experiences is a complicated planning and organizational responsibility. Taking a class to a resource area requires the teacher to know exactly what is available at the site. Details such as adequate supervision by trained personnel, transportation schedules, fees, permission slips, lunch arrangements, culminating activities, and evaluation procedures are done by the teacher ahead of time. There are three critical periods in the actual field trip.

Before the Trip
1. Take care of all details.
2. Prepare the students. Prior reading and discussion will set the trip in their mind. They will also make a list of specific things they want to see, do, or learn about. Set the objectives.

3. Prepare the people at the site. Let them know what you are expecting from them. Give them a copy of the lists your students made.

4. Take care of all the details. Yes, this is the second time we said it. If you fail to do this, unpleasant surprises will mar your trip.

During the Trip
1. Be aware of safety. Nothing ruins a good trip like an accident.

2. Point out specific things that are on your list. Make sure that the children do not accidentally miss what they wanted to see.

After the Trip
1. Hold a critique. Review what the children saw or heard. Go over the list and review each point. Discuss the trip.

2. Write thank you notes. This is a courtesy that cannot be overemphasized. Businesses or sites will post them in a prominent place and keep them for a long time. Good public relations is important if you want to go back again.

Artifacts, Real Things, and Models

There are many things that qualify as learning resources for social studies. Teachers are great collectors of these various "things" that help them to do an effective job of teaching. Artifacts, real things, and models can be used for hands-on learning experiences.

Look at this example from a western movement unit. The role of the Conestoga wagon in the westward movement was critical. Textbooks commonly picture pioneer families sitting up front holding the reins for a team of horses or walking beside a yoke of oxen. Students of all ages readily recognize the cov-

Table 10-2 Examples of Resource "Things"

Artifacts (Simple objects showing human workmanship)	Real Things (Actual objects)	Models (Copies or images of a real objects)
Pottery fragment	Tools—axe, saw	Wagon
Arrow point	Clothing	Tipi or wickiup
Woven basket	Coins or paper money	Windmill
Stone oil lamp	Ethnic food	Ship
Wood and bone carvings	Live animals	Animals
Stone axe	Butter churn	Rocket
	Spinning wheel	Dolls
	Toys	

ered wagon as an important part of our heritage. How many could describe the inside of the wagon and understand how a family could live in one for months on end? This is an important concept to be learned. The teacher brings in a model of a Conestoga wagon. Students can lift off the top and examine the floor plan. Where was everything stored? Where did everyone sleep? How many belongings could it carry? These and many other questions can be answered when a model of the real thing is introduced and thoroughly examined.

Obviously, many real items cannot be brought into the classroom. However, many others can be located, borrowed, and used by resourceful teachers. Reading about a tool such as a branding iron is a good experience; actually seeing and handling one adds another dimension (tactile-kinesthetic) to the event. Table 10–2 lists some examples of "things" to be used as resources.

Current Events as a Source

Current events are happening everyday. One merely has to tune in to the evening news to witness, almost firsthand, history in the making. Many of the local, national, and world events will directly affect the world our students will inherit as adults. These current events are the social studies of today and the social

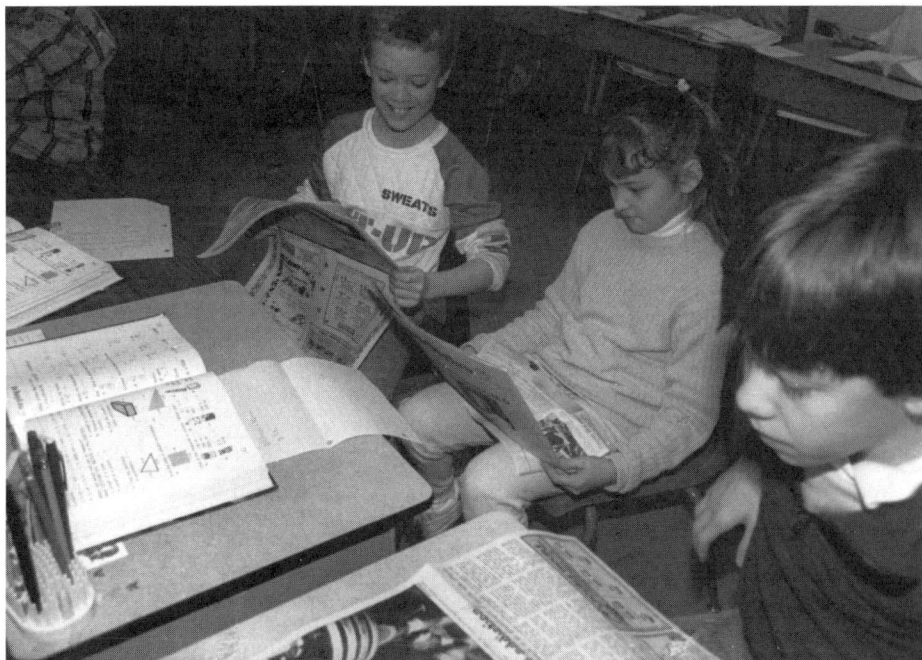

Reading the newspaper should be a part of any social studies program.

studies content material of tomorrow. When the American hostages were released from Iran in January 1981 the entire country (indeed, the free world) was elated. Yellow ribbons, the symbol of freedom, were everywhere. Students of all ages wore yellow ribbons to school that day. Playbacks of the airport scene were viewed in classrooms all over the country. In January 1986 the country witnessed the explosion of the Challenger space shuttle moments after lift-off. Seven Americans lost their lives, one of them a teacher. School-aged youngsters were acutely affected by this event. It was something they will remember for a lifetime.

Events occur almost daily that are resources for the classroom. Students need to be aware of what is happening at this point in their lives. Much of the textbook-based information will be forgotten soon after the school experience is completed. The current events that happen during those school years may remain vivid and intense for a lifetime if they are studied.

Sources of Current Events

There are three primary sources of current events: *newspapers, radio,* and *television.* They report the news and keep us informed of ongoing developments.

Newspapers are published daily and can give details of major stories that are not found in broadcast news. They also report many less-known events as well as local events. Major television news will not report on a local historical reenactment, but the local newspaper will. Most of the larger newspapers have an educational staff that will work with you and provide all types of suggestions for effective use of a newspaper in a classroom. There are, among other ideas, research activities, games, reading comprehension exercises, and current events quizzes. You usually can purchase classroom quantities of newspapers at a nominal fee. Teach your children how to read the newspaper as a part of your reading program and how to use the newspaper as part of your social studies.

Radio brings instantaneous news in a capsule summary. Fast-breaking news stories are almost always heard first on radio. Almost everyone, including preschoolers, has access to a radio, whether at work or play. The portable radio and headphones are almost a national trademark. It is easy to have a radio in the classroom. Many teachers keep one on hand all of the time, using it for music, weather, and news whenever warranted. If an event of importance has occurred, turn on the radio and let your students keep up with what is happening. When President Kennedy was assassinated, most radio stations broadcasted a continuous account, not only of what happened but what was happening at the moment. If you had been teaching on that day, would you have turned on your radio?

Television is a very popular medium for obtaining news. Correspondents and camera crews are stationed all over the world and can get to any news story very quickly and, through satellite, relay it instantaneously back to the home studio for broadcast. The evening news is one of the most viewed television productions. Television shows us the actual events as they happen, as well as repeating them at later times. Children watch television news with their parents or when there is an exciting story or event taking place. They are familiar with many names of places around the world. On some occasions when a historical event is about to occur, you will want to have a television set in the classroom. Videotapes of news telecasts are an excellent way to bring in special current events. You can tape the broadcast and show it in the classroom. *A word of caution*: Be sure you are aware of the copyright laws and how they affect your use of taped material.

Selecting Current Events

Current events are used to teach and reinforce social studies concepts. When current events are taught as an isolated series of events that happen in the world, they tend to become just that—isolated events with little or no real meaning. The outcome for many students is "So what?" When current events are an integral part of the social studies program, they assume a whole new role. They are an almost daily part of the social studies lesson. Topics such as economics, human rights, government, war and peace, ecology, and world population are real issues on the world scene. In some cases, a current event may be the impetus for a series of lessons that is not covered in the textbook. Some very creative teaching sequences result from these situations.

Current events are used in three ways. First, they are used to reinforce or supplement a lesson. You plan a lesson and find a current event that goes with it. Care must be used to select an event that the students can relate to as well as understand. If the event is beyond their comprehension, it will not be of much value. For example, a news article about a war in a small, distant country may not mean much to a third-grade student who is trying to understand the concept of community unity.

The second use of a current event is to develop an awareness of the news of the day. This is used to teach about current events and how to know what is happening in the community and the world. Students may select events to share with the class or you may select some events. Be advised that students look for the unusual. Their idea of a good current event may be quite different than yours. You look at something like "Political leaders caught lying"; they look at "Shark bites man in Australia." The main criteria here is to select for interest or to select for particular types of events. This is when you need newspapers in the classroom.

The third use of a current event is to follow an ongoing news story of world, national, or local importance. For example, a major earthquake has destroyed a city. We will want daily reports on fatalities, damage, rescue operations, humanitarian aid, aftershocks, or anything else that will keep us informed.

A local issue such as problems with the disposal of garbage may be worth spending some time on. You may select the events or let the students report the news of the day.

Teaching with Current Events

There are many activities that involve current events. Here are only a few:

1. Pretend your classroom is a radio or TV station. A team of two or three students will select news items and prepare a short daily news report for the class. Teams may change daily or weekly.

2. Hold a panel discussion on a current topic. Each member uses newspapers to prepare for the discussion.

3. Go on a buying spree. You have just won $1000 in a contest. What will you buy with it? You must spend it all, with none left over. Use the newspaper ads as your source for prices.

4. Plan a shopping trip to the grocery store. Use the ads in the newspaper to find the best bargains. You may give the students a prepared list or let them develop their own.

5. Keep records of a story from beginning to end. Use a currently breaking story. Make a time line of the events as they occur.

ACTIVITIES

In this chapter you were introduced to several different learning resources. Now you will examine a textbook for examples of Bruner's "Ways of Knowing," review your research skills, and make a learning game. These activities allow you to see the theoretical as well as practical applications of some of the resources available to you.

10.1 *Ways of Knowing*

Examining and previewing current textbooks is one way of determining the content, concepts, and processes of social studies. This activity will give you an opportunity to examine the enactive, iconic, and symbolic modes of presentation as they are integrated into textbooks.

Go to the curriculum materials center and check out a primary and an upper-grade teacher's guide. Choose two units of special interest to you. Carefully read through the units to locate examples of enactive, iconic, and symbolic student activities. Consult other resources if you need more clarification on the specifics of each mode. Use the following list to record your findings.

Textbook publisher:

Title and grade level:

Describe the activity:

Enactive activities:

Iconic activities:

Symbolic activities:

Comments on the activity:

Now reexamine your work. How many different activities did you locate for each of the three modes of presentation? Was any one of the three used more than others? How did the primary and the upper-grade activities compare? Textbooks that meet the learning needs of students at varying stages of development will have well-designed activities for all students to perform. Check with your instructor if you are unsure of any classifications.

10.2 *Research Skills and Current Events*

Reading and researching social studies materials is an important skill for students to learn. Learning some researching skills is one part of becoming an independent learner. If students do not learn these research skills from you, they may not learn them anywhere else.

Research is nothing more than looking for information. You may look in books, newspapers, or magazines or you may listen to reports or watch a film, videotape, or a television program. Any source that will give you information is acceptable. It is important that you know what you are looking for before you start looking. When you find it, record it in some usable form.

Do a research project using a current event. Find a continuing news story and then discover all you can about it.

Topic:
1. Where?
2. What?
3. Who?
4. When?
5. Why?

Summary of the story:

List five facts:
1.
2.
3.
4.
5.

Background information (What the story doesn't tell)

Make a time line

Start_____End

Make a projection (What will happen now?)

10.3 *Learning Games*

Learning resources is an area that gives teachers room for creative expression. This activity gives you an opportunity to use your creative skill.

Go to the university library and research learning games. Take special note of such things as usage, design, format, strategies, and evaluations. Visit the university curriculum materials center and preview some social studies games. Now that you are familiar with games as a resource, design a game for the grade level of your choice. Select the specific skill(s) your game will highlight. Will this game be an introductory resource, a guided practice resource, or an informal evaluation tool? There should be three rules for your game. Be prepared to share your game with your instructor and classmates. Prepare a rationale for using this game in a classroom and a brief description of your game. Share a copy with your classmates.

Summary

The multidisciplinary framework of social studies requires that a variety of learning resources be used. The learning styles and requirements of an average group of students are diverse. Some students learn best from reading the textbook and performing the suggested activities at the end of each lesson. Other students perform more successfully when they can participate in several different kinds of learning experiences. To meet these various learning needs, it is necessary to have the appropriate materials for students to use. Planning and preparing those materials is an important responsibility of the social studies teacher.

This chapter has examined a very small number of the learning resources that are available to teachers. Maps and globes, supplementary reading materials, current events, resource people, field trips, and artifacts, real things, and models were presented. Some ideas for using each of these resources were included.

READING RESOURCES

Ellis, Arthur K. *Teaching and Learning Elementary Social Studies,* 3rd ed. Boston: Allyn and Bacon, 1986.

Martorelli, Peter. *Elementary Social Studies: Developing Reflective, Competent, and Concerned Citizens.* Boston: Little, Brown and Company, 1985.

Michaelis, John. *Social Studies for Children.* New York: Macmillan Publishing Company, 1988.

Savage, Tom, and Armstrong, David. *Effective Teaching in Elementary Social Studies.* New York: Macmillan Publishing Company, 1987.

Schug, Mark, and Berry, R. *Teaching Social Studies in the Elementary School.* Glenview, IL: Scott, Foresman and Company, 1987.

Schuncke, George. *Elementary Social Studies: Knowing, Doing, Caring.* New York: Macmillan Publishing Company, 1988.

Welton, David, and Mallan, John. *Children and Their World.* Boston: Houghton Mifflin Company, 1988.

Woolover, Roberta, and Scott, Katherine. *Active Learning in Social Studies.* Glenview, IL: Scott, Foresman and Company, 1988.

ENDNOTES

1. Bruner, Jerome; Goodnow, J.; and Austin, E., *Studies in Cognitive Growth* (New York: John Wiley and Son, 1966).

2. Maxim, George, *Methods of Teaching Social Studies to Elementary Children* (Columbus, OH: Charles E. Merrill Publishing Company, 1977).

3. Dunn, Rita, and Dunn, Kenneth, *Practical Approaches to Individualizing Instruction* (Englewood Cliffs, NJ: Parker Publishing Company, 1972), p. 189.

11
New-Tech
Media Resources

PROJECTIONS

The role of media resources in the social studies curriculum is significant now, and will continue to expand in the 1990s. Both the content and the hardware for elementary students is improving steadily. Teachers are looking for resources that require students to use thinking skills, divergent strategies, creativity, and higher-order reasoning. Publishers and writers are trying to provide these in formats students can use comfortably.

Technology will continue to affect the curriculum, the teaching methods, and the expectations for student performance. The academic community does not expect technology to replace teachers as the primary source of instruction; however, it does expect teachers to use technology to prepare students for active participation in society. To ignore the role of technology as one part of educating youth is to deny them access to an important skill they will need as adults. Educational computing will continue to have a major role in the academic environment.

Teachers are always searching for materials that will help students to learn. This constant search frequently results in the creation of new and exciting materials. Administrators and school boards must be cognizant of one important issue—teachers need time and funds to design and assemble the various resource materials they need to teach the social studies. New teachers must be aware of the fact that this is one of their professional responsibilities: to make teaching materials. Experienced teachers frequently comment, "I could have designed this in a better way." Indeed, teachers do have many creative skills to prepare very good materials. This could include such things as video lessons, computer programs, interactive television (IATV) courses, and many others. Teachers anticipate the availability of time to work on projects to increase the inventory of pertinent media resources for social studies.

A comprehensive social studies program is augmented by a strong support system. One part of that support system is the resources that are usually available in each school building and the district's central offices. Media resources are the audiovisual communications services and printed materials that teachers use to teach social studies. Without a variety of pertinent instructional materials, social studies lessons can easily revert to textbook reading and teacher talk.

We use the media to introduce, reinforce, and, in some cases, reteach social studies material. Teaching students how to use the library, the computer lab, and other learning centers is very gratifying. Teachers use resources as instructional tools, modeling the appropriate use of a resource as part of the social studies experience. Social studies teachers should be aware of and use the many advantages tht new high-tech media present.

Various items are included in a resources inventory. The first one that comes to mind is the elementary school library. Traditional audiovisual equipment, such as filmstrip projectors and cassette recorders, continue to be standard equipment for elementary classrooms. Advances in technology make the newer media more accessible in the classroom and easier to use. This technology is grouped under four categories:

1. *Equipment.* The area of advanced electronics has opened a new field in audiovisual presentations, such as VCRs (video-cassette recorders and playback), large-screen televisions, video (laser) disks, camcorders, tap recorders, and computers.

2. *Printed Materials.* Fast reproduction of printed materials allows handouts of many kinds. Electronics allow easy transfer of information between the school and other schools, the central office, libraries, businesses, and homes. Many textbook series now include computer disks as a part of their program. Books and reference materials (dictionaries, encyclopedias) can be stored on disks.

3. *Centers.* Central areas are being developed for specific purposes. Media centers specialize in distributing materials, libraries contain references and information, learning centers teach specific knowledge or skills, and computer centers provide computer access.

4. *Teaching Strategies.* New technology has allowed new ways to teach. Interactive teaching using a conference call network on the telephone, an audio-video hook-up, or connecting computers are only a few of the possibilities.

These resources enable teachers to improve their instructional techniques by using technology to expand select communication experiences into the social studies lesson. This chapter serves as a review of media resources that are available in elementary schools. The applications for teaching social studies will be examined.

New-Tech Equipment

Technological advances demand that educational systems bring instruction into the new-tech age. Advanced instructional systems are available and should be implemented now, especially in the intermediate grades where the students are mature enough to grasp the procedures and processes needed to utilize their potential.

Audiovisual Equipment and Materials

Traditional audiovisual equipment consisted of a record player, a filmstrip projector, and a viewing screen. Both the record player and the filmstrip projector are quickly being replaced with newer equipment such as video disks, talking computers, cassettes, and interactive television.

Audiovisual equipment is used to supplement other instructional media. Filmstrips with accompanying cassettes and a cassette recorder with plug-ins for headsets is a basic requirement for the elementary classroom. These two items work well for small groups of four or five students to view and listen at the audiovisual table, or for an individualized enrichment or reteaching activity.

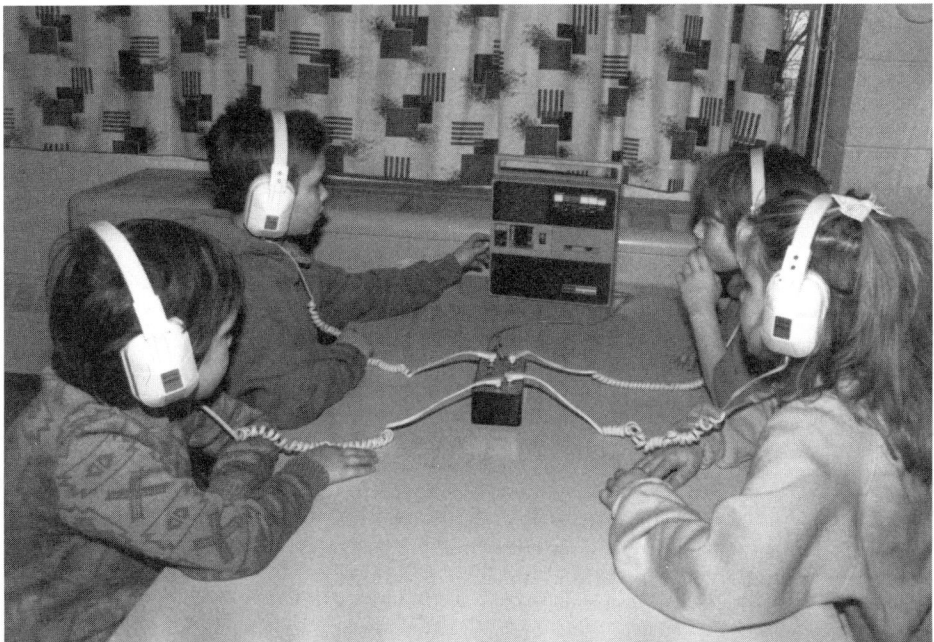

Students are using the visual and auditory modalities at the audiovisual station.

Computers

The personal computer is the mainstay of new technology in the educational system. Computers have one major purpose: to store and retrieve information. This capacity for storage and instant retrieval is significant. The computer as a teaching tool and resource has made its impact in all curriculum areas, including art and music. In many cases, computer technologies make teaching and learning more productive. Computers provide students and teachers with more freedom—freedom to make a mistake without personal embarrassment or ridicule. The computer accommodates trial-and-error methods. If a mistake is made, an error message appears on the screen and you simply try again.

Computer technology is an important tool to move educational practice into the 1990s. Instructional computer software is the critical factor. Selecting good software is the initial step in determining the output you can expect from students. Software is available from public domain sources. MECC (Minnesota Educational Computing Corporation) is an organization that started in 1973 to assist schools in the implementation of educational computing. This group prepares and distributes software, in-services teachers, and provides other services. MECC handles courseware primarily for the Apple family of computers. More information can be obtained at the following address:

MECC
3490 Lexington Ave. No.
St. Paul MN 55126

Computer companies such as Apple Computer, Inc., IBM, and Tandy manufacture hardware that is used in elementary schools. In addition to the hardware, they also develop software and support materials. These specialty support groups produce software specifically for their hardware, and the programs may or may not be compatible with other manufacturer's products. More information can be obtained at these addresses:

Apple Computer, Inc.
20525 Mariana Ave.
Cupertino CA 95014

IBM DIRECT
PC Software Department
One Culver Road
Dayton NJ 08818

Other education specialty companies manufacture and sell a variety of materials (books, reproducibles) including software. Some companies specialize in educational software. Three such resources are:

SoftWare House
West Acres Shopping Center
Fargo ND 58103

Beckley-Cardy
1645 Downs Drive
West Chicago IL 60185

Scholastic Inc.
904 Sylvan Ave.
Englewood Cliffs NJ 07632

Video-Cassette Recording (VCR)

One of the most practical, serviceable, new-tech audiovisual resources is the video cassette recorder/player system—the VCR. It is quickly replacing both the filmstrip and the traditional 16mm film equipment. To view a prerecorded video, you simply insert the cassette into the video tape deck, push the designated controls, and the movie is transmitted to the television monitor. Many of the companies that supplied films now have the same titles on tape. Almost all new productions are on video tape rather than film because tapes are cheaper, easier to produce, and easier to use.

Commercial and public television stations have many quality educational programs. Programming ranges from the creative arts (music, art, dance, theater), science, language arts, and several themes that correlate with the social sciences. The problem is these programs are frequently scheduled during school hours, and therefore are inaccessible to the intended audience. Programs that are scheduled in the evening are accessible, but many students are unable to view them for various reasons. The result is that educational programs are not always an available resource. The VCR allows teachers to use special television programs in the classroom. This is done by recording directly from the television and playing back at a later time. But before you do this, read the copyright laws. You do not want to inadvertently become a "pirate." It is not a violation of copyright laws to record for personal or educational use, provided viewing fees are not charged, cassettes are not sold, and tapes are promptly erased after use. Yes, you do have to include all commercial messages and credits.

The VCR has some distinct advantages over the traditional 16mm movie equipment. Teachers and students can record educational resources that are otherwise unavailable. Recording educational programs directly from the television is an important advantage. Once the program is on a cassette, it can be viewed more than once for observing and critiquing different aspects of the content. The cassette is easily shared with other classes or buildings in the school district.

A cassette system is easier to handle than 16mm film. The complicated process of loading a film into the standard projector is eliminated. Cassette recordings are durable and they occupy less storage space than large film canisters. The tape that is enclosed in a cassette is less likely to become brittle, scratched, or broken. VCR systems are the preferred method for classroom viewing. There are many good tapes produced by businesses and special-interest groups that are available free or for a nominal charge. Modern Talking Picture Service (5000 Park Street, N., St. Petersburg FL 33709) acts as a clearing house for commercial films and videotapes. Contact them for a catalog of resources and services.

The National Aeronautics and Space Administration (NASA) has a very extensive educational program on tape. Videotapes of almost any topic are available from NASA resource centers at a nominal duplication cost. These are public domain materials and can be used and copied without special permission. NASA is not exclusively related to science. It has a lot to offer in the social studies, especially in the areas of weather, maps and mapping, and geography.

Video Disks

State of the art in audiovisuals is the video disk. A laser optic system scans the surface as the disk rotates, converting the digital information into picture and sound on the video monitor. An enormous number of pictures (more than 20,000) can be stored on one disk. The advantages of video disk systems include: a high resolution (sharpness), compactness for easy storage, and durability. The disadvantages are that they have a very high initial cost and they cannot be altered by the user. Newer technology is beginning to allow the interconnection of video disks and computers so that the computer can control the selections on the disk. You can program your picture selections to correspond with your lessons.

A video disk system is a good resource to use for information or programs that remain standard. Topics such as geography, history, anthropology, or economics principles are practical to have in the system. An inventory of historical literature or dramas that relate to particular periods is a valuable asset to the social studies curriculum.

Video Cameras

Teachers frequently enjoy filming their students performing various activities in the classroom. The video recorder enables teachers to do this on a regular basis. The term *film* is still used by many when they really mean *videotaping*. (Old habits are hard to break.) Camcorders (*cam*era re*corder*) are very easy to use, lightweight, and portable. A blank cassette is inserted and the operator is ready to begin videotaping. Fourth graders can easily be trained to use the equipment.

The camcorder has many classroom applications for social studies. Teachers may videotape student performance for evaluation, or tape a process or event to bring into class. A social studies teacher may videotape a variety of lessons and activities. Here are some possible uses to consider.

1. A sixth-grade class is preparing a panel discussion to be presented for an intermediate grades assembly. The teacher videotapes the practice session. The teacher and the panel members view the videotape and take note of

such things as diction, enunciation, emphasis, eye contact, pitch, and other aspects of presentation.

2. A kindergarten teacher videotapes her students roleplaying an activity (e.g., How to Use the Playground Equipment Safely, Me and My Family, Things I Can Do Well).

3. Second graders are learning how to work in a cooperative learning setting. The teacher videotapes the class as they work in groups. They view the videotape at another time. The teacher points out all the ways each group shows cooperative behaviors. She also makes a mental note of students who need more direction or intervention during group activities.

4. A small group is preparing a demonstration for the social studies fair. The activity is videotaped so the participants can see how each step of the process will be seen by the audience.

5. The teacher videotapes himself or herself delivering a lecture-style lesson and evaluates his or her teaching as well as the students' on-task behaviors. The stationary camcorder works well for this stype of lesson.

6. Guest speakers may be videotaped. Some excellent resource people are unavailable when we need them or for some other reason cannot come to the school. A 95-year-old person may not be able to come to us, but she has a lot of history to share. If individuals cannot come to you, go to them.

7. A specific right-brain activity is videotaped to provide staff members with some insights into the ways these style-preference students approach particular tasks. This is a good staff inservice project.

8. Videotape a social studies class to evaluate questioning strategies, think time, and student responses.

9. Students make a videotape of their school or community for a pen-pal exchange with similar-aged students in another school. (I had great success with this when my fifth-grade class started corresponding with a group of fourth through eighth graders in an Eskimo school in Alaska. They started with pen-pal letters, added tape recordings with occasional narrated slides, and then added videotaping. They learned a lot about each other through an almost face-to-face experience. JME)

These and other situations are defensible uses of the video media for social studies. This medium has significant potential and is limited only by your imagination. What you can't think of, your students will.

Media Centers

Media centers are central locations designed for specific purposes such as collecting and distributing materials, providing specific learning activities, and sharing equipment. Three of these centers are the library, learning centers, and computer centers.

Library

The elementary school library is a vital source for the reading materials needed by teachers and students. The library is dramatically changing to meet contemporary educational requirements. Books, magazines, newspapers, and other printed material are very important, and they will continue to be so, but educational practices now provide students with experiences and activities that are not limited to reading. Some students examine books for recreational reading, others research information to complete classroom assignments. Study carrels are a fixture in the library for students to work independently. A headset station provides opportunities to use the auditory modality for listening activities or to gather topical information. One or two computer stations may be located in the library for students to use. Films, videotapes, filmstrips, and recordings are becoming standard items in the library. These learning-based materials contribute toward making the school library a contemporary resource.

Learning Centers

Learning centers are specialized areas that provide special learning programs which are usually developed and staffed by fully certified teachers. The learning center is a satellite to the social studies classroom. Social studies materials, units, and other resources are available for teacher and student use. The teacher is an important component of an effective learning center, serving as a resource person to all other teachers on the staff, or planning and teaching special themes. She or he locates, designs, and makes materials the teachers need to teach social studies.

A learning center has a remedial and an enrichment function. Students who fail to achieve lesson or unit objectives may go to the learning center for reteaching. Students who are ready for enrichment activities may also go to the center for that purpose. The whole class may go for a special presentation, and the teacher may go for information and materials for the classroom lesson. Students and teachers benefit from the expertise of the learning center teacher.

An effective learning center has access to a variety of materials. Those that are needed for social studies would include: books, magazines, pamphlets, maps, globes, tapes, cassettes, filmstrips, computer courseware, movies, videos, artifacts, models, games, and any other materials that can be purchased, made, or borrowed. Schools with learning centers have a central location, such as the school library, where materials are stored, cataloged, and distributed. The learning center teacher is a proactive person who initiates, plans, and helps to make those materials that energize the curriculum in positive ways.

Social studies teachers use the learning center in several ways:

1. To consult with the learning center teacher for an innovative unit opener, bulletin board idea, and so on

2. To request remedial or enrichment materials for the classroom

3. To request organizational assistance for a social studies fair, program, or exhibit

4. To use the learning center teacher as a speaker, demonstration teacher, or small group advisor

5. To allow students to view a filmstrip, play a game, or use a social studies computer program

6. To allow lower-performing students to receive additional instruction on a regular basis

7. To use as a resource for visual, auditory, and kinesthetic materials

8. To use as a place to donate social studies materials, ideas, lessons, or units that can be used by others

A learning center enhances social studies instruction. Teachers plan how and when it will be used and in which ways it can be most beneficial for a particular class. Figure 11–1 shows a diagram of a classroom arrangement that accommodates a variety of teacher and student activities. Simultaneous activities with a variety of media and resources is encouraged. Learning centers are staffed and supplied for one major reason—to be used. The learning center teacher and the classroom teacher are comembers of the instructional team that plans and delivers complementary social studies experiences.

Computer Centers

Computers may be used in the individual classroom or in a computer center. Computer centers allow more students to use a limited number of machines. Special teachers can also be available in a computer center to teach computer literacy and to provide special help for students who are less proficient in computer operation.

A computer center in the elementary school is an immediate possibility, partially due to declining enrollments in many areas. An empty classroom is readily transformed into a computer center with modest electrical adaptations. Placing a number of computers in a central location has several advantages:

1. All classes have access to use the center.

2. The computer programs, manuals, and accompanying courseware are readily available.

3. The teacher can work with an entire class or a small group.

4. Small groups can pair with a student mentor.

Figure 11-1 Room with Learning Centers

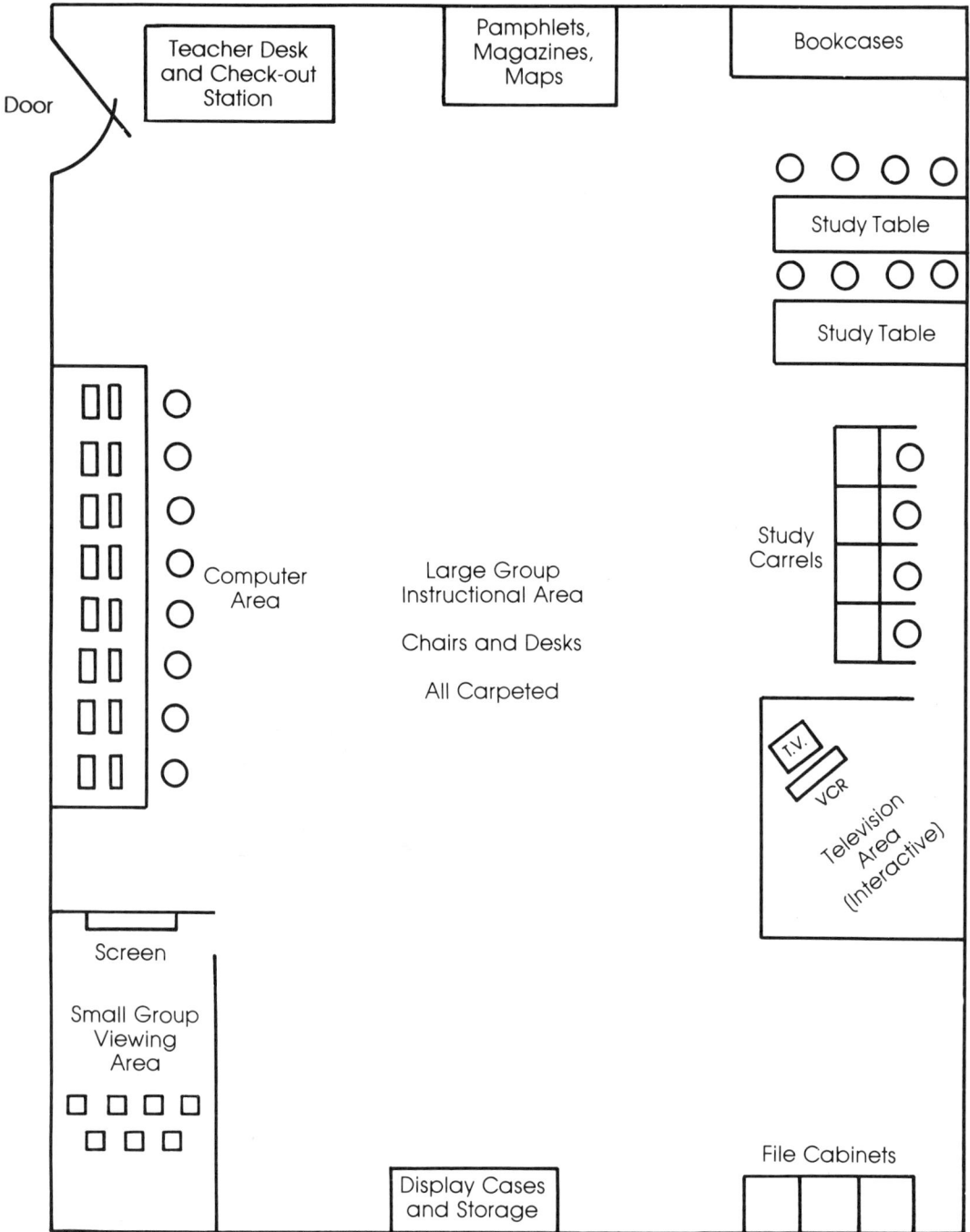

Door

Teacher Desk and Check-out Station

Pamphlets, Magazines, Maps

Bookcases

Study Table

Study Table

Study Carrels

Computer Area

Large Group Instructional Area

Chairs and Desks

All Carpeted

T.V.

VCR

Television Area (Interactive)

Screen

Small Group Viewing Area

Display Cases and Storage

File Cabinets

5. A computer center enables students to work with fewer external distractions.

6. The central console enables the teacher to monitor individual student responses.

7. The console enables the teacher to intervene almost immediately when a student needs help.

8. A computer center is a valuable resource for community education classes.

Schools with a computer center soon realize that a user's schedule is immediately necessary. Everyone wants to be there! A schoolwide schedule gives each classroom specified times to use the center. The teacher can plan ahead to incorporate computer time into the social studies lessons. Primary teachers must do a significant amount of training with the students to be sure they are familiar with basic computer operations. Loading the program is a major task for young children. When the basic operational skills are learned, the teacher can move the class directly into social studies material. Beginning social studies programs focus largely on identification, recall, location, and other introductory skills. Primary teachers use the computer center for guided practice or evaluation-culmination activities.

Teachers of intermediate grades find the computer center to be a rich re-

The computer lab can accommodate two students at each monitor and keyboard.

source for instruction. Upper-grade students are able to work on concentrated activities for longer periods of time. One-hour periods are commonly scheduled, whereas half-hour sessions are planned for primary classes.

There are many social studies programs available from the textbook publishers as well as from computer courseware companies. Topics range from U.S. presidents, to space-age technology, to community planning. It is exciting and encouraging to read the computer catalogues and discover how much courseware is actually available.

The computer center, like all other media resources, is only as effective as the teacher who uses it. Ironically, many students know more about computers than do their teachers. Many homes have computers and the children have been using them for years. These students can be of great help to you if you will use their talents. A teacher who is only moderately skilled at using the technology may only get moderate results from her students. The teacher who becomes computer-literate feels secure enough to lead the students beyond the computer-toy-games philosophy. All teacher candidates should take a course in computers before they start job hunting. Many school districts are beginning to insist on computer knowledge as a condition of employment.

Once the students have a demonstrated knowledge of computer usage, the teacher must decide how to use the computer center to enhance the social studies program. Computer technology is effective at almost every stage of instruction. Introductory activities, practice lessons, testing, and enrichment all have possibilities. Your scheduled time largely determines which activities will occur at the computer center and which will occur in the classroom.

Upper-grade students enjoy programs that are open-ended and permit them to use divergent thinking processes. Making decisions and following through with the consequences is a valuable human relations skill that students need to learn. Computer graphics enable students to practice and use the chart and graph skills, as well as other commensurate social studies skills. A computer center in the elementary school is one resource that is a minimal requirement to prepare students for the technology that is already in the workplace.

New Instructional Techniques

Interactive Video

Interactive video consists of a videotape cassette that utilizes the conventional VCR system. It differs from interactive television in that the viewer responds to a prerecorded learning set as it appears on the monitor screen. Interactive video presents a graphic representation on the monitor. The student responds by entering a keyboard response or by manipulating a mouse or joystick. The responses are analyzed in various ways that are written into the program.

Prerecorded tapes are a good resource for simulation activities. The tapes provide a means for practice and training in the observation skills. The teacher who plans a particular field trip experience for his or her class with the express purpose to use observation and recording skills may elect to use an interactive video for guided practice opportunities. The intermediate grades typically study the age of technology and its effect on our daily lives. Space exploration is a large part of the technology industry. Interactive video enables students to experiment with scale modeling of various kinds. Building a rocket is one possibility. Interactive video provides the classroom teacher with an alternative activity for students who need to work alone for a period of time. It also provides opportunities for both left- and right-brain preference learners to experience an activity that may not be in their preferred mode. Interactive videos are an example of new-tech iconic learning.

Interactive Television

Instructional television has been available for many years. One basic premise for using instructional television was to bring specific courses to areas that were unable to provide them. This premise utilized teaching expertise and staffing resources in cooperative ways. Teaching television was innovative at the outset and it was effective for some types of classes. One major drawback was the one-way communication style where the teacher talked and demonstrated and the students listened and watched—in other words, no interaction.

The new electronic application of television in the classroom is IATV, interactive television. The interactive television system enables the teacher to communicate with the students (at several different locations if necessary) and the students to communicate with the teacher. There are three basic methods for transmitting the television signals: the UHF broadcast signal, the cable system, and the satellite. Due to the relatively low cost of tying into the cable or telephone franchise, the cable transmission is accessible virtually everywhere. The hardware needed for interactive television includes microphones, monitors, camcorders, and cassettes. These are needed at both the home site and the remote site.

Interactive television enables students to have instructional experiences they otherwise may not get. These instructional experiences might include courses, resource people, lectures, visual field trips, and various other enrichment activities. IATV uses the television teacher to teach classes to her or his own group of students (the home site class) as well as another group of students at a different location (the remote site group) simultaneously. Some practice and training is necesary to become an effective, poised televison teacher. An enthusiastic, competent classroom teacher makes this transition rather easily. IATV is another example of shared time between schools. One building shares human resources with another academic site. The students at both the home site and the remote site benefit by having access to the expertise of the television teacher. Cooperation, flexibility, and coordination are very important for IATV to be successful at both locations.

Adopting any innovation into the academic arena is preceded by establishing a rationale. A major element in this rationale is that IATV delivers service to a greater number of students. To expand and deliver instructional choices is one of our goals as educators. It is agreed that elementary social studies includes a number of major instructional areas. Interactive television enables teachers to use the electronic media to share instructional resources. It is possible for staff members in one district or educational service area to team teach by using the IATV as the medium.

Social studies education allows many applications for interactive television as a viable learning resource. IATV is a good medium for students with specific communications or language development handicaps. The electronic media is a resource students enjoy using without feelings of inadequacy, embarrassment, or peer rejection. They are practicing and using their communications skills in a different environment. IATV is a resource for teaching specific social studies skills for the special education students. The high-potential learners benefit from

The computer, VCR, and a telephone modem provide a powerful combination for sharing information.

opportunities to converse and interact with other students of similar academic abilities.

IATV enables school districts to provide instruction for special-interest groups. One teacher may develop and plan a course on Archeologists and Anthropologists and teach it to the surrounding television audience. Another teacher may organize a class on problem-solving skills for students who need reteaching or enrichment in that area. There are many possible uses for IATV that directly relate to social studies. Classroom applications are limited only by the creativity and planning skills of those teachers who use the medium for instructing students.

ACTIVITIES

An important part of preparing to teach social studies is knowing how and when to use resources. Audiovisual courses provide background information and opportunities to use standard and state-of-the-art classroom equipment. The decisions regarding when to use these resources will be made by you, the social studies teacher. The social studies teacher's guide, classroom experience, and your professioal judgment are factors that help you make these planning decisions. Media resources are important tools for teaching social studies.

11.1 *Educational Television*

Many educational programs are available on public and commercial television. These programs are geared for all age groups, toddlers to adults. Educational television is a good resource for social studies teachers and their students.

This activity is a title search for educational programs that are scheduled for a particular week or month on commercial television. You will need a copy of *T.V. Guide* from several viewing areas. One of them should be for a large metropolitan area. You are looking for all programs that could be used for teaching social studies. Include regularly scheduled programs and specials that could be used directly with students, as well as those thay may be used as resources for the teacher. The chart shown in Figure 11–2 can be used to help you tabulate your findings. You may list the basic stations and the cable offerings separately in order to show the limitations for homework assignments.

You may be pleasantly surprised at the number and quality of programs that can be used in the classroom. Some programs may be assigned as homework and critiqued in class the next day. Part of the teacher's responsibility is to determine which programs have merit and which ones do not. Using the television

Figure 11-2 Viewing Log for Educational Programs

Channel	Program Title	Day(s)	Audience	Time	Content Area
ABC	"Nightline"	Fri.	Grades 4–6	10:30 P.M.	Current events
NBC	"Inherit the Wind"	Sun.	Grades 4–6	8:00 P.M.	History, government

medium demands a time commitment: Does this particular program warrant a 45-minute class period? Being generally familiar with a specific program format is very helpful. A certain "trust in content" is readily established by programs such as the National Geographic or Jacques Cousteau series.

What about regularly scheduled programs that are unfamiliar to you? In this case, it is suggested that you preview several telecasts before using them with your class. When you have determined the relevancy to social studies objectives, reading the previews will be a sufficient preparation.

This title search is a first step to using commercial television as a resource for social studies. Now you and your classmates will work in small groups to view programs that are currently being aired. Each group member will select a number of programs to view. Your objective is to determine the value of the programs for social studies education. Would you use them in the classroom? Your group will design a set of criteria to guide you in this investigation. Each group will make a short presentation of the results at a time designated by the instructor.

11.2 *Tape-Slide Shows*

It is helpful to have actual hands-on experience with a particular medium before attempting to use it with a classroom of students. This activity gives you and your classmates an opportunity to make a tape-slide presentation. A group of five or six is workable. Before you begin this project, review the cooperative learning skills as outlined in Chapter 9. Adults need guidelines too!

Tape-slide presentations are valuable resources for social studies teachers. They provide an audiovisual message that may be otherwise unavailable. Teachers have opportunities to visit places and do things that students do not. This is the basic premise for your tape-slide project. Consult with the university audiovisual or instructional materials center for the equipment you need. These are some organizational points to help you get started.

Making a Tape-Slide Presentation

The Plan
Major Theme:
Minor Theme(s):
1.
2.
3.
Grade Level:
Objective(s):
1.
2.
3.
Evaluation:
Due Date:

The Personnel	Name of Person	Tasks Performed or Duties in Production
Project Chairman		
Director		
Photographer		
Narrator		
Script Writer		
Presenter		

Present your slide-tape project to the class or submit it to the instructor. What are the particular benefits of this medium? Were there any problems with equipment, selecting a theme, or choosing appropriate vocabulary for the narration? This firsthand experience will help you recognize some potential problems, as well as the enjoyment teachers experience using this particular resource.

11.3 *Piracy*

By definition, a copyright is "the legal exclusive right which an author, musician, or artist has to print, publish and sell his own works during a certain period of time."[1] Copyright laws, permissions, and violations are issues that concern not only authors and publishers, but teachers and other school personnel as well. Illegal copying of electronic materials is called *piracy*. The ease with which electronic materials can be copied, legally or illegally, has created a very real ethical problem. Which materials can be copied and used, and under what circumstances? The legal and ethical ramifications of the copyright laws are frequently unclear at best, especially for new teachers.

Search the literature for articles, books, monographs, and pamphlets on the subject of copyrights. Specifically concentrate on the area of educational materials. Prepare a report. Your instructor will provide the format, which may be either a research-based paper or an oral report to the instructor or the class. Include information that will be particularly helpful for new teachers. Some topics you might investigate are: the copyright laws of the United States, writings of authors, steps to secure a copyright, fees, infringements, and jurisdiction of the courts.

Your instructor may invite a copyright attorney or a publishing house representative to give a presentation on the subject of educational copyrights.

11.4 *Potpourri*

These are some other activities you may do:

1. Plan and prepare a videotape lesson.
2. Observe an interactive television simulcast.
3. Search the educational materials catalogues for social studies video disks. Make a list of those designed for elementary students.
4. Interview a social studies teacher who uses computer technologies to a large extent.
5. Visit an elementary school learning center for a day.
6. Visit an elementary school library.
7. Visit a public television station. Interview the program manager and/or elicit information on educational programming for elementary children.

Summary

Suitable media resources are inherent to a good social studies program. Teachers are not expected to know everything or to be the students' sole source of information. If that were the case, our students would be denied access to many sources of learning. The media are a vital part of our contemporary life-style. Both the electronic and the print media influence us in many ways. They penetrate our lives in ways that cause us to pause and think, to consider, weigh, evaluate, judge, and meditate. The media resources that are available in the classroom provide students with opportunities to do the same.

New-tech media resources are part of the traditional learning format for students of this decade and the next. Using technological innovations is as much a part of a typical school day as going to lunch. The skill and comfort level of even the youngest elementary student is encouraging to witness. It is encouraging from the standpoint that teachers, administrators, parents, and community members are making the commitment to focus on the future, to make a positive response to the educational applications of innovation.

READING RESOURCES

Kastenmeier, Hon. Robert W. *Congressional Record* E4751, daily edition, October 14, 1981.

ENDNOTE

1. *Webster's Dictionary,* edited by John Gage Allee (Baltimore, MD: Harbor House Publishers, Inc., 1984), p. 77.

12

Teaching the Special
Needs Student

PROJECTIONS

Teaching special needs students in the 1990s will be no easy task, but it can be accomplished by careful planning, foresight, and empathy. Our society takes pride in providing (and even requiring) an education for *all* children. It is important to note that *all* children have special needs, but our main focus will be on children with special needs in one or more of six areas: physical handicaps, mental impairment, emotional impairment, language impairment, culturally different, and gifted and talented.

The social studies teacher of the 1990s will have to be alert to the needs of all of these special needs children because they will be in the classroom. Mainstreaming is an important concept for mentally and emotionally impaired children, allowing them to function as much as possible within a normal environment. Most certainly, some year you will have to modify the physical arrangement of your classroom to accommodate a physically handicapped youngster. Equally certain, you will be presented with the task of challenging and motivating gifted and talented students.

The greatest challenge that social studies teachers will face in the 1990s is coping with the child who has little or no fluency in the English language. Children of all nationalities and cultures, speaking a variety of languages, will be in our classrooms. It will be essential to learn how to work with the ESL (English as a Second Language) child. This is a golden opportunity to really teach social studies, using the child and his or her cultural experiences as examples.

The social studies teacher will work with a variety of special needs children who will need a skilled and empathetic teacher who will meet their individual needs.

New and experienced teachers are frequently dismayed or discouraged when a special education student is assigned to their regular classroom. Some teachers are equally concerned when a truly gifted student appears on the class list. The term *special needs* is used here in reference to those children who qualify for special education services under the auspices of P.L. 94-142. This includes the learning disabled, the physically handicapped, and the emotionally disturbed.

Academically talented students are also special needs students. They have needs that are not met in a normal classroom. Classroom teachers must use their own unique understanding of the particular student(s) and must adequately meet or even exceed the academic needs of these students.

Teaching the Special Education Student

Public Law 94-142 requires the public schools to provide an education for all handicapped children. This law has affected the education of all children, handicapped and nonhandicapped, significantly. The public schools comply with the tenets of this law by providing instruction with special education staff and classroom teachers. Handicapped students are an important part of our student population. They are part of everyone's teaching responsibilities.

The student identification process, child study or staffing, determines the specific handicap(s) of the student. It may be a physical, learning, or emotional/behavior disorder, or a combination of special needs. The child study team establishes an Individual Education Plan (IEP) which guides the instructional plans of the special education teacher and the classroom teacher. The IEP determines the level of service for which the student qualifies. The level of service states the amount of time (or subject areas) the student can be serviced with the special education teacher, as well as the specific instructional responsibilities of the classroom teachers.

Special needs students want to learn. It is the teacher's job to do everything possible to help them achieve their goals. It is probable that a special needs student will be in your classroom. What are the responsibilities of the social studies teacher for instructing this student? In most cases, these children assimilate easily into classroom activities and routine procedures. Some children require more direct supervision or special accommodations. Some special responsibilities of the mainstream teacher will be discussed in the following segments.

The Individual Education Plan (IEP)

An IEP is an important part of a student's file, along with test results and other educational information. The format can be confusing at first glance, with many columns, boxes, and unfamiliar educational terms and jargon. It is important that you become familiar with the format of a standard IEP. Determine what is critical for the mainstream teacher to know, and what information is primarily for the special education teacher.

The student's IEP clearly states the long-range objective(s) as determined by the teachers, parents, and other people assigned to the case. An objective may be a behavioral, academic, or physical goal the child study team determines is appropriate and achievable. The responsibilities of the classroom teacher, the parents, the special education teacher, the therapist, and others are clarified. An example of a parental responsibility might be: The parents will perform a given set of adaptive exercises with the child for 15 minutes each day. (This would be for a child with a specific physical handicap.) An academic goal set by the teacher might be: The child will complete a midyear social studies test with 50% accuracy.

In addition to stating the objectives for the student, the specific strategies, methods, materials, or adaptations may be given. Writing an objective for the student is necessary. Determining how the objective will be achieved is essential to ultimate goal achievement. Referring to the student IEP periodically during the year will keep the student's objectives clearly in mind.

Direct Instruction

Mainstream education implies that handicapped students can be properly educated with other nonhandicapped students in the regular classroom. Functioning as a member of the class to the degree they can have a successful learning experience is the goal of mainstream education. Students who have physical handicaps or emotional/behavioral disorders are not necessarily learning disabled.

Educators believe and support the philosophy that special needs students clearly benefit from the interaction and instructional episodes that occur in the mainstream of a school. It is in the best interest of special needs students to service them in the special education setting only when necessary. When is it necessary? These are some of the situations when removal from the class is beneficial and necessary:

1. The student is scheduled for therapy or adaptive physical education.
2. The student receives daily instruction for a specific content area as identified on the IEP.
3. The student is exhibiting severe maladaptive behavior that is disrupting the class. This may be an emotional or physical reaction that could result in personal harm or harm to others.
4. The student needs one-to-one assistance to complete a project successfully.
5. A required learning sequence is clearly above the ability of a particular student.
6. The student is scheduled for some other services in the special education department.

It is clear that direct instruction of special needs students is the responsibility of the classroom teacher with supportive assistance from the special education personnel. Special needs students can perform well in the class most of the time. The teacher must do some restructuring and adapting to meet their needs, while at the same time keeping the lesson moving and avoiding segregation from others.

The General Learning-Disabled Student (GLD)

There are some very basic things that can ease the process of accommodating special needs students. The teacher's organizing, managing, and planning skills are very critical here. To teach a learning-disabled student successfully with the regular class, it is necessary to carefully determine the student's level of achievement or skill in the content area. This can be done by referring to formal test results, by consulting with former teachers, and by using your own formal and informal evaluation techniques. Once the performance level is established, the teacher plans specific objectives for that student. Placing him or her at a study carrel and assigning some irrelevant, unrelated task *is not mainstream education.*

Once the objective is clear, then plans to implement it are needed. Some things teachers do for implementation are:

1. Allow the student to read the textbook with another person.
2. Give the student many opportunities to use manipulative materials.
3. Have various audiovisual materials readily available.
4. Confer with the special education teacher for any special materials she or he may have on your topic.
5. Collect various materials from the instructional materials centers that are at the student's level of comprehension.
6. Assign the student a partner for the entire unit.
7. Expect the student to accomplish his or her objective.
8. Include the student in all activity or project groups.
9. Make an effort to incorporate any special talents of the student into the lesson sequence.

The classroom teacher must make every effort to provide the direct instruction that will enable the student to experience success.

The Physically Handicapped Student

The needs and requirements of a physically handicapped student can be minimal or extensive depending on the special circumstances. One child may require assistance going up and down the stairs, another may need help with eating and using the lavatory, while still another may only need help getting into and out of the wheelchair. You may be asking yourself at this point "What has all this got to do with teaching social studies or math?" Perhaps nothing, but the point is that this child has these special needs and you must recognize and meet them. It is part of the mainstream responsibility. You must take care of these matters before you can begin teaching lesson content.

To reiterate, a physically handicapped student is not necessarily learning disabled. Teaching a class with a handicapped student can become routine once the special needs are identified and met. A student with a severe vision problem may require large-print textbooks and reading materials. The teacher will seat this person near the front of the room or very near chalkboards and viewing screens. A hearing-impaired student must be able to hear the teacher's voice, audiovisual materials, and the other students. Where would you seat this person? These are some of the classroom management concerns the mainstream teachers must address for physically handicapped students. Assuming the mental capabilities of the student are within grade-level expectations, the teaching of content can proceed normally. Once the physical needs are managed, the teacher must get on with the task at hand. Dwelling on the handicaps or physical limitations is unnecessary and unproductive for you and the students.

The Student with an Emotional/Behavior Disorder (EBD)

Perhaps the biggest special education concern of teachers is dealing with emotional and behavior disorders. *Emotionally disturbed* and *emotionally handicapped* are other names for the child who cannot control himself or herself. Emotional and behavior disorders are very complex. This very complexity is the source of much of the frustration teachers experience when attempting to teach and fulfill all their professional responsibilities. The stress on the teacher and the other students can be considerable. Nevertheless, these students are mainstreamed and must be taught.

EBD students are not acting-out or displaying inappropriate maladaptive behavior all of the time. When they do, appropriate action must be taken immediately in the best interest of the child and others in the class. This appropriate action is predetermined as part of the student's IEP. Traditionally, teachers have concerned themselves with ways to prevent these behaviors from occurring. It is a valid concern but perhaps not always achievable. Teachers frequently feel it is their fault when a student loses control. Finding fault is not the issue here— meeting the student's immediate needs is. However, there are some commonsense things teachers do to create a learning atmosphere wherein the inappropriate behavior is less likely to occur. Here are some recommendations:

1. Have all elements of the lesson well planned and organized. Students perform better when the lesson progresses smoothly with a clear focus.

2. Establish a discipline policy. Students can behave when they clearly know what you expect.

3. Keep interruptions at a minimum; they can be very disconcerting to an EBD student.

4. This student needs more rewards than the other students. Reward the correct, appropriate, acceptable things she or he does. Use behavior modification procedures.

5. Be aware of the social interactions in the room. Is this child included?

6. Establish achievable goals for this child; try to minimize or eliminate the frustration level.

7. Be aware of any classroom-environmental factors that affect this child in negative ways.

8. Be aware of any developing situations; you can do an intervention and perhaps prevent a full-blown incident.

9. Be more available for this child; he or she needs you more than the other students. Stay close without hovering.

10. Be approachable for the parents. They need you too.

There are many other techniques teachers use on a daily basis to encourage and promote classroom success for EBD students. Working in close cooperation with the EBD teacher will increase the probability that this will indeed happen. Additional study in this area is recommended.

Attitudes and Perspectives

What is your attitude toward teaching special needs students? Is it positive, condescending, or ambivalent? Do you accept the general philosophy of mainstream education? Establishing and maintaining a positive, supportive attitude toward this teaching responsibility is very important. The power of a positive attitude is significant. If you firmly believe that you can teach special education students, and you have an equally strong belief that they can learn, then chances are both of these will actually occur in your room. A positive, supportive attitude provides the necessary impetus to make the adaptations special education students require.

Elementary teachers have many responsibilities: teaching children with special needs is one of them. It is unrealistic to assume these children will somehow be on someone else's class list. An attitude of avoidance is unprofessional. It is important to keep all teaching responsibilities in a proper perspective. You chose to become a teacher. With that choice comes the reality of teaching all kinds of children, not just the high performers or those from backgrounds similar to your own. This can be a harsh reality for beginning teachers, but it must be confronted. Interacting with students is what teaching is all about. Accepting all of them and doing the best job you possibly can is the mark of a true professional.

A positive attitude toward special education students includes the human relations matter of establishing a personal relationship with them. Are you teaching them because you have to or because you want to? There is a big difference between the two and children are very adept at distinguishing the difference. It is important for all students to know that they are liked by their teacher. This includes your special education youngsters. You will find they are generally very pleasant children to have in the class. The relationship you establish with them is an important part of their academic experience.

This is a brief overview of teaching special needs children in the classroom. It is not a substitute for special education courses or for actual experience with special education children. The mainstream process has affected many changes

Recognizing the student who seldom responds can eliminate a potential management problem. Be aware of his or her need for reinforcement.

in our school systems. Some changes were organizational, philosophical, personal, and attitudinal. Teaching children who learn in ways that are perhaps different from the average child has forced teachers to carefully examine, evaluate, and modify many instructional strategies and methods. This type of self-examination is critical and should occur at regular intervals if teachers are to remain current and effective. All students in the class benefit from updated instructional techniques.

Teaching the High-Potential Student

Gifted and talented, academically advanced, superior, high potential, and *high track* are some of the labels used to identify those students who are capable of performing academic skills at levels significantly higher than their peers. Academically superior students are identified by scores on standardized tests, classroom performance, interviews, and teacher judgment. It is common practice to identify students with exceptional math ability or reading abilities in the content areas, or those students who demonstrate artistic or musical talents in the creative arts area, or those with exceptional athletic ability. Why not identify students with particular skills in the social sciences?

Scores on standardized achievement tests are one tool that teachers use to identify the students who have scored well above national norms on particular subtests. Such a subtest for the primary grades may have a generic title such as "Environment." The specific test items may include such categories as: laws, play-group situations, jobs, problem solving, family roles, choices, needs, and wants. Item analysis for the intermediate grades shows more emphasis on content and concepts of a higher order. Tests such as these provide an indication of the student's grasp of social studies principles. These principles are learned from academic instruction, family, and environmental influences.

Classroom teachers are well aware of those students who consistently perform tasks exceptionally well. The high performers will complete all the work that is assigned and then seek additional things to do. These activities and projects are frequently divergent, creative, or atypical. A well-organized, well-designed learning center may be available for these individuals. They may use the study carrels and the computer stations to satisfy their curiosity for meaningful activities.

Teachers must recognize the fact that these youngsters do not always have to be busy. It is a misconception that if students are not doing something (often meaning paperwork) they are not using instructional time appropriately. When questioned "What are you doing?" high performers may sometimes answer, "I'm thinking!" Think time is a very necessary, productive, and defensible use of class time. High-potential students are capable of deep thought that frequently precedes their actions. Having time to think through a plan of action, steps, or procedures is an important attribute to preplan for them. *Think, Plan,* and *Do* is a good classroom theme.

Teachers recognize students who consistently exhibit outstanding abilities in both cognitive and affective situations. A heterogeneous classroom may have an individual who frequently assumes the role of leader, problem solver, organizer, risk taker, inquisitor, and other multidimensional character roles. The comprehension and contributions of these students are beyond the majority of their peers.

Students who exhibit special capabilities in the social studies benefit from a differentiated educational program. Their unique educational needs can be met in two major ways: with a "pull-out" program and a specially trained teacher (concentrated work in gifted and talented education) or with acceleration and enrichment planned and supervised by the classroom teacher.

Enrichment models offer a variety of broadening experiences and activities that center around the primary unit objectives or some specific part of a unit. The whole class works on the same basic unit. The high-potential students remain integral members of the learning cluster but they are working on different aspects of the objective. This is referred to as *horizontal enrichment.*

Acceleration models move students through the curriculum at an accelerated rate. This can be done but at some point there are consequences. What will these students do when they complete the elementary curriculum in the fourth or fifth grade? Will they then go to the high school for social studies? Enrichment or moderate acceleration is clearly a better choice for the average classroom situation.

Providing meaningful, purposeful classroom experiences and activities for high-potential children is largely the responsibility of the mainstream teacher. It is part of providing for individual differences. These activities evolve from the basic social studies curriculum. The creative energies and talents of these students are channelled by providing opportunities to work with intellectual peers at least some of the time. Cross-age and cross-grade groups work, explore, and achieve goals together with the guidance and supervision of a supportive, creative teacher. Staff cooperation and coplanning is absolutely vital for this to happen with smooth transitions.

Some of the enrichment activities teachers use are suggested in the guides that accompany the textbooks series. Specific topics may include such things as: discussion, writing (reports, creative extensions), vocabulary development, research, topical recreational reading, demonstrations, or a combination of related activities. Social studies activities kits are commercially available. They are convenient, organized, and can easily become an important part of a social studies learning station. Teacher resource books are also valuable aids to locate just the right activity for a particular lesson or student. There are many books of reproducible paper-and-pencil activities available from school supplies stores but these should be used with discretion. Students quickly tire of paper production.

You should have a functional plan for teaching the high-potential students in the classroom. Some important factors are:

Identification

1. Administer an achievement test (i.e., Stanford Achievement Test).
2. Administer an abilities test.
3. Examine records from previous years.
4. Administer the Scales for Rating Behavioral Characteristics of Superior Students.
5. Participate in a child study.
6. Establish the student's proficiency in the basic curriculum.

Program Delivery

1. Incorporate higher-level thinking skills (Bloom's taxonomy).
2. Incorporate opportunities for problem-solving activities.
3. Provide for development of creative skills.
4. Compact the curriculum whenever feasible.
5. Provide opportunities for independent study and research.
6. Incorporate a computer literacy component.
7. Use acceleration and enrichment strategies.
8. Use curriculum differentiation when appropriate.

Program Evaluation

1. Select a method(s) for evaluating.
2. Evaluate the objective(s) and the product. (What did you plan for the students? How well did they do it?)
3. Is the program defensible?
4. Interview the students and evaluate with them.
5. Solicit comments and reactions from parents.
6. Share your data with your supervisor or principal.
7. Use your data to plan ongoing activities.

This basic three-step model (identify, deliver, evaluate) is a usable approach for beginning teachers who are committed to meeting the learning needs of high-performing students. This model can serve as a guide and a starting point to begin addressing the educational potential of adaptive instruction for these children. It can be implemented with relative ease and minimal disruptions.

The reality for many teachers is that if you are committed to teaching the high-potential students who are in your class, then you will probably have to plan and administer the program yourself. To assume they will be serviced somewhere else is presumptuous. Some school districts have established programs but many others do not. Planning for (and with) high performers is a definite challenge. Your creative powers will be stretched. Your organizational and managerial skills will be strengthened as you begin to implement your program. And, most importantly, your students will enjoy a more satisfying academic experience.

ACTIVITIES

Special needs students are an integral part of our school population. Both the academically advanced and the lower-performing children comprise this special population. The following activities target their social studies academic needs.

12.1 *Research*

Research the literature on the topic of special education or gifted education. (Note: Education for the gifted and talented is categorized under several different labels.) Look specifically for research on teaching social studies to these children. Programs, materials, practices, trends, methods and strategies, testing, and evaluation are some things to look for. Prepare a written or oral report for the class.

12.2 *Panel Discussion*

Prepare a short panel discussion on one of the following topics:

1. Mainstreaming practices for the GLD students
2. Social studies adaptations for the low-performing child who does not qualify for special education
3. Social studies challenges for the high performers
4. Dealing with the high-ability, low-performing child
5. A topic of your choice

12.3 *Visitation*

Make arrangements to visit a social studies class that has one or more special education students, or visit a special education room during social studies. The building principal or administrator may recommend a teacher who accommodates these students particularly well. Use the following form to record your observations.

> Grade:
> Unit:
> Lesson Topic:
> Activity:
> Special Methods or Strategies:
> Adaptations or Accommodations:
> Student's Level of Participation:
> Problems:
> Evaluation:

Interview the teacher after class. Discuss any preconceived notions you had prior to the visit. Were they verified or nullified? Question the teacher regarding her or his plans for this student, parental support, school policies, available instructional materials, collaboration with the special education teacher, and so on. Your objective is to gain as much information as possible from a resource person who teaches special needs children on a daily basis. Are you willing to do the same?

12.4 *Materials*

This activity enables you to design and construct instructional material(s) for either a high-performing or a special education student. (You may consider a high-potential student with a physical handicap for a real challenge!) Work alone or with a partner. Your project can be a game, an activity, or a paper-and-pencil lesson. Choose the grade level your target student is in, the social science category (geography, sociology, anthropology), and other information the instructor must know to judge the value, relevancy, and usability of your project. Demonstrate your project for the class.

How did you do? Were your directions or plans clear and specific? Is your project realistic? Challenging? Too long? Too short? Did your classmates understand your objective in choosing this particular activity? What was the most difficult part of this activity for *you*? These are some of the questions classroom teachers face every time they prepare special materials for their students!

Summary

This chapter has briefly discussed the responsibilities of teachers regarding the special needs students that may be in your classroom. Special education and high-potential students have particular instructional requirements. Meeting individual differences in social studies and every other subject is part of the teacher's job. How well this is done directly affects the social and academic progress of children.

Courses in special education for the learning disabled and the academically advanced children are very valuable. They offer various philosophies, strategies, methods, and program management ideas for general classroom use. Such courses increase the expertise of both new and experienced teachers. Using the knowledge gained from these courses increases the motivaton, knowledge, and application skills of those special students.

All students benefit from good teaching. The learning disabled, the physically handicapped, and the high-potential students are special: laws and legislation have labeled them so. There are many students in the average classroom who are equally special in their own way. They also enjoy and benefit from activities that are specially planned and designed for them. Remember these special students as you plan your social studies lessons!

READING RESOURCES

Alvermann, Donna. "Strategic Teaching in Social Studies," in Beau Fly Jones et al., eds., *Strategic Teaching and Learning: Cognitive Instruction in the Content Areas.* Alexandria, VA: Association for Supervision and Curriculum Development, 1985.
Gallagher, James J. "Social Studies for the Gifted," *Teaching the Gifted Child,* 3rd ed. Boston: Allyn and Bacon, 1985.

UNIT V

The New Teacher

13
Preparing to Teach Social Studies

PROJECTIONS

Preparing to teach social studies in the 1990s is clearly a challenge to be embraced by those teachers with commitment, enthusiasm, energy, and flexibility. Undergraduate academic preparations provide the basic foundations to meet degree program and licensing requirements. In effect, these are commencement preparations, as teachers are continually "preparing" themselves to teach.

The personal, implicit preparations that enable you to enter the classroom and teach social studies to contemporary students are very critical. These preparations are the criteria that will determine your success or failure as a professional educator.

National and world events, cultural changes, environmental issues, political issues, and various community matters require the social studies teacher to be informed and capable of instructing students in a variety of topics. Community mandates commission the educational institutions to teach students what potential informed citizens need to know. It is not too early to begin preparing yourself to accept this responsibility. What do first graders already know about a clean environment, and what should they know? What do fifth graders need to learn about national politics? Ask yourself some questions. Make a mental plan for ways to teach these things to a group of students. Preparing to teach social studies includes mental (thinking) and active (doing) exercises.

Very soon you will be entering your first teaching assignment. Starting out as a new teacher is a great adventure—an adventure that carries a great deal of responsibility and joy. How the school year begins from the first day determines the atmosphere for the entire year. Beginning the year on a positive note with preparation and organization will be satisfying for you and the students.

This chapter presents some information that will ease the transition from university student to professional educator. Being prepared for this metamorphosis allows a smooth transition to occur. Everything you do from this point on is preparing you to be a teacher. Your knowledge of the curriculum, methods, strategies, planning skills, attitudes, and theories are an important part of the skills package you bring into your teaching career. Your application period is when you start teaching.

Preparing and gathering teaching materials is largely your responsibility. This job will be time consuming the first year. However, some preliminary preparations can begin now.

Getting Started

Preparation for your first teaching assignment is integral to your education. You will make decisions about many things to use or discard. You will examine some very realistic activities that are useful for the first week of the school year. Let's begin to look ahead at some teaching materials you will need.

Looking Ahead

The first thing you need to do is to look ahead at all you must do in the upcoming year. Your textbook or curriculum guide will help you to outline the content areas and give you a sense of timing. A yearly calendar will help you plan ahead for specific needs such as films and resource people. By choosing approximate starting and ending dates for each unit or chapter, you can watch your timing. Are you going too fast or too slow? Running out of things to do is just as much of a problem as not being able to complete the work you expect to do.

Gathering Materials

Textbooks.   The social studies textbook you will use has been adopted by your individual school board. That basic textbook must be used; however, an adopted series does not preclude the use of other books in the classroom. Many supplementary materials are used by social studies teachers, and it is convenient to have additional books available. Curriculum guides tell you which specific goals and objectives must be taught for your particular grade level. The textbook addresses these goals and objectives to a greater or lesser degree. If you have additional textbooks available, you can use them to supplement particular units or skills. Using more than one basic text gives students the opportunity to see a different point of view, to use a book that is perhaps more readable, and to use comparing and contrasting skills.

Social studies teachers need to collect things such as trade books, pictures, maps, magazines, slides, and artifacts. School storerooms and bookrooms frequently have off-inventory books, company samples, teacher guides, and other printed materials that are not being used. These items can be used as is for particular students to gather information. Teachers frequently remove a chapter from an off-inventory book, put it in a folder, and use it for a learning station activity. Some older textbooks have very good sections on a specific topic such as citizenship and values. Other teachers use supplemental textbooks as reading materials for individual students who simply like to read social studies. Other textbooks are especially effective as an additional source of information for research group activities. Use textbooks to enhance and supplement, not supplant, the basic textbook series.

Resource Files.   Starting a resource file is an enjoyable task. Although it may seem inconsequential to you now, it will prove to be a valuable teaching tool when you are teaching social studies. What is a resource file and where do you begin? A resource file is a collection of things that will eventually help you teach social studies more effectively. How do you begin? Go to an office or school supplies store and purchase two or three accordion-style file folders. Now you are ready to begin!

Organizing your resource files for easy access increases the probability that you will actually use them. It is helpful to establish some categories for things; the categories you choose will to some extent determine what you put into your files. One method of categorizing (labeling) is: People, Places, Events, General. Another is: Teacher Things, Student Things. Choose titles that work for you and attach gummed labels to the tabs on the file folders. The Table of Contents in the social studies text may provide categories for your file.

Your resource files are an invaluable tool—a ready resource—for you to pull quickly just the right thing to add flavor and interest to a particular lesson. Start to select magazine and newspaper articles that discuss social studies issues in creative ways. Mount them on heavy paper, laminate them, and write the footnote information on the back. You may wish to write the publisher for additonal copies of the article later on. In your readings you may find a good teaching objective for a particular social studies skill. Write it down and put it in your file. Make a notation of research articles you want to study. Bibliographies, pictures, ideas, and other memoranda have a place in your resource file. It is your file and you can put anything you want in it.

Bulletin Board Ideas.   Attractive bulletin boards and display cases are an important part of a pleasant room atmosphere. They are also important teaching aids. Functional bulletin boards and displays are more important than beautiful ones. Designing and preparing these display areas is one of your responsibilities, but you can let the children design the displays to show their work. Start looking for attractive, functional social studies displays and ideas as you observe in various classrooms. Make a sketch for your collection and note particular uses for each one. Be sure to write enough information. Too often you will write a quick note, thinking that is all you need, but six months later when you look at it, it won't make sense—another good idea lost.

Some bulletin boards serve as a motivational device, for example, a unit opener. Other boards are activity-oriented wherein the students perform a task directly on the display area. It may be helpful to organize your bulletin board files into primary and upper-grades sections. Display and functional bulletin boards are both used for social studies. You do not really appreciate a good bulletin board file until you need an idea and cannot think of one.

Activities.   The activities file is for learning activities of various kinds. Individualized lessons, group project ideas, topics for panels, lesson plan ideas, evaluation suggestions, things you have observed during demonstration lessons or methods classes, synopses of various kinds—any of these can be put here. This file is the one that will help you directly in planning what the students will do during a special lesson. Also be sure to collect sources of these various activities.

Bibliographies.   It is helpful to have a separate resource file for bibliographies. There are numerous lists of social studies books and reading material. Some are for teacher use and others are for student use. They might be categorized by subject titles or concept titles. These bibliographies are very handy when you need a ready reference. For example, a book on pioneer villages can be located quickly and easily by referring to your file. When you need materials from the public library, it is handy to have a specific bibliography available to readily locate what you want. If bibliographies are available from local bookstores or the university library, take one of each. It will save time for you later. Add to your bibliography file whenever you find a new entry.

The First Day/Week

The preschool workshop and inservice time is important for all teachers, but it is especially critical for new teachers. The first few days of professional service, before the students arrive, must be used wisely. This is the time to get the classroom ready for the students in terms of placing things where you want them, getting your bulletin boards put up, organizing your learning centers, gathering and ordering supplies and books, arranging furniture, and getting other materials from storage areas.

This is when you set aside a block of time to study your curriculum. Write some long-range plans, goals, and objectives for yourself. Know where you are going. Read the IEPs (Individual Education Plans) for any special education students on your class list, and arrange to confer with the teacher of the previous year. Using your workshop time wisely helps you establish the habit of using your planning time wisely all through the year.

The first day of school is very exciting for students and it will be equally exciting for you. Never again will you experience your first day in your very own room. It is important to set the tone you want on this first day. Establish your discipline policy. Be positive and firm. Set your expectations for the year by telling the students very clearly what your standards are. It is helpful to have a handout ready for the students to take home so the parents will also know. This handout can present a clear explanation of your discipline plan as well as an overview of your social studies curriculum objectives.

Some teachers make personal contact with every child's parents the first week of school. A short telephone call is very meaningful to parents. It starts the year with a positive feeling and establishes the foundation for a working relationship between the home and the school. This initial contact with parents is not a conference, however.

Learn every student's name as soon as possible. In self-contained classrooms this can be done the first day. Perhaps you will want to start a 3 × 5 card file for every student in your room.

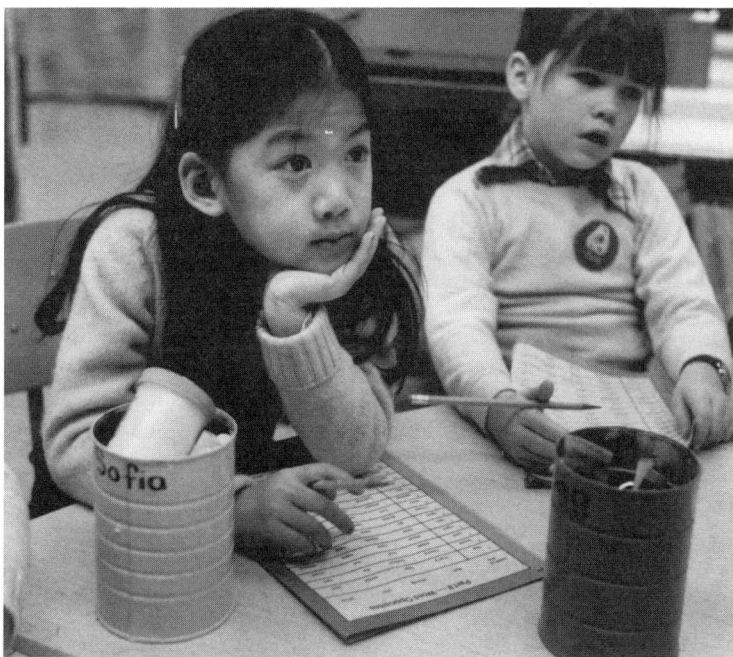

As you prepare to teach the social studies, be cognizant of the visual clues the learners give you. What can you anticipate from these visual clues?

The first week of school is a good time to investigate your school community. Knowing which community resources are available for you and your class is helpful when you begin particular units. Familiarize yourself with the media center, the computer lab, the library, and other special rooms in your building or school district. Become aware of special procedures and schedules. Take some time to preview any computer programs for social studies that are for your grade level. (A third-grade program may not be entirely appropriate for your third graders.)

The first week of teaching social studies should be dynamic and interesting for the students. Social studies may not be the favorite subject of everyone in your class. If you plan your first week's lessons primarily around book reading, their assumptions will be verified: "I knew it would be boring!" These initial lessons should contain a variety of activities that appeal to the students' interests and result in active involvement.

Plan some project groups and some brief research activities, show a film, get the students actively involved in helping to plan your first out-of-school experience or field trip, ask for volunteers to design and construct a bulletin board, plan a creative writing lesson that focuses on some aspect of the first social studies unit. There are a number of excellent activities that give clear messages that social studies is as interesting as we, teacher and students as a team, make it. And finally, invite your building principal or immediate supervisor to stop by your room.

Getting Your Students Involved

Active student participation and involvement is a major ingredient in every lesson plan and presentation. Consecutive lessons that demand little more than passive reception from students reap little more than passive learning! Do not mistake active participation for a laissez-faire state of disorganized confusion. Lessons that are planned to get students actively involved require a commitment to plan thoroughly and precisely for exactly what you want each student to do. There is always a place for student flexibility. Preparing two or three separate activities for the students to select is even more demanding from a planning standpoint. Activities for student involvement must be clearly organized.

Social Studies Fair

One large-scale idea for getting students involved in the curriculum is a social studies fair. It is an event for students and teachers to share and interface with the school community. It is an opportunity to show the many different ways students learn social studies. A fair provides a real audience for students to display their individual and group projects in creative ways. It is a very effective method for reporting to parents in a nonconference setting.

What are some suggested components for a successful social studies fair? The primary one is to exhibit children's work. These exhibits can be in several formats, all of which project learning in slightly different ways. Some ideas that are used for a fair are: panel discussions, debates, computer program demonstrations, samples of creative writing, short music sketches, a physical education component (i.e., a demonstration of children's games from the colonial period), videos the students have planned and directed, oral reports, a listening station for "students on cassettes," flat displays, and three-dimensional items. With components such as these, a social studies fair communicates clearly that this curriculum is truly dynamic and varied.

A successful social studies fair encourages the participation of all grade levels. Even kindergartners enjoy displaying their work. Working through the curriculum committee and the coordinators, the planning and preparations for a fair start at the beginning of the year. A general theme can be established for each grade level, or it can be left to the discretion of the individual teachers. It is important to involve every student in some way, either through a live performance of some kind or by displaying a piece of work.

Some schools have their fair on a scheduled PTA night, an open house day, or some other special evening. The social studies fair can utilize the entire building or it can be confined to certain areas. For example, in art-show style, room dividers, movable chalkboards, and free-standing panels may be used in the halls or gymnasium to display the flat pieces students have done. The library or media centers may have all the textbooks and instructional materials on display for parents to examine. The computer lab may be open for students to demonstrate their fluency with social studies programs. The audiovisual center is where audiovisual activities will be available; the music room is for music-related activities; the auditorium is for skits or panels; and classrooms are used for other particular activities. The planning and coordinating of a social studies fair is one way of actively involving both students and teachers.

Involvement Projects

Students who are actively involved soon realize that social studies is interesting and challenging. Involvement projects are all the numerous activities and projects that students *do*. They range from paper-and-pencil lessons, to three-dimensional items, to performance projects of various kinds. These involvement projects are what you exhibit at a social studies fair and on bulletin boards or in showcases throughout the year.

Student involvement in a particular project can be short term, such as one social studies period, or it can be long term over a period of days, weeks, or months. For example, a particular time line or graph may be extended or expanded on over the entire year. These projects have value beyond the display aspect, however. Some of those values are the following:

Have you ever wanted to create your own castle?
These girls have.

1. Projects give students the opportunity to work alone or with others.
2. Projects permit learning to occur in new and innovative ways that supplement textbooks and other materials.
3. Students learn step-by-step approaches to complete assignments.
4. Projects give students opportunities to use various thinking skills in conjunction with creative endeavors.
5. Some projects give students the opportunity to work with their parents.
6. Projects give students opportunities to use community resources.

These are only some of the values students learn and experience through involvement projects. Involvement projects of varied levels of difficulty are an integral part of social studies education.

Learning Skills Centers

What are learning skills centers? A skills center is a place where students work on a specific social studies skill as directed and prescribed by the teacher. The skills center can be a special room in the building that is staffed by a certified teacher or supervised by trained volunteers and assistants. However, the skills center in the classroom is perhaps more universal in elementary schools.

The physical design of a skills center can be as simple as a study carrel or a long rectangular table with chairs, or it can be something purchased from the school supplies store. The design itself is inconsequential as long as students can use it easily. Student involvement occurs when an individual student or a small group uses the center to increase proficiency in a specific skill. Elementary teachers involve students in the skills center in different ways. Some plan and design a skills center for high-potential students only; others use the skills center as an enrichment-reinforcement vehicle for everyone; still others use them for guided practice and reteaching purposes.

A skills center has many and varied materials for the students to use. Much of this is planned and prepared by the teacher with the necessary topics, objectives, directions, and evaluation procedures. Self-checking materials work especially well in a skills center. Supplementary materials from the textbook publisher can be placed in a skills center. Other materials are available through school supplies catalogues.

If students are to use a skills center appropriately, it must be used as directed by the teacher. Determining which skill a student needs to learn is part of planning and evaluating. Both of these are the teacher's responsibility. Planning and developing a quality skills center is an important, functional part of classroom management. Included here are some reasons for using a skills center as part of your instructional and organizational plan.[1]

1. A skills center has manipulative materials the students can handle.
2. The activities involve more than underlining and crossing out responses.
3. The activities in the center are designed to use more than one modality as often as possible.
4. Skills center materials are easy to make and can be monitored by volunteers or the students themselves.
5. A skills center provides students with many opportunities to practice a skill.
6. A skills center is different from other large group activities.
7. The materials are visually appealing when care is taken to make them so.
8. A skills center provides one way of subgrouping within the classroom.
9. Skills center materials (folders, boxes, etc.) are easily stored and retrieved as needed.
10. Certain activities and lessons are self-correcting.
11. Skills centers provide varied independent activities for students who need to work alone.
12. Skills centers materials are designed and prescribed for particular students by the teacher.

13. Skills centers may have materials that are appropriate for students with poor reading skills; it gives them an alternative to experience success.

14. Skills centers are designed to review, enrich, drill, practice, and motivate. They are not designed to teach new content and concept material.

It is advisable to begin thinking about how a skills center fits into an organizational plan for getting your students involved. It is not too early to start planning and designing some activities for various grade levels, focusing on some general skills, to use when you start teaching.

You and Your Community

Learning about Your Community

As a new professional you will want to learn about the school community where you are teaching. Being familiar with the community will add understanding to your teaching effectiveness and will help you to be more comfortable with your students, their parents, the administrators, and other school officials.

As soon as time permits, it is recommended that new teachers make a sincere effort to learn about the community. What is the socioeconomic situation? Are there certain values systems that are prevalent? What businesses are within school district boundaries? Is their a high mobility rate? Some schools and districts maintain a historical account of significant educational events. If such an account is available, read it. These evolutionary events are a source of great pride for the school neighborhood.

Learning about your school community serves the purpose of allowing you, the new teacher, to accept, to adapt to an environment that may be drastically different from your own, and to be a supportive public employee. Being visible in the community is important. Parents and local businesses support the schools in various ways. Parents want their children to learn and are very supportive of teacher efforts. When they feel that teachers are an integral part of their community, the critical home/school relationship is unquestionably strengthened. Building and maintaining that relationship is an ongoing process.

School Organizations

School organizations exist to support, enhance, and promote quality education. The role of these organizations in the elementary school is invaluable. Support of school programs can be as discreet as a few parents who ask "What can we do to help you (the teacher) or our kids?" It can also be highly structured and organized such as the National Parent Teacher Association. The objectives of the PTA are:

> *To promote the welfare of children and youth in home, school, community, and place of worship*
>
> *To raise the standards of home life*
>
> *To secure adequate laws for the care and protection of children and youth*
>
> *To bring into closer relation the home and the school, that parents and teachers may cooperate intelligently in the education of children and youth*
>
> *To develop between educators and the general public such united efforts as will secure for all children and youth the highest advantages in physical, mental, social, and spiritual education.* [2]

The objectives of this school organization reflect an extensive focus. The concerns range from politics (getting needed legislation) to the many facets of raising youth in our society.

A typical elementary school has other organizations that help its program in special ways. There are school support groups that can be informally organized. There are advisory committees, councils, task forces, and other groups that perform specific functions in the community. Some are required by state law, others are mandated by the school board, and some develop out of needs and concerns.

What is the role of teachers in relation to school organizations? Remember: School organizations exist to work for the school in various ways. Cooperation, support, encouragement, and recognition are some of the expectations for teachers. The level of participation in these groups varies from school to school. Be aware of this expectation in your particular building. Get involved. You work with them and they will work for you. Knowing the specific goals of each group is a good initial step for new teachers.

Community Organizations

Service Organizations.   Learning about your school community requires that you investigate outside the boundaries of the school itself. The existing school organizations are important to the management and operation of a successful learning environment. The schools are important institutions in the community, and the service organizations are interested in an active relationship. Some of the more well-known service organizations are the Lions, the Jaycees, the Rotary, and the Chamber of Commerce. These and others have a full agenda of services they perform for and within the community. You can make inquiries at their local offices or by phoning.

Cultural Organizations.   Some organizations in your community will have a cultural basis. The mission statement of some cultural organizations is clearly the promotion and propagation of specific cultural values. Such organizations may have various ethnic backgrounds. Other cultural groups are supportive of the arts such as community theater, youth symphonies, and dance. Friends of the library, the local historical society, and the museum foundation are other groups that perform valuable services. Knowing the roles of the various cultural groups in your school community is an important part of your portfolio. They are very social studies oriented.

Political Activities

Your choice of teaching as a career indicates that you are a responsible, serious person. One of the privileges that responsible persons exercise is participation in political activities. Engaging in political activities involves not only voting, but other things as well. Teachers are role models for young people. Being politically active demonstrates to youth that political freedom is more than a nice sentimental idea. If teachers get involved, it must be important.

State and National Politics.   Participation in state and national political activities is a constitutional right. As members of the school community, teachers should feel absolutely free to participate actively and openly. Attending caucuses, running for office, serving on political action committees of various kinds, and other choices are within your realm. Participation in political conventions and meetings is both a privilege and a right from the standpoint that it clearly demonstrates to students how the system works, how decisions are made, and how things get accomplished in our democracy. Teaching our political system is a large part of social studies. Teaching by personal example is invaluable. Participation in the political system may involve voting, working as a voting judge, volunteering for voter registration, taking surveys, or submitting articles for the local newspaper.

Involvement in Issues.   Involvement in issues, especially controversial ones, is a concern of teachers that evokes both positive and negative opinions. In some cases teachers have been reluctant to express publicly their personal and professional ideas on controversial issues. In some areas there are still vestiges of the philosophy that teachers are public servants. However, teachers are public *employees* and, as such, are a vital part of the community where they are employed.

Involvement in public issues can be handled professionally without being offensive. Activities and statements must not give the impression that you are speaking officially for the school or the district, unless that is specifically the case. Professional involvement in crucial issues might include such things as a certain area of study that has been designated by the school board to be taught in the public school, book selections, professional staffing situations, or other matters that arouse differing opinions.

Professional Organizations

Membership in various professional organizations make you a part of the professional community of teachers. National membership in subject area organizations, such as the National Council of Social Studies, will provide you with updated curriculum materials and teaching ideas. Membership in state content organizations provides opportunities to meet and share ideas with teachers of similar interests and concerns in your state.

You should become a member of your state and national teacher associations. The AFT (American Federation of Teachers) and the NEA (National Education Association) are the main ones. They address such issues as ethics, working conditions, and educational standards. Your membership and participation in both national and local levels gives you a say in your profession.

Resources—Check Them Out

Community Resources

Community resources that enrich your teaching come in many forms—some are people, some are places, and some are things. Every community has resources. Perhaps the extent of those resources will vary with the size and the complexion of the area, but there are resources nonetheless. One of the most important and frequently underutilized resources in a community is the *people* who live there. It seems relatively simple, but teachers tend to overlook parents and other community residents as a very handy resource.

Places in the school community include such obvious things as the library, museums, public parks and recreational areas, public service buildings, stores, businesses, community centers, arts and sciences facilities, and many others. *Places* as a resource can be a specific building or a site location of some kind. The school property is a resource. Checking out the places in the community and their possible uses for social studies teaching will give you some immediate resources to use.

Things as a resource for teaching covers a wide range of ideas. A specific collection of books at the library, a display of Civil War clothing at the museum, a family photo album, a personal antique collection, a collection of letters or newspaper articles—all of these are resources that might be available in your community. How do you find out about them? One method is to ask other teachers in your building. Another method is to make a list of many different things you might need during the year, then ask parents where they might be found. You might ask a school volunteer to investigate for you.

Out-of-Building Resources

The field trip is a traditional resource for the social studies curriculum. Going to an on-site location for a learning experience is clearly valuable for both teachers and students. Locating possible out-of-building resources in your community and nearby locations can be as simple as using the phone book. Inquiries are necessary, of course, to determine whether or not school groups are permitted, what the level of supervision is, and the educational value for your specific group of students. Some schools have listings of these resources for all new staff members. This does not preclude your individual investigation of other possible resources. Checking on these community resources includes both resources for teachers and students.

ACTIVITIES

Teachers need many materials to do a thorough job of teaching. Whether the lesson is math, reading, or social studies, many different teaching aids are needed. Social studies encompasses a number of topics and disciplines; therefore, more materials are required to teach them well. New teachers who enter their first teaching assignment with a variety of materials in their files are better prepared to teach than those who only have a textbook. The following activities are designed to give you a headstart on preparing materials for social studies. Your section may decide to have a mini social studies fair so everyone can share projects. This could be planned with your instructor for a specific date.

13.1 *Materials*

Prepare a bibliography of concept books (books or booklets that teach to a single concept such as family, careers, ethnic groups, or self-concept) for teaching social studies to the primary grades. Your objective may be to teach a different grade level; however, it is possible that the reading and comprehension level of some students will be lower than grade-level expectations. Include the following information in your bibliography:

Concept
Title
Author
Publisher, Date
Grade Level
Synopsis

13.2 *Trade Books*

The elementary library and the children's section of the public library are both rich resources for teaching materials. This activity gives you another avenue to pursue in using children's literature to teach social studies. Using the format shown in Activity 13.1, prepare a bibliography for multicultural and multiethnic education in modern realistic fiction. Focus on both the treatment of controversy and stereotypes.

Extension of the Activity.   Now extend this activity further. Think of how you could incorporate these books into a social studies unit in the classroom. Prepare three sequential lesson plans for the grade level of your choice in which you will use particular books. Be sure to include all the parts of a lesson plan, as given in Chapter 7. State clearly what you will do with the literature as a resource.

13.3 *Skills Centers*

This activity gives you a headstart on a learning skills center for your classroom. Select a social studies topic at the grade level of your choice. Determine which skills are needed for the average student to complete a unit successfully on that topic. Now prepare skills center activities for that topic. There should be activities that use the three modalities of learning as well as some items that can be used for the three stages of a lesson (introductory, midpoint, and culminating). You may decide to use the folder idea, or a decorated box, or any other receptacle for your skills center project. Refer to the section on learning skills centers as needed.

Summary

This chapter gave an overview of some helpful suggestions to assist you in your preparations to teach. University courses and experiences with children are very important factors in this process of preparing for a career in education. A teacher must know the content before she or he can teach it to someone else. This strong foundation is obtained through the numerous courses you have taken at your university. When taken seriously and conscientiously, all of the courses contribute to the essential background that is required.

This foundation helps to prepare you for your first clinical experience or student teaching assignment. This part of your preparation gives you opportunities to actually teach students under the close supervision and guidance of an experienced teacher. It is a time to try some of the strategies and methodologies you have studied in your coursework. Supervising teachers traditionally are very generous in sharing their teaching materials with student teachers. In addition to these, you will be preparing your own materials and sharing them with other student teachers. Having a large portfolio of teaching materials is very helpful when you start teaching your own class.

Preparing to teach involves comprehensive preplanning. Right now you are planning for the kind of teacher you will be. This planning is both on the conscious and subconscious level. The elective courses you choose are conscious decisions: Are they heavily focused toward elementary curriculum and learning theories, or are they generic? Other professional decisions that you are making, opinions that you are forming, values that you are clarifying—these and other matters may be almost second nature by comparison. Both levels of formation contribute significantly to the educator you are becoming.

Thinking about teaching may seem trite but teachers need think time for planning and preparation. How you perceive the role of teachers is important. Your role is one of facilitating and enabling—facilitating by providing material and direction, enabling by providing a positive learning atmosphere. An important part of your preparation for teaching is taking time to think and plan for the kind of teacher you want to be.

READING RESOURCES

Kaplan, Sandra Nina. *Change for Children*. Santa Monica, CA: Goodyear Publishing Company, Inc., 1973, chapter 2.

ENDNOTES

1. Adapted from Dr. Vicki Jacobson, College of St. Thomas, St. Paul, Minnesota.
2. *The National PTA Handbook 1985–1987,* The National PTA, 700 North Rush Street, Chicago, IL 60611. Page 5. Reprinted with permission.

APPENDIX

Sample Script Tape

The coach uses a script tape or audiovisual tape to record what is happening during the lesson. Some coaches write the observed behaviors (verbal and nonverbal) to be discussed at the postvisit conference. (*Note:* It is important that the notes are written; it is easy to forget the many "right" things teachers do!) During the instructional conference the coach and the teacher review the notes together.

This is an exact copy of a script tape made during an observation. Note that the observer did not try to write everything—just enough to keep a record of what was observed. Note also the circled comments that were made for future reference.

You will need the following key to read the script.

T   Teacher comment
S   Student comment
T/S Teacher and student discussion
T/C Comment on teacher action
C   Comment by observer
+R   Positive response by the teacher
−R   Negative response by the teacher

		(20 min.) Molly B. 3-27-88 12:15
	T	Would you like to come up and join us
	S	I can watch from here (Team)
	T	Oh? I need you up here
	T	I would like legs crossed all listeners
	T	Boys could you leave that on the floor
		we don't need it now - helper later
	C	Takes something from Ricky (nice disciplinal Technique)
Strategy Objecting		We are going to do four things
		Nathan will share
		Look at Big pictures
		Story
		Quiz - a short little test (lowers anxiety - good!)
	T	Before we get to that Nathan is going
		to share
	S	Nathan shares
	S	States a few comments
	T	Whats its name?
	T/S	T _____ R _____
	C	Teacher directed questions to help
		discussion (Purposeful questions)
	T	Anything else .... should we go
		to the next one

T/S	Teacher Comments
T	What about this one
T/S	Nathan discusses
C	(Keys: defending • objective speed • plant/meat)
C	Cute pictures + student displays
C	Nathan leaves
T	Short test ... would you sit down please
(Sets expectations)	Directions for yes/no questions Passes out test questions
T (-T-R)	Ryan, let me shake your hand .. that was very nice .. I'm going to tell Mrs. Johnson
T ↓	We are going to spend two more days to end this unit "Earth Long Ago
T/S	Informal discussion while cards are passed out
C	A little confusion the first time through
T	Instead of taking test alone we are going to do it all together
T	test practice -- oral directions
(+R) T	Oh aren't we good listeners

S/T	yes
T	That's correct because it means
good question	to dig up (Possible check for understanding)
T/S	questions about dentist & paleontologist
T	We have had 12 questions
(TR)	I think (we) did very well (Teamwork)
C	Cited two boys (nice touch)

Objectives: Students previewed how prehistoric animals defended themselves, ate, and moved by allowing Nathen to "Show and tell"

Students would check their understanding of the concepts taught in a social studies unit by using an "every student" response testing technique.

Nice room atmosphere
Relaxed Learning environment
Clear expectations set for Lesson

- Job well Done!

T/C	Background on questions	
T	People on earth?	
S	NO	*Good use of time*
(4R) T	Everyone got it right..great	
T	First life started in water	
S	Yes	
T	OK	
T	Did the DINOS all die?	
S	Yes	
(4R) T	Very good	
T	Scientist arent sure why	
S	No	
T	Are there still Dinos alive?	
S	No	
T	Heres the next one!	
↓	etc.	
S	yes	
T	Why, Jeremy *mind stretching*	
S	So big	
S	And fat	
T	Fossil means to dig-up	
S	Yes/no answers	

Glossary of Educational Terms

This glossary is designed to be a usable, easy-to-understand reference for selected educational terms. Some items are given a regular definition, whereas others are assigned a commonly used classroom explanation. Specific social studies terminology and other general education terms are included.

Accountability: teachers and schools are held responsible for achieving specific objectives; accountability is often equated with raising pupil scores on standardized tests.

Active learning: the student role is to use all activities, materials, methods, strategies, and resources to learn a skill; students *do* the lesson; there is a continuous focused interaction between the teacher and the students.

Affective skills: the thinking skills and the problem-solving skills are commonly identified as affective skills.

Balance: the teacher keeps all professional duties and responsibilities in perspective: students, parents, lesson planning, paper correcting, testing, conferencing, effort, methods and strategies, time allotments, and so on. Emphasizing only what is enjoyable or successful and ignoring others is not acceptable.

Behaviorism: the study of observable changes in behavior.

Censorship: judging curriculum materials and textbooks on the basis of special interests, values, codes, biases, standards, or religious principles.

Chaining: a sequential relationship from one lesson or learning sequence to another; connecting facts, ideas, and experiences to establish relational patterns. Chaining is used to establish a knowledge base for young children.

Chapter 1: a federal program that provides funding to educate disadvantaged children. It was formerly called Title I.

Classroom management: the instructional and organizational skills required to manage and teach children. Organizing for teaching and learning is an important part of good classroom management.

Closure: the culminating point of a lesson or unit when all the processes and skills converge toward a successful completion of the specified learning objective. A test, a project, or a skill demonstration are frequently parts of a closure technique.

Computer center (lab): a room designated for computer literacy instruction and access.

Computer literacy: to have a basic working knowledge of how to run programs on a computer. Elementary students should use appropriate computer vocabulary and preprogrammed disks.

Concept: a category or filing system for facts.

Concrete experience: activities that physically involve the students in learning, doing, experimenting, and building. The direct opposite of passive reception.

Concrete operations: the learning period wherein children need concrete, real opportunities to experience what they are expected to learn (the whole body stage). Manipulative materials are particularly important and effective at this time.

Content: all the facts, concepts, skills, and subject matter that you are required to teach for each curriculum area; the "what" of teaching.

Coping skills: those skills that enable children to function and survive various social situations. The ability to call upon a number of learned skills to solve problems.

Core curriculum: the basic required skills that must be taught in each content area. The core curriculum is supported and enriched with many other supplementary materials and activities.

Curriculum committee: a group of parents, teachers, and administrators that determines the direction of a particular subject area. Establishing short- and long-range goals, selecting textbooks and other teaching materials, evaluating the testing program, and assuring compliance with local, state, and national directives are some of the responsibilities of a curriculum committee.

Deductive learning: the learning process that starts with a generalization and proceeds toward gathering all the pertinent usable facts to support it.

Discovery teaching: the students gather the tools, materials, and information they need to answer a question or solve a problem.

Entry behaviors: all the skills a student must have before he or she can learn a given skill.

Ethnics: the study of various races or peoples, their social customs, origins, peculiarities, habits, and values systems.

Expository teaching: the teacher presents the information the students are to learn.

Formative evaluation: methods, strategies, and activities the teacher uses to determine if the students are moving toward mastery learning of content material. It is an ongoing process of monitoring learning.

Futurism: the process of teaching the skills students will need to function successfully as adults dealing with the impact of technology and as yet unknown social, political, and environmental factors.

Generalizations: the core or basic idea of a lesson or unit based on the facts and concepts therein.

Global education: the interdependence of all peoples and countries on earth which focuses on responsible decison making and shared values.

Goals: long-term expectations for learning and instruction (e.g., the students will learn to read political maps).

Guided practice: the part of the lesson where students practice the new skill under the direct supervision of the teacher. The teacher can determine whether or not the skill is being performed correctly.

Hemispheres: in-brain research and its educational applications; the hemispheres refer to the left and right sides of the brain and their unique processing capabilities.

Human relations skills: the skills children need to develop and maintain acceptable human relationships; the skills needed to function successfully in various personal and social groups.

IEP: an individual education plan that clearly specifies the learning objectives for a student. Every special education student must have an IEP as part of his or her case study. The special education teacher, the parents, and the classroom teacher work cooperatively to establish achievable goals for both home and school experiences.

Incidental teaching: using a true teachable moment to teach without previous planning; teaching that emanates from a spur-of-the-moment incident or happening.

Inductive learning: the learning process that proceeds from facts toward making generalizations.

Instructional sequence: a series of lesson plans, activities, materials, and teacher behaviors that will lead students toward successful completion of an instructional objective. The teacher performs instructional sequences, and the students perform learning sequences. Typically, an instructional sequence will cover several class periods.

Knowledge set: all the information you have on a particular topic or subject that prepares and qualifies you to teach it to others.

Learner outcomes: the expected, observable behaviors and skills students should exhibit as a result of your teaching and instruction.

Learning: a change caused by some experience.

Learning center: a room designated to provide specialized programs, experiences, and materials for one or all curricular areas.

Learning resources: all the materials teachers use to present, reinforce, or evaluate social studies lessons (e.g., books, pamphlets, games, media, charts, simulations, etc.).

Learning sequence: a series of activities that will lead students to perform a given behavioral objective.

Learning style: in educational literature and conversation this term has acquired several meanings. Some of them are: refers to a preferred left- or right-brain method of processing new information; an individual's preference for working alone or in small or large groups to learn new information; a dominant style of learning most efficiently using one modality over another; the domains of learning—cognitive, affective, psychomotor.

Left brain: the left side of the brain receives and processes information in a logical, analytical, verbal, and sequential manner.

Lesson design for students: a four-step process that students are expected to perform during instruction: reading, thinking, doing, and evaluating.

Lesson design for teachers: the elements of planning a lesson that includes objectives, motivational techniques, an introduction, lesson development, evaluation, and provisions for special needs students.

Lesson integrations: the strategy of combining particular curriculum elements from one subject into another; applying the principle of transfer in many different ways.

Mainstreaming: the process of educating handicapped children with nonhandicapped children to the degree they can perform successfully in the regular classroom.

Major emphasis topic: history, geography, and government have traditionally formed the core of elementary social studies; a major emphasis topic is the most important element of a chapter or unit.

Mapping: a strategy for teaching a specific skill, lesson, or unit; it is frequently presented to the class in a process chart format with sequential steps that lead to skill mastery.

Mastery learning: the student will successfully learn (master) a predetermined objective or skill at a given level of accuracy (e.g., the student will correctly solve 100 two-digit addition problems with 98% accuracy).

MECC: Minnesota Educational Computing Corporation; an organization that assists schools in the implementation of educational computing.

Methodology: the procedures and processes used to teach lessons.

Modality: the manner or methods children use to help them learn. The tactile, auditory, and visual modalities are the three modalities beginning teachers should incorporate into their lessons as frequently as possible. These three modalities are often called VAT.

Modeling: demonstrating or practicing a skill or behavior the teacher expects the students to learn. Teacher modeling enhances the probability that the skill will be learned correctly.

Monitor and adjust: the teacher observes students performing a skill and makes the necessary adjustments for them to learn efficiently and effectively.

Multicultural education: studying and having access to the various cultures that comprise our present U.S. society; providing students with the necessary skills to function in a variety of social cultural environments.

NAGTE: the National Association for Gifted and Talented Education provides information, seminars, and workshops for teachers and parents of gifted children; generally promotes the importance of and methods for appropriately educating the gifted and talented.

NCSS: the National Council for the Social Studies.

New-tech media resources: the audiovisual communications services and printed materials used for instruction. Equipment, printed material, centers, and teaching strategies are part of the new-tech media.

Objective: the specific observable skill the teacher expects the student to demonstrate as a result of her or his lesson presentation. The objective may include an acceptable criterion, time limits, or other performance standards. The objective validates a good lesson plan.

On task: the term used to determine the amount and quality of time the student attends to a given task. Effort, concentration, attention span, and work production are some of the factors that contribute to a student being "on task."

Open enrollments: a policy that allows students to attend school outside their home district, thereby expanding course offerings for students.

Passive reception: the student role is to observe, remain seated, watch the teacher "do the lesson," or listen; there is little or no interaction between the student and the teacher.

PL 94-142: the federal law that requires the public schools to provide an appropriate education for all handicapped students. It is commonly referred to as "the special ed law."

Power actors: persons in the school community who initiate and affect change.

Process chart: a diagram that shows ordering of specific information, skills, or processes.

Process teaching: teaching for the process skills (how you do it) rather than a specific answer. Much problem solving is the result of effective process teaching.

Product teaching: teaching for an answer or product being the important goal. Much teaching of factual information is product teaching.

Questions: statements of inquiry that call for a reply from the student(s); in this text questions are used in both interrogative and declarative statements.

Resource person: any knowledgeable person who can share information or experiences with your social studies class.

Right brain: the right side of the brain processes information in a visual/spatial, perceptual, creative manner.

Roleplay: the student assumes the identity or role of another person and tries to act and react the way that person would in various situations.

Rule-Example-Rule-Application: a four-step procedure for teaching a concept: rule—define the concept in usable detail; example—use examples and obvious nonexamples to illustrate the rule; rule—give the rule or definition again; application—find ways for students to use the concept in a meaningful way.

Scope and sequence: the established pattern of skill instruction and the degree of mastery for each, how much and at which level appropriate for the grade or age group.

Script tape: a written documentation of observable teacher behaviors during a lesson presentation: verbal, nonverbal, body language, etc.

Selective listening: the student hears everything but commits portions to long-term memory and other things to short-term memory.

Self-contained classroom: the traditional classroom setting with one teacher and a group of students.

Simulation: an activity wherein students react, solve problems, and practice self-awareness skills within a given situation with certain conditions or rules established.

Skills center: a part of the classroom designated for students to work on specific social studies skills as directed by the teacher.

Social skills: the skills children need to function successfully in their school, home, and community.

SQ3R: a practical, usable method for teaching children to read in the content areas: survey—scan the material and observe headings and titles; question—formulate questions about the material; read—read the text and get answers for your questions; recite—orally answer your questions, talk it out; review—reread the text, reinforce your answers.

State assessments: statewide testing of specific grade levels, frequently fourth and sixth, for achievement in a particular content area such as social studies, math, or reading. These testing programs are conducted at predetermined intervals; the schools that are to be tested either volunteer or are randomly selected. Test results are frequently used to set programs and to determine special funding allotments.

Summative evaluation: a closure process or activity that determines if goals or objectives have been met; frequently this takes the form of a posttest.

Task analysis: identifying all the sublearnings that are integral to a new skill. Performing a task analysis helps to establish realistic, achievable learning objectives.

Teaching strategy: a plan for achieving an educational goal or objective; what the teacher does to teach children.

Test-out: a common conversational term among teachers. Students test-out of a given chapter or skill requirement and are provided with a supplementary activity or task, frequently an outcome of pretesting procedures with higher-performing students (e.g., the student received a score of 100 on a pretest; he already knows all the material).

Textbook tasks: reading the book, answering study questions, doing the activities, taking chapter tests, knowing special vocabulary, and able to use glossaries.

Think time: the period of time after the teacher poses the question but before the student is required to respond.

Tracking: the process of moving students through a predetermined set of skills or lessons; some programmed materials are designed this way. At the secondary level, students choose the track they will follow: academic, general, or vocational. At the elementary level, assigning a student to the low, average, or high group with limited mobility.

Transfer: establishing and maintaining the relationship of one skill to another (especially a new skill to one the student already knows). Focusing these ''connectors'' gives relevancy to skill learning.

VAT: a shorthand version of the visual, auditory, and tactile modalities of learning.

Ways of Knowing: enactive—action oriented, doing things, using real objects; iconic—images, uses representations of real things, builds the foundation for symbolic learning; symbolic—the most abstract mode, uses language as the main focus.

Index